Dalí and Disney

DESTINO

The Story, Artwork, and Friendship Behind the Legendary Film

David A. Bossert

Disney Editions
Los Angeles • New York

"Dave Bossert gives us an insider's look at the production of a paramount achievement in animation and art. We learn about the culture of Disney studios through the years and the remarkable meeting of Disney and Dali which comes to feel destined. Further we get original insights into the character of Dali – at once, agreeable, hard-working, as well as eccentric."

—Hank Hine, Executive Director, The Dali in St. Petersburg, FL

"Walt Disney and Salvador Dali were among Andy Warhol's favorites and he probably would have loved their collaborative film, *Destino*. Certainly the marriage of art and commerce, painting and film that *Destino* represents was at the center of Warhol's artistic practice. Dave Bossert lovingly reconstructs the decades spent conceiving, executing and eventually bringing the film to the screen. Perhaps most moving and important, however, is the evident pride the contemporary Disney team took in bringing the project to fruition. As Bossert quotes Roy Disney regarding *Destino*, "Our roots are in art, in that side of the world rather the commercial side. It's important that we keep remembering that."

—Patrick Moore, Deputy Director, The Andy Warhol Museum

"Dave, as a key player in helping Roy Disney bringing this lost jewel back from oblivion, has a great responsibility in educating the public, especially the younger generations, as to the importance of the magic collaboration between Disney and Dalí, and what it means to art today. Thanks to him the story is now told. And good story tellers are the best educators."

—Juan M. Sevillano, Managing Director
Gala-Salvador Dalí Foundation

"For fans it is no surprise, and for students it should be a lesson, that there is no better source for what we were up to in the latter era of Disney Animation than Dave Bossert. Roy Disney's trusted colleague and a deep veteran of countless films, Dave has the clearest POV on all things Disney Animation of anyone I know."

—Tom Schumacher, President of Disney Theatrical Productions

"It is truly an amazing sight when giants collide. Sometimes, they fight. Sometimes, they make beautiful art together. Dave Bossert gives us a delightful glimpse into two spectacular lives. Few know that the splendiferous surrealist painter, Salvador Dalí and the towering American icon, Walt Disney, collaborated to make the *Destino* film. Bossert's book is a compelling and mirthful behind-the-scenes look at genius, hijinx, American culture and these two seemingly worlds-apart epic souls."

— John Boston, Author of *Naked Came the Sasquatch and Adam Henry*
Journalist and Will Rogers Lifetime Humanitarian Achievement Award recipient

"Dali and Disney: Destino is fascinating from beginning to end. Two gifted artists and showmen come together in mutual admiration, attempt to blend their very different styles on the basis of shared surrealist elements, and leave their project incomplete. A half century later, in the conviction that their founder was on to something, a team of Disney artists, combining state-of-the-art technology with deep knowledge of Dali and Disney, fulfill in a triumphant and almost magical way the possibilities latent in the drawings remaining from the original collaboration. This is a great read for anyone who cares about Disney or animation."

—Dr. Steven Lavine, President California Institute of the Arts

"This profusely illustrated book explores one of the 20th century's least likely artistic collaborations -- between Walt Disney and Salvador Dali. Personal correspondence, production memos, rare conceptual and finished art, photos and artifacts (even Dali's studio paycheck voucher) take readers behind-the-scenes of a truly surreal animation project."

—John Canemaker, Oscar-winning animation director, and author of
The Lost Notebook: Herman Schultheis and the Secrets of Walt Disney's Movie Magic

Destino

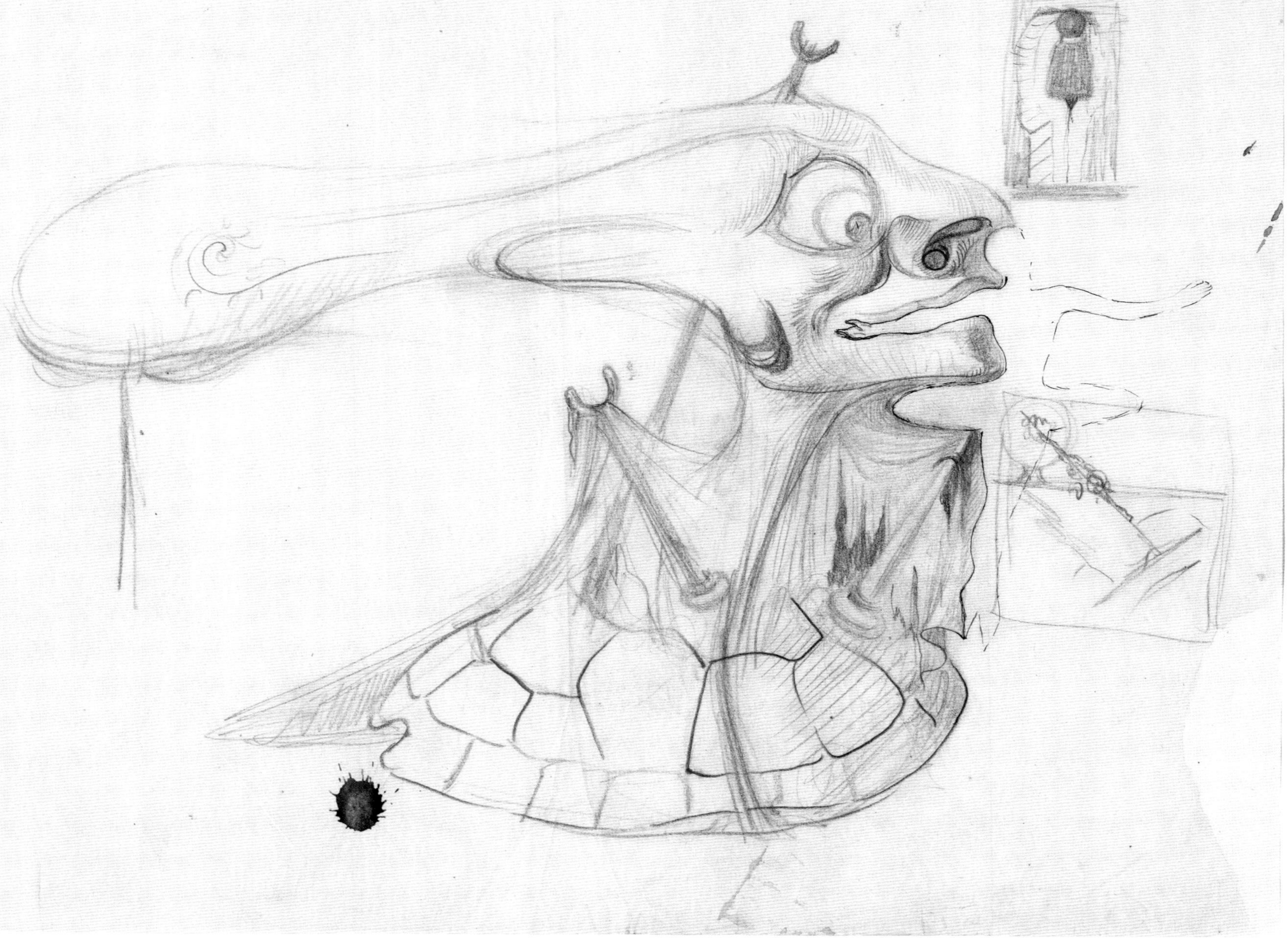

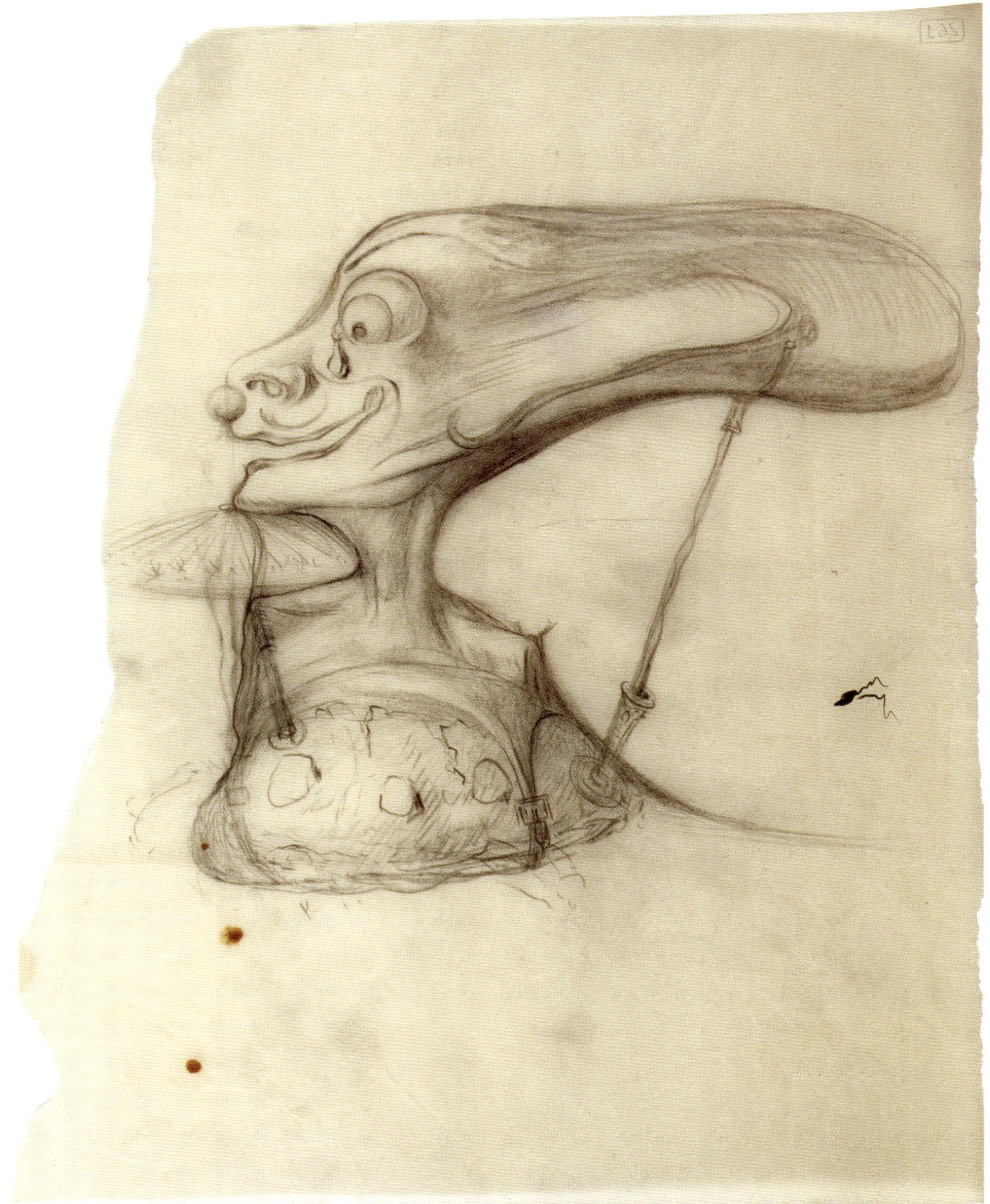

Pages 4–5: Visual development of the fate heads by Salvador Dalí. Courtesy of Fundació Gala-Salvador Dalí.

Page 7: Image from the final film, *Destino*.

Page 9: Story sketch by Salvador Dalí.

For information address Disney Editions,
1101 Flower Street, Glendale, California 91201

ISBN 978-1-4847-0713-5
FAC-029191-15205
Printed in Malaysia
Reinforced binding
First Hardcover Edition, October 2015
10 9 8 7 6 5 4 3 2 1

Visit www.disneybooks.com

D23
The Official Disney Fan Club
Disney.com/D23

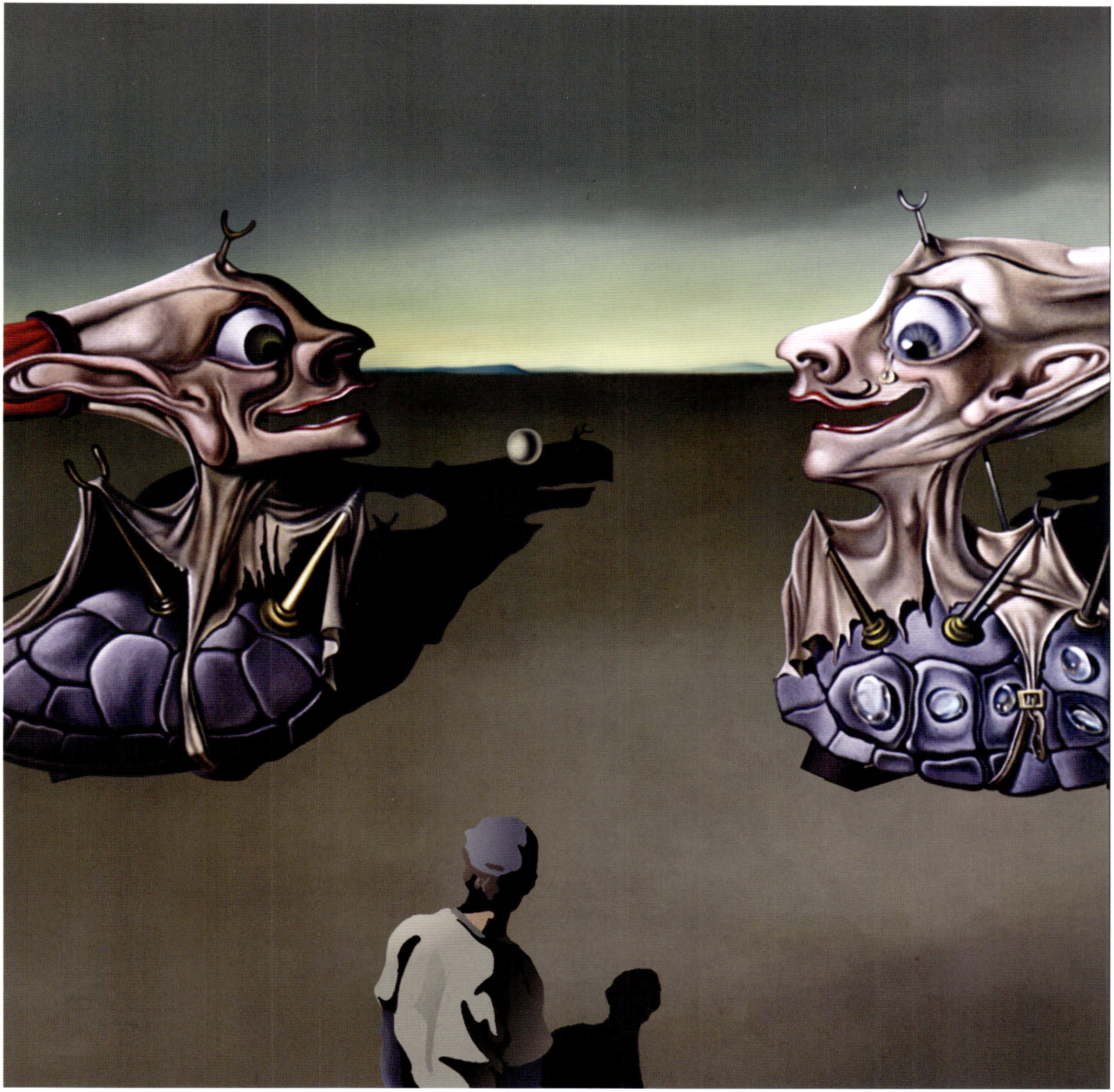

Dedicated to the loving memory of my brother

Col. Phil Bossert, Jr. (USAF)

July 6, 1959 – October 3, 2013

Aim High . . . Fly, Fight, Win!

P-212 (R-1)

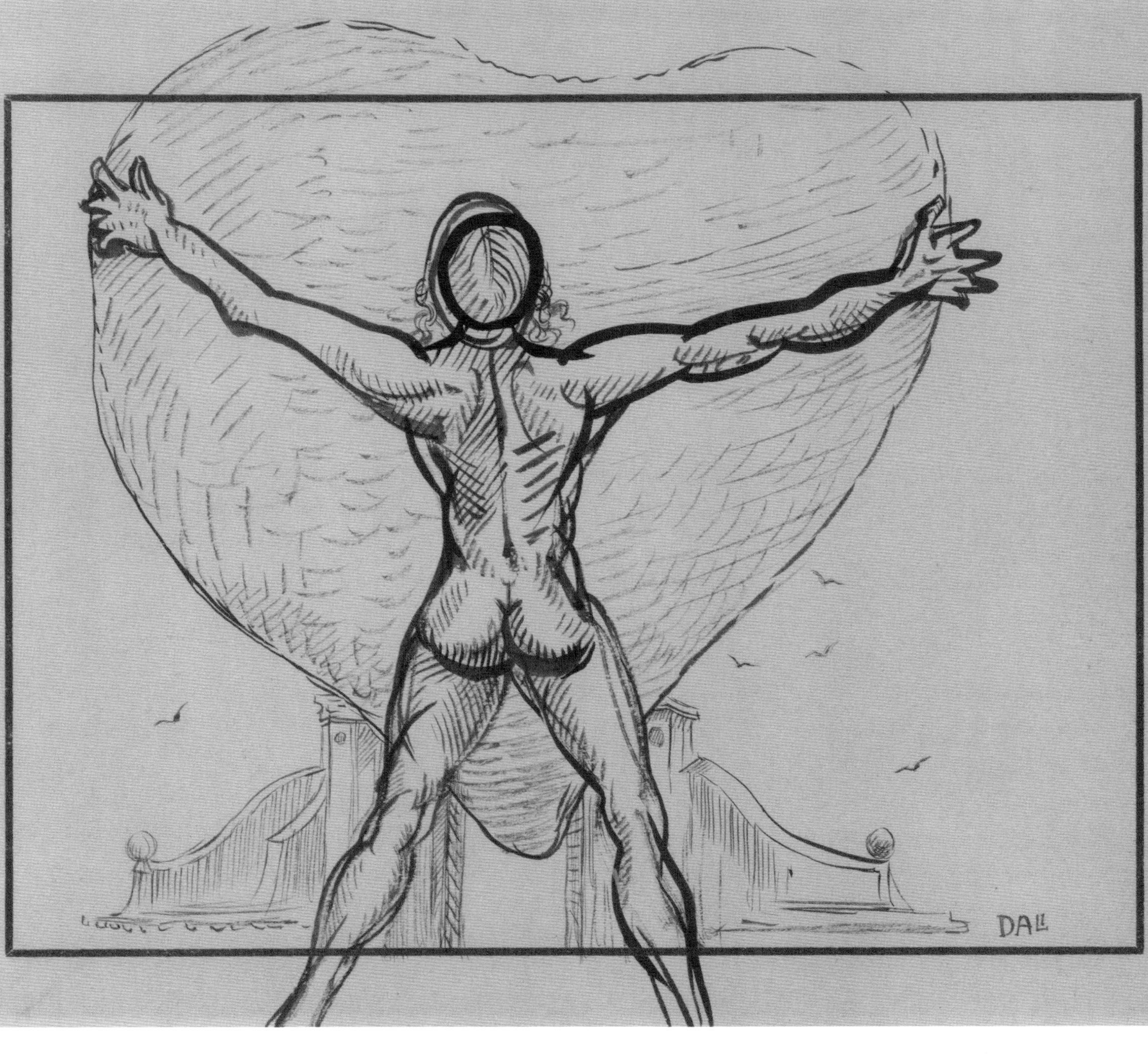

Salvador Dali   Walter E Disney

TABLE OF CONTENTS

Limited edition serigraph of *The Girl and the Eyeballs*; *Destino* No. 67. Print by Michael Young and Tim Dickson with Collectors Editions, Inc. This is HC print, number 10 of 10, and was signed by Roy E. Disney and given to the author as a gift.

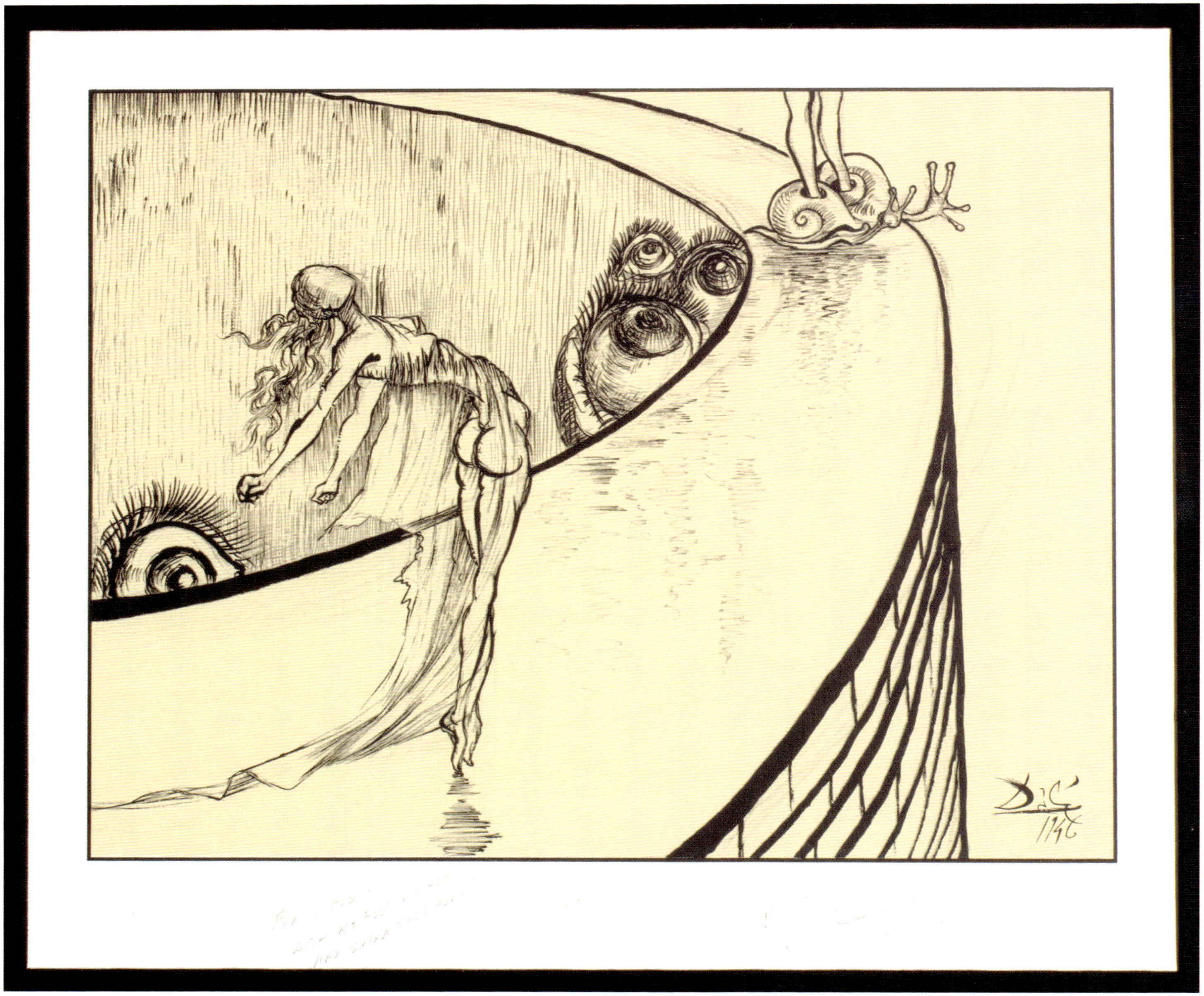

ACKNOWLEDGMENTS

My journey in writing this book is rooted, unbeknownst to me at the time, in the production of *Fantasia/2000*, the thirty-eighth animated feature film from Walt Disney Animation Studios. It was during my time on that film that Roy E. Disney described the *Destino* project and the treasure trove of art associated with it. I am eternally grateful for his friendship and his tenacity in completing this project fifty-eight years after it was started.

Edward Nowak, Deputy General Counsel for The Walt Disney Company, deserves a very special thank you for all his legal expertise in clearing the way for the film to be completed. Without his expert guidance and sage advice, we may never have enjoyed what is *Destino*! Also in the legal department thanks goes to Claire Robinson, Michael Horn, Catherine Bridge, John McGuire, Heiko K. Schultz, Christine Chrisman, and Sylvia Haro.

Montse Aguer, director of the Centre for Dalinian Studies at the Fundació Gala-Salvador Dalí in Figueres, Spain, has been a wonderful, enthusiastic, and invaluable help in filling in some missing holes in the *Destino* chronicle. Montse along with Juan Manuel Sevillano, the managing director of the Fundació Gala-Salvador Dalí, were early supporters and very cooperative with this project right from the inception. Mr. Sevillano's introduction to this book is both gracious and succinct. I am forever grateful for their permission to include some rare early sketches of *Destino*–related iconography and other associated material from the Fundació Gala-Salvador Dalí collection. Thanks also goes to Anna Otero and Mercedes Aznar at the Fundació Gala-Salvador Dalí for their help as well.

My friend, author and humorist John Boston, has always said that writing is a muscle that gets stronger the more you use it. That's true, but it also helps to have some great friends that are established writers and professionals that you can relay on for honest, knowledgeable feedback. That is what I got from John and my friends, filmmaker and author John Canemaker, as well as Patrick Moore, deputy director of The Andy Warhol Museum, and Hank Hine, executive director of The Dalí Museum in St. Petersburg, Florida; they gave me some excellent suggestions and support. I greatly appreciate their willingness to read an early draft of the manuscript for this book and giving me superb comments.

Special thanks to The Walt Disney Family Museum for granting permission to use the image of the Dalí painting that hung in Walt Disney's Palm Springs home. The museum and the Disney-Miller family have been gracious in their cooperation. They continue to preserve, display, and share Walt Disney's achievements, memories, and legacy in their beautiful museum facility at the Presidio in San Francisco.

I would also like to thank my friend Wendy Lefkon. She is an amazing and wonderful publishing executive who has been editor on this and my other books, *Remembering Roy E. Disney: Memories and Photos of a Storied Life* and *An Animator's Gallery: Eric Goldberg Draws the Disney Characters*. Wendy continues to be a great partner with her candid advice and thoughtful guidance. She has taught me much about the publishing world, all with a wonderfully dry sense of humor and great intellectual depth. I can't imagine doing these books without her. Also, her colleague, Jennifer Eastwood, has been an amazing partner on this project with her terrific insights and assistance.

The book's layout and design was done by our Disney colleague Tamara Khalaf. She is a talented member of the Walt Disney Animation Studios' Animation Research Library group. She is part of the team headed by Mary Walsh, who lovingly cared for and preserved all the animation art going as far back as the mid–1920s. Tamara is always a joy to work with, and her talent is evident by how she exquisitely designed this book. And thanks to the entire staff at the Animation Research Library, especially the Collections, Research, and Image Capture teams.

I also want to acknowledge my Walt Disney Animation Studios' Special Projects colleagues Cameron Ramsey, Ashleigh Bateman, and my assistant, Minnie Chen, for all their help. Also, thanks to Rebecca Cline, Kevin M. Kern, and Justin Arthur in the Walt Disney Archives for their assistance in research, documents, and photos. And thanks to Kent Gordon and Mike Pucher for their expert image scanning.

I wrote the majority of this book while traveling, on weekends, and in the upper mid-coast region of Maine, a wonderful place to write!

Finally, last but not least, a heartfelt thanks to my family: Nancy, Sydney, and Marlee; my parents, Philip and Virginia, as well as my siblings, Phil Jr., Caroline, and Alison; my sister-in-law, Anita, and my nephew Andrew and niece Stephanie, for all their love and support.

Dave Bossert
Burbank, California
2015

Exterior of the Centre Fundació
Gala-Salvador Dalí in Figueres, Spain.
Photograph courtesy of Dave Bossert.

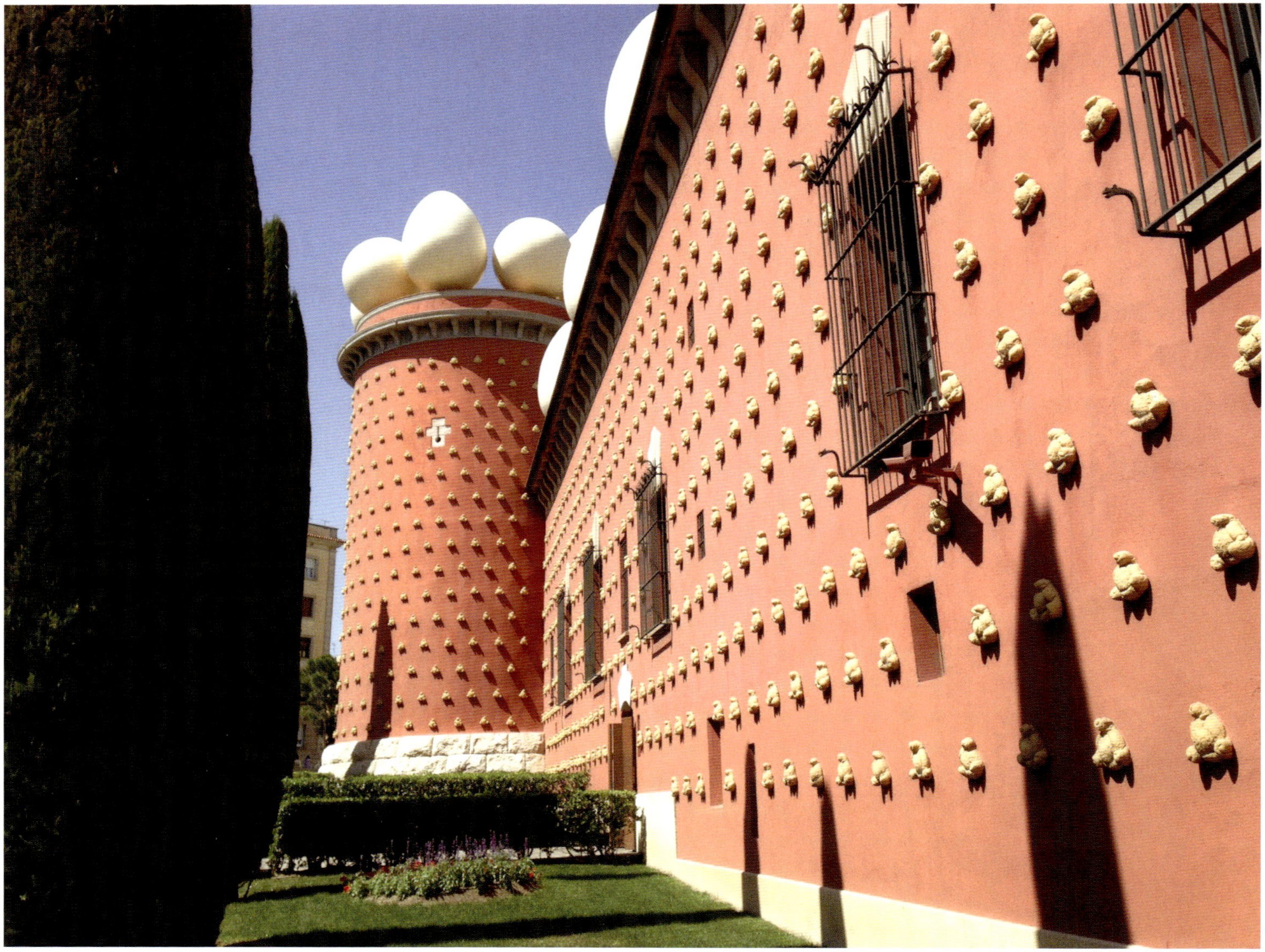

FOREWORD

I met Roy E. Disney in Barcelona, Spain, in February of 2004, at the opening of the "Dalí and Mass Culture" exhibition. This was one of the two central exhibitions organized to commemorate Salvador Dalí's centennial, and very notably, the first comprehensive study of Dalí's role as a pioneering twentieth-century artist, who explored and understood better and earlier than most the new dimensions to art which the new century brought with it.

The exhibition presented a scholarly review of Dalí's work in an array of fields, such as theater, cinema, television, printed mass media, industrial design, fashion, dance, music, and publishing (just to name a few). It was a fascinating, expansive wave of creative genius beyond the boundaries of artistic orthodoxy, which finally was being seen in a coherent light.

Organized by the Fundació Gala-Salvador Dalí and the Fundació La Caixa, "Dalí and Mass Culture" was inaugurated by the then Crown Prince Felipe, today His Majesty King Felipe VI of Spain. It immediately became a huge success and went on to be shown in Holland (at the Museum Boijmans Van Beuningen, in Rotterdam), Spain itself (in Madrid's Museo Nacional Centro de Arte Reina Sofia), and the United States (at The Dalí Museum in St. Petersburg, Florida). Most importantly, it opened a whole new perspective on scholarly research about Dalí, and became a starting point for other successful and highly relevant exhibitions, such as "Dalí and Film," which was shown in London (at the Tate Modern); St. Petersburg, Florida (at The Dalí Museum); New York (at the Museum of Modern Art); and Los Angeles (at the Los Angeles County Museum of Art). *Destino* was prominently featured at each exhibit.

Roy E.'s understanding of this context and his total support for having *Destino* showcased in "Dalí and Mass Culture"—the first time outside the specialized cinema festival circuit—was of great importance to the success of the exhibition. *Destino* is a work of art, and as such became the hidden jewel in a discourse full of extraordinary surprises.

Since then *Destino* has been shown in some of the most important projects organized by the Gala-Salvador Dalí Foundation around the world. It plays a crucial role as a hybrid creation fusing filmic and painterly arts and in helping people understand Dalí's fascination with the new media of the twentieth century. Further, it allows curators to present the once almost-forgotten story of a magic encounter of geniuses, which developed into a lifelong friendship.

The American (and generally the Western for that matter) establishment has been reluctant to grant Walt Disney proper consideration as a highly relevant twentieth-century artist in his own right; a man well ahead of his time, who found in Dalí very much a soul mate—and vice versa. They were both geniuses, pioneers, game changers; and eventually they were both extremely successful. Yet for much of their lives they found themselves quite alone with their visions. Arguably, it is difficult to explain the art of the twentieth century, from a modern perspective, without considering these two men.

The day after the opening of the "Dalí and Mass Culture" exhibit, the foundation hosted a dinner for Roy E. Disney and his party at the Círculo del Liceo—a historical private club—in Barcelona. It was there, in a very small group, surrounded by a superb collection of Catalan nineteenth- and early twentieth-century paintings, and some of the finest examples of modernist craftsmanship, that we had the chance to get to know Roy better and his account of *Destino*'s rescue from oblivion. It was a memorable evening during which I discovered this man's respect and fierce devotion to his uncle's legacy, his love for the Disney corporation, and the pain and worry he was experiencing due to the turbulent battles the company was going through at the time.

The production of *Destino* turned out to be a fascinating story of curiosity, tenacity, and excellence embodied in an outstanding human team. Roy would not hide his pride in them and the satisfaction he drew from the exquisite job they had carried out with *Destino*.

Dave Bossert's book tells us this story in full detail. With all his insights and researched information, it is enormously relevant and rigorously reflects what constitutes the highlight and focal point of the artistic interaction between Dalí and Disney. His work gives an interesting, thorough account of *Destino*'s story and undoubtedly will be of great help in the effort to overcome the same conventionalisms and narrow-mindedness which much of the academic and art world has traditionally shown toward the geniuses of their own time.

Dave, as a key player in helping Roy bring this lost jewel to life, has a great responsibility in educating the public, especially the younger generations, as to the importance of this magic collaboration and what it means to art today. Thanks to him the story is now told. And good storytellers are the best educators.

Juan M. Sevillano
Managing Director
Fundació Gala-Salvador Dalí
Figueres, Spain
December 2014

Roy E. Disney and Thomas Schumacher at the premiere of *Fantasia/2000* at Carnegie Hall, 1999.

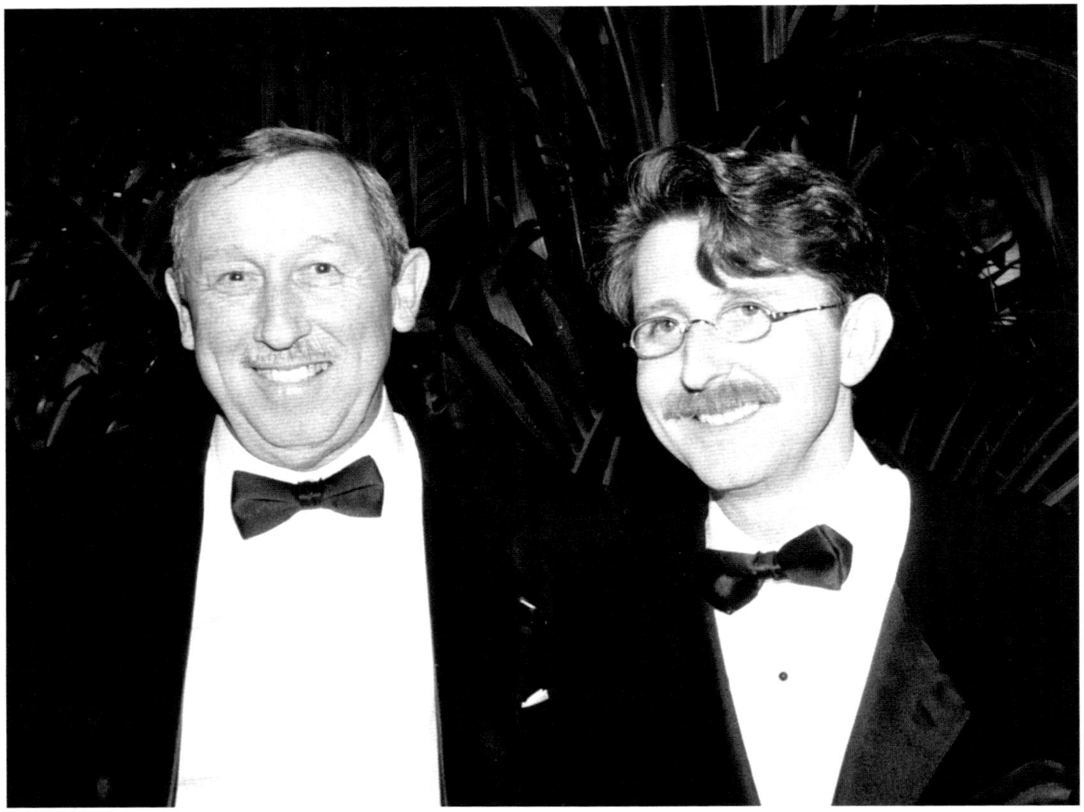

PREFACE

I'm always interested in how people perceive art. I recall I once wrote a paper on Salvador Dalí during high school. He was one of the first artists whose work I liked and felt some connection to. For my research, I had a bunch of Dalí books spread out all over our kitchen table. I loved the melting clocks, giant eyeballs, and the confusing abstract imagery.

My very sweet and very funny grandmother, who was born in Italy in 1902, sat with me at the kitchen table while I showed her what I was working on. I adored my grandmother, who was an open-minded and curious woman. She was a real rock for me.

She looked at page after page of the books I showed her. She kept looking and turning the pages. She didn't dismiss anything. She took it all in.

Finally, she said, "What sort of mind thinks of this?"

And that's when it occurred to me that my affection for Dalí might be outside of the ordinary.

Years later, when I was leading Disney Animation, I was delighted to find that Dalí and Walt Disney had been both creative collaborators and friends. It was a complete surprise to me because I, like so many people, had a fairly singular view of Walt that centered on his American Main Street aesthetic.

It therefore makes sense that this connection of Dalí with Disney typically turns heads and raises eyebrows—because it belies the conventional wisdom that a man of Walt's broad popularity just couldn't also be intellectual, or sophisticated, or an important artist. But Walt, it turns out, frequently sought out who might be considered unusual collaborators.

For example, English writer and philosopher Aldous Huxley worked for Walt on a script for a film called *Alice and the Mysterious Mr. Carroll*. Another, American artist and muralist Thomas Hart Benton, developed an early version of Davy Crockett for Disney. For *Fantasia*, Walt brought German-American abstract animator, filmmaker, and painter Oskar Fischinger to the studio.

Even aerospace engineer and space architect Wernher von Braun developed a series of television programs for Walt in the 1950s. Walt's curiosity and desire to collaborate with great minds was vast.

By the time Dalí came to the studio in 1945 to work on what would become *Destino*, Walt had brought the surrealist possibilities of animation to life in the "Pink Elephants on Parade" sequence in *Dumbo* and the Oscar-winning short *Der Fuehrer's Face*. Afterward, surreal and fantastic animation would continue to be featured in projects such as *The Three Caballeros*, *Melody Time*, and *Alice in Wonderland*.

The marriage of Dalí's highly imaginative, unusual, and grandiose visual world with the filmmaking touch of Disney's seemed to fit perfectly with Walt's notion that "Animation can explain whatever the mind of man can conceive."

After their initial meeting, Dalí and Disney quickly developed a productive working relationship and ease of collaboration. Work between the two moved smoothly, with little conflict reported between them. Walt's typical demand for absolute creative control changed, and—for the first time—his studio staff felt the influence of other artistic forces. Walt's affection for Dalí was out of the ordinary, too.

Sadly, the realities of the film business and the studio's need for more surefire commercial success spelled the end of the *Destino* project. Walt later said that it was "no fault of Dalí's that the project . . . was not completed—it was simply a case of policy changes in our distribution plans."

It all might have just been an obscure and curious footnote in Disney history, if not for Walt's nephew and the godfather of the renaissance of Disney animation, Roy E. Disney. His passion for the art of animation, understanding of the importance of the Dalí work that remained archived at the studio—and most of all, commitment (much like his uncle's) and belief that, in some cases, profitability cannot be the sole motivation for filmmaking—were all vital.

Completing this long-ago vision of two artistic giants, and getting the story of its making and the stunning artwork created for it in front of the public, became a passionate enthusiasm of Roy's, and in many ways is emblematic of the culture of the Animation division at the Walt Disney Studios under his stewardship.

It was also a point of great controversy. Just as Walt had been encouraged to shut the project down, Roy was under great pressure from corporate forces to do the same years later.

In this volume, Dave Bossert has recounted the full arc of the creation of this one-of-a-kind film, plus covered the talents, personalities, and relationships that weave through that story from the 1940s to today. For animation fans, it is no surprise—and for students it should be a lesson—that there is no better source for what we were up to in the latter era of Disney Animation than Dave Bossert. As Roy E. Disney's trusted colleague and a veteran of countless films, Dave has the clearest POV (point of view) on all things Disney Animation of anyone I know.

I think that after reading this authoritative and entertaining work, my grandmother might have a clearer answer to her question, "What sort of mind thinks of this?"

Thomas Schumacher
President, The Walt Disney Theatrical Group
New York, NY
February 2015

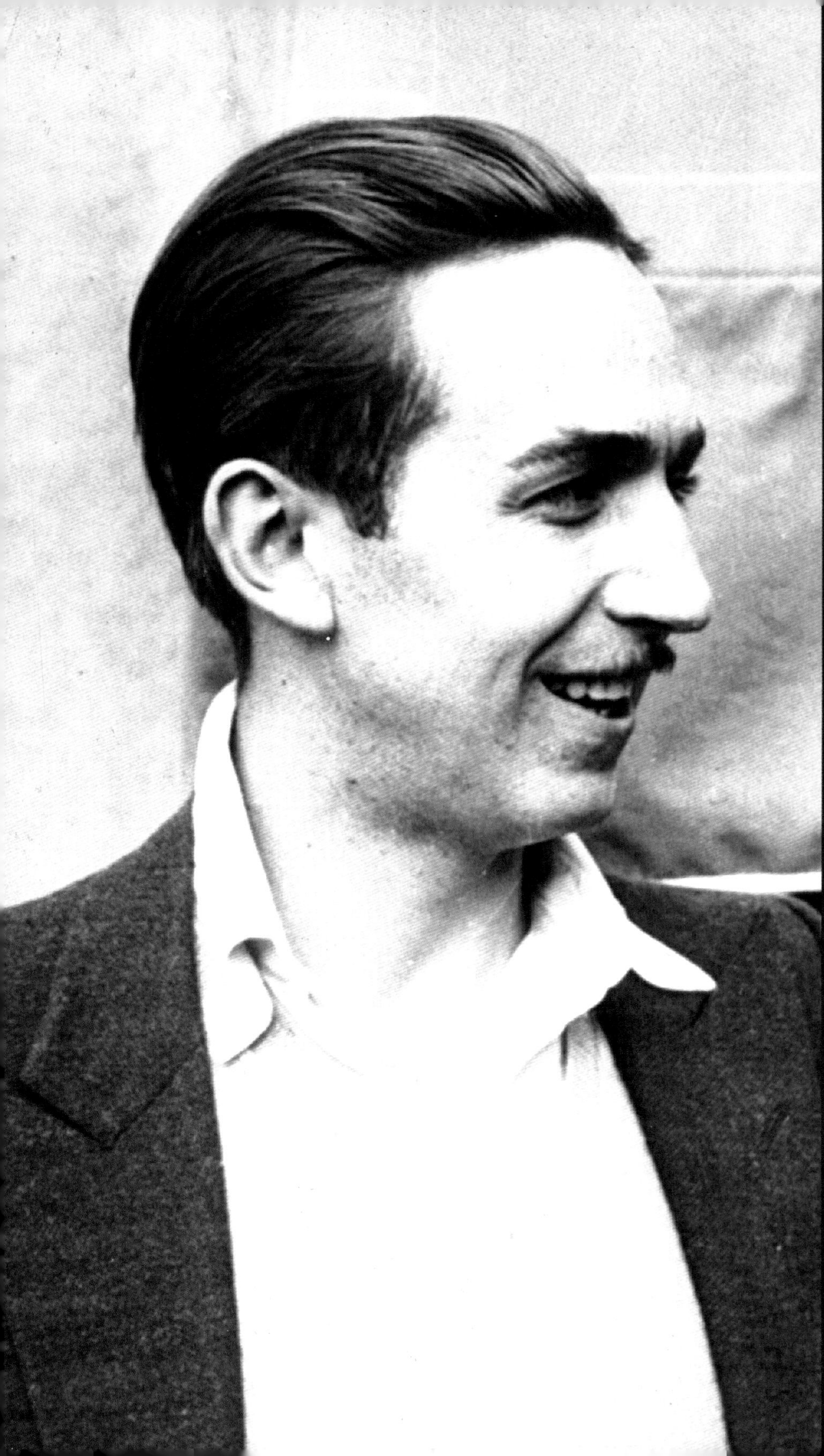

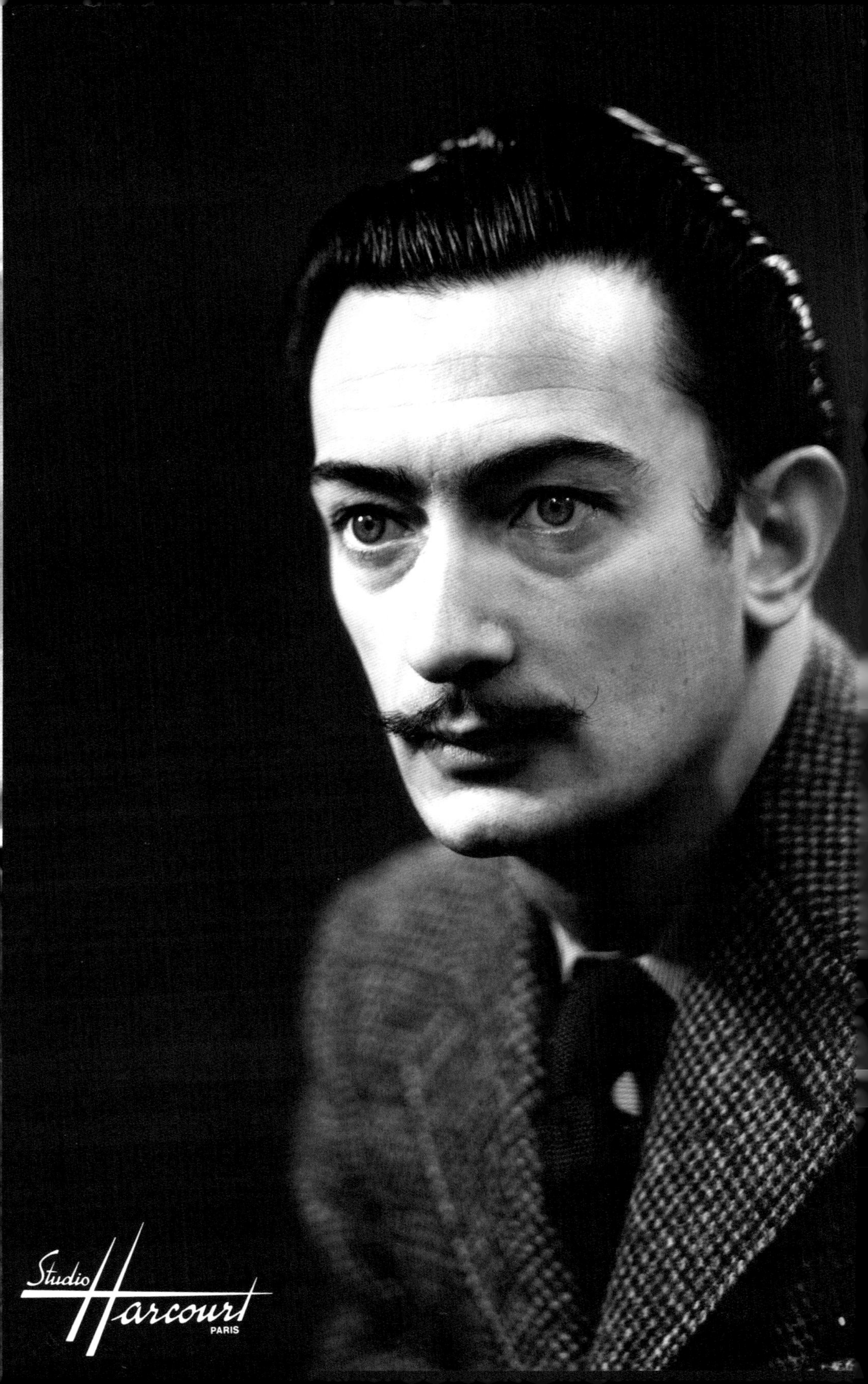
Studio Harcourt
PARIS

ACT I:
Artists on Parallel Paths

In 1998, when I first listened to the original, early 1940s Dora Luz recording of "My Destiny of Love," it sounded horrible. The tone was distant and hollow, full of scratches, pops, and hisses. In fact, it was one of the worst recordings I had ever heard. That was the first day of an incredible, multiyear adventure to finish a rare gem of a short film started by two of the most renowned artists of the twentieth century.

The film was *Destino*. And thanks to the advancements in digital technology, we were able to salvage that original recording so well that it was used for the final production of this short—nearly sixty years later. However, that is but a small footnote to the larger story of the origins of this wonderful film.

For, it is not only a story of the destiny of true love, but it's also a story of Walt Disney and Salvador Dalí who, through mutual admiration and happenstance, would collaborate on a short film that would ultimately take nearly six decades to complete. That short film was originally planned to be a segment for a *Fantasia*-like film, which is commonly known as a packaged picture.

In 2003, Roy E. Disney stated that people would be dumfounded when they heard, "Walt Disney and Salvador Dalí? This must be crazy! Yet on the other hand, it always seemed to me that they were both really relentless self-promoters and [that] they must have seen something of that in one another."

There is no doubt that they did see something in collaborating together on an animated project: the common ground of art.

Disney and Dalí reportedly met for the first time at a dinner party in the home of Jack Warner of Warner Bros. fame in August 1944, when Dalí was working on Alfred Hitchcock's *Spellbound*. Dalí was a houseguest at Warner's home. It was during his time in Los Angles that Dalí got to know many of the Hollywood luminaries of the day. He became friends with Harpo Marx, as well as other Hollywood stars, and painted portraits of Warner and his wife. Walt Disney was one of the individuals he admired and thought of as "one of the great American surrealists." After the first meeting, Disney and Dalí would go on to forge a lifelong friendship.

There are no known photographs or documentation of that chance meeting, just the lore passed down over the years and verified by Dalí's main collaborator at Disney, John Hench. It was in a later interview that Hench recalled Walt telling him that he had met and asked Dalí if he would like to do some work at the Disney Studio.

But it was the parallel paths that these two artists were on that seemed to speak to the fact that they eventually would meet. In a sense, it was their destiny.

That destiny took root years earlier during the 1920s, a time of innovation and invention—it was, by all accounts, the decade during which the modernization of America took hold. Those ten years reaped the birth of Jazz, the invention of the television, the first commercial radio station, the founding of the surrealist movement in art, and synchronized sound in motion pictures. Bookended by the end of World War I and the Great Depression, the decade's still commonly known as the Roaring '20s.

In Spain, Salvador Dalí was attending the Real Academia de Bellas Artes de San Fernando in Madrid to study art in 1922. He quickly proved himself to be an accomplished draftsman and painter with the work he produced for his classes. By 1924 he'd created a series of illustrations for his friend and classmate, the poet Carles Fages de Climent, and his published collection of Catalan poems titled *Les:Bruixes:de:Llers* (*The Witches of Liers*).

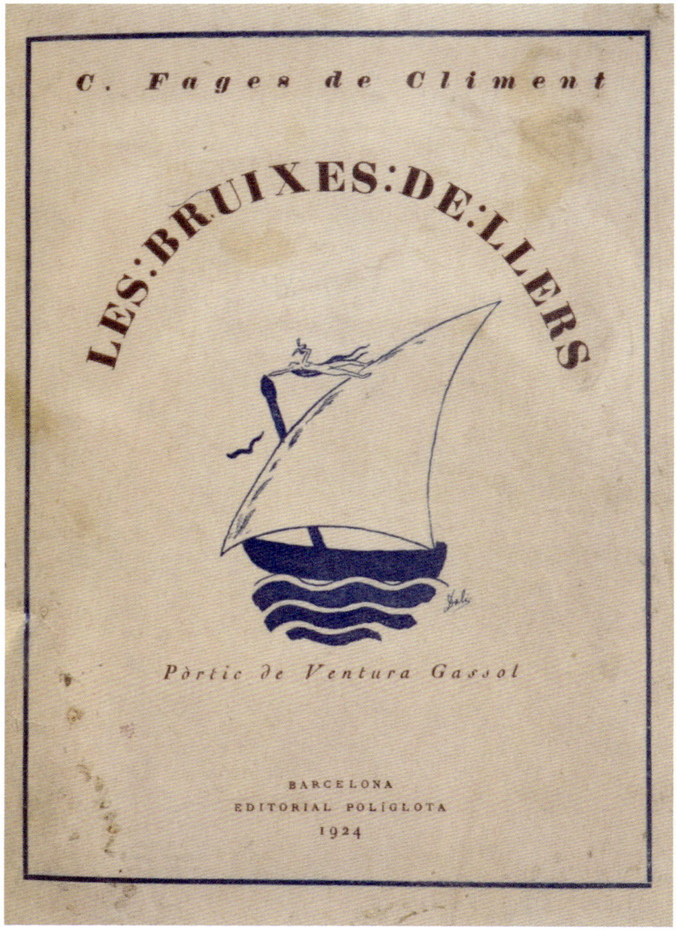

Page 18 (left): Walter E. Disney, circa 1928.

Page 18 (right): Salvador Dalí, 1936. © Studio Harcourt Paris / Ministère de la Culture - Médiathèque de l'architecture et du patrimoine.

Carles Fages de Climent's booklet of Catalan poems titled, *Les bruixes de Llers* (*The Witches of Liers*). Illustrations by Salvador Dalí, 1924.

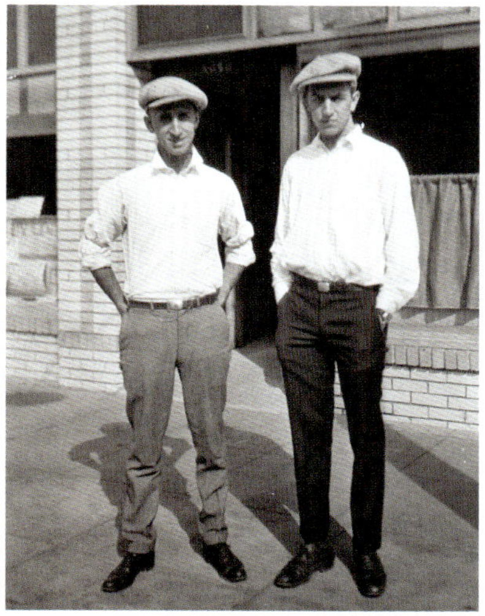

Above: Roy and Walt Disney, circa 1923.

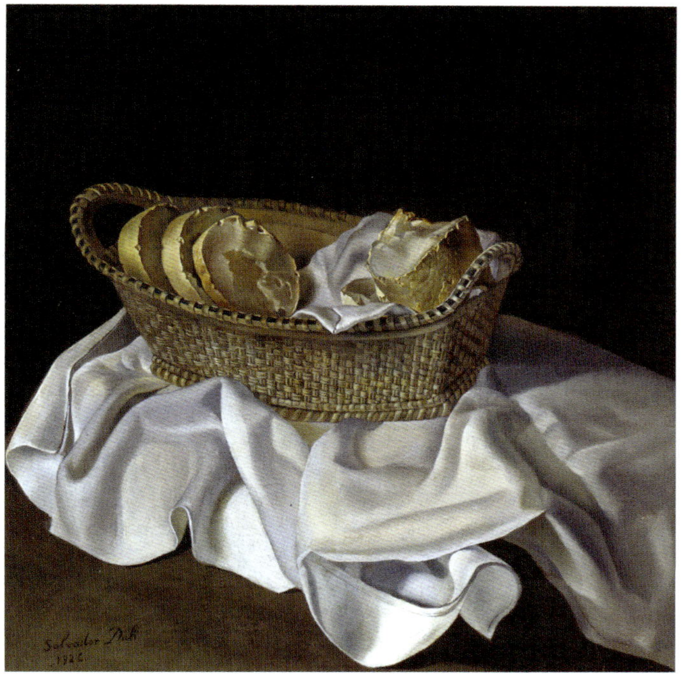

Right: Salvador Dalí's painting, *The Basket of Bread*, 1926. Courtesy of The Dalí Museum, St. Petersburg, Florida.

That year Dalí led the protest against an unpopular professor being appointed to the art academy and was charged with inciting a student insurrection. He was suspended from school for a year and briefly jailed for the disruption. Dalí was imprisoned twice more for short periods on charges of antimonarchist activities.[1]

Dalí's first one-man show was staged in Barcelona, Spain, in 1925. By 1926 Dalí's unparalleled painting skills were further confirmed with the completion of *The Basket of Bread*, which showcased his discipline and technical expertise for realism. Despite his talent, Dalí was permanently expelled from the renowned art school because he refused to take an exam in his art history class.

In 1923, Walter Elias Disney was heading up the Laugh-O-gram Films studio in Kansas City, Missouri. After making a new short titled *Alice's Wonderland*, however, the studio went bankrupt. Walt bought a one-way train ticket and headed to Los Angeles to live with his Uncle Robert and older brother Roy Oliver Disney.

Walt and Roy founded the Disney Brothers Cartoon Studio soon after in the fall of 1923. Their venture started out in the garage of Uncle Robert's home in the Los Feliz neighborhood of Los Angeles. In October of that year, the brothers moved down the street to a larger storefront location on Kingswell Avenue. Their studio would near bankruptcy a number of times in the ensuing years but would always manage a comeback.

The Disney brothers produced a successful series of live-action/animated shorts known as the Alice Comedies based on the *Alice's Wonderland* short Walt had completed in Missouri. These were one-reel films, which were typically ten-minute short subjects that played as part of a movie theater program. This was a series that originally starred Virginia Davis as Alice, with her sidekick Julius, an animated cat. Disney eventually got a distribution deal with Margaret Winkler, and the series went on to be successful for several years with a total of fifty-six shorts being produced.

By 1927 the popularity of the series began to wane and the series became more dominated by the animated characters. Their next series, however, proved to be quite popular as well. It focused on Oswald the Lucky Rabbit, who starred in short cartoons created with the backing of producer Charles Mintz. He was married to Margaret Winkler and ran Winkler Pictures, which was based in New York and distributed the Oswald shorts through Universal. Oswald proved to be the true breakout success that the brothers needed, but it was a very short-lived triumph.

Walt Disney ultimately lost the rights to Oswald the Lucky Rabbit after directing twenty-six short silent cartoons that featured the character. Unbeknownst to Walt till he visited New York, and his distributor Mintz had not only taken control of Oswald, he'd also signed away most of the Disney Brothers Studio's artists except for Ub Iwerks, who refused the offer to leave Disney.

That setback led Walt Disney to create a new character on the train ride back to Los Angeles, which followed that meeting in New York. He initially named the new character Mortimer Mouse, but his wife, Lillian, had the good sense to persuade him to change it to Mickey Mouse. The rest is history.

Always pushing the envelope of new technology, Disney was determined to be the first to release an animated short with synchronized sound. Walt had developed three silent Mickey Mouse shorts—*Plane Crazy*, *Steamboat Willie*, and *The Gallopin' Gaucho*—while finishing his contractual obligation for the Oswald shorts. His wife and his sister-in-law Edna, Roy O.'s wife, were painting animation cels on their kitchen tables for the new shorts at night while helping to finish the Oswald shorts during the day. True to his pursuit, *Steamboat Willie*, starring Mickey Mouse, became the first

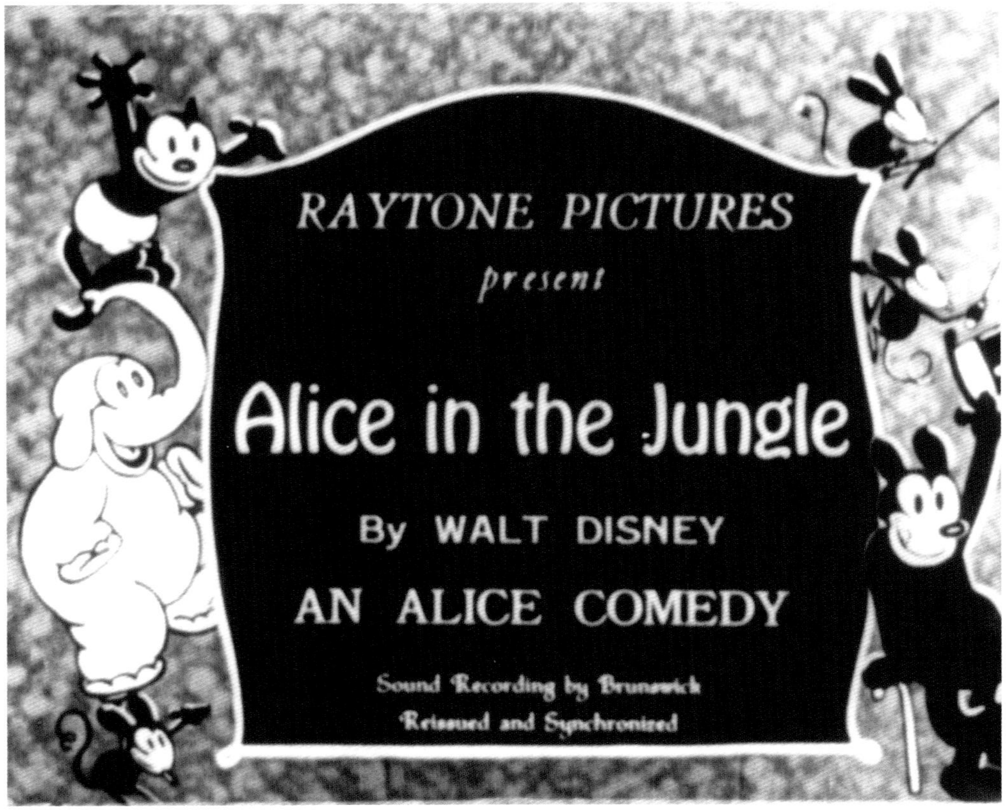

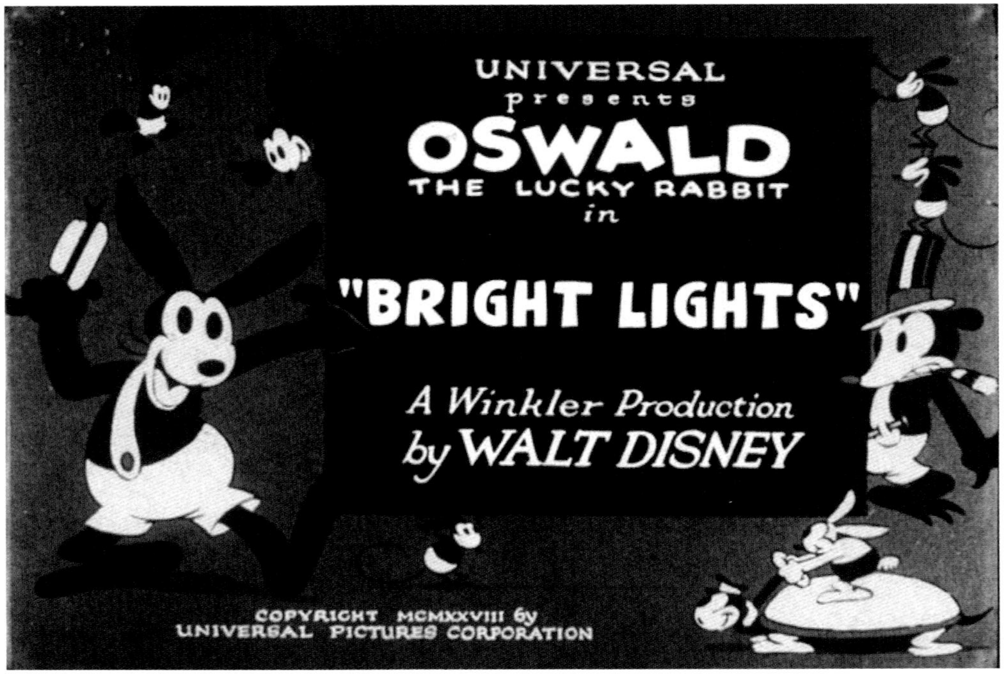

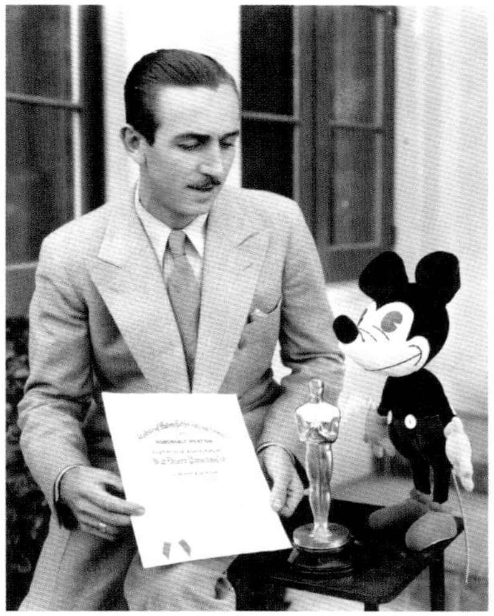

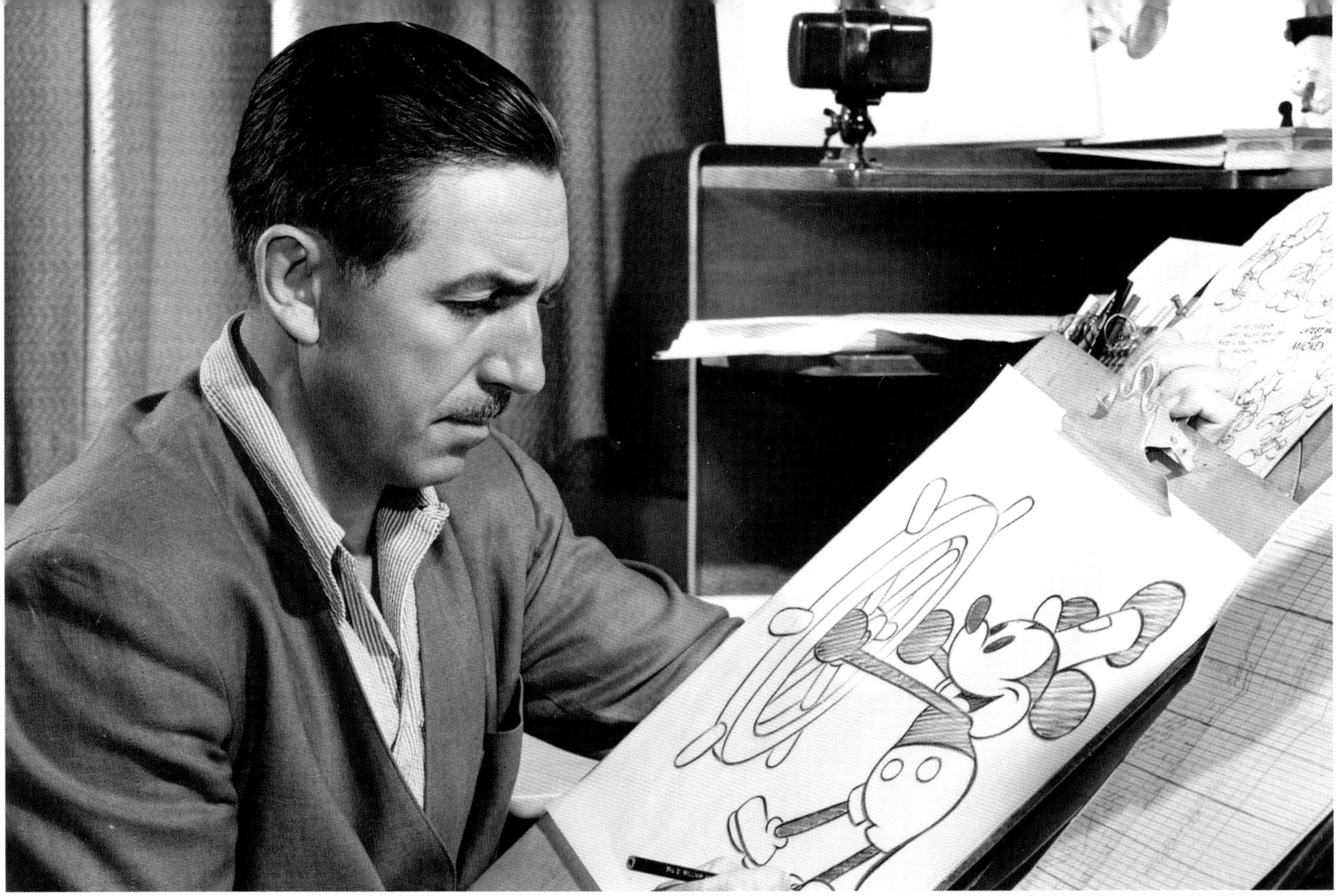

Page 22: Title cards for the Alice Comedy, *Alice in the Jungle* (1925), and the Oswald the Lucky Rabbit short, *Bright Lights* (1928).

Above: Walt Disney poses in a publicity shot with a Mickey Mouse doll and an honorary Oscar awarded for the creation of the inimitable mouse. The certificate is the Academy Award in the category of Best Cartoon for the short film *Flowers and Trees* (1932).

Right: 1947 publicity photo of Walt posing with a sketch of Mickey Mouse as Steamboat Willie.

cartoon short to premiere with synchronized sound on November 18, 1928.

Mickey Mouse was an instant success and quickly eclipsed the popularity of Felix the Cat and Oswald the Lucky Rabbit in the late 1920s. Mickey's popularity skyrocketed in the early 1930s, and by 1932 Walt was honored with a special Academy Award for his creation. That same year he would win another Academy Award for the first color cartoon, *Flowers and Trees*.

Half a world away, surrealism was formally being founded in 1924 in Paris by French writer and poet André Breton. Breton published his *Surrealist Manifesto*, in which he "advocated automatism; that is, the unchecked expression of the unconscious mind in speech, writing, or any other medium. Surrealism, with its emphasis on dreams, was based on Sigmund Freud's psychoanalysis."[2]

In late 1926, Dalí left Spain for Paris for his first visit to the French capital. Once there he met Pablo Picasso, whom he admired greatly, as well as another artist, Joan Miró.

A few years later, in February 1929, Dalí and Spanish film director Luis Buñuel completed the sixteen-minute short *Un Chien Andalou*. The film contained a shocking opening sequence in which it appears a woman's eye is sliced open with a straight razor. The film also contained images that became part of Dalí's visual language in the ensuing decades, examples of which can be seen in numerous paintings and drawings. These included ants (insects), long cast shadows on barren landscapes, bicyclists, and time represented by a watch. It was a success, at least with the "French bourgeoisie," and resulted in Dalí and Buñuel becoming the first filmmakers welcomed to the ranks of the surrealist movement.

By August of 1929, Dalí was fully engulfed in the surrealist movement. He then met his muse and future wife, Gala, a Russian immigrant, who was married to surrealist poet Paul Éluard at the time. She eventually divorced Éluard. Although they lived together beginning in 1929, Dalí and Gala did not marry until 1934. The two remained together, inseparable, for the rest of their lives. Dalí once wrote, "Every good painter who aspires to create authentic masterpieces must before anything else marry my wife."[3]

In the summer of 1930, Dalí and Gala rented a fisherman's cabin in Portlligat, Spain. They eventually purchased the property and gradually expanded it into a larger villa with a studio. Portlligat is a beautiful, picturesque village in the Costa Brava region on the Mediterranean, about sixteen miles from the French border. From 1929 to 1932 the couple split their time between Portlligat and their flat in Paris or visiting friends in Spain and Paris.

It was in early 1931, in Portlligat, that Dalí painted what is now considered one of his greatest masterpieces, *The Persistence of Memory*. The painting is aptly named, as it is quite memorable to see in person not only for the imagery within the painting but also for the size it is. The painting is only nine-and-one-half inches by thirteen inches. It combines hard objects that become inexplicably soft or limp in a barren, dreamy landscape where ants crawl around on metal as if it is decomposing flesh. It was an abstract idea of what he called "the usual paralyzing tricks of eye-fooling." Dalí painted with what he referred to as "the most imperialist fury of precision," but only, he said, "to systematize confusion and thus to help discredit completely the world of reality." It is the classical surrealist ambition, yet some literal reality is included too: the distant golden cliffs are the coast of Catalonia, Dalí's home.[4]

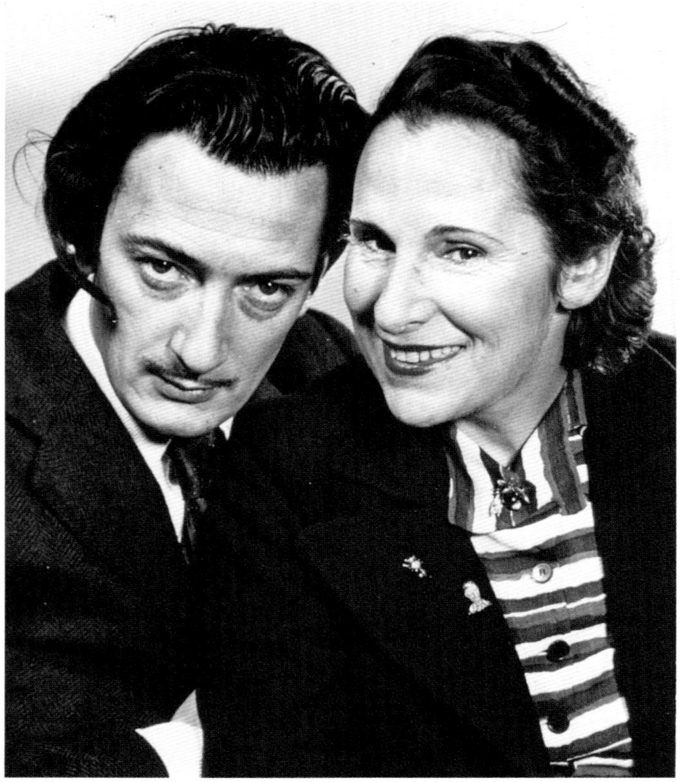

Surrealist artist Salvador Dalí with his wife Gala. Photograph by Eric Schaal, Courtesy of Fundacio Gala-Salvador Dalí, Figueres, 2015.

Top: Modern-day photograph of the Dalí's home in Portlligat, Spain. Courtesy of Dave Bossert.

Center: Statue of Dalí in Cadaqués, Spain. Courtesy of Dave Bossert.

Bottom: Cape de Creus, Spain. Courtesy of Dave Bossert.

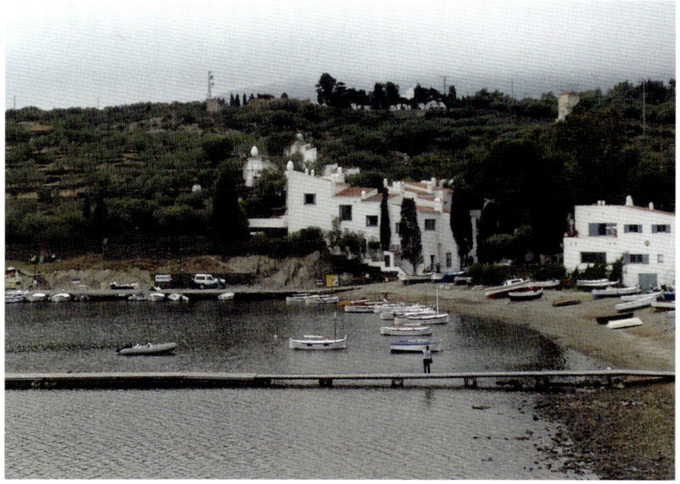

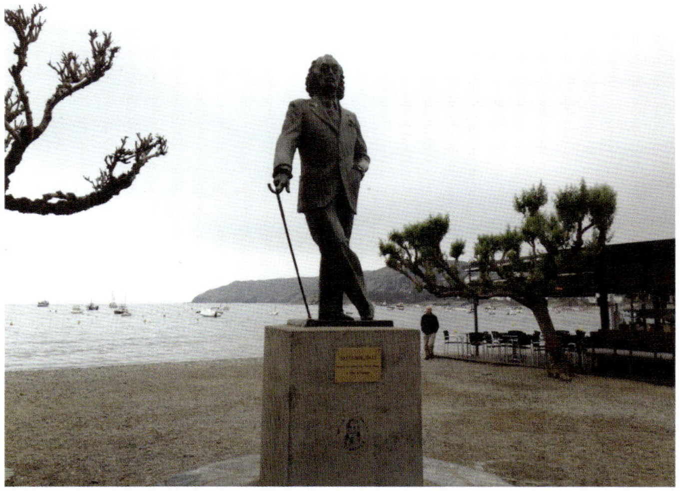

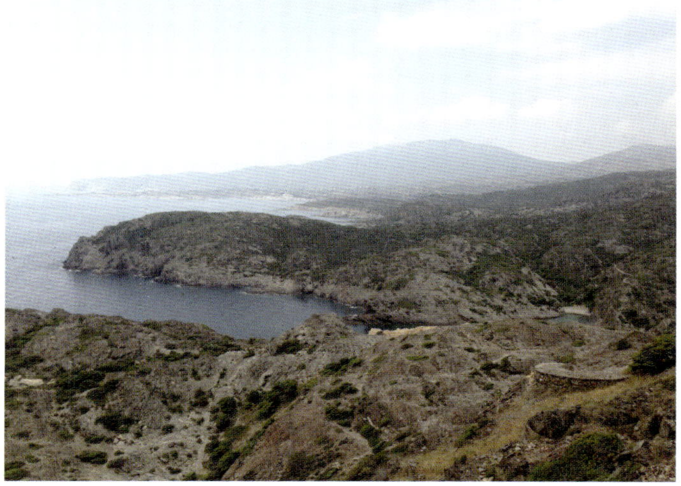

Dalí would refer to the soft watches as "the Camembert of time." To him, time loses all meaning. The use of ants or insects is a common subject in Dalí's work and represents the putrefying or rotting of flesh and hard objects becoming "grotesquely organic." The image in the center of the painting draped with a soft watch is a caricatured profile of Dalí's face; "its long eyelashes seem disturbingly insect-like or even sexual, as does what may or may not be a tongue oozing from its nose like a fat snail." Toward the distant horizon are the rocks inspired by those in the Cap de Creus peninsula, near Dalí's Portlligat home.[5]

When asked about the soft watches and what they meant, Dalí commented to John Hench in a 1968 interview, "Well, it means that sometimes you're waiting for somebody and the time stretches, becomes a long time; other times you're having a good time, and time's very fast. That's all it means." Oftentimes, Dalí would give very straightforward descriptions of what he meant by an image in his paintings. To him they were simple ideas.[6]

The Persistence of Memory contains elements that are recurring themes throughout many of Dalí's paintings. The grotesque, fleshy creature in the center of the painting, which represents Dalí, is similar to the one found in his 1929 painting *The Great Masturbator*. Self-portraits, ants, soft watches, telephones, bell towers, the bleak rocky peninsula of Cap de Creus, and stark shadows on barren landscapes are all iconography found repeatedly in Dalí's works. These symbols can also be found

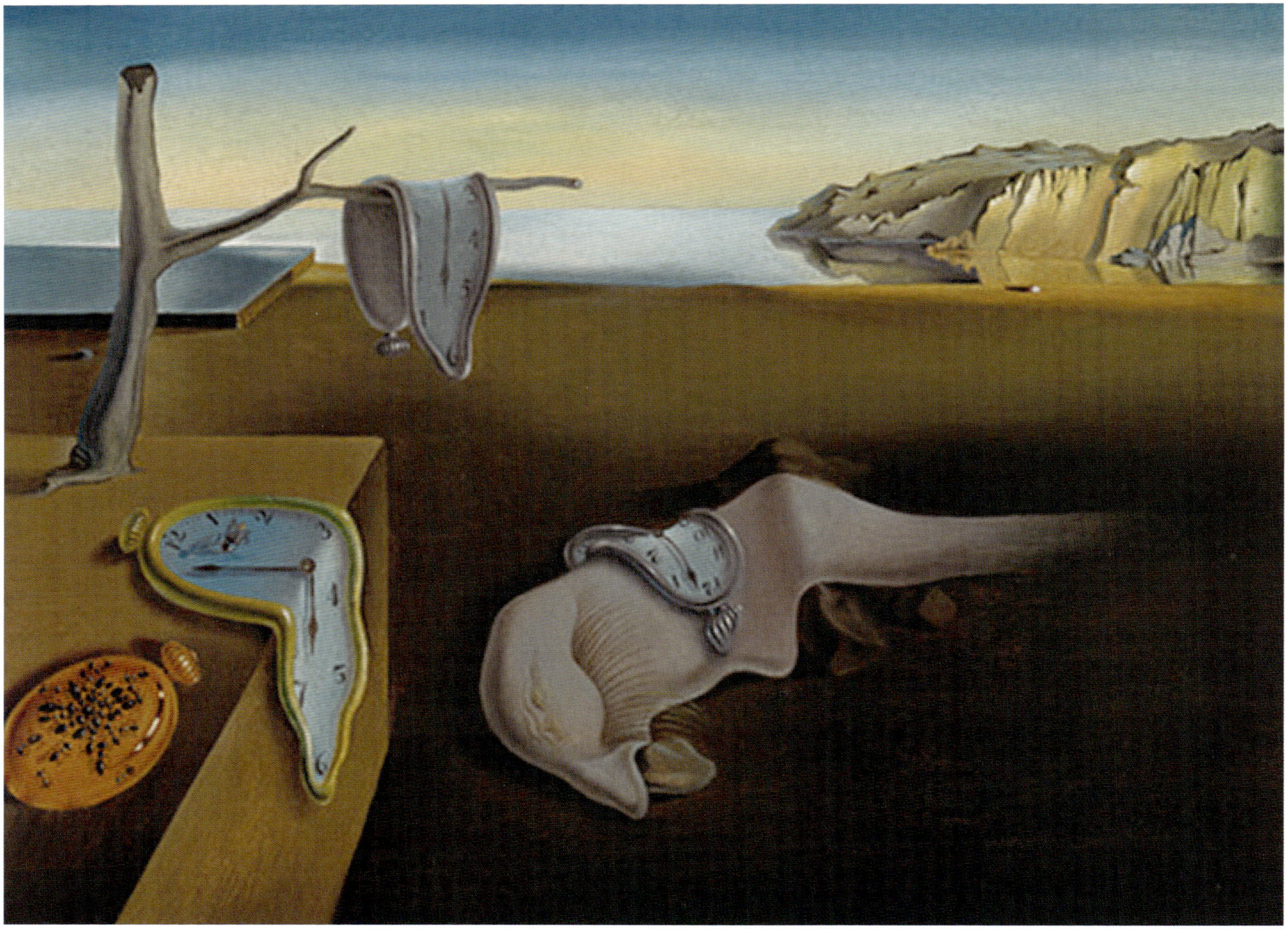

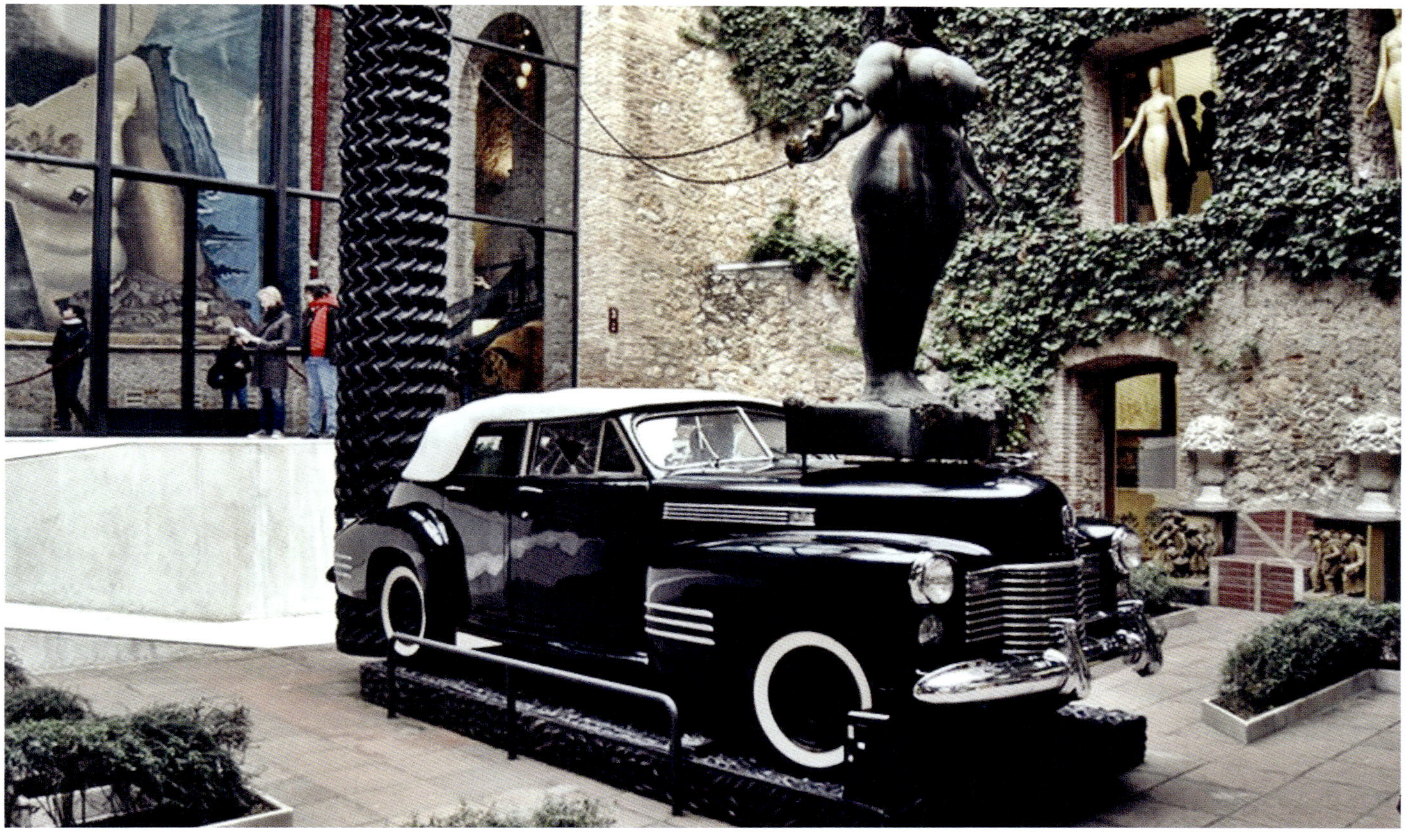

Page 26: *La Persistance de la memoire (The Persistence of Memory)*, 1931, by Salvador Dalí, courtesy of the Museum of Modern Art (MoMA) collection.

Rainy Taxi installation, 1938. Photograph courtesy of Fundació Gala-Salvador Dalí.

throughout the development, production, and final version of *Destino*.

The introduction of *The Persistence of Memory*, at an exhibition of Dalí's paintings at the Julien Levy art gallery in New York City in 1932, created an instant sensation and much notoriety for the Spanish artist. Throughout the rest of the 1930s, Dalí participated in various showings of his works, including the London International Surrealist Exhibition in 1936.

At the Galerie Beaux-Arts in Paris during the Exposition Internationale du Surréalisme in 1938 (which was organized by Breton and Éluard), Dalí unveiled *Rainy Taxi*, a three-dimensional piece of artwork. The *Rainy Taxi* consisted of an actual taxicab with two mannequin occupants that were actually being rained on inside the vehicle. (The piece is now part of the collection—and is on display—at the Dalí Theater-Museum in Figueres, Spain.) The rain was coin operated.

The Disney brothers had had their greatest success to date in 1928 with the breakthrough Mickey Mouse vehicle *Steamboat Willie*, the first synchronized sound cartoon. It further set the stage for many more firsts for the Disneys during the 1930s, including the first color cartoon, the 1932 Silly Symphony cartoon *Flowers and Trees*, which used the new and first-time-used (in a cartoon) 3-strip Technicolor film process. The Technicolor process used three

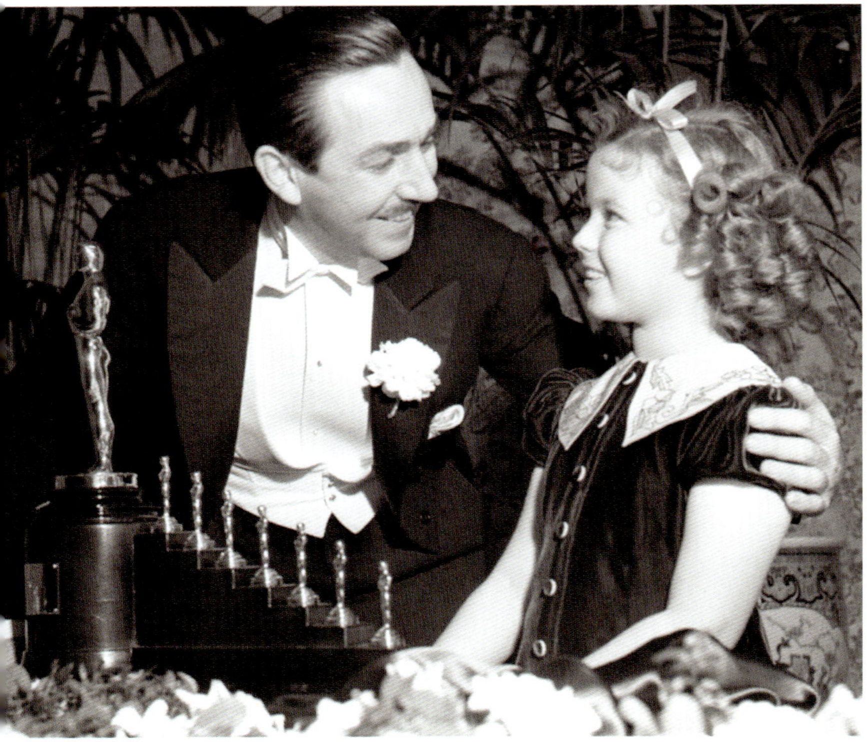

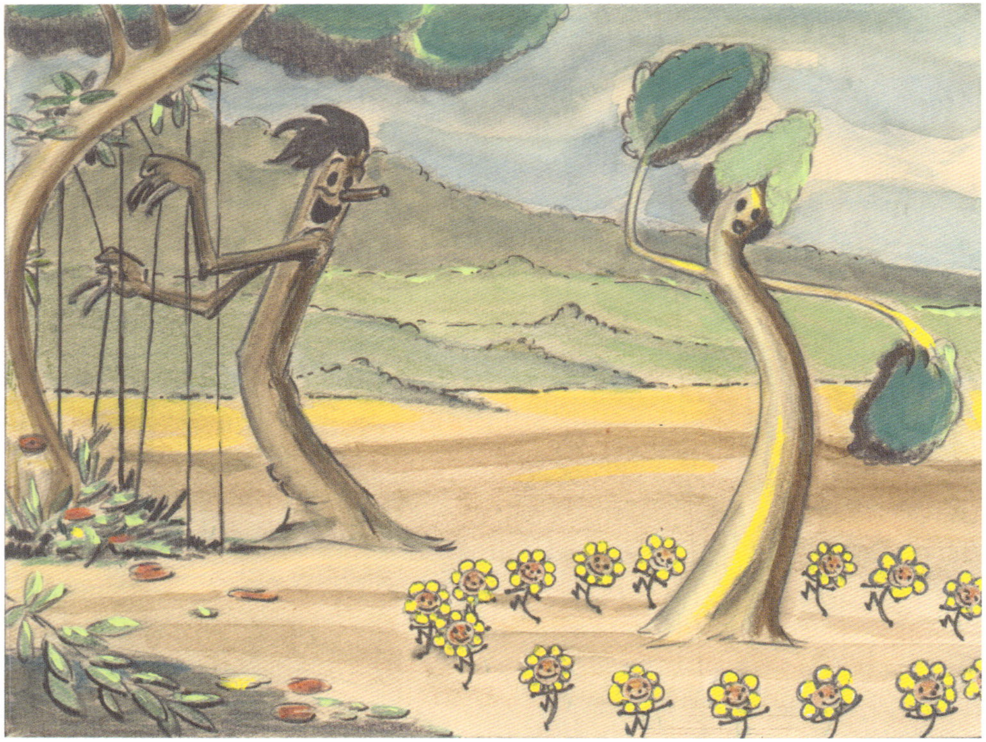

separate negatives that would be combined to create a single full-color projectable print. Walt and Roy were shrewd and negotiated an exclusive contract for the three-strip process that prevented other cartoon studios of the day from using it until 1936. The color Silly Symphonies were so popular during this period that they often eclipsed the popularity of the feature films they preceded.

The studio won an Academy Award for *Flowers and Trees*. In fact, Disney would go on to win seven more Oscars before the decade was complete, plus a very special award for *Snow White and the Seven Dwarfs*.

Both Walt Disney and Dalí saw a meteoric rise in their respective careers during the years of the Great Depression. The similarity in their parallel paths is striking, as these two artists became masters of their respective, yet still separate, disciplines. However, by the end of that decade world events would help lead to those paths eventually crossing.

Dalí painted *Soft Construction with Boiled Beans* (*Premonition of Civil War*) in 1936, which was considered by many a foreshadowing of the conflict brewing in Europe. The first signs of this occurred in Dalí's homeland. Between 1936 and 1939, Spain would be engulfed in a brutal civil war that pitted the Nationalists against the Republicans. It was a particularly grim conflict of deep political divisions and noted for horrific atrocities that were committed by both sides.

Top left: Walt Disney poses with Shirley Temple in 1939 with his Oscar and seven mini Oscar-ette statues for *Snow White and the Seven Dwarfs*.

Top right: Concept artwork from the short film *Flowers and Trees*, for which the studio won its first Academy Award, in 1932.

Page 29: Salvador Dalí's painting *Construction Molle avec Haricots Bouillis (Soft Construction with Boiled Beans)*, 1936. Courtesy of the Philadelphia Museum of Art, part of the Louise and Walter Arensberg Collection.

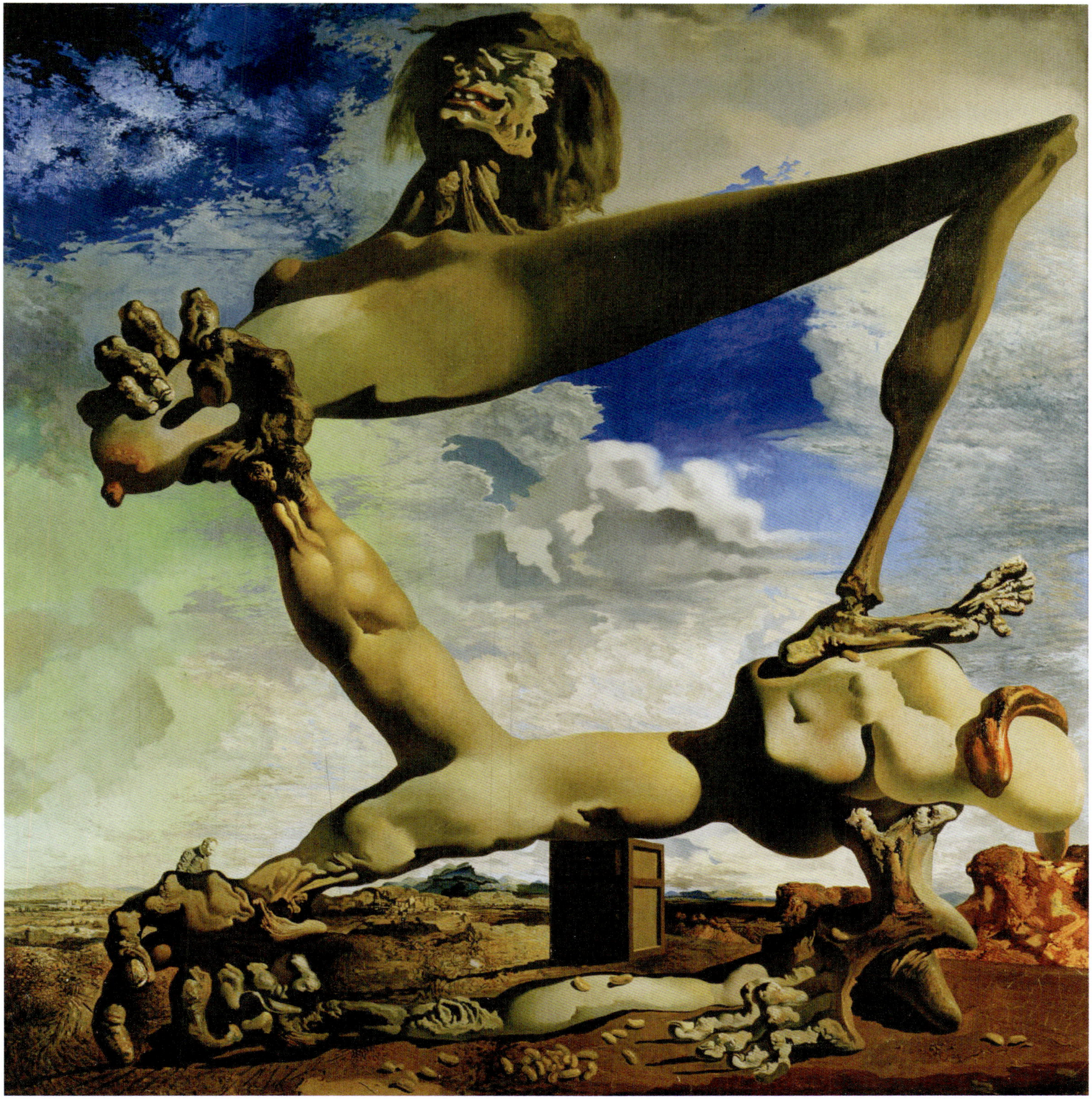

Many of Spain's artists were either taking sides or going into exile abroad. Dalí and Gala had fled the country and were spending much of their time between New York City, London, and Paris during this chaotic period.

By the end of Spanish Civil War, Europe was beginning to be torn apart by the start of World War II. In June of 1940, Dalí and Gala were able to escape from Europe and the invading German forces with visas issued by Aristides de Sousa Mendes, the Portuguese consul in Bordeaux, France. They went to New York City first via steamship, where they took up residency at The St. Regis Hotel. They would live in the United States for the next eight years splitting their time between New York City, Los Angeles, and the Hotel Del Monte in Monterey, California.

Dalí had already dabbled in film years earlier with the sixteen-minute short *Un Chien Andalou* and a number of other unfinished film projects. He was interested in working again in film, so while in Los Angeles the artist immediately established friendships, made contacts, and continued to explore the medium.

For Dalí, ". . . film was a medium in which he could draw both his visual and his verbal skills in the service of his imagination, according to Dawn Ades, a professor of the history of art at the Royal Academy of Arts in London. "And there is a constant triangulation formed by the flow of film, painting, and text," observes Ades, who is also a former trustee of the Tate galleries in Britain and has organized a number of exhibitions on surrealism, including the Centenary of Salvador Dalí at the Palazzo Grassi in Venice, Italy, in 2004.[7]

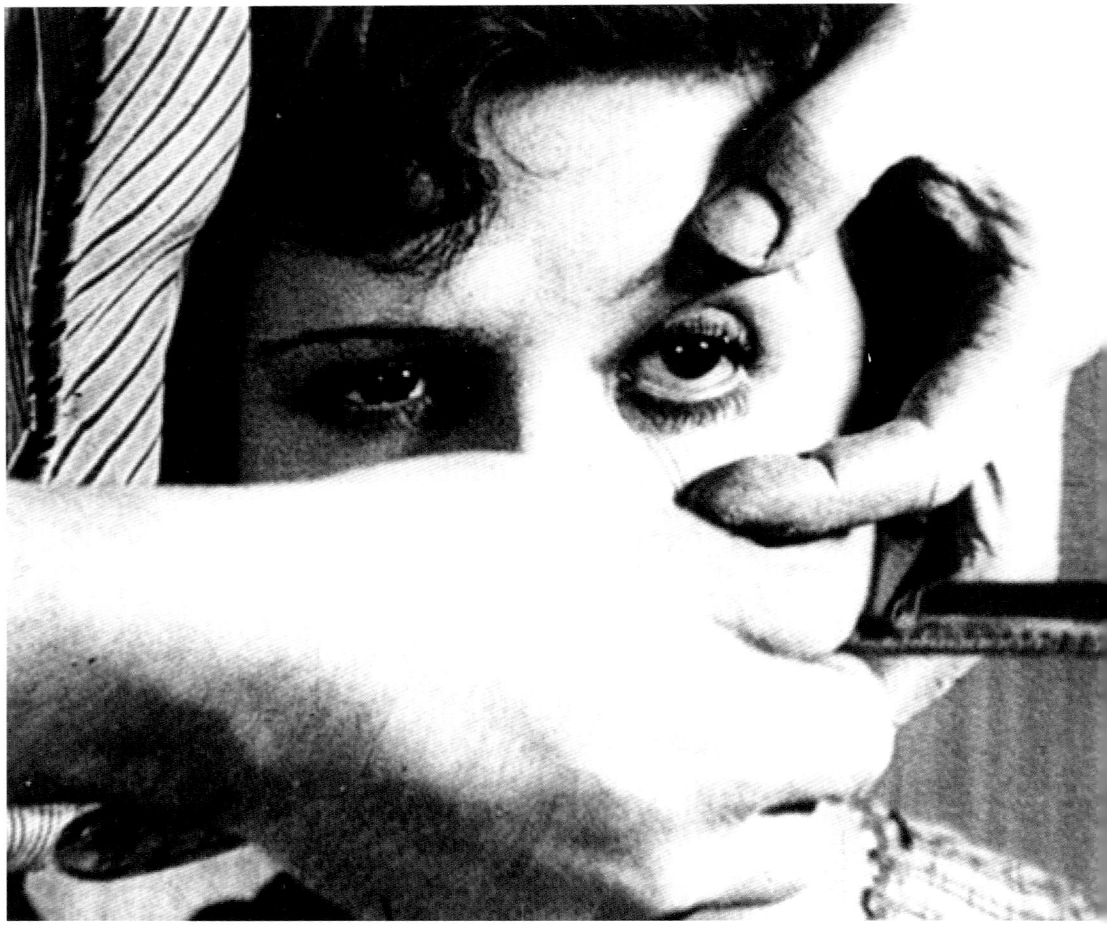

Page 30: Still-frame photograph from the film *Un Chien Andalou* (1929). Courtesy of Contemporary Films.

Salvador Dalí's painting *Le Grand Masturbateur (The Great Masturbator,* 1929, courtesy of the Museo Nacional Centro de Arte Reina Sofia, Madrid.

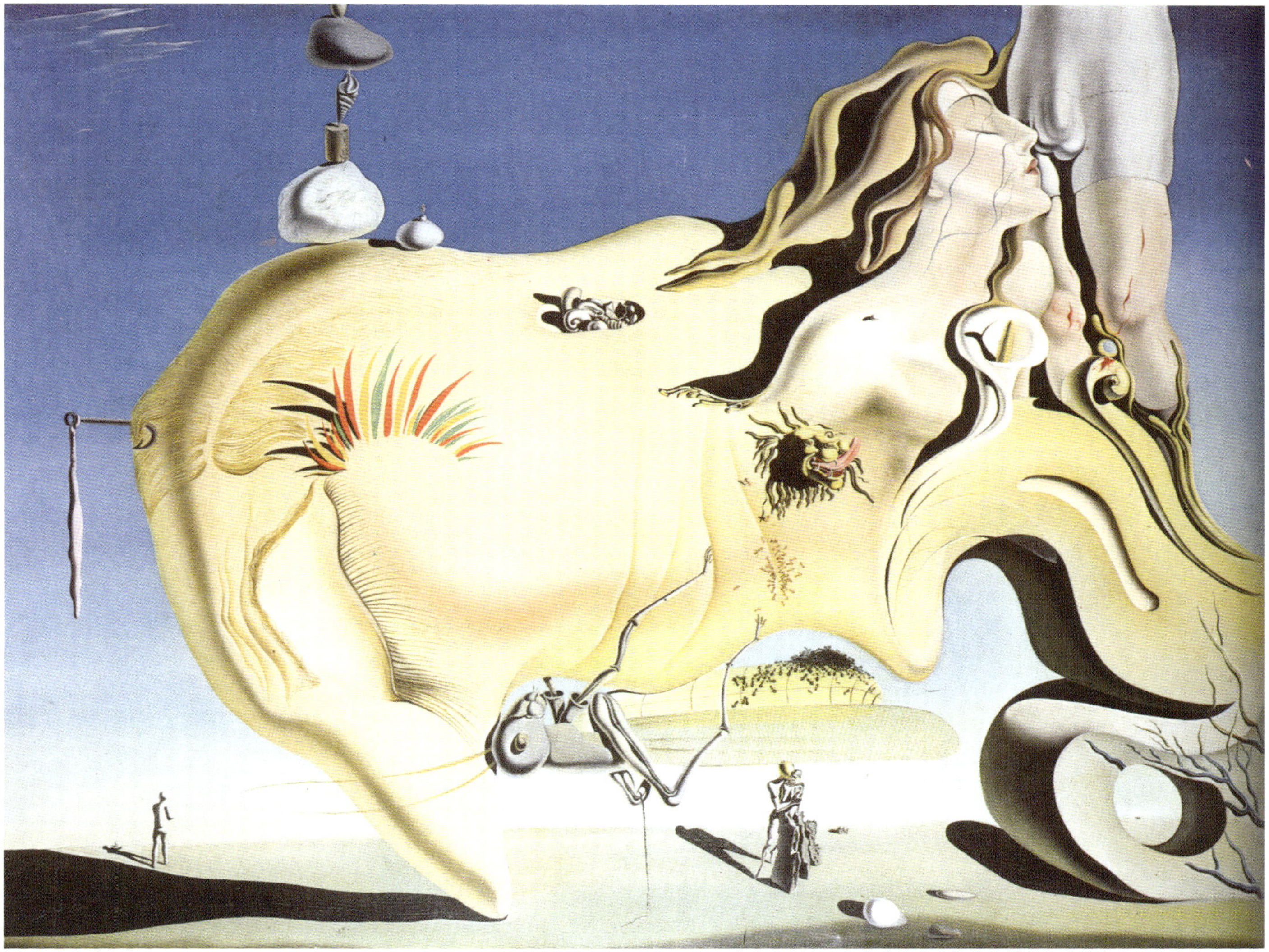

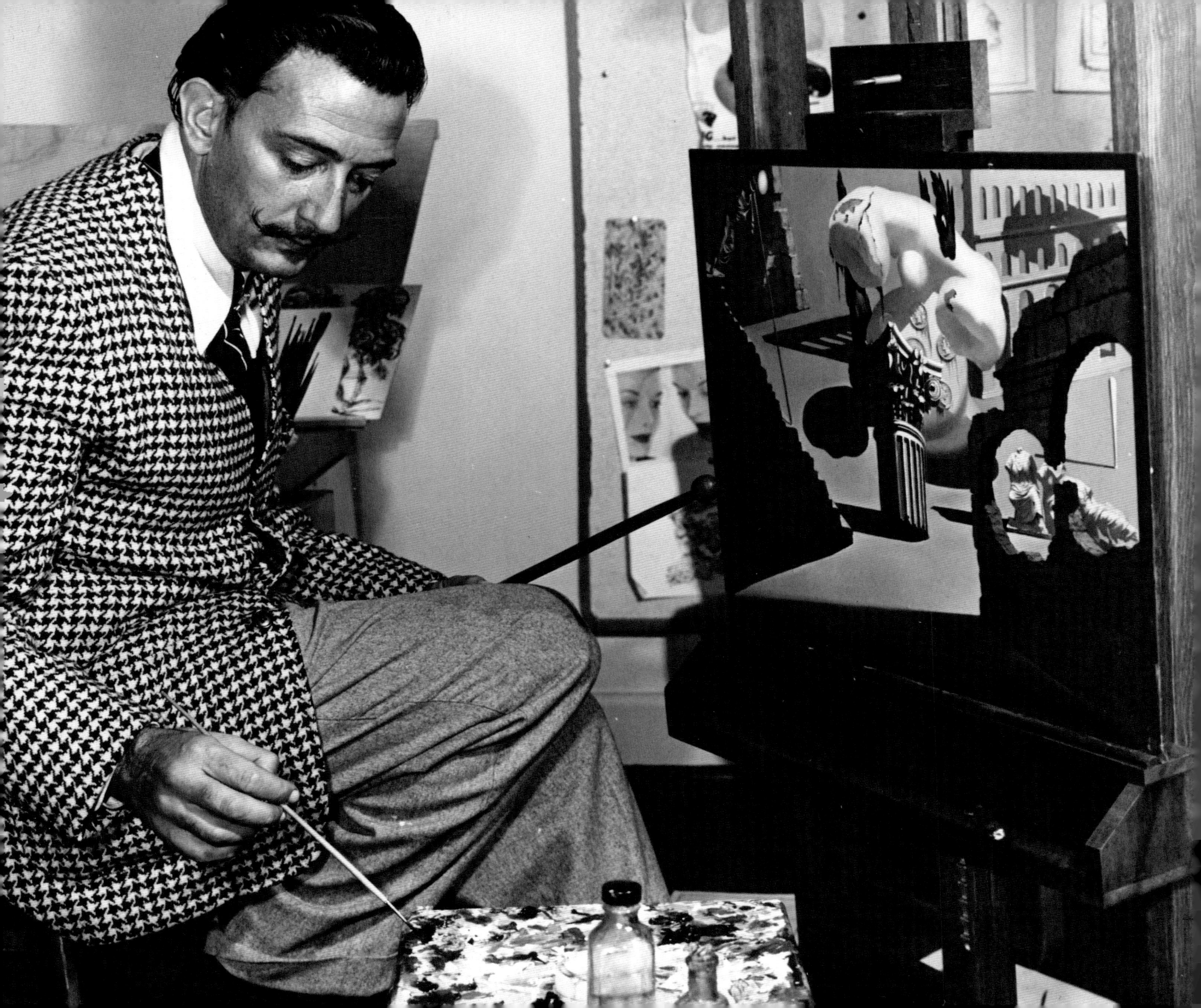

ACT II:
Disney & Dalí Meet and Collaborate

The script for the Warner Bros. film *Spellbound* was finalized in July of 1944. Director Alfred Hitchcock wanted to work with Salvador Dalí on the dream sequence in the film. Hitchcock commented years later in an interview that, "What I was after was . . . the vividness of dreams . . . All of Dalí's work is very solid and very sharp, with very long perspectives and black shadows . . ."

Dalí was "the best man for me to do the dreams," the director further noted, "because that is what dreams should be." In August Dalí signed a contract to "create, draw, and paint all sketches and/or designs required in connection with *Spellbound*'s four paintings."[1]

When Walt and Dalí met through Jack Warner, they discussed working together on a project. Dalí later wrote to Walt the following: "Very dear friend: I think constantly and with enthusiasm of our future collaboration[,] and every day I figure out new ideas . . . There is enormous curiosity in New York about our future collaboration. Good day."[2]

By February 1945, Dalí and his wife, Gala, sent this note to Walt saying, "We're back from New York at Hotel Del Monte, where we plan to stay a while—Dalí works so well here . . . How are your projects coming along? Dalí is always thinking about that collaboration you spoke about. How is it going?" The note is signed, "Your friend, [Mrs.] Dalí—and Dalí joins with me."[3]

There is a wonderful sense of warmth that comes through in these letters. It gives the impression that these two artists established an instant bond when

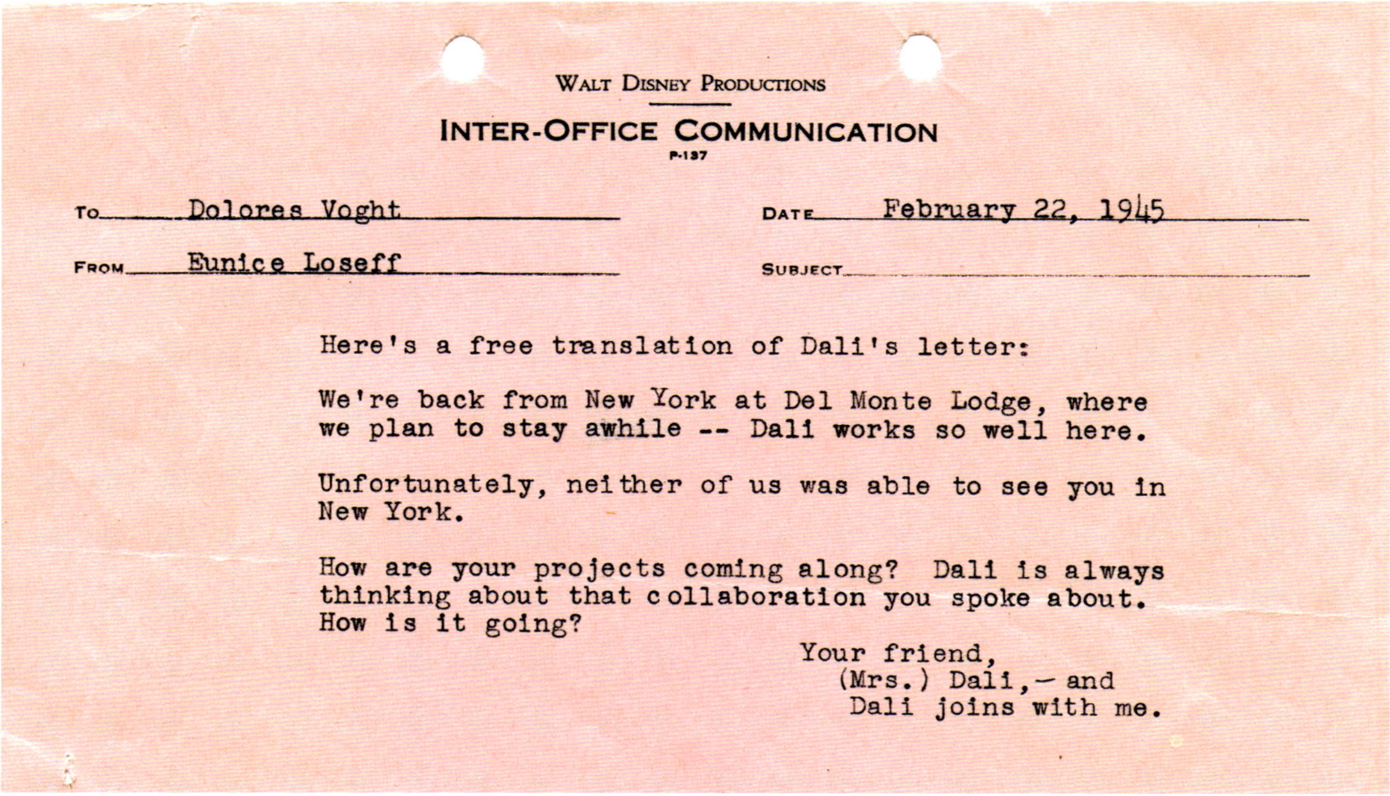

WALT DISNEY PRODUCTIONS

INTER-OFFICE COMMUNICATION

P-137

TO Dolores Voght DATE February 22, 1945

FROM Eunice Loseff SUBJECT

Here's a free translation of Dali's letter:

We're back from New York at Del Monte Lodge, where we plan to stay awhile -- Dali works so well here.

Unfortunately, neither of us was able to see you in New York.

How are your projects coming along? Dali is always thinking about that collaboration you spoke about. How is it going?

Your friend,
(Mrs.) Dali,– and
Dali joins with me.

Page 32: Photograph of Salvador Dalí working in his studio.

Interoffice memo receipt from Eunice Loseff to Dolores Voght regarding a translation of Dalí's letter to Walt Disney on February 22, 1945.

they met. This is not uncommon in the arts as many artists are inspired by their peers and the work they are producing.

Walt had always been interested in the concepts of other artists in various fields, including Oskar Fischinger; Thomas Hart Benton, the American painter and muralist; Norman Rockwell; Leopold Stokowski; Igor Stravinsky; and others. Walt would work with some of these artists and even hired Rico Lebrun, the Italian-born painter and sculptor, as well as others, to teach drawing classes to his animators during the making of *Bambi* and other features at the studio.

One day, in 1944, Walt stepped into animator Marc Davis's office and noticed a book on surrealism that featured artworks by Dalí. Marc Davis was one of Walt's "Nine Old Men" and is noted for designing Tinker Bell, Maleficent, the Pirates of the Caribbean attraction at Disneyland, and many other familiar things at Disney. According to Davis's widow, Alice Davis, Marc had checked the book out of the studio library. Walt borrowed the book and ultimately bought his own copy, which he eventually sent off to Dalí to be autographed.

At the time, John Hench, another Disney artist, felt that surrealism wasn't understood that well partly "because it was not made for laughs; it wasn't exactly amusing." He would go on to say, when interviewed years later, that "The juxtaposition of things that are contradictory, of course, we exploited . . . for years; barren landscapes, long shadows." There are some

Original letter that was translated from page 34.

RECEIVED
FEB 22 1945
WALT DISNEY PROD.

DEL MONTE LODGE
PEBBLE BEACH, CALIFORNIA

18 fev 45

Cher ami et monsieur Disney,

nous voici de retour de New-York à Del Monte Lodge où nous pensons rester pas mal de temps - Dali y travaille si bien -

Malheureusement à New-York ni l'un, ni l'autre nous n'avons pas eu le temps de vous voir -

Quels sont vos projets Dali pense toujours à cette fameuse collaboration qu'en dites vous?

Amicalement
votre Gala Dali
et Dali se joint à moi

Very dear friend:

I think constantly and with enthusiasm of our future collaboration and every day I figure out new ideas.

I am sending a statement of everything you desired that I should say from your side to the journalists because I promise in this matter a series of articles.

My regards to your wife.

Gala and I are sending to you .... Salvatore Dali

Remember me to Joe Grant. I am also saving for him some surprises.

There is an enormous curiosity in New York about our future collaboration. Good day.

CLASS OF SERVICE
This is a full-rate Telegram or Cablegram unless its deferred character is indicated by a suitable symbol above or preceding the address.

WESTERN UNION

1220

A. N. WILLIAMS PRESIDENT · NEWCOMB CARLTON CHAIRMAN OF THE BOARD · J. C. WILLEVER FIRST VICE-PRESIDENT

SYMBOLS
DL=Day Letter
NT=Overnight Telegram
LC=Deferred Cable
NLT=Cable Night Letter
Ship Radiogram

The filing time shown in the date line on telegrams and day letters is STANDARD TIME at point of origin. Time of receipt is STANDARD TIME at point of destination

SD22 NL PD=NEWYORK NY DEC 26 1945

MR & MRS WALT DISNEY=

=MEILLEURS VOEURS POUR NOUVELLE ANNEE ATTENDONS AVEC GRANDE ILLUSIONS NOUVEAU MONDE QUI NAITERA DE NOTRE COLLABORATION AFFECTIONS A VOUX DEUX=

=VOS GALA ET DALI. (839AM

a New York une curiosité enorme sur notre future colaboration! Bon jour!

CABLE ADDRESS "SAINTREGIS NEW YORK"

Hotel St. Regis

Fifth Avenue and Fifty-fifth Street

New York

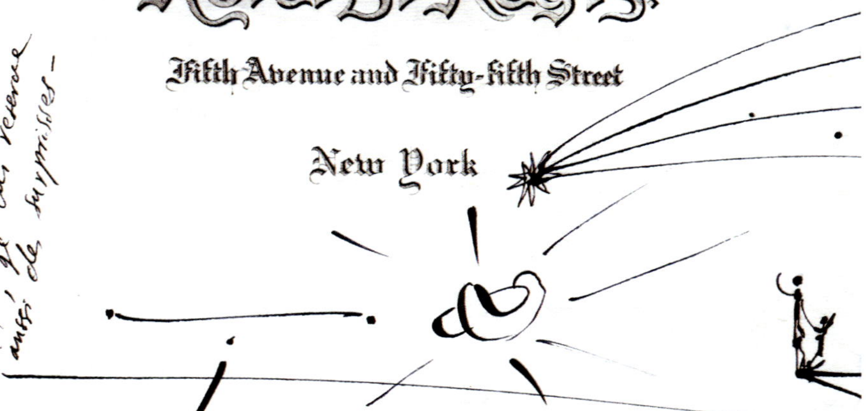

Tres cher ami, ge pensse constenment avec entusiasme a notre future colaboration, et j'anote deja tous les jours des nouvelles ideas!

ge m'envoi un statement, de tout ce que vous dessire que ge disse de votre part aux journalistes, car ge promis a ce suget une serie de reportages!

Hommages a Votre femme

Gala et moi vous envoyons notre afection votre Salvador Dali 1943

mes souvenirs pour Joe Grant, ge lui reserve aussi des surprisses—

Page 36 (top left): Translation of Salvador Dalí's letter (right) to Walt Disney.

Page 36 (right): Dalí's original letter to Walt, written on stationery from The St. Regis Hotel in New York, 1943.

Page 36 (bottom left): Telegram from Dalí to Walt and Lillian dated December 26, 1945. The translation reads, "Mr. and Mrs. Disney, Best wishes for the New Year. We await with great hope this new world that will be born from our collaboration. Affections for you both.
Yours, Gala and Dalí"

Walt's letter to Dalí about their plans to collaborate, dated December 24, 1945.

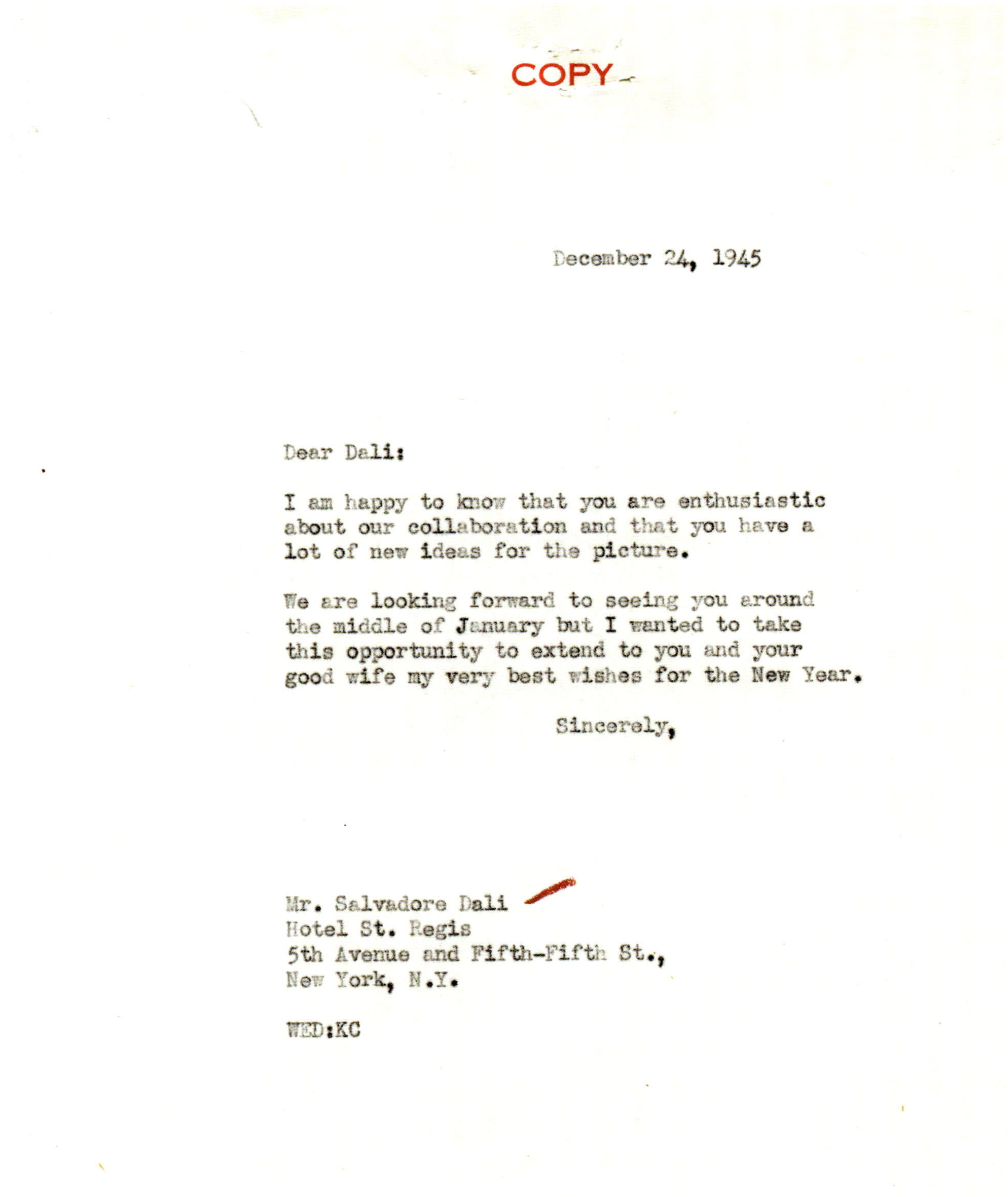

COPY

December 24, 1945

Dear Dali:

I am happy to know that you are enthusiastic about our collaboration and that you have a lot of new ideas for the picture.

We are looking forward to seeing you around the middle of January but I wanted to take this opportunity to extend to you and your good wife my very best wishes for the New Year.

Sincerely,

Mr. Salvadore Dali
Hotel St. Regis
5th Avenue and Fifth-Fifth St.,
New York, N.Y.

WED:KC

of these types of surrealist elements in Disney films, such as *Hell's Bells* (a 1929 Silly Symphony), the "Pink Elephants on Parade" sequence from *Dumbo* (1941), and *Alice in Wonderland* (1951). You can even see the influence of surrealism in the 1936 Mickey Mouse short *Thru the Mirror*, in which inanimate objects come to life after Mickey falls asleep reading a copy of *Through the Looking-Glass* by Lewis Carroll. John added that Walt "would exploit any style he thought was effective. That was his obsession—to communicate well."[4]

To some it may seem like an odd pairing of personalities; Walt was a popular filmmaker whose work appealed to the masses, and Dalí was a leading fine artist who was a founding member of the surrealist movement. They both had something, personal attributes, that the other admired and wanted to emulate. Walt was elevating animation techniques from cartoons to an art form; he was constantly striving to improve the abilities of his entire artistic staff and wanted to be viewed as a more serious fine artist.

The artistic progression of Disney animation through the 1930s is evidence of Walt pushing his artists to hone their draftsmanship skills. It's particularly visible in the evolution of Mickey Mouse from the crude, flat drawings in the black-and-white short *Plane Crazy* to the first color Mickey cartoon, *The Band Concert* in 1935, to the very dimensional Sorcerer's Apprentice sequence in *Fantasia* in 1940. There is a clear visual progression of refinement to the animation craft, the development of the Disney house style, from 1928 through the release of *Fantasia*.

Although Dalí was getting notoriety in the late 1930s as a fine artist with paintings such as *Metamorphosis of Narcissus* (1937), *Swans Reflecting Elephants* (1937), *Inventions of the Monsters* (1937), and *The Burning Giraffe* (1937), he was not garnering the mass appeal that he craved. He fell in love with the American media and was a favorite of the press in return for his antics and unique persona. Although he reveled in his own eccentricity, he yearned for even more attention on a grander scale than his artwork

From left to right: *Plane Crazy* (1928), *The Band Concert* (1935), and *Fantasia* (1940).

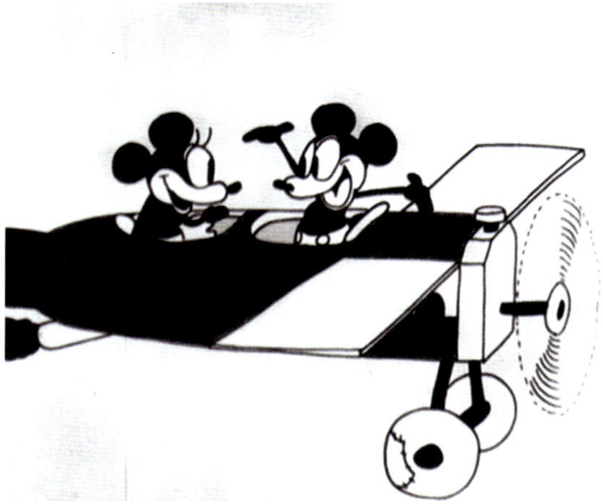

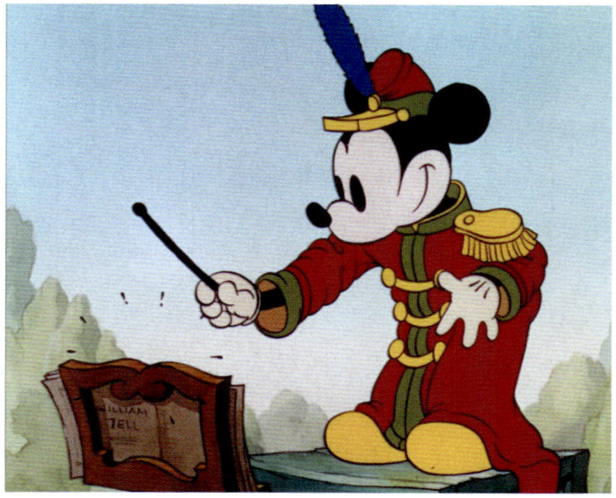

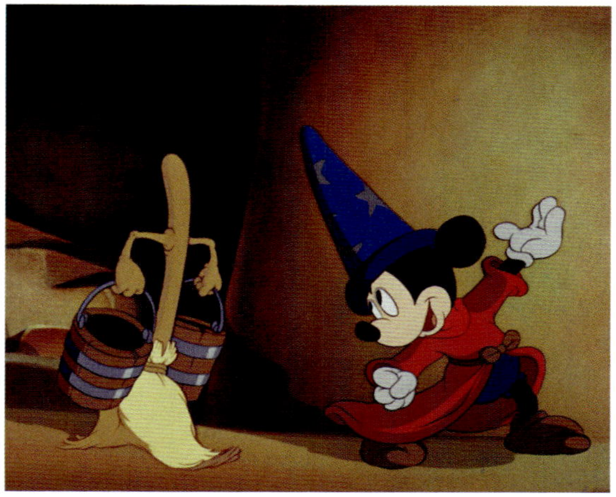

Clockwise from left: Piano keys morph into a caterpillar on a Dalí-esque landscape in the "Bumble Boogie" sequence from *Melody Time* (1948); Alice runs across a Dalí-esque barren landscape with long, cast shadows; "Pink Elephants on Parade" sequence from *Dumbo* (1941), which is often referred to as a Disney film that used surrealist imagery and themes.

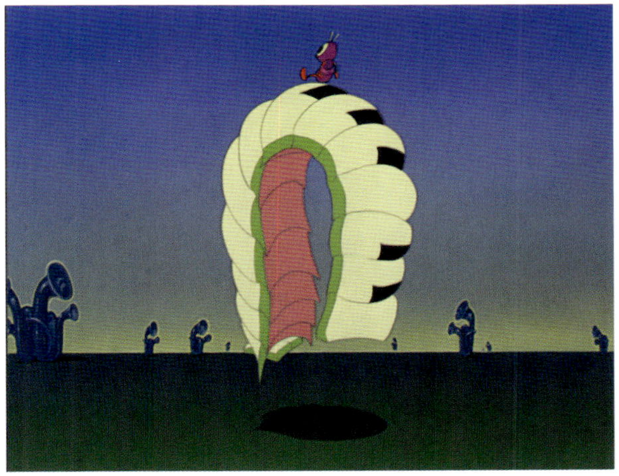

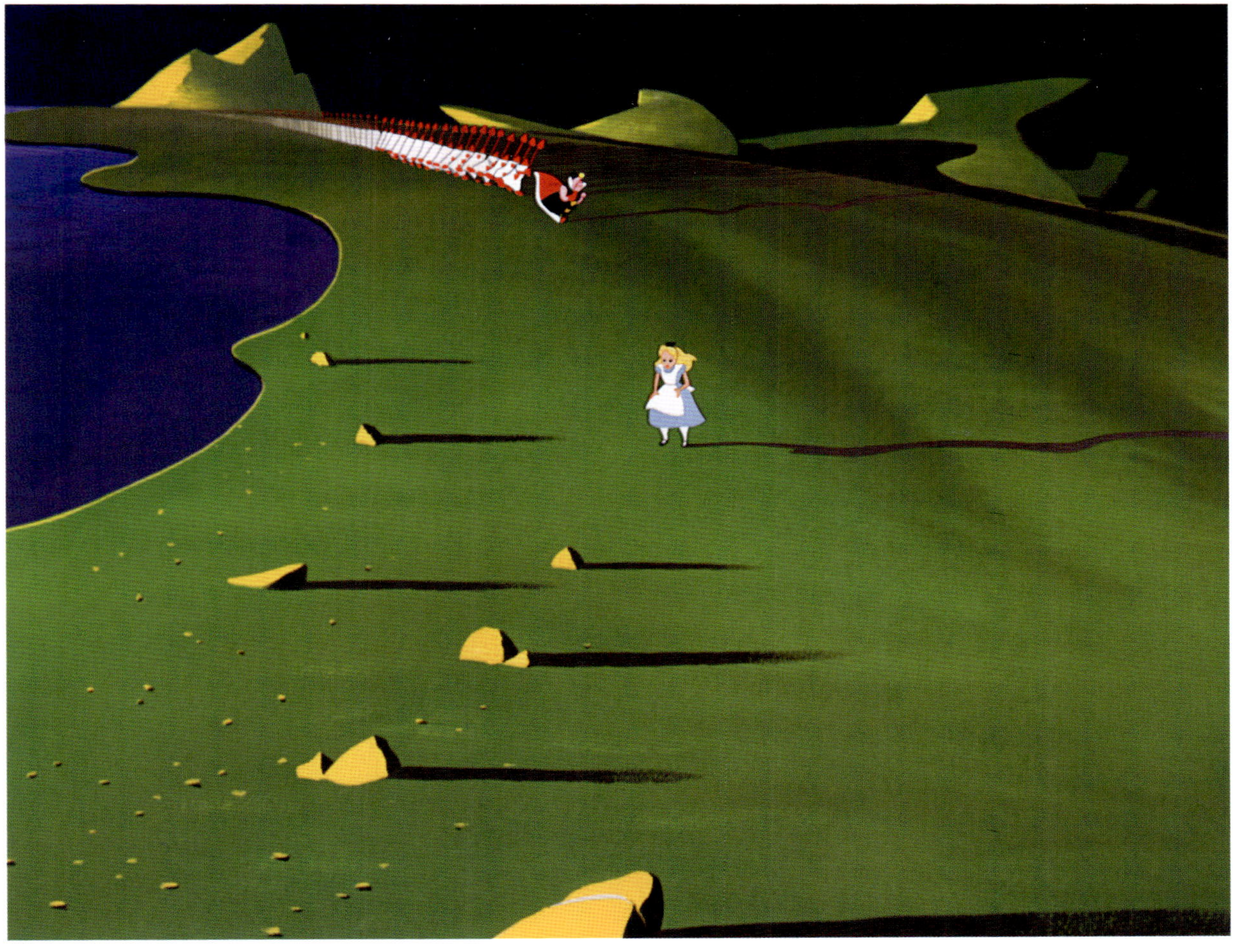

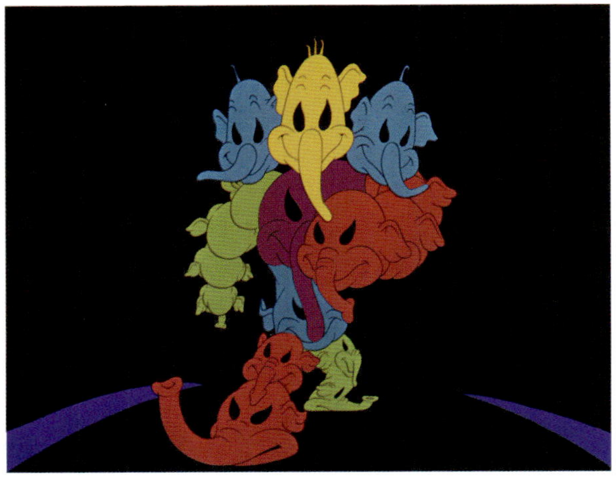

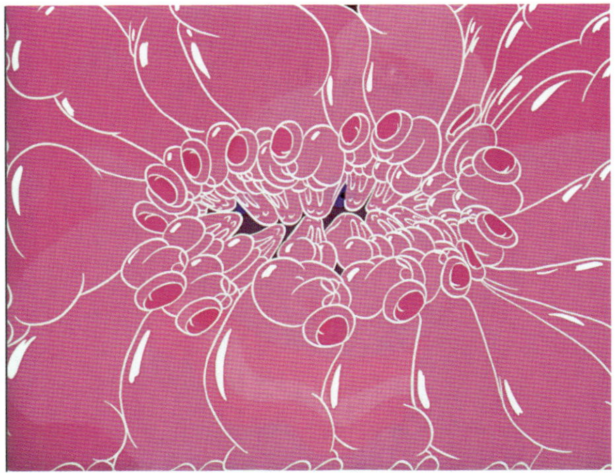

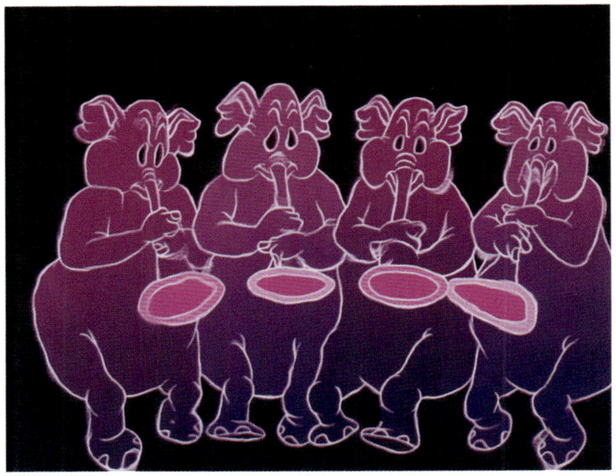

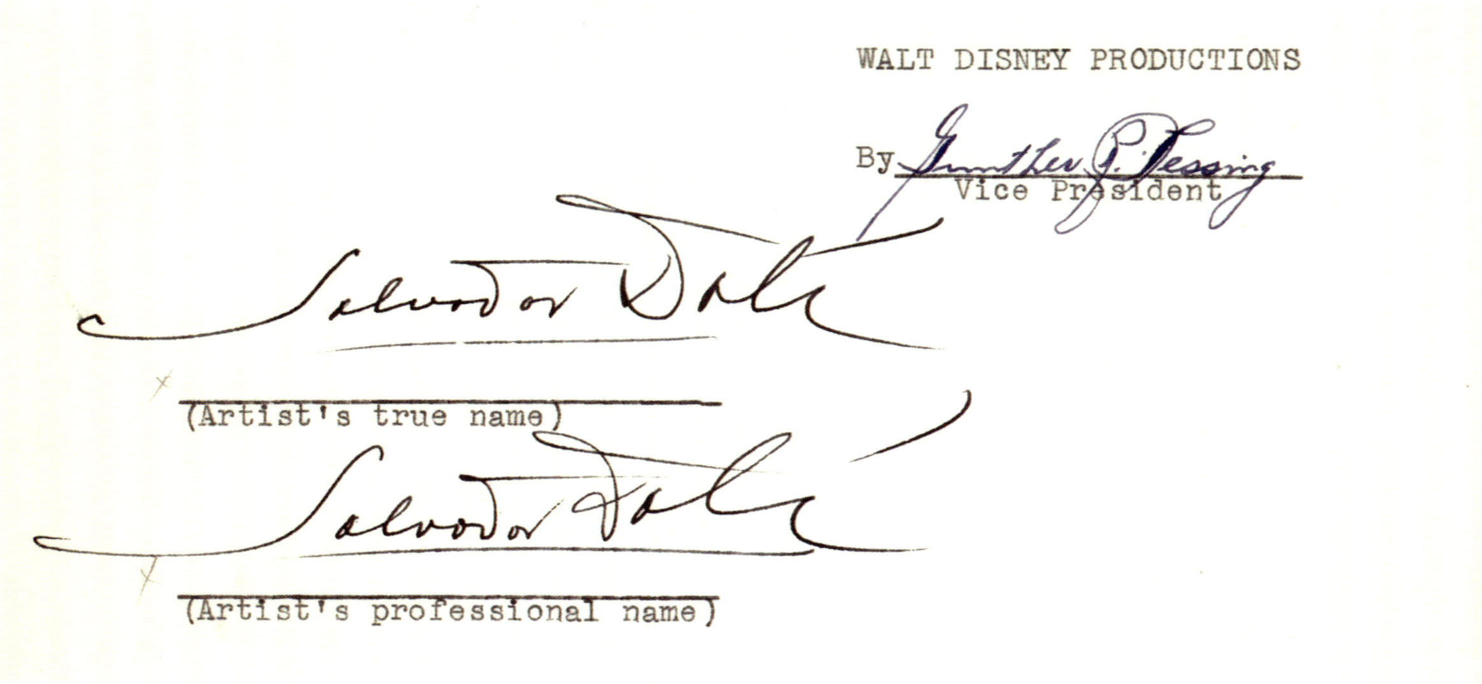
WALT DISNEY PRODUCTIONS

By____________________
Vice President

(Artist's true name)

(Artist's professional name)

Close-up of Salvador Dalí's signature on his employment contract with the Walt Disney Studios in 1946.

had attained at that point. He was in search of the mass appeal Walt Disney enjoyed. In some sense, the old idiom of "opposites attract" came into play, and the two artists became friends—and maintained a friendship that lasted a lifetime.

To Disney artist Joe Grant, Dalí and Walt Disney understood art and commerce. "There was that commercial side to both of them for that matter," Joe said. "Of course, that was a necessity. I mean, that term, 'poor artists', it still meant something!" At the time, Walt and Dalí had already achieved great financial success. It was a fusion of art and commerce that created an ecosystem that they both felt comfortable in.

In a letter dated December 24, 1945, sent to Dalí while he was back at the St. Regis hotel in New York, Walt wrote:

> Dear Dalí: I am happy to know that you are enthusiastic about our collaboration and that you have a lot of new ideas for the picture. We are looking forward to seeing you around the middle of January[,] but I wanted to take this opportunity to extend to you and your good wife my very best wishes for the New Year.[5]

Walt and Gala had worked out the arrangements as she usually acted as Dalí's business agent. There was a contract drawn up that stipulated all of the details. One interesting note: Dalí typically retained ownership of his artwork at the end of a collaborative project such as the one with Disney. That was not the case with *Destino*.

Dalí did not require any "persuasion as he long believed in the special power of animated images to evoke ideas," according to Hench. He was quite excited by the idea of working at the Disney Studios.

Salvador Dalí's paycheck stub totaling $2500.00 for his work from January 15, 1946, to February 4, 1946.

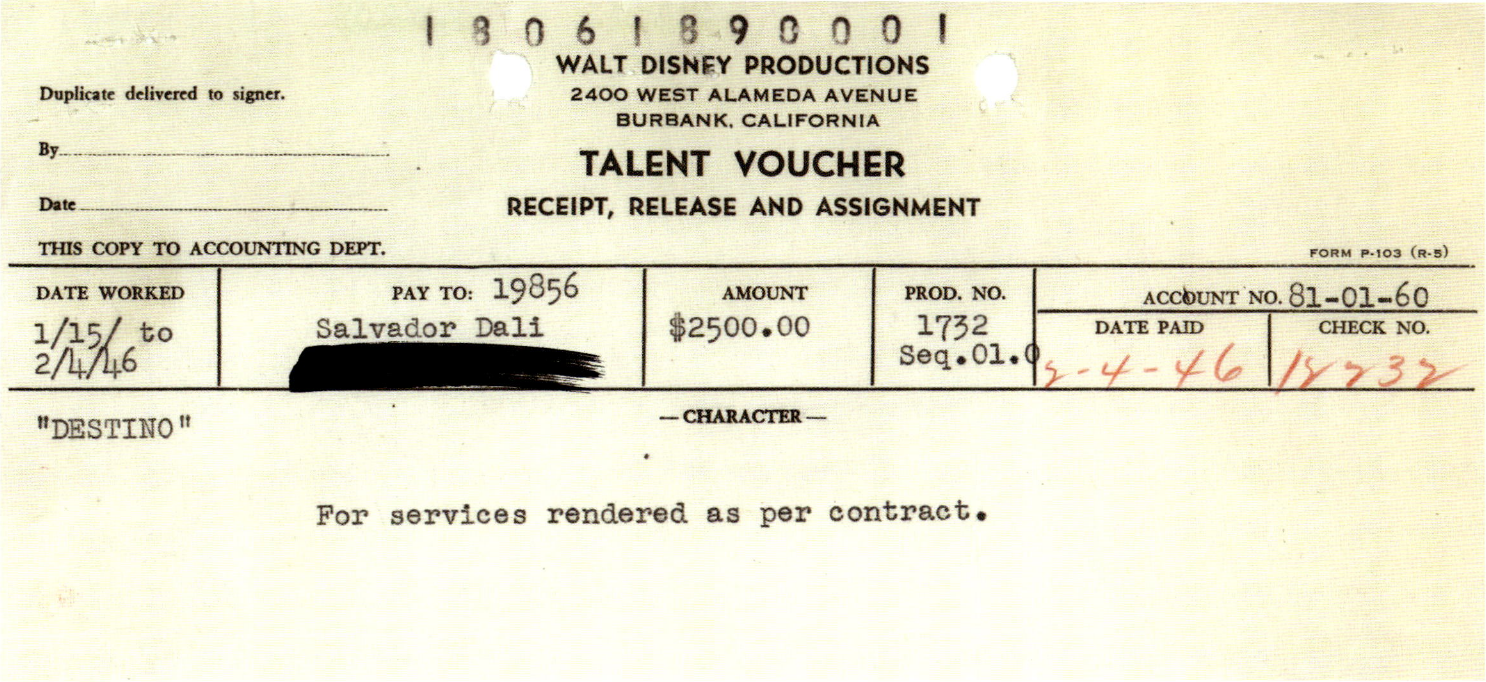

1 8 0 6 1 8 9 0 0 0 1

WALT DISNEY PRODUCTIONS
2400 WEST ALAMEDA AVENUE
BURBANK, CALIFORNIA

Duplicate delivered to signer.

By

Date

THIS COPY TO ACCOUNTING DEPT.

TALENT VOUCHER

RECEIPT, RELEASE AND ASSIGNMENT

FORM P-103 (R-5)

DATE WORKED	PAY TO: 19856	AMOUNT	PROD. NO.	ACCOUNT NO. 81-01-60	
				DATE PAID	CHECK NO.
1/15/ to 2/4/46	Salvador Dali [redacted]	$2500.00	1732 Seq.01.0	2-4-46	18732

"DESTINO"

— CHARACTER —

For services rendered as per contract.

Although Dalí came to the Disney Studios to begin work on January 15, 1946, he did not actually sign an agreement until April 1946. The talent contract was signed between Salvador Dalí and Walt Disney Productions for "Artist and other services in connection with *Destino* (Prod. #1732 Seq. 01.0)."

The date of the agreement was April 15, 1946, but the contract covered the "principal period" from January 15, 1946, to "July 31, 1946[,] or later as may be extended, but not between April 9, 1946[,] and April 14, 1946." The contract also stipulated an option based on mutual agreement that extended the agreement out to the "30th day of April, 1948."

Dalí was paid handsomely, by 1946 standards, for his services in connection with the *Destino* project. Under "salary rate," the contract notes a salary of $17,909.09 "total payable as follows: Artist acknowledges receipt of $11,909.09 the aggregate of all installments due up to April 30, 1946; $2,000.00 due on or before May 31, 1946, $2,000 on or before June 30, 1946[,] and $2,000 upon expiration of agreement."

The first payment of $2,500, verified by the "Talent Vouchers" which were the payment receipt and time sheets on file at Disney, began when Dalí arrived at the Disney Studios on January 15, 1946, and covered the period through February 4, 1946.

Contrary to a popular myth at the studio, Dalí did not punch a time clock, which many of the artists did during that time period—and continued to do until the mid-1980s. Although Hench commented that ". . . I don't think that he'd have minded punching in. He liked ritual."[6] Hench later recalled that he shared a table and the space with Dalí, and he was very prompt. "He arrived at eight every morning or eight-thirty; we

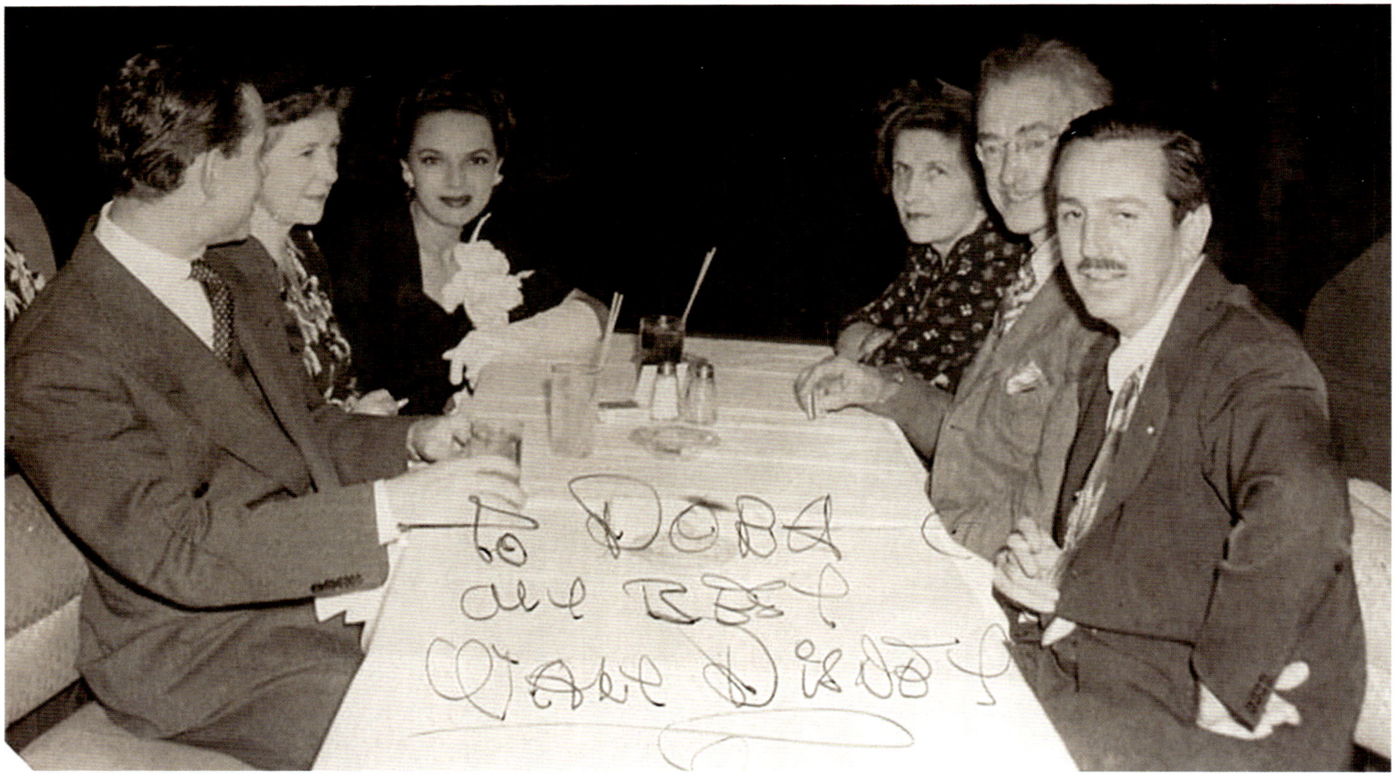

From left to right: An unidentified man, Harriet Wolcott, Dora Luz, Lillian Disney, Charles Wolcott, and Walt Disney dining at the Hollywood Palladium. Photograph courtesy of phil-sears.com.

had lunch together, and we said good night at five-thirty or six or seven."

The *Hollywood Daily Reporter* would publish a notice with the headline DALI WORKS AT DISNEY several months after Dalí arrived at the studio. The brief article states the following:

> Salvador Dalí, the surrealist artist, yesterday checked in at the Walt Disney Studios, where he will work for eight weeks "styling" Disney's forthcoming production, *Destino*, based on Armando Dominguez's famous Mexican tragic song, for which Ray Gilbert wrote the English lyrics. It will be a boy-meets-girl cartoon film done in the surrealist mode.[7]

At the time Dominguez was a well-known Mexican composer and arranger, as well as a popular songwriter of the day. He was a founding member of the Society of Authors and Composers of Mexico and had worked on at least twenty Mexican films, plus recorded several popular albums.

Walt had purchased the song "Destino" in the early 1940s. (This is standard practice at studios even today; they purchase songs, scripts, books, and other material for possible use in or development of a film.) The American lyricist Ray Gilbert, best known for his Oscar-winning song "Zip-A-Dee-Doo-Dah," from the Disney film *Song of the South*, wrote the English version of the song titled "My Destiny of Love." Gilbert had also written the English lyrics for

Story sketches by Salvador Dalí.

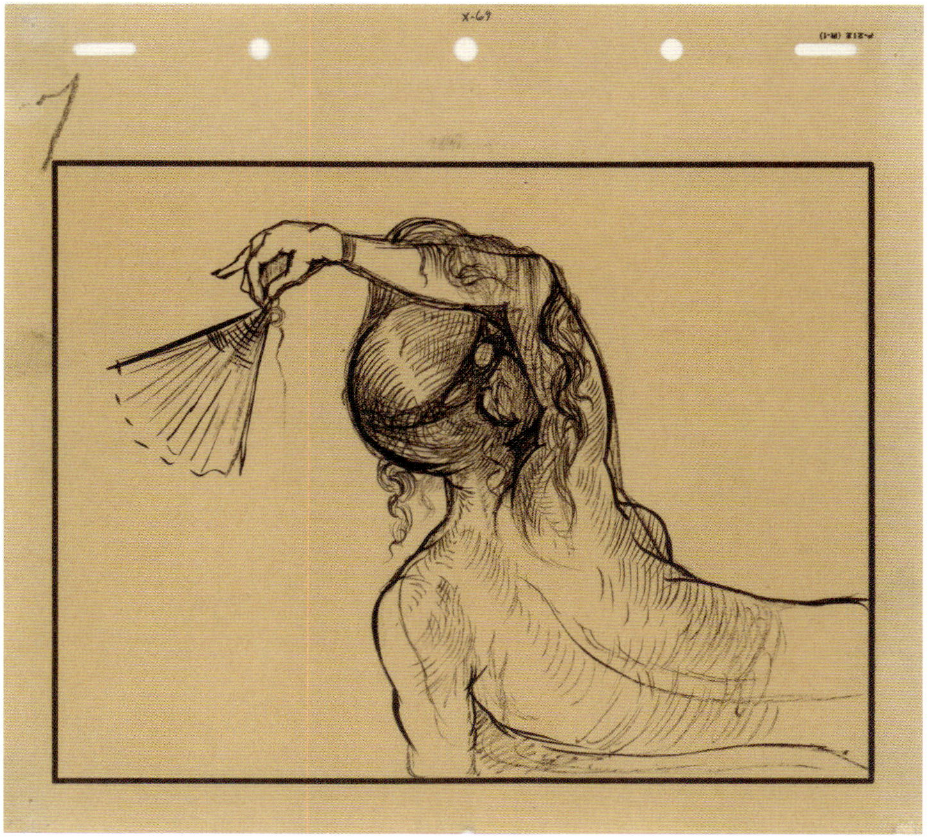

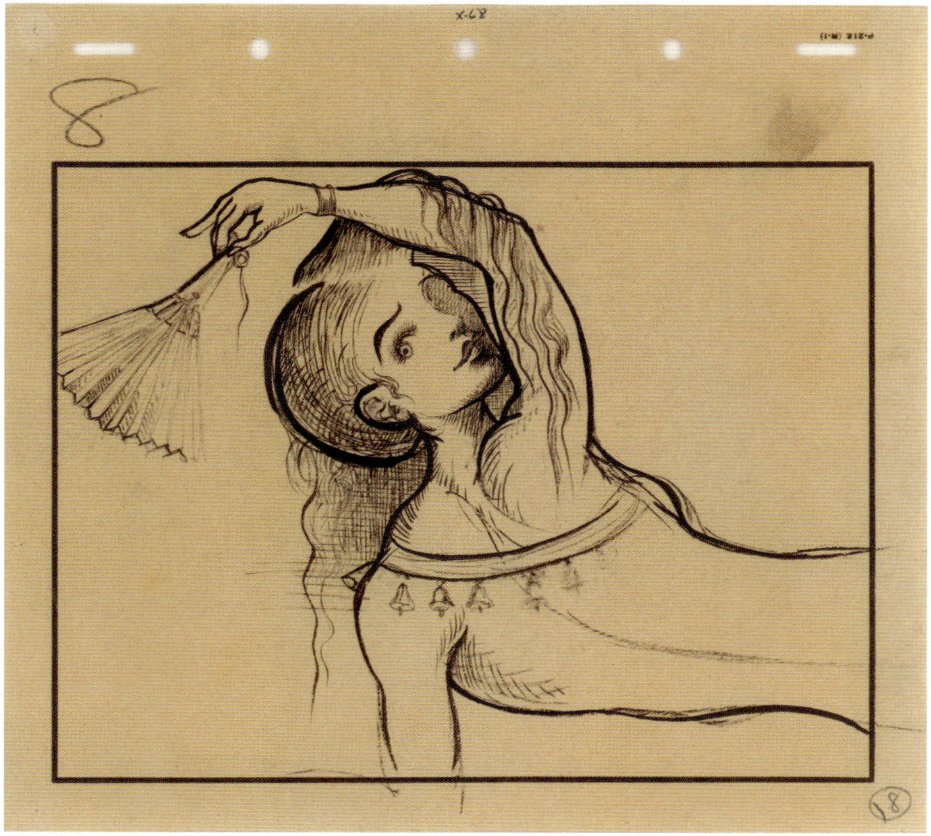

"My Destiny of Love"

Lyric: Ray Gilbert Music: Armando Dominguez

Verse:

My lonely tears were in vain,
Like tears that fall in the rain;
But now fate has brought you my way,
Now I can smile and say

Chorus:

Destino,
My heart was sad and lonely;
And knowing that you only,
Could bring my love to me.

Destino,
This heart of mine is thrilled now;
My empty arms are filled now,
As they were meant to be.

For you came along,
Out of a dream I recall;
Yes, you came along to answer my call,
I know now,
That you are my Destino;
We'll be as one for we know,
Our destiny of love.

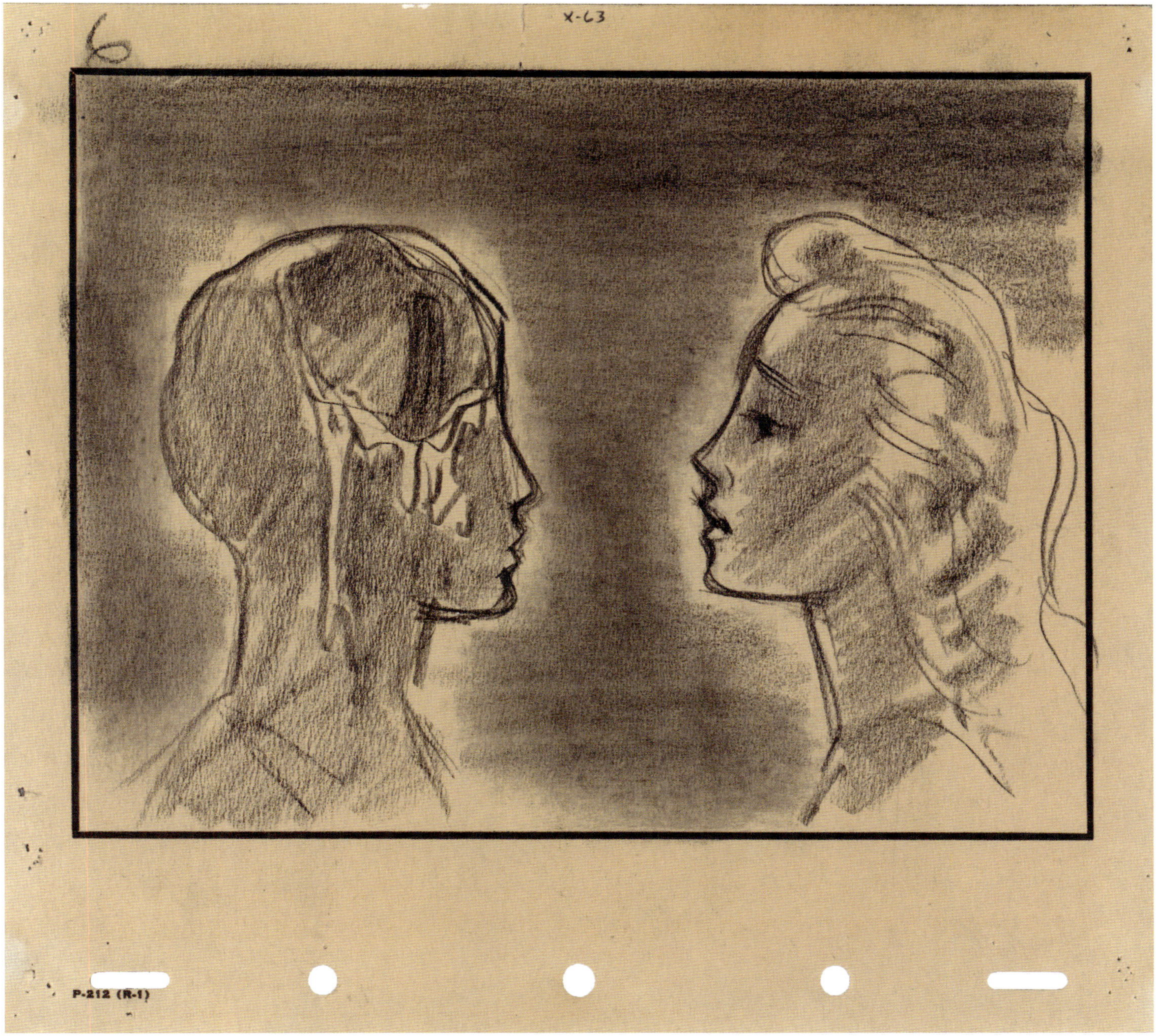
6
X-63
P-212 (R-1)

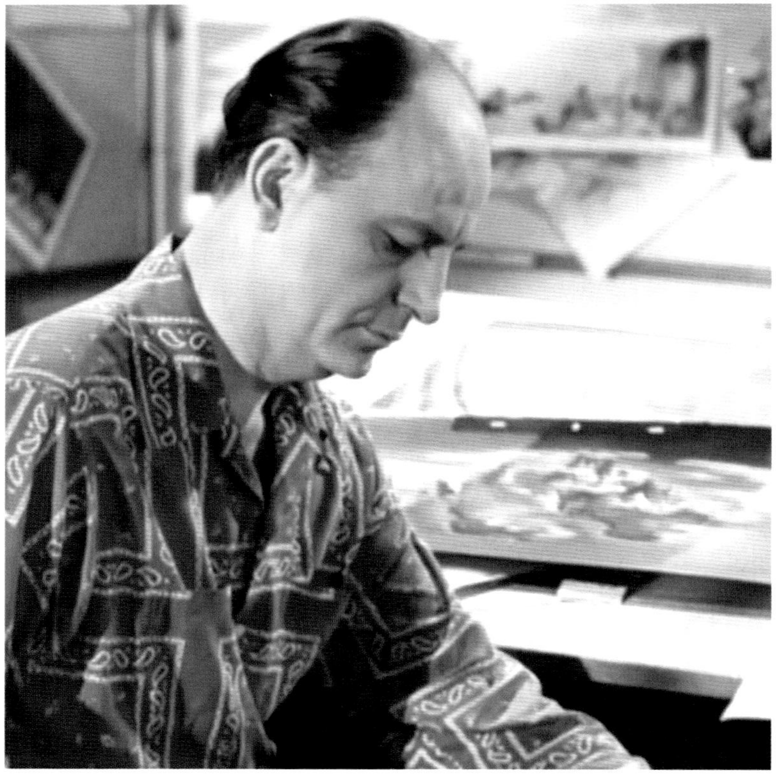

the title track to Disney's *The Three Caballeros* and had worked on the Disney films *Make Mine Music* (and the "Blue Bayou" segment), *Melody Time*, and *The Adventures of Ichabod and Mr. Toad*.

Based on some early storyboard concepts and some of the early treatments for *Destino*, the film was first conceived as a live-action/animation combination. The Disney Studios developed much of the technology that allowed the artists to create live-action/animation combination pictures like *Song of the South*, *The Three Caballeros*, and *Saludos Amigos* in a very effective and convincing way. The film was to star Dora Luz, who was the Latin American actress and recording artist who played herself in the 1944 Disney film *The Three Caballeros*.

Luz recorded the sound track vocals for *Destino*, but Walt decided not to make it a live-action/animation combination picture with her as the star. Instead he would collaborate with Dalí on the project. Apparently Dalí gravitated to the song because of its title, which he liked very much: "My Destiny of Love."

Dalí was attracted to the song because he thought something that harbored *destiny* would be interesting. Even though the song was extremely "banal" according to Hench, Dalí felt that he had a predetermined destiny and he was "working on it."

Although Dalí did not speak English, he and Disney were still able to communicate. It was primarily because Walt spoke some French from his days as an ambulance driver in Europe during World War I. Some at the studio cynically joked that the reason why Dalí and Walt were friends was because they "couldn't understand each other!" But there was the common language of art, which does transcend language and cultural barriers. If you look at many of the early Disney cartoons and even a feature like *Bambi*, there is very little dialogue. The visual images carry the story which bridges the language divide.

Ultimately Walt selected John Hench to work with Dalí because he was the only other person at the studio who could speak French well enough to communicate with Dalí in order to effectively move the project along. John liked to say, "My French wasn't any worse than his English."[8] Hench was a versatile draftsman, a true artist in every sense of the word. While working on *Destino*, he had the uncanny ability to mimic Dalí's drawing style to the point

Page 45: Story sketch by John Hench.

John Hench working at his desk, 1952.

From left to right: Salvador Dalí, Bob Cormack, and John Hench discussing storyboards for *Destino*.

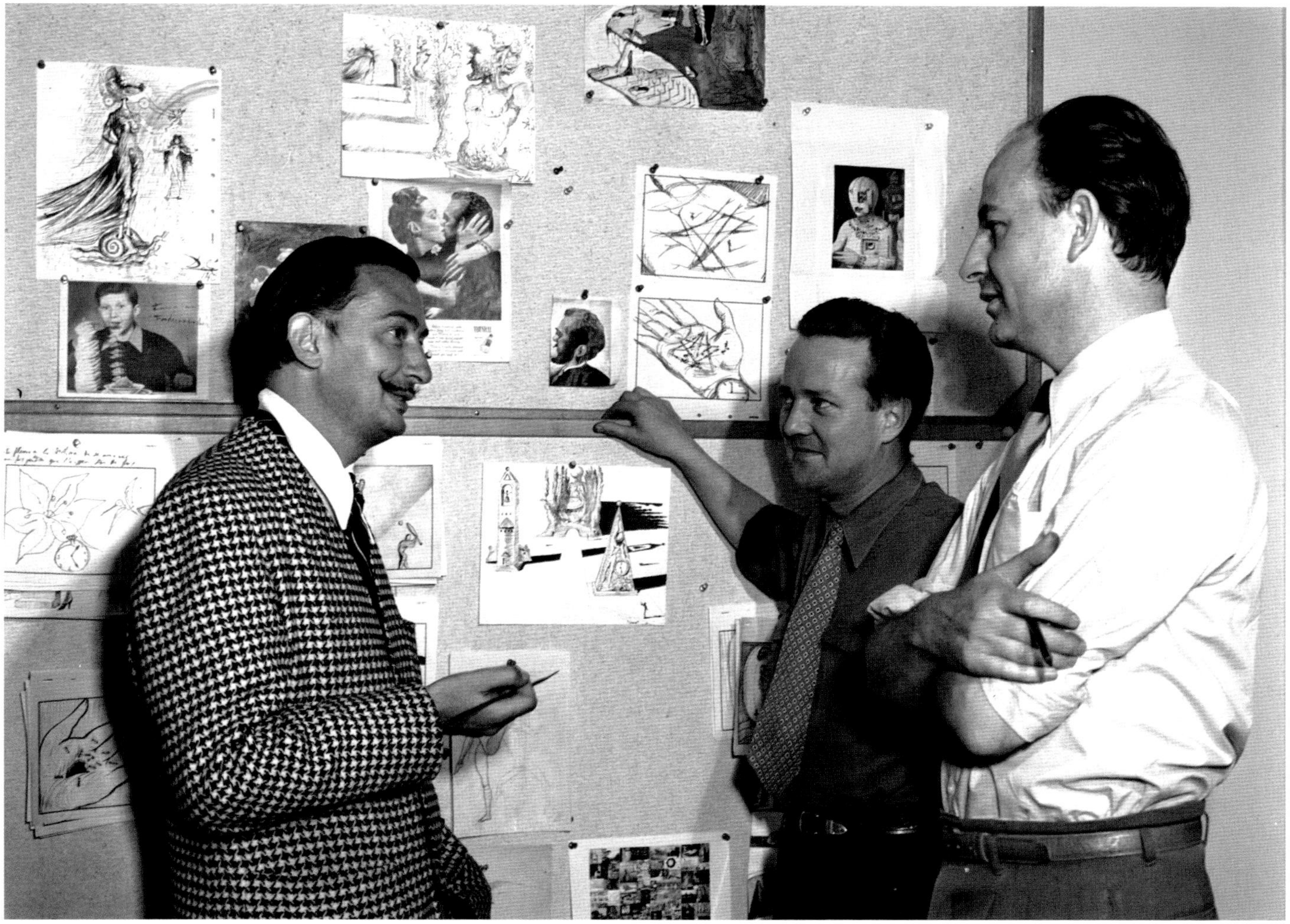

where Dalí at times could not tell the difference between his drawings and Hench's. In fact, years later, Hench was brought in to attribute each of the individual storyboard drawings for *Destino*. There were even a few of the images he had to really study before determining if they were his or Dalí's. It was not a common practice to sign artwork in the early years. Animators often put their names on exposure sheets associated with a scene from a film that might contain fifty or a hundred drawings. But it wasn't the norm for individual drawings and paintings to be signed by the artist.

Today at the Walt Disney Animation Research Library, much more importance is placed on attributing artwork. It is not uncommon for artists now to note their name on the back of a piece of art or in a saved digital file. It's important from a historical and archival standpoint to keep clear and concise records of the thousands of pieces of art that are generated on each Disney animated film project.

Hench reflected years later that "Dalí was genuine. There was no pretense about him at all. Privately, he was the same as his public image . . . He was really quite an innocent person, I thought a real Renaissance man; he could do so many things."[9]

The great Disney story artist Joe Grant commented in 2002, "To find yourselves in that atmosphere was very satisfying, and I think it was pretty much mutual. Dalí was just as interested in us as we were in him. It was a great union." Dalí, Grant further noted, "was more or less represented as a very bizarre character, but in truth, he was just like anybody else, except he had this extraordinary mustache. So he and his wife, Gala, were just people, but with great talents." Joe was working at the studio in 1946 when Dalí was there, and he was working at the studio when he was interviewed about *Destino* in 2002. It was a real treat to have several artists that knew Dalí personally still working with us all these years later.

In an October 2006 letter to her cousin Roy E. Disney, Diane Disney Miller wrote about her father and the Spanish artist joining forces: "Dad [Walt] was very delighted with Salvador Dalí, as an artist, and as a unique personality . . . Dad was very enthusiastic about having Dalí at the studio, and giving his artists the opportunity to work alongside him, to be inspired by him. [John] Hench, of course, found it especially thrilling."

Roy had written to Diane about being interviewed for the documentary *Dalí & Disney: A Date with Destino* we were planning on making. The film explores the collaboration of the artists and the completion of the film. Diane felt that she didn't have much to contribute since she was only in her teens at the time Dalí was at the studio and politely declined the invitation to be interviewed.

Hench worked to bring story continuity to Dalí's ideas. The story sketches were all done in black and white, with Hench the principal "assistant" to Dalí. Bob Cormack was also involved in the effort, doing additional story-continuity work. This is a very iterative process in which the story artists are generating many story sketches and pinning them up, reviewing them, and tearing them down and/or rearranging them. Even with today's filmmaking, this is still very much the process; it's a constant putting up and tearing down of ideas with the goal being that a very strong story eventually emerges.

Dalí would work on the key scenes, the establishing shots, or ideas for the film, which he then refined with India ink and watercolor washes to help set the mood for a particular sequence. Today this is primarily the function of the visual development artists and production designers on an animated picture. Dalí would also do full-color paintings that were intended to be used as backgrounds for the final film. "He brought in his own paints and palette," Hench remembered. "He was serious about what he was doing." Most of these paintings would eventually be used in the completed film decades later.[10]

Hench further recounted that he had once brought Dalí some animation bond paper with the

Top left: Salvador Dalí's *Metamorphose de Narcisse (Metamorphosis of Narcissus)*, 1937. Courtesy of the Tate Modern, London.

Center: Dalí's *Inventions of the Monsters*, 1937. Courtesy of the Art Institute of Chicago, Chicago, Illinois.

Bottom: Dalí's *Swans Reflecting Elephants*, 1937. Courtesy of a private collector.

Far right: Dalí's *The Burning Giraffe*, 1937. Courtesy of a private collector, on long-term loan to the San Francisco Museum of Modern Art, San Francisco, California.

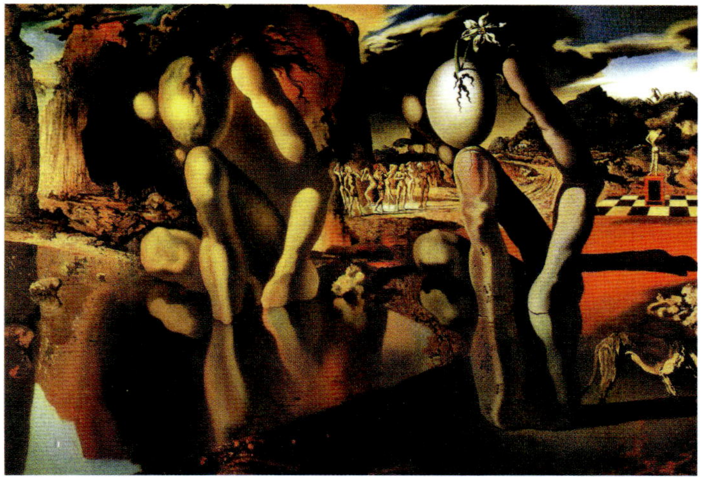

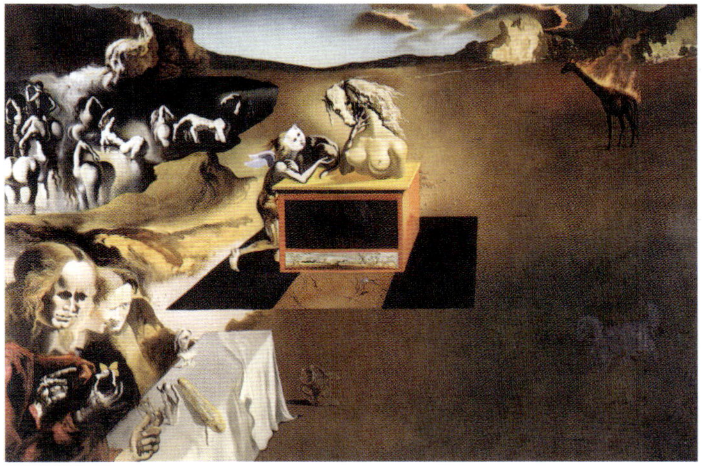

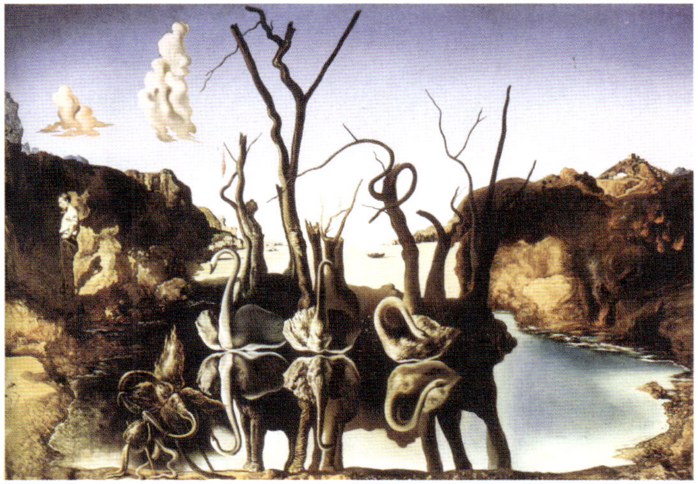

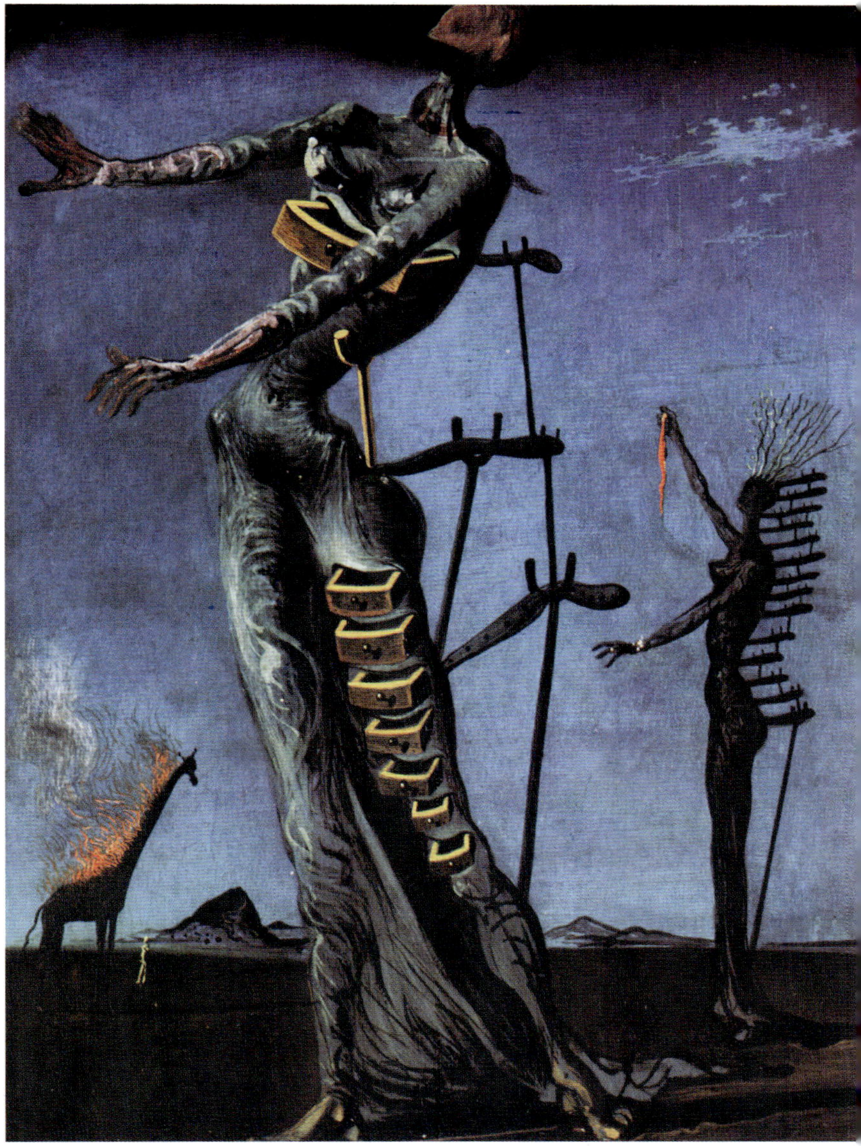

Page one of the eleven-page handwritten manuscript for *Destino*. Courtesy of Fundació Gala-Salvador Dalí.

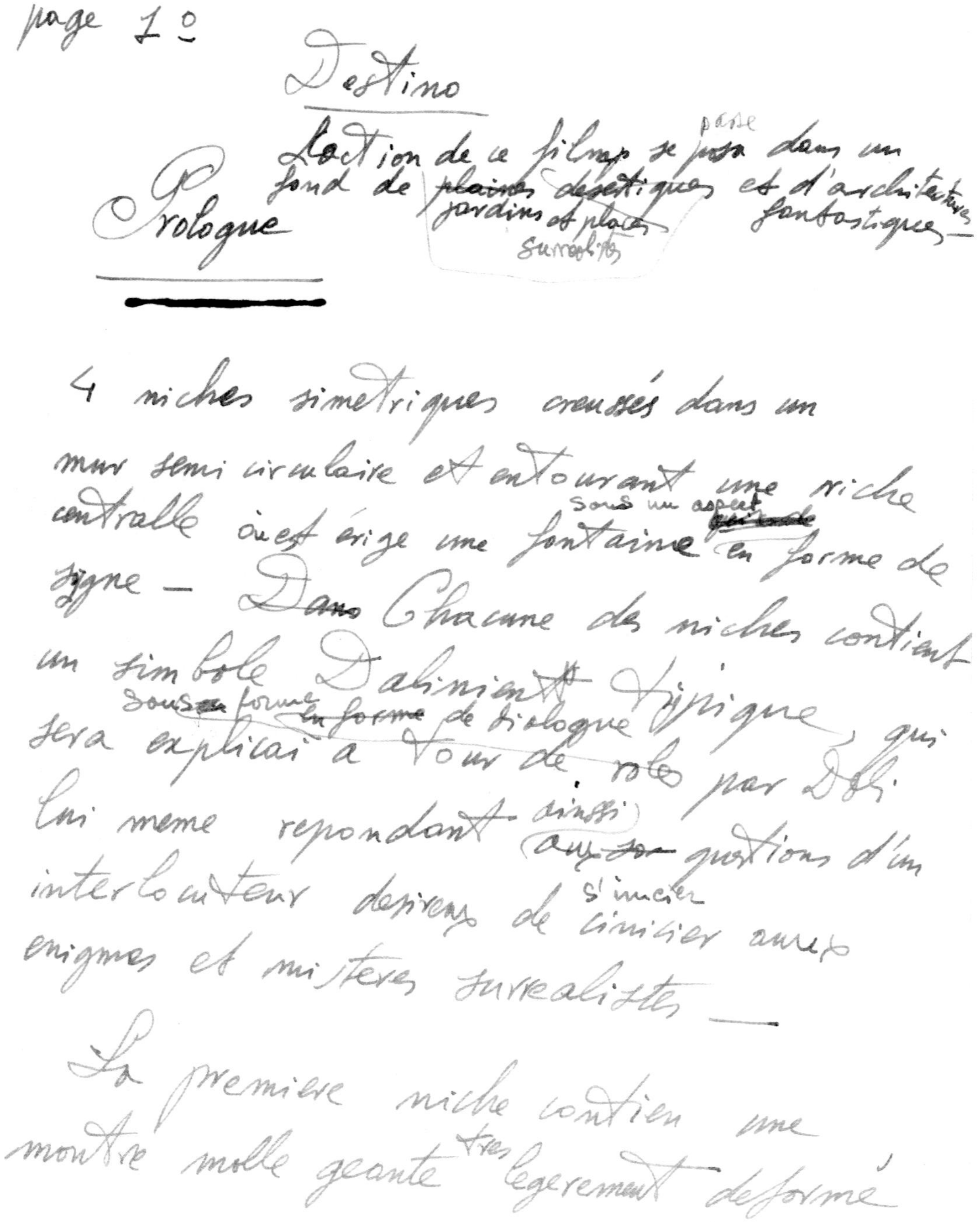

page 1º

Destino

Prologue

L'action de ce film se passe dans un fond de ~~plaines désertiques~~ jardins et places surréalistes et d'architectures fantastiques —

4 niches simetriques creusées dans un mur semi circulaire et entourant une niche centralle où est érigé une fontaine sous un aspect en forme de signe — ~~Dans~~ Chacune des niches contient un simbole Dalinien typique, sous forme de dialogue qui sera expliqué à tour de rôle par Dali lui meme repondant ainsi aux questions d'un interlocuteur desireux de s'initier aux enigmes et misteres surrealistes —

La premiere niche contien une montre molle geante tres legerement deformé registration holes already punched into it, and that the guest artist refused to use it. Dalí, according to Hench, stated that it was "already complete. 'It's started already. There are elements here on this paper, on all this paper.'" Dalí, Hench noted, wanted paper that was completely blank, without any design elements at all. Of course, working at the animation studio in those days, virtually all the paper that was readily available was animation bond paper. By the time that paper got to the artists, it was already punched with a sequence of holes along the bottom to allow for a secession of animation drawings to register to one another.

"Working with Dalí was a most unusual experience. Ordinarily good story ideas don't come easily and have to be fought for," Hench said. "But with Dalí it was exactly the reverse. Every morning there were so many new ideas that the allotted film footage couldn't contain them." For example, "the musical score was stretched twice," recounted Hench. "It was somewhat like trying to contain fast-growing yeast that every morning was entirely too much for its container.

"And not only wonderful ideas for the picture, but, in fact, they spilled into all directions as machines, furniture, jewelry, visual, or optical apparatus, which included an extraordinary device to indicate when a painting was finished," Hench added.

By all accounts, John Hench and Salvador Dalí worked very well together. Dalí's wife, Gala, handwrote a note to Walt saying, "We have had a visit with John Hench[,] who is truly a perfect collaborator for Dalí . . . He understands Dalí." Dalí went on to spend more than eight weeks working at the Disney Studios and continued to create artwork and ideas for *Destino* at the Hotel Del Monte at Pebble Beach, in California. Hench made several visits to the Pebble Beach location to work with Dalí and progress on the *Destino* film project.

There are several synopses from this time period, but one in particular by Dalí describes the film best. The translated English version, typed on bond paper, was found at the Fundació Gala-Salvador Dalí (Gala-Salvador Dalí Foundation) in Figueres, Spain. A handwritten French version was also rediscovered in the Disney Archives during the research of this book.

According to Salvador Dalí, the main theme for *Destino* is the "search for true love, to find one's destiny." It was intended to be a love story. "The awakening of love between two people," Hench said. "It starts out with destiny being a matter of time." The film was originally intended to start and end with live action, with Dalí himself explaining Dalínian symbols. It is not surprising that they were planning for live action to be mixed into *Destino*, since the studio had already done a number of live-action/animation combinations by that point. But as with all films, it went through multiple iterations and that idea eventually faded away.

The following is the entire story synopsis written by Dalí as it was left off in 1946:

Translated and typed page from the *Destino* script. (The entire script is written out on pages 51 through 60). Courtesy of Fundació Gala-Salvador Dalí.

DESTINO

The action of this picture takes place against a background of surrealistic places and gardens with fantastic architecture.

PROLOGUE

We see a broad expanse where construction is being terminated on the location sets for the picture "Destino". An heterogenious assortment of objects are strewn about in startling combinations : gigantic crutches, bicycles, architectural fragments etc. lie pell-mell in the path of the carpenters and electricians who go about the usual business attending film production.

Four symetric niches have been built in a semicircular wall framing a central niche where a swan-shaped** fountain is erected. Each of the other niches contains typical Dalinian symbols to be explained in turn by Dali himself in the dialogue between him and an interlocutor anxious to be initiated into the enigmas and mysteries of surrealism. The first of these niches contains a giant limp watch, slightly distorted.

In a far corner, a boy (Eglevsky ?) amuses himself with a baseball and bat. Pretty soon his play leads him out in front of the semi-circular set described above. The

**(note : this may be the fountain from which the elephant comes later)

DESTINO

The action of this picture takes place against a background of surrealistic places and gardens with fantastic architecture.

PROLOGUE

We see a broad expanse where construction is being terminated on the location sets for the picture Destino. An heterogeneous assortment of objects are strewn about in startling combinations: gigantic crutches, bicycles, architectural fragments[,] etc. lie pell-mell in the path of the carpenters and electricians who go about the usual business attending film production.

Four symmetric niches have been built in a semi-circular wall framing a central niche where a swan-shaped fountain is erected ** (note: this may be the fountain from which the elephant comes later). Each of the other niches contains typical Dalínian symbols to be explained in turn by Dalí himself in the dialogue between him and an interlocutor anxious to be initiated into the enigmas and mysteries of surrealism. The first of these niches contains a giant limp watch, slightly distorted.

In a far corner, a boy (Eglevsky ?) amuses himself with a baseball and bat. Pretty soon his play lands him out in front of the semi-circular set described above. The boy stares in blank amazement then exclaims, pointing to the limp watch:

BOY:

What in the name of sense is this thing?

A gum-chewing workman, who is adjusting the watch with indifferent deliberation, replies.

WORKMAN:

It's all part of the surrealist picture Destino.

BOY:

I don't get it.

WORKMAN:

Neither do I. That's not my department.
You'll have to ask Mr. Dalí over there.

Turning to Dalí[,] who is re-reading his script, the boy inquires:

BOY:
Can you tell me what all this is about?

Dalí:
What you see there are just symbols. Surrealism is like a new language.
Every object means something other than what it actually appears to be.
This watch, for instance—it symbolizes the relativity of time.
Depending on the circumstances, in love for instance, one minute of
waiting may seem like a thousand years. . .
Or, an hour may pass as quickly as if it were a few seconds.

(The watch contracts)

The time of human beings is different than mechanical time.
It's flexible and viscous, like the time in dreams.

(The watch melts and spreads on the floor)

BOY:
(pointing to the second niche)
And, this awful creature?

Dalí:
This awful creature symbolizes a chimera, a monster: four antagonistic
personalities living in the same body. It is of the same species as the
mythological beings of antiquity—the centaurs, mermaids, etc.
The head of a philosopher, the bestial body of a rat, and the
delicate legs of an exotic bird. . .

BOY:
That's easy to understand.

(They walk without further explanation past the fountain)

BOY, CONT'D:

But, what's the meaning of this strange creature with drawers?

Dalí:

This creature represents the stream of life: the head of flowers means Spring, and the drawers encased in the body hold symbols of the things life keeps in reserve. Some of the drawers are already full of jewels[;] others hold sentiments such as tenderness . . .

(We open a drawer glittering with jewels)

In another, bees have built a hive. In yet another, there is a bird's nest. Some are still empty, awaiting Destino's decisions.

BOY:

And, this sculptured hand?

Dalí:

That is the mysterious Hand of Destiny. Those ants symbolize the life of human beings as they search their way along the channeled lines of the palm. Whenever the hand remains static for a time, we say it is asleep. And, when a sculpture animates, it is covered by the ants of life.

(The hand is covered with ants and becomes alive)

BOY:

Fascinating! It's too bad there aren't more symbols whose secrets we could read.

Dalí:

Well, there is still the symbol of the fountain to explain. It is the rarest, because in it, invisible destiny can suddenly be seen, thanks to the miraculous hazard of circumstances. Just watch . . .

(The water in the fountain stops.
Its reflected image appears, identical, in focus)

The boy whoops with delight, pets the little elephant which leads them on ** (details of walk undecided) to a huge silhouette of a young girl projected on a stereoscopic screen. The boy utters an appreciative whistle.

Dalí:
Do you understand this?

BOY:
Rather! But, what about the thing shoving inside of her?

Dalí:
That's the fountain of young Chronos, God of Time.

BOY:
And, does the fountain, too, have its symbol, its destiny?

Dalí:
Yes. Everything in the world has a "destino"

BOY:
What is the fountain's destino?

Dalí:
Its destino is love.

BOY:
(bewildered, scratching his head)
It's all too much for me.

Dalí:
Maybe not . . . maybe the whole thing has to do with your own destino. In the dream-time of surrealism, an antique statue can very well become a young baseball player just like you.

Let's sit here and watch. . .

(From this point forward, the picture itself unfolds.)

Visual development by Salvador Dalí.

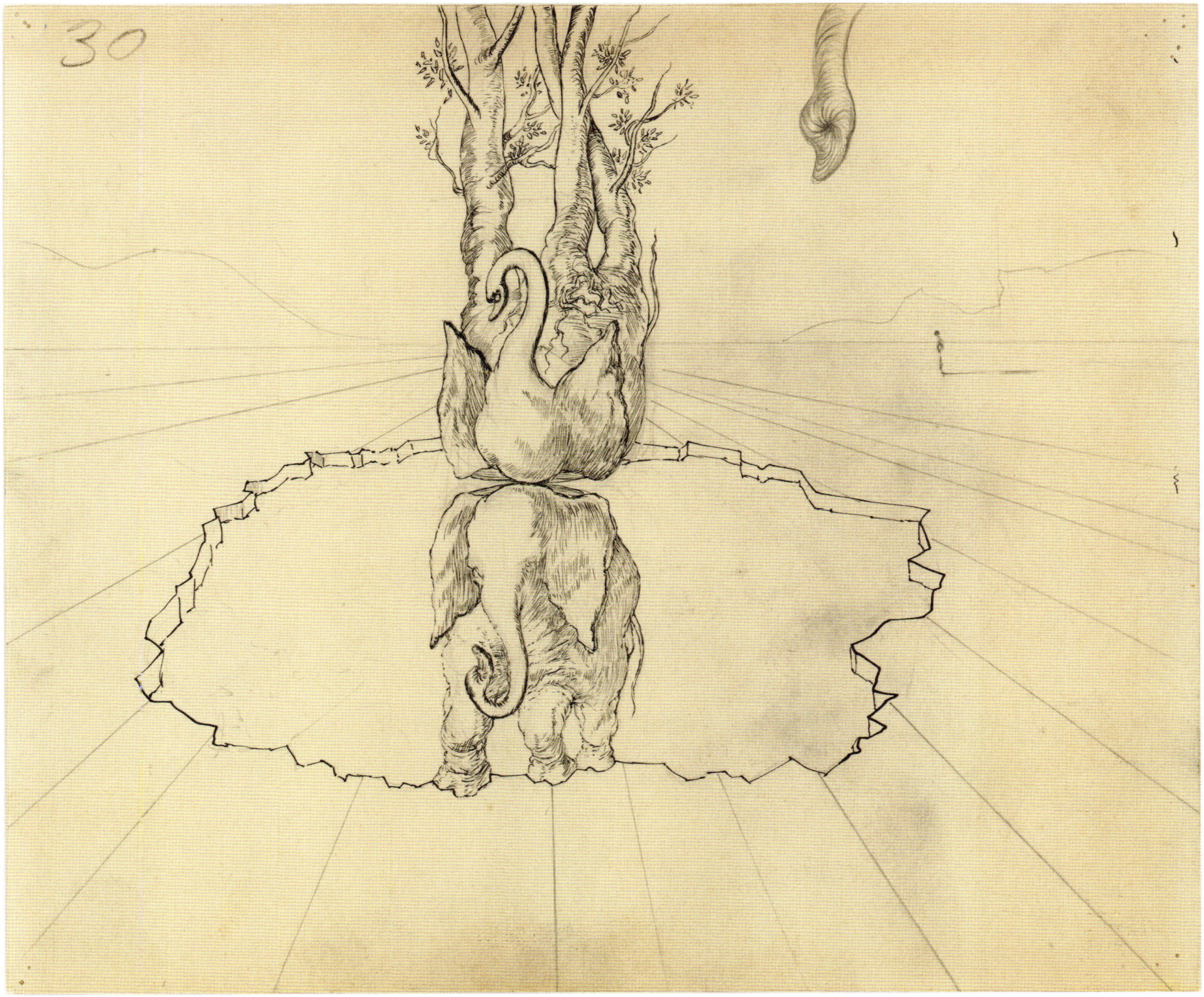

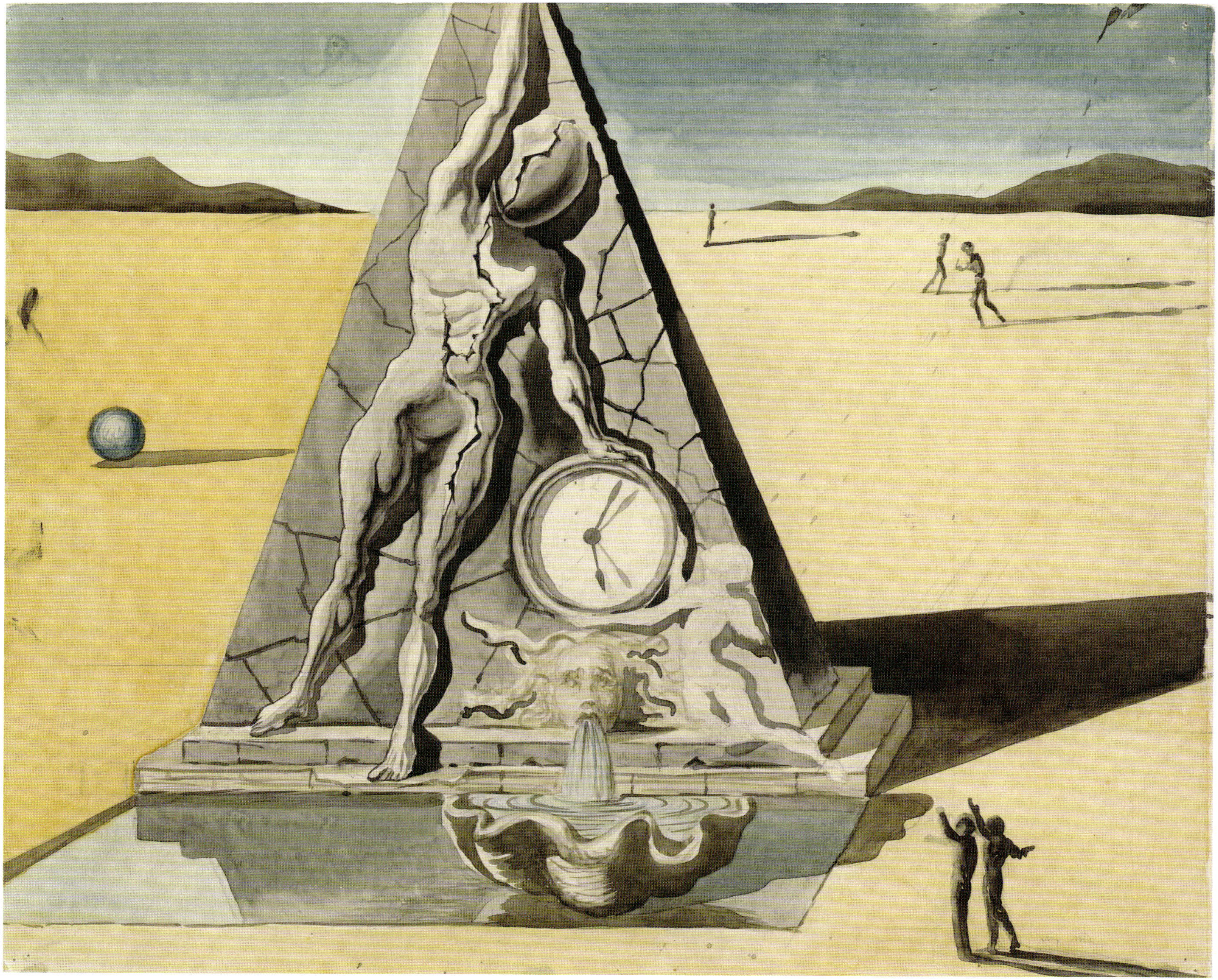

Page 58: Visual development by Salvador Dalí.

The pyramid-like shape of the fountain blends into the endless road of existence. Upon its stark emptiness appears the figure of the young girl, in melancholy dance. We now notice that the road skirts a frightening abyss, that it is slippery, treacherous, lined with the thorny vegetation of temptation and frustration. The eyes of public opinion thwart the girl in her every attempt to achieve happiness—they flash at her with sudden magnesium flares. Newspapers with scorpion feet and tails pursue her. Progressively stripped of her veils, the girl takes refuge in a shell. But, all the while, she moves closer and closer to the precipice. Her balance is failing—she totters, plunges into emptiness. . .

As she falls, the girl becomes detached from her old personality and travels onward in a fantastic journey through space. Finally, she reaches the limitless plane where she will meet her true destiny. Here, she is immediately entranced by the shadow of a bell[,] which appears to her symbolic of the purity within herself: she clothes herself in this shadow.

The metamorphosis takes place before the unseeing eyes of the statue of the God Chronos—eyes which only seem alive when they are met and kindled by the fire of the young girl's glance. As soon as the girl steals the shadow of the bell, the statue of Chronos softens, bends[,] and takes on a semblance of life, although it is clear that in its somnambulistic movements, it is still bound to its original state. Groping like a blind man, Chronos seeks the beloved shadow which has disappeared, and when he cannot find it, he seems to relapse once more into stone's eternal torpor, while limp watches gather, clinging, binding, as though seeming to immobilize him.

Story sketch by Salvador Dalí.

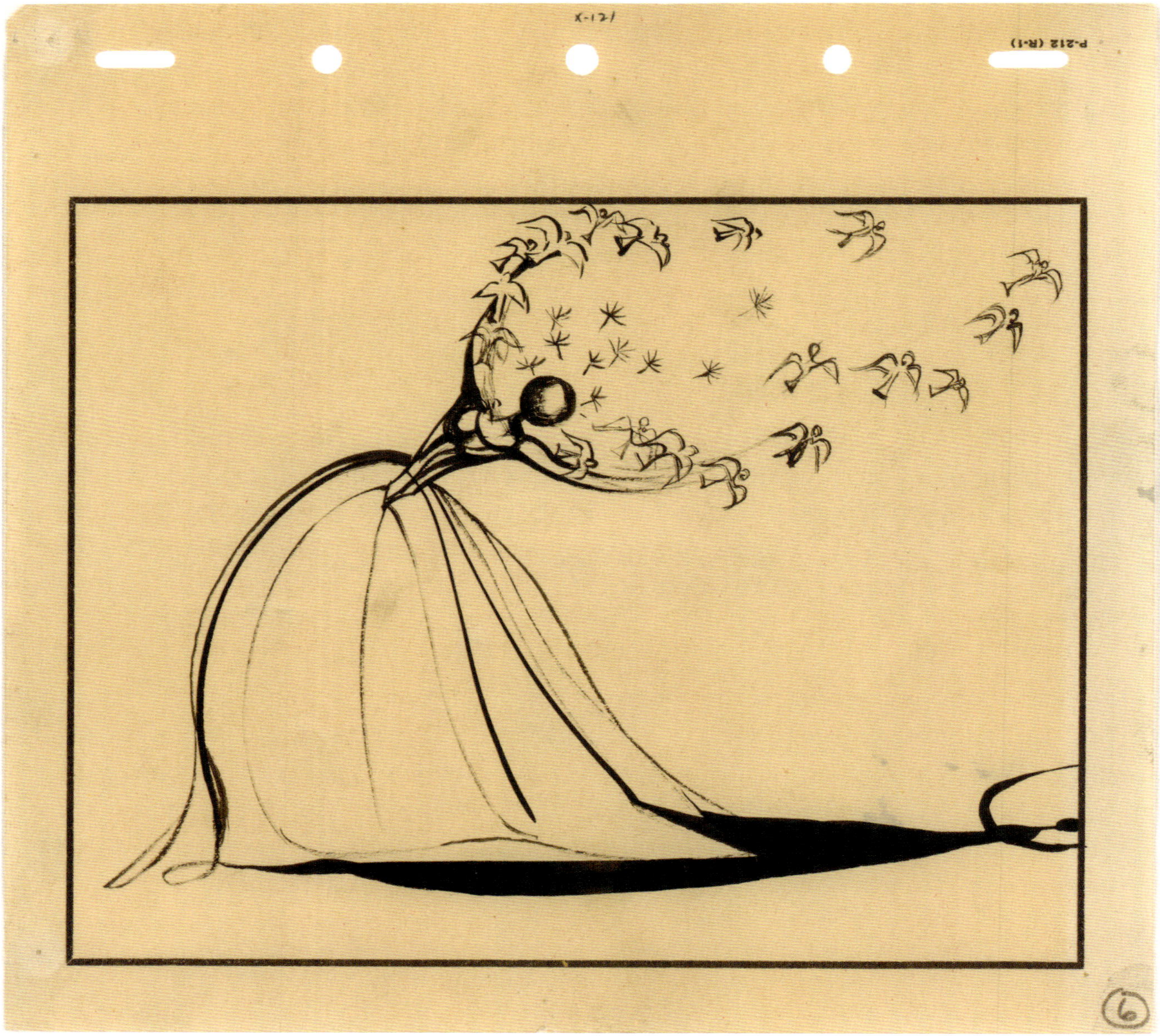

The young girl now dances far away, separated from Chronos by a river of limp watches. But, with every gesture, she tries to wake him, draw him to her, and thus, free him from the bonds of time. In her efforts to communicate, she sends him the effulgence of her love—the spin-drift of dandelions, wafted from her head. When the hopelessly enmeshed Chronos feels its downy touch, he gathers new life, new strength to tear away the watches clinging like leeches to his body. Finally set free from time, he can become a modern being. Chronos now seizes a baseball bat to try out his new-won liberty of motion.

He wastes no time: armed with his bat, Chronos steps into the labyrinth whose involved ways are traced in the lines of his own palm and where the girl for whom he is destined already awaits him.

LABYRINTH SCENE: Using a 'pas-de-deux' (type of dance step executed by a couple) the choreography is based on movements executed in the game of baseball. The magnificent exit from the labyrinth takes place through the kindly protecting face of Destiny itself.

From here, we break into a mad race toward Happiness, whose portals open one by one, leading on to the final goal: a vast heart supporting the majestic Temple of Love.

Crags, great crystal masses, the very sea gives way to the force of Destiny. In the center of the great divided Heart, we see the couple embracing amid glorious flights of birds—rising skyward to form once more among the clouds, the smiling face of Destiny.

We dissolve back to the first picture of the fountain of the god, Chronos. CAMERA PANS AND HOLDS on a hole in the statue where, in place of its heart, there hangs the little bell.

THE END.

Visual development by Salvador Dalí.

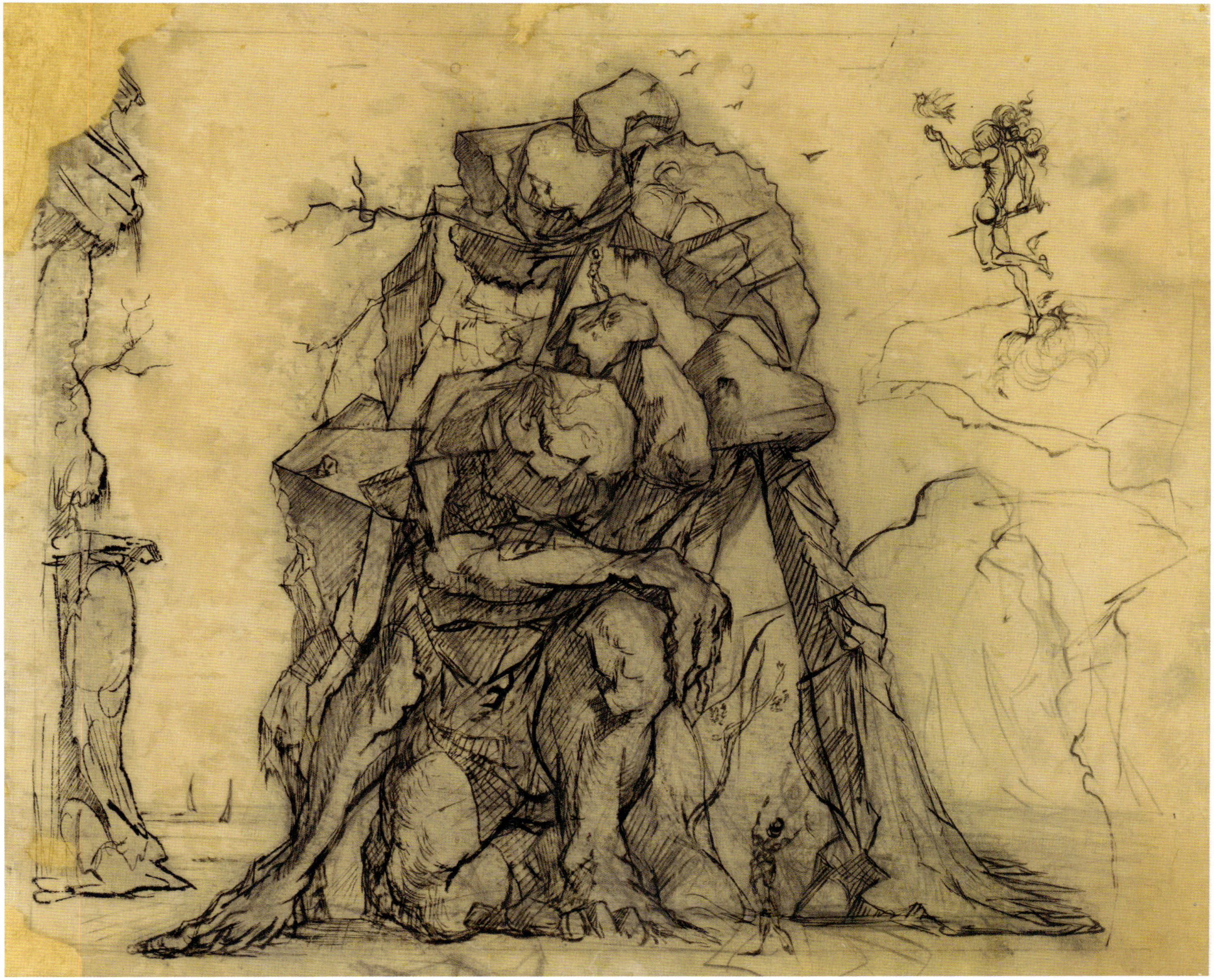

X-125

13

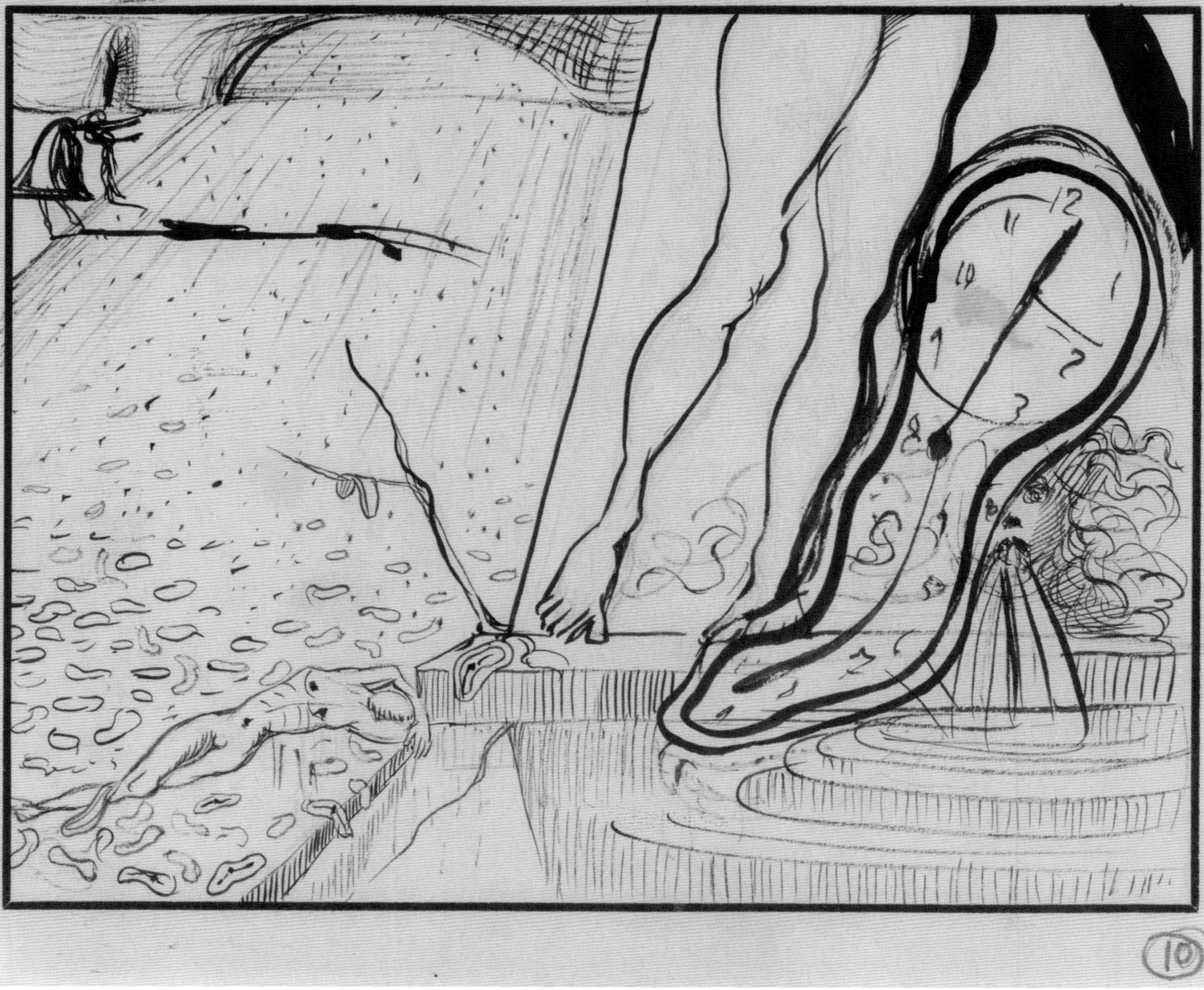

(10)

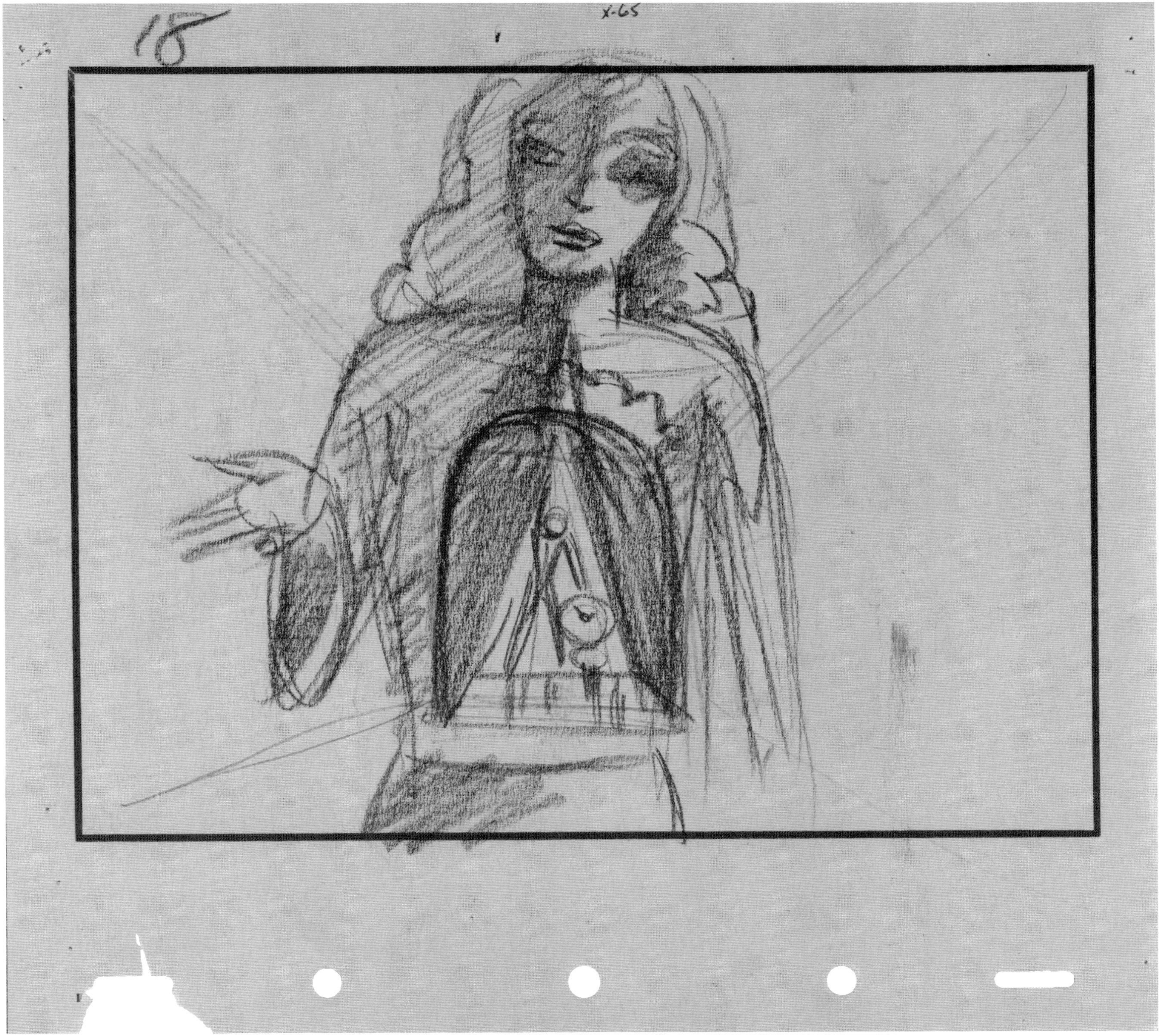
18
X-65

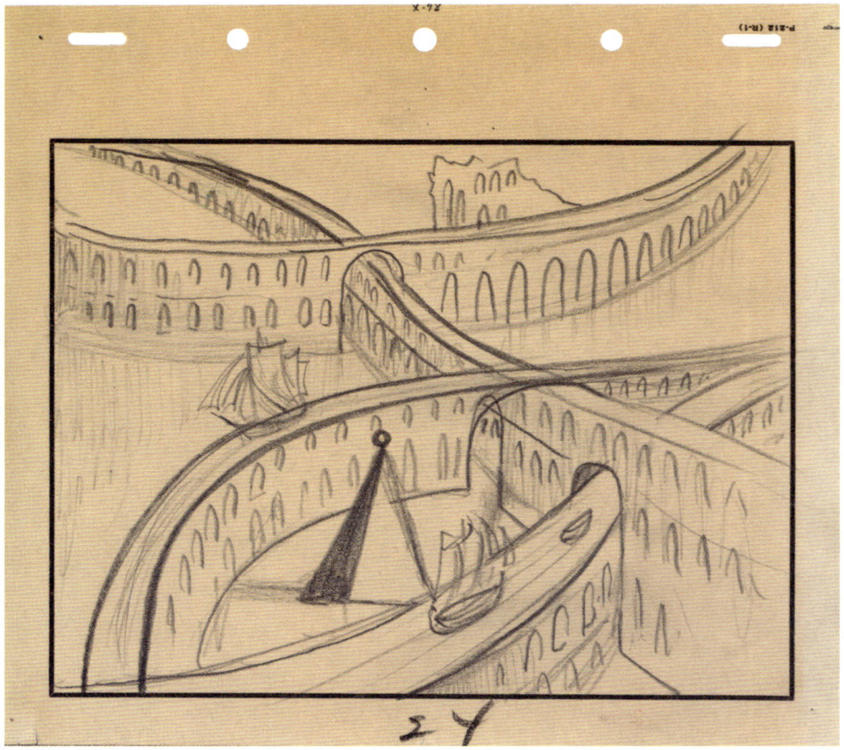

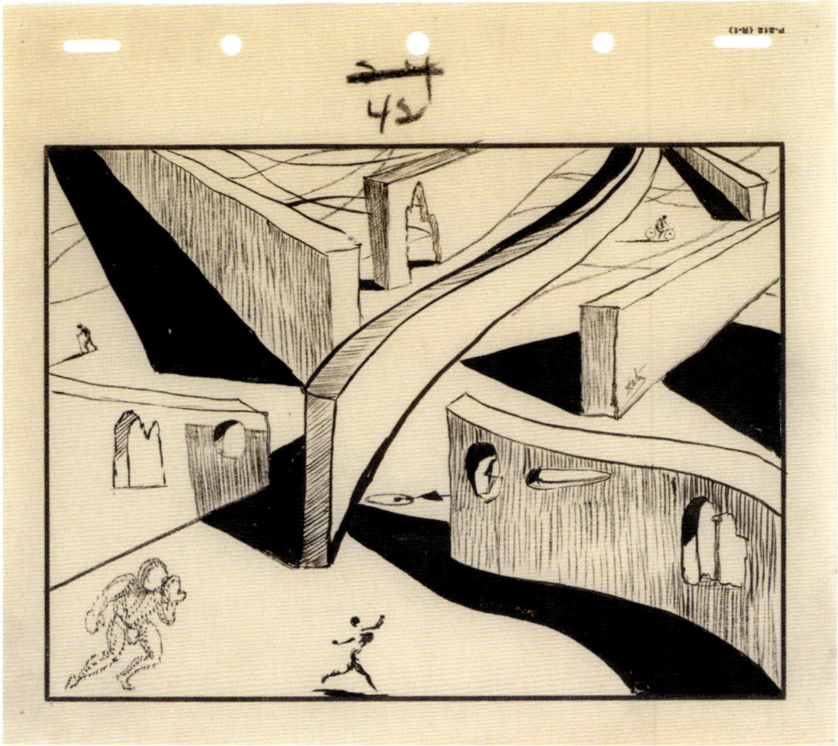

Page 64: Story sketch by Salvador Dalí.

Page 65: Story sketch by John Hench.

Above: Surrealist walls separate the lovers. Story sketches by Salvador Dalí.

There are several other treatments and outlines in the archives that are slight variations of this version. But the basic theme is the same: the search for true love, to find one's destiny. To achieve "the working out of girl's destiny" would require a "series of symbolic experiences that are revealed as temporary seductions and not her true destiny," as Dalí emphasized in the prologue. "These illusions build to an apex where she reacts in violent flight. The girl, free of her obsessions, takes on a state of purity, unaware of the nearness of her true destiny now released by her act from the bondage of time. The boy steps out of the fountain in his true personality [a baseball player?] and looks for the girl. They are separated by a maze constructed of surrealist walls which are a barrier and are unable to come together."[11]

Writing in 1957, Hench commented that ". . . along with the usual profusion of Dalíana, iconic Dalí imagery, Dalí had conceived, for the first time, I believe, of using, American baseball as a ballet form." Chronos, the hero and lover in *Destino*, emerges toward the end of the film as a baseball player symbolizing his newfound freedom. The ballerina disappears leaving only the head, which is a baseball that Chronos hits with his baseball bat. The ball travels into another realm, the temple of love, hitting a catcher's mitt, which transforms into a heart, a symbolic home run.

The visual styling for this "series of symbolic experiences" borrowed liberally from Dalí's previous creations in which he had established a visual design language; his signature iconography, the symbols which repeat through many of his works. The heroine

Ballet-inspired baseball scene.
Story sketch by John Hench.

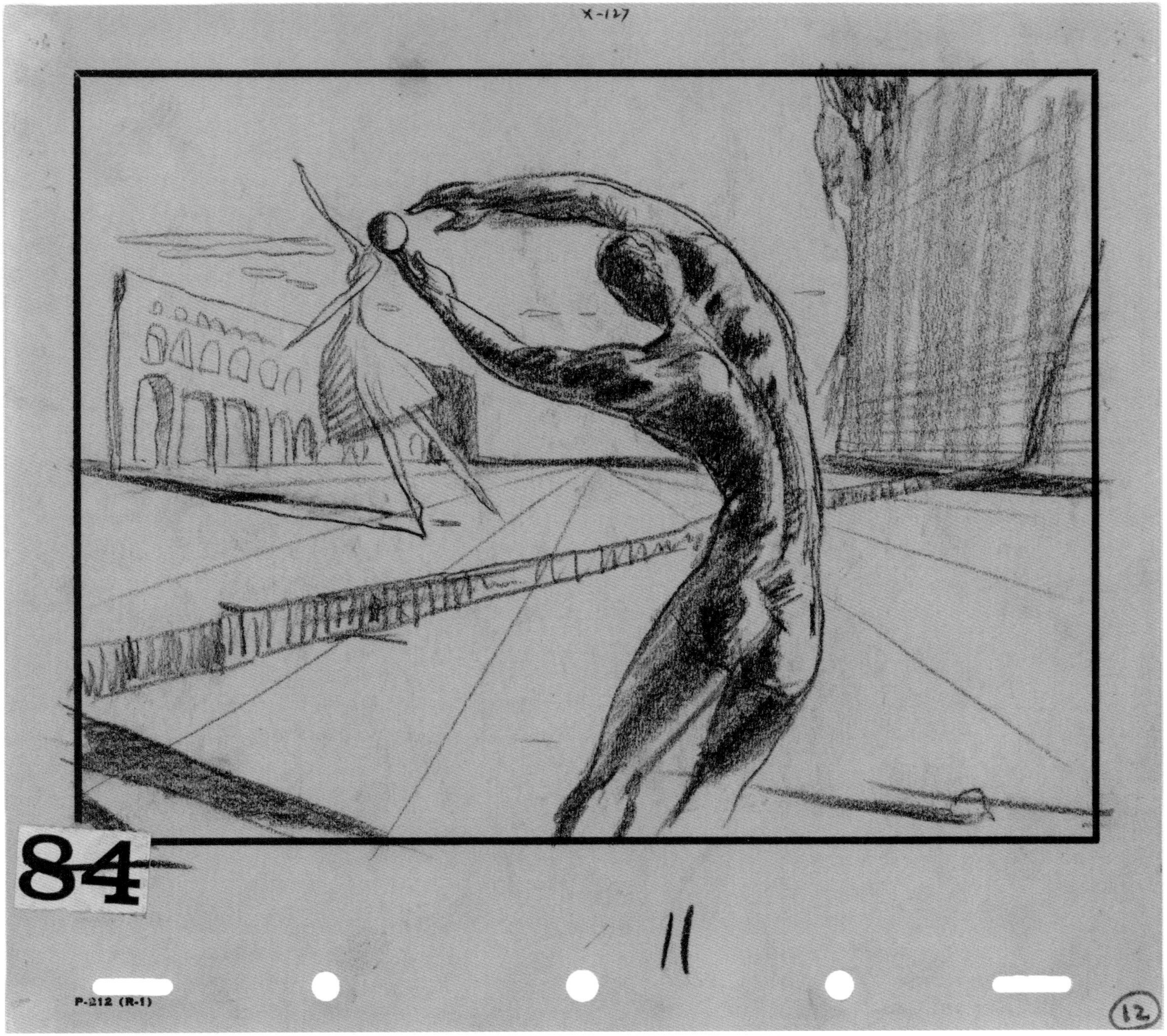

Chronos as a baseball player.
Story sketches by Salvador Dalí.

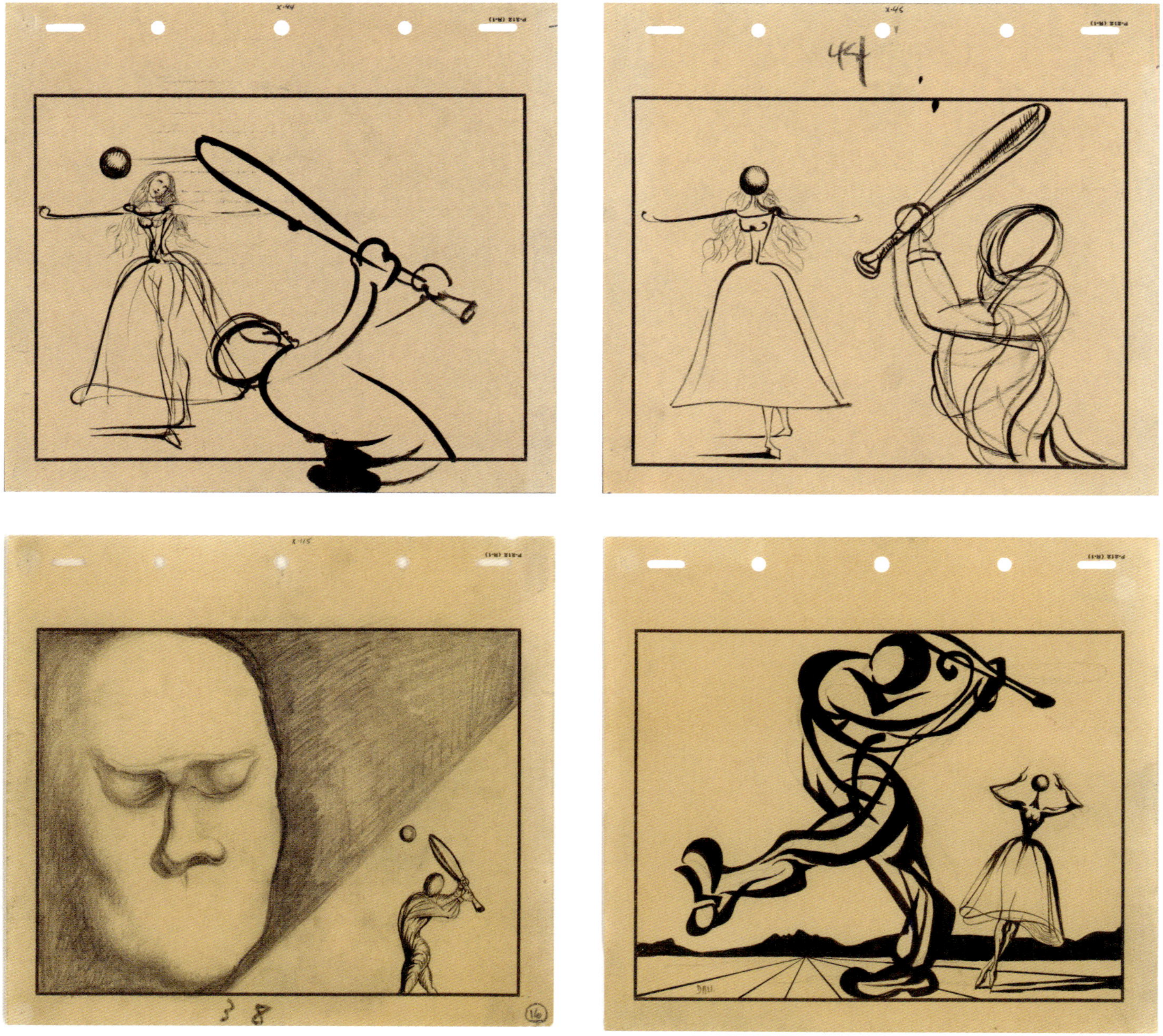

The girl, entranced by the shadow of the bell tower, clothes herself in its shadow. Story sketches by John Hench.

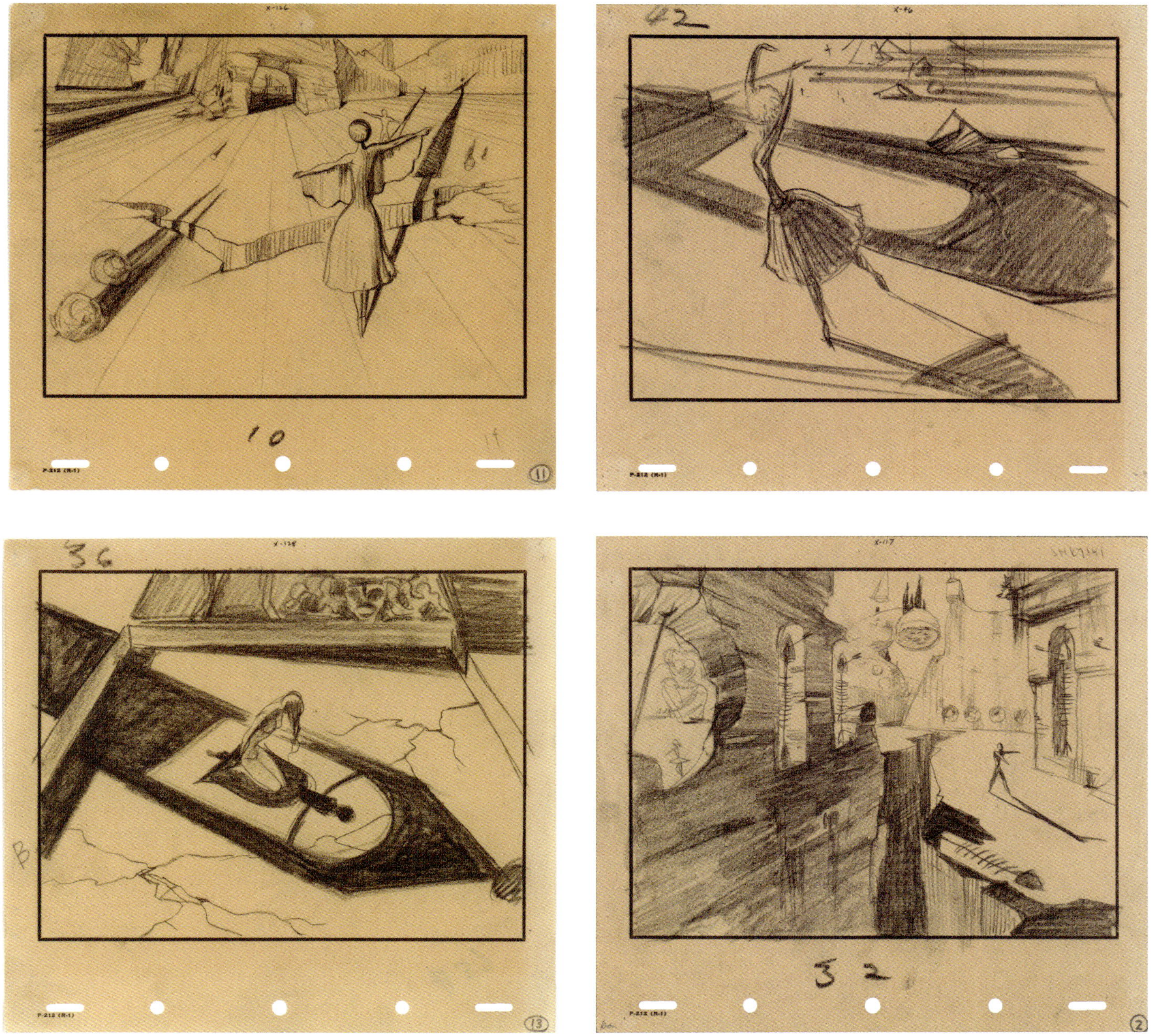

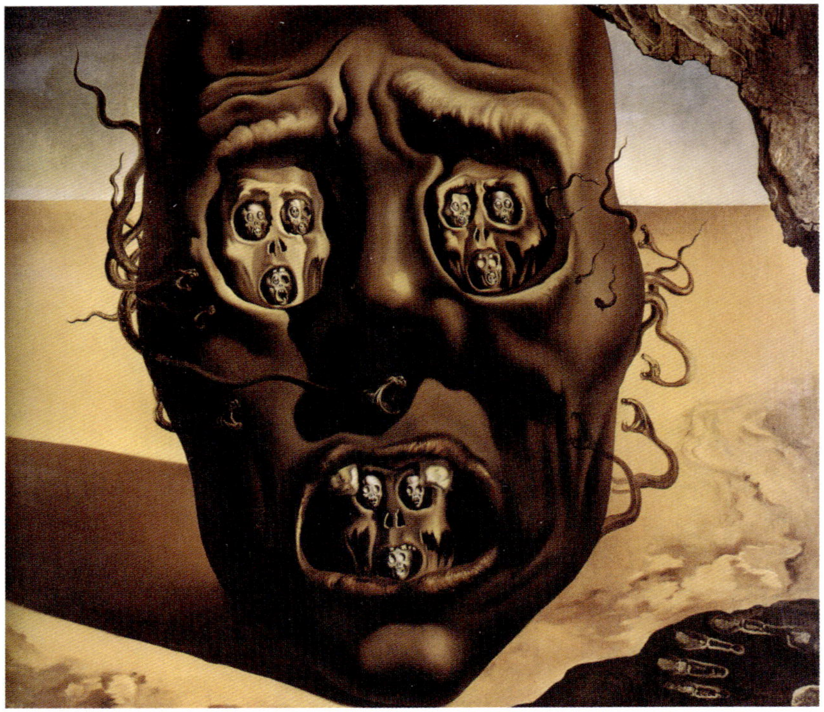

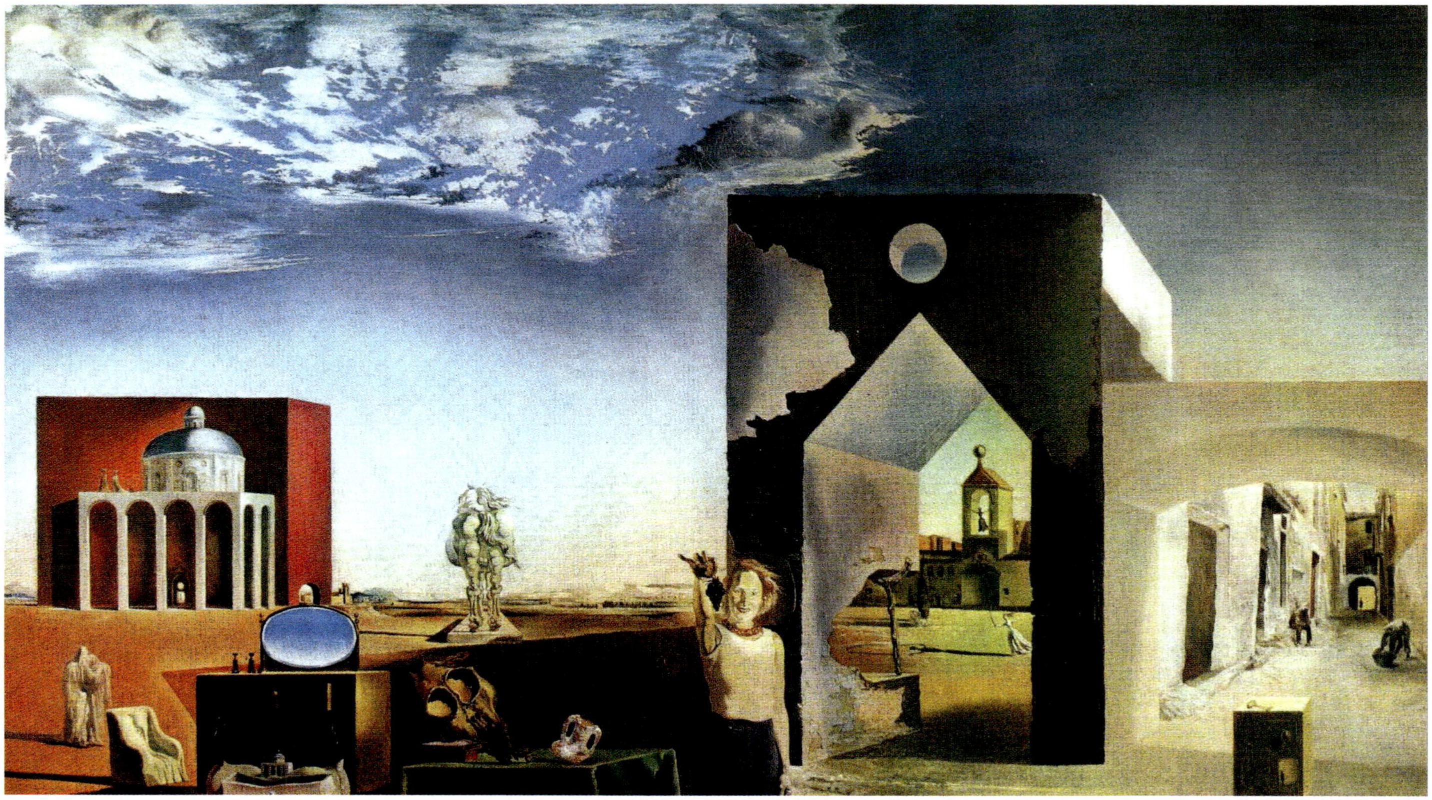

Top: Salvador Dalí's *Le Visage de la Guerre* (*The Face of War*), 1941. Courtesy of the Museum Boijmans Van Beuningen, Rotterdam, Netherlands.

Bottom: Dalí's *Suburbs of a Paranoiac Critical Town, Afternoon on the Outskirts of European History*, 1936. Courtesy of a private collector.

The bell tower, as inspired by paintings in Salvador Dalí's earlier works, such as *Suburbs of a Paranoiac Critical Town* (page 70). Story sketch by Salvador Dalí.

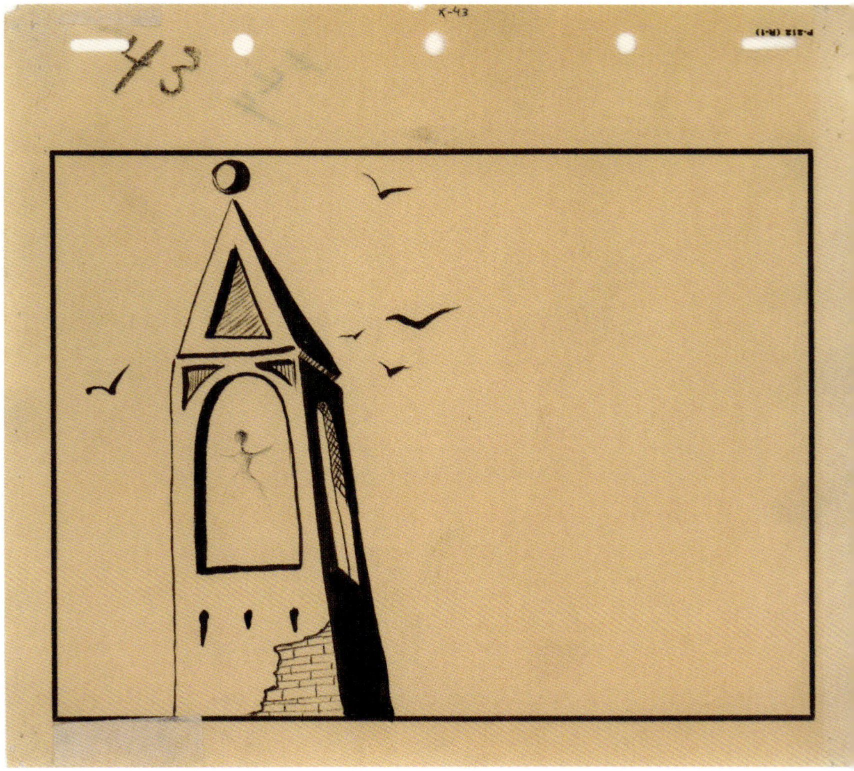

is a young girl drawn in such a way that her dress resembles the shadow of a bell in a church tower, and was referenced from a painting he had done a decade earlier, *Suburbs of a Paranoiac Critical Town, Afternoon on the Outskirts of European History* (1936).

The long cast shadows are seen in various works, including *The Face of War* (1941) and an earlier cited work, *The Great Masturbator* (1929). The use of those shadows, along with the craggy rocks, reminds one of Cap de Creus, near Dalí's beloved Portlligat, Spain, which he often referenced as visual elements in many of his paintings. The shadowing, whether cast or used as shading for the purposes of lighting, are evident in many of Dalí's paintings. His technical skill was such that he did very photo-real paintings that were highly rendered and mimicked strong light sources.

Dalí explained the opening of *Destino* as, "The girl's search for destiny, to find her true love—a series of symbolic experiences revealed as false destinies on the route of life. Confusion, temptation, social conflict end persecution (there is no rose without thorns) is the theme of this section. The apex is reached (the Tower of Babel—the city), the girl reacts (crawls into her shell), and as her position becomes instable . . . and precipitates, her into a fantastic flight—(evasion, escape)."[12]

The idea of the sculpture coming to life was originally conceived for *Spellbound*, Dalí's much-publicized 1945 collaboration with Alfred Hitchcock. For the dream sequences in that film, Dalí envisioned Ingrid Bergman as a statue coming to life and also planned to cover her with ants. That idea was "vetoed" by the actress. But it was resurrected in *Destino* with Chronos, the male lead, breaking free of the constraints of time. Again, there is a continuous recycling of images and ideas, oftentimes being flushed out more each time they appear.

One new concept for the Disney project was not deemed as radical: it was a scenario that involved a group of baseball players whose actions were to be choreographed to resemble a ballet. Dalí no doubt had a fascination with American baseball.[13]

Insects, and ants in particular, are an often-repeated iconography in many of Dalí's works. There are ants on the back of the "hard" timepiece in the lower left quadrant of his most famous painting,

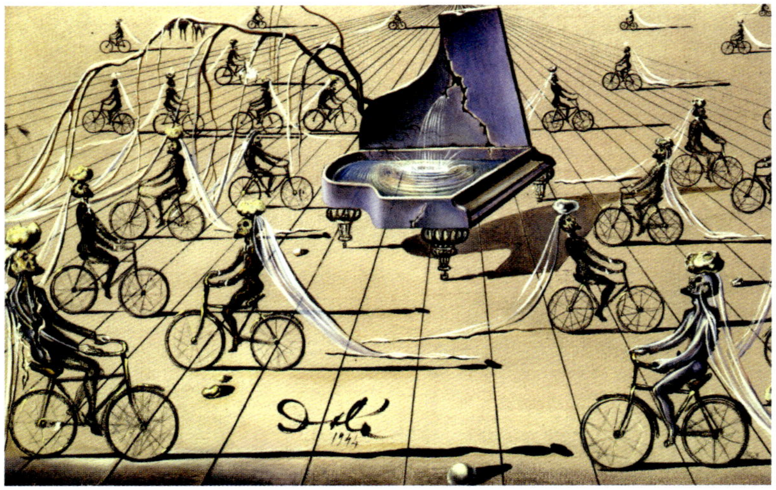

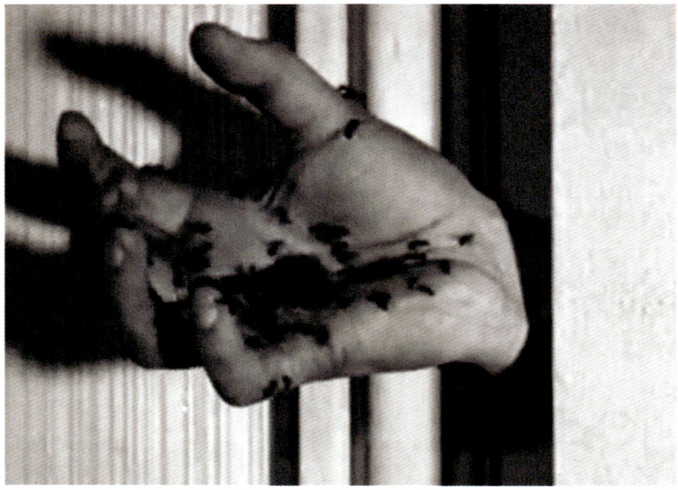

Left: Painting of bicyclists, *Study for Sentimental Colloquy* (1944). Courtesy of the Salvador Dalí Museum, St. Petersburg, Florida.

Right: A still-frame image from *Un Chien Andalou* (1929). Courtesy of Contemporary Films.

Page 73: Ants crawling through a hole in the hand, as seen in *Destino*. Story sketch by John Hench.

The Persistence of Memory (1931). To Dalí, the ants represented rotting or "putrefaction" and can also be seen emerging from a hand in *Destino*. This is a very similar idea and is staged in a nearly identical manner to a scene in the film *Un Chien Andalou* (1929). The difference is that these ants actually transform into male characters riding bicycles with baguettes on their heads in the final version of the film.

This was a mistake that John Hench pointed out to the production team in 2003 as we were finishing the film project that had been shelved and uncompleted for years. The baguettes were in fact supposed to be rocks on the heads of the bicyclists, but John smiled and said with a laugh, "I rather like the baguettes instead!"

It was wonderful to have John in the production process to get these insights, comments, and his approval. It is a rare occasion when nearly sixty years after a project was started that one of the principle artists would not only still be available, but still working at the studio.

The image of the bicyclists also appeared in a number of earlier works by Dalí. In *Illuminated Pleasures* (1929), he painted the bicyclists with round stones on their heads; it was loaves of bread in *Babaouo* (1932), and heavy stones that hold down the ends of veils in *Study for Sentimental Colloquy* (1944). In the paintings *The Little Theater* (1934), *Perspectives* (1936), or *Medium-paranoiac Image* (1935), there are bicyclists as part of the composition, both as minor elements or focal points in the images.

Bicyclists were to appear earlier in *Destino* in a cathedral-like structure riding around the edge of the reflecting pool. This changed, as did many of the story concepts during development, as Dalí was a "continuous fountain of ideas." I think it is worth noting that bicycles were a standard mode of transportation in Europe and still are today. They were also prevalent on the studio lot as an easy way to move around the property. Even today you will find bikes and bike racks all around the Disney studio; this author has his bike hanging in a storage closet and uses it frequently to get around the property.[14]

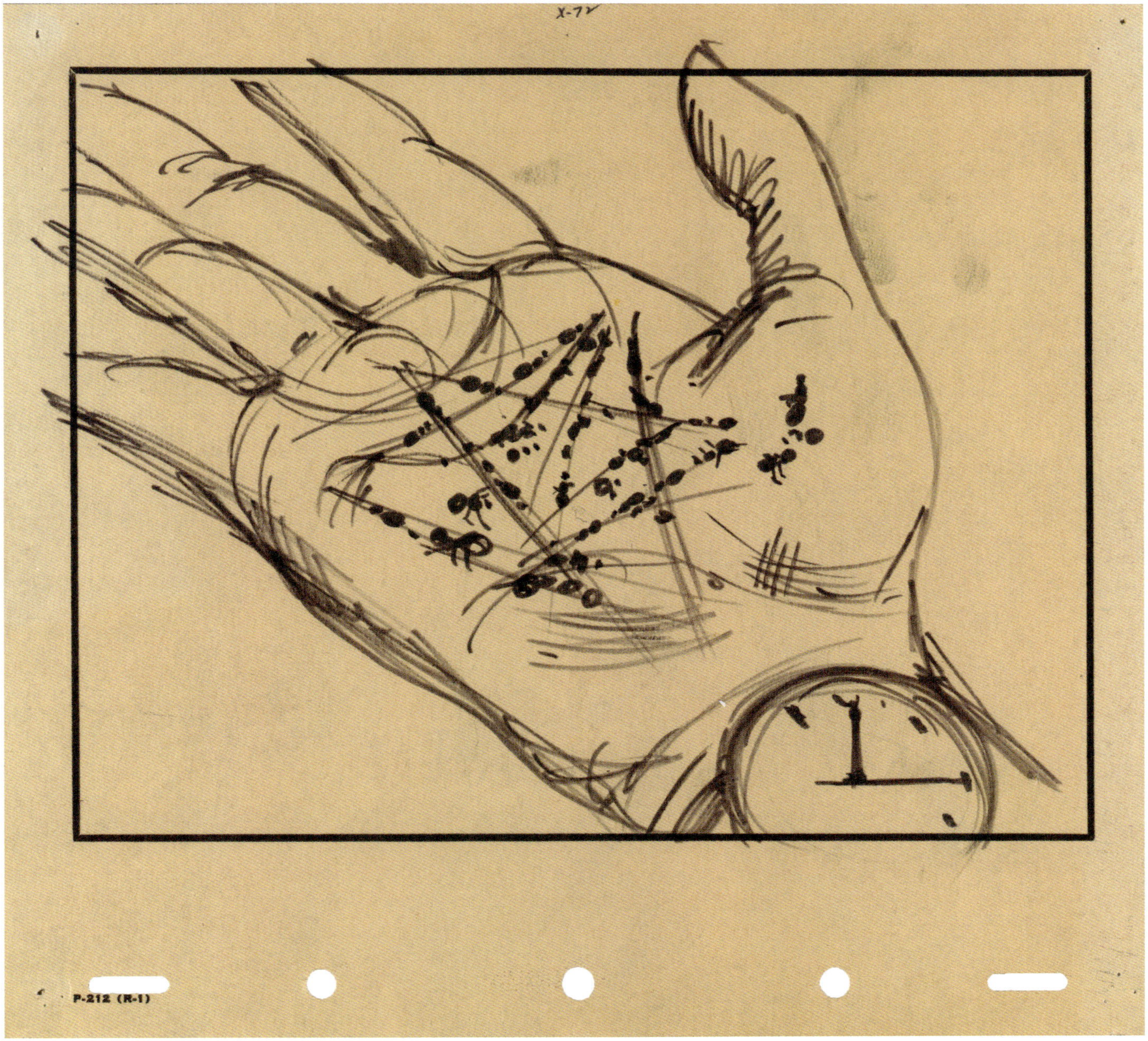
X-72
P-212 (R-1)

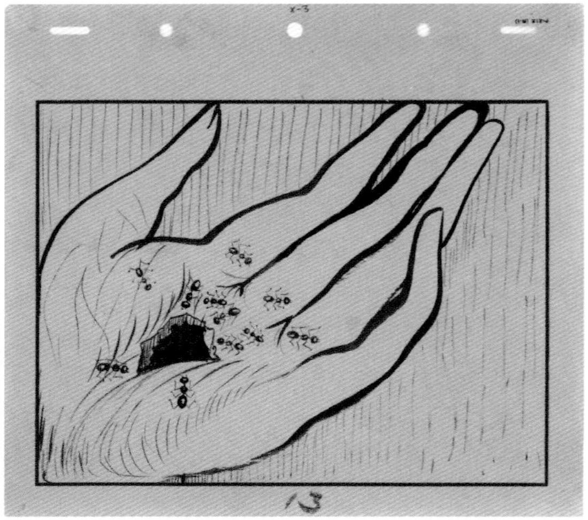
13
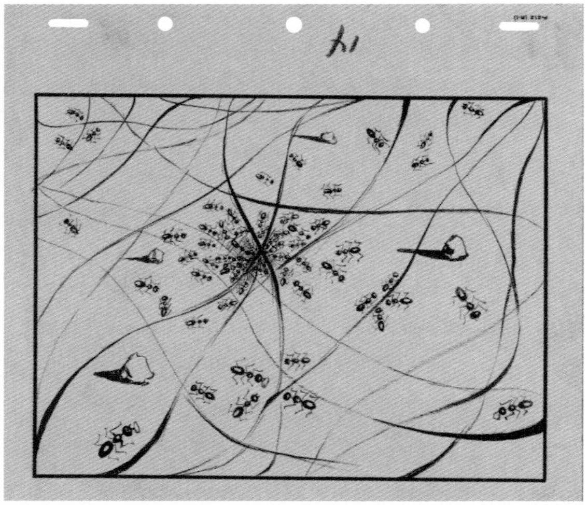
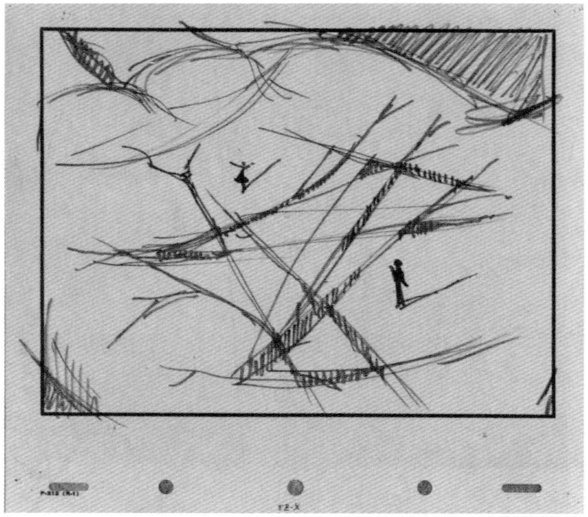
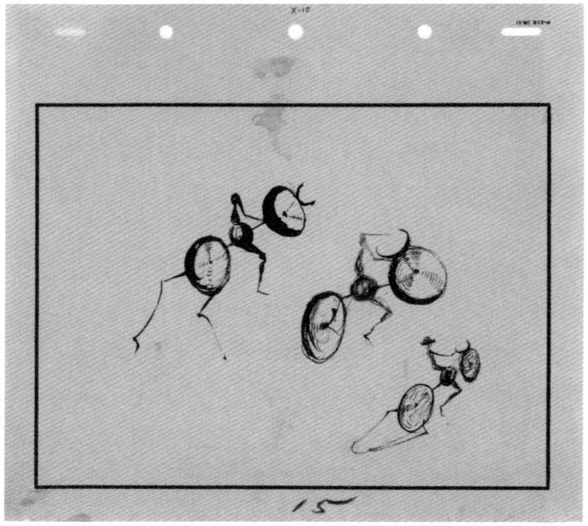
15
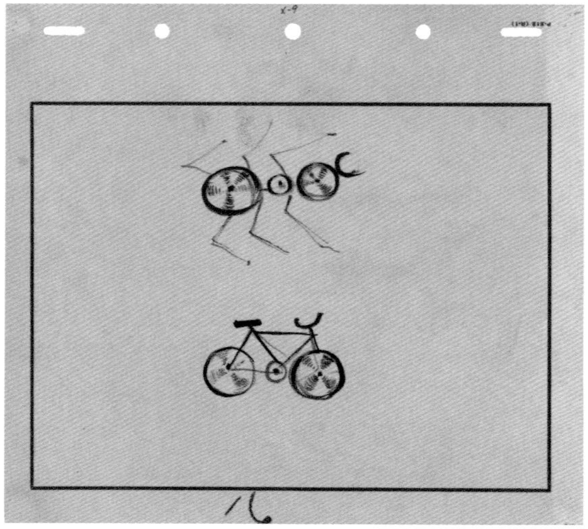
16
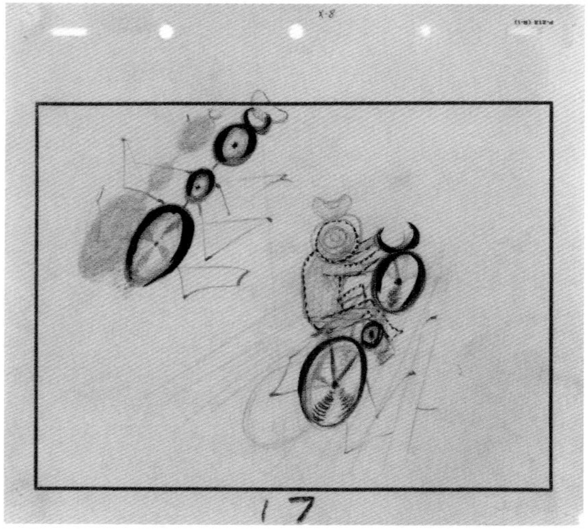
17
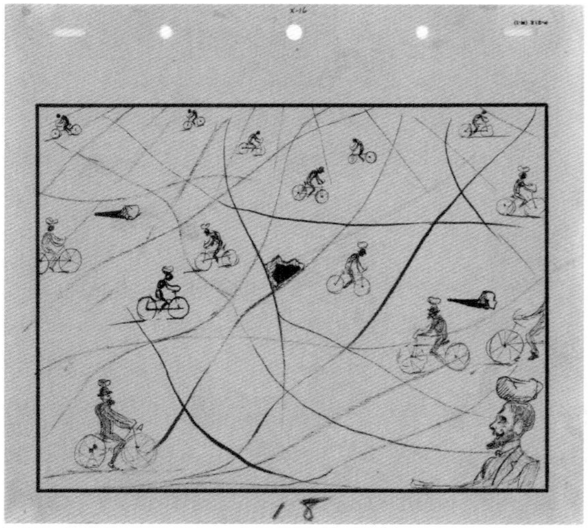
18
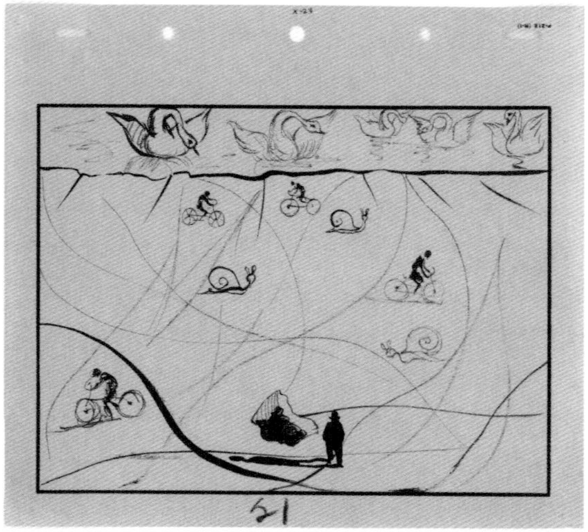
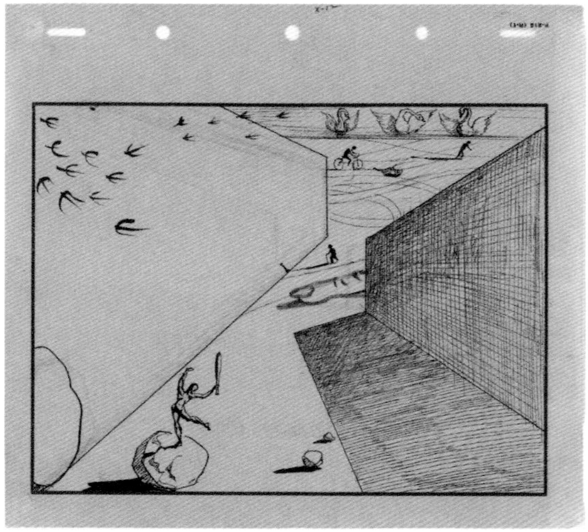

Page 74: Story sketches of ants crawling through a hand. Story sketches by Salvador Dalí with the exception of the top center and top right images, which were created by John Hench.

Image from the film, *Destino*.

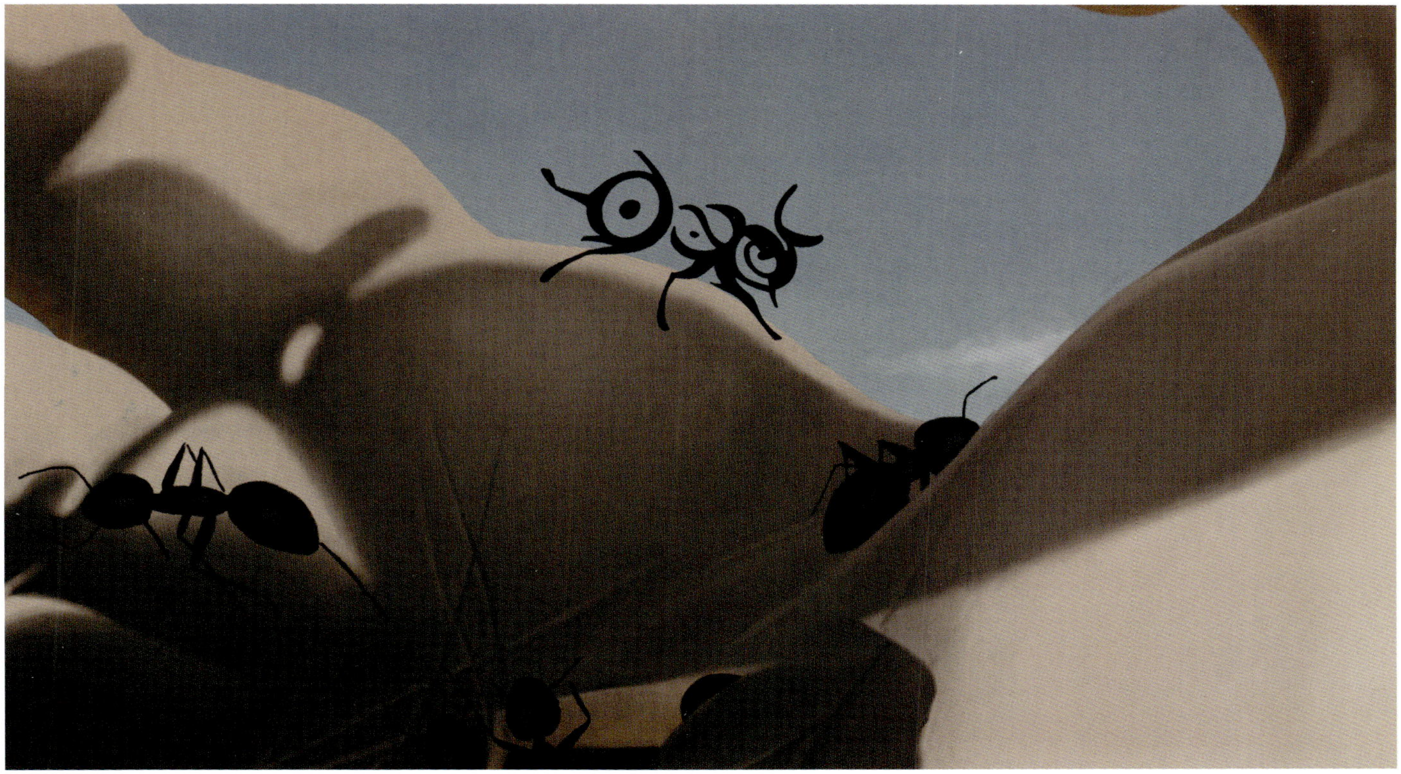

Dalí had a fascination with telephones as well, and in 1936 he created the Lobster Telephone sculpture for English poet Edward James, who was a collector of surrealist artworks. Art critics have said it "is a classic example of a surrealist object, made from the conjunction of items not normally associated with each other, resulting in something both playful and menacing. Dalí believed that such objects could reveal the secret desires of the unconscious." It is a similar conjunction of unrelated items being combined in animation, like adding eyes to the car in the 1952 Disney animated short *Suzie, the Little Blue Coupe* or the cartoon gag of a boxing glove popping out of the end of a gun barrel and punching a character.

The telephone image appears elsewhere in Dalí's works, including his 1938 paintings *Imperial Violets*, *Beach Scene with Telephone*, and *The Sublime Moment*. In several of these paintings, the telephone is propped up with crutches or attached like a rope to a zepplin, which are also repeating elements in Dalí's works.

Crutches were a very iconic design element of Salvador Dalí's and appear in numerous works throughout his career: *The Enigma of William Tell* (1933), *Sleep* (1937), *Soft Self-Portrait with Fried Bacon* (1941), and *The Burning Giraffe* (1937). Dalí wrote that ". . . the 'pathetic crutch' [was] the prop of the first crime of my childhood, as the monstrous development of certain atmospheric-cephalic skulls, crutches immobilize the ecstasy of certain attitudes of rare elegance, . . . [and]

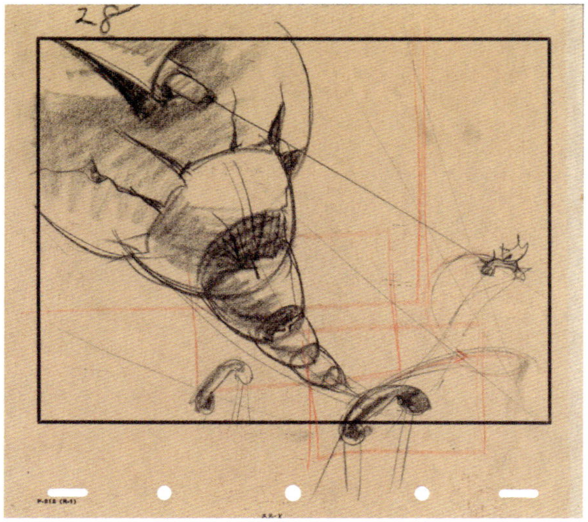
28
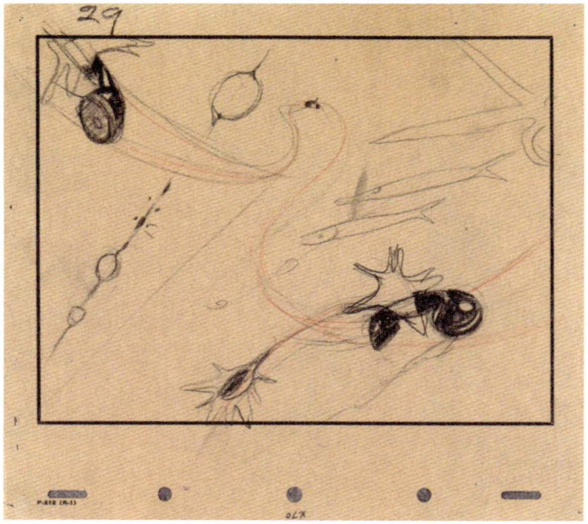
29
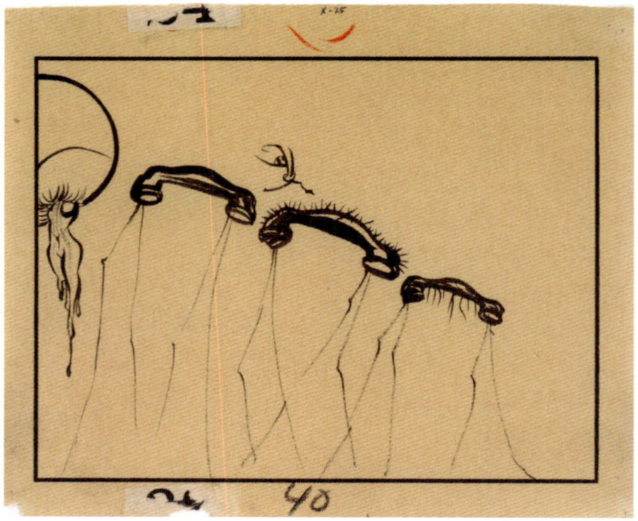
40
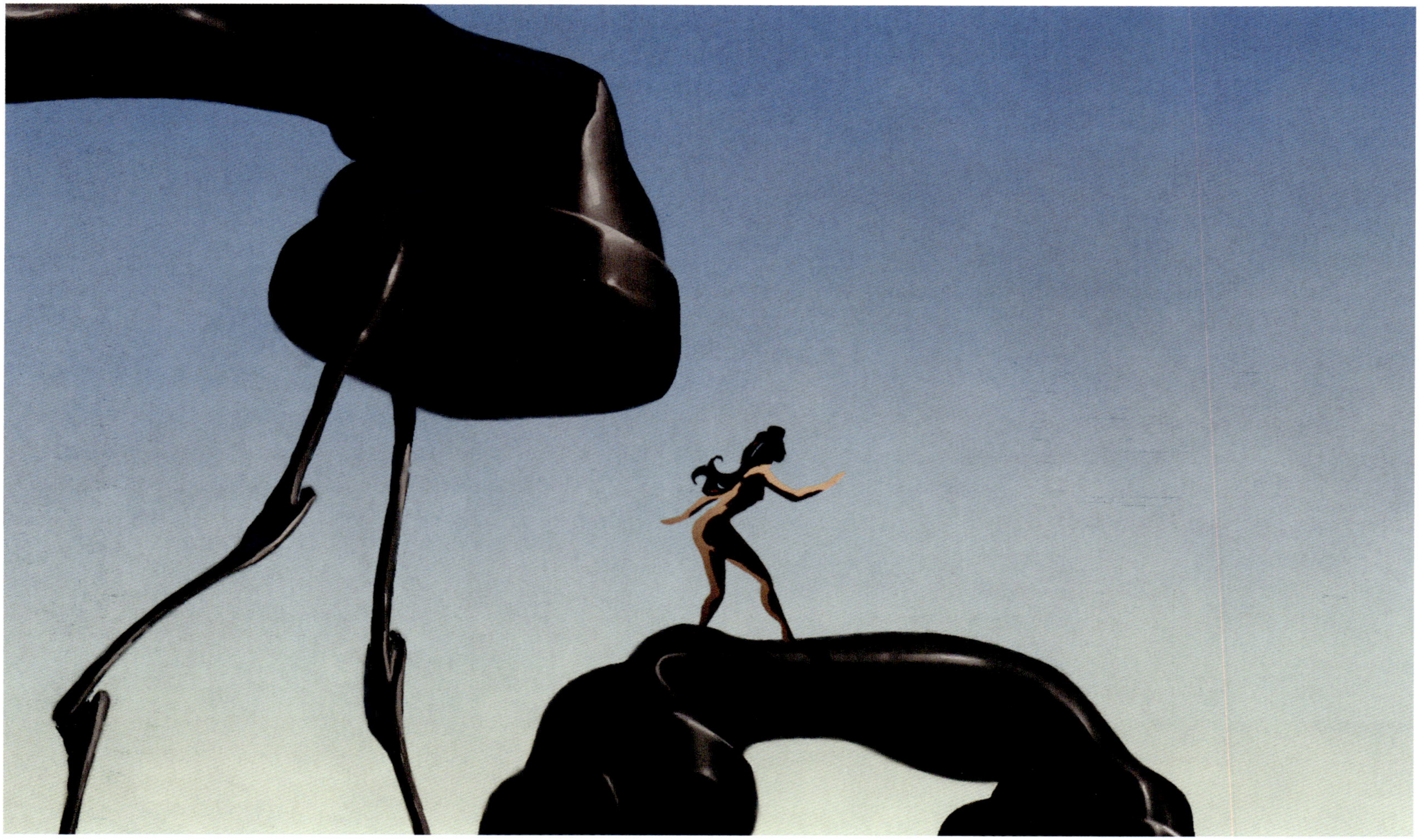

Page 76 (top row): Story sketches Nos. 28 and 29 are by John Hench. Story sketch No. 40 is by Salvador Dalí.

Page 76 (bottom): Image from the film *Destino*.

Top left: Story sketch with crutches by Dalí.

Top right: Dalí's watercolor painting (done in 1946) is based on the story sketch and visual development pieces from *Destino* (on pages 108 and 109). These images incorporate the artist's fascination with crutches and the merging of the human form with inanimate objects. Courtesy of the Walt Disney Family Foundation.

Bottom: Image from the film *Destino*.

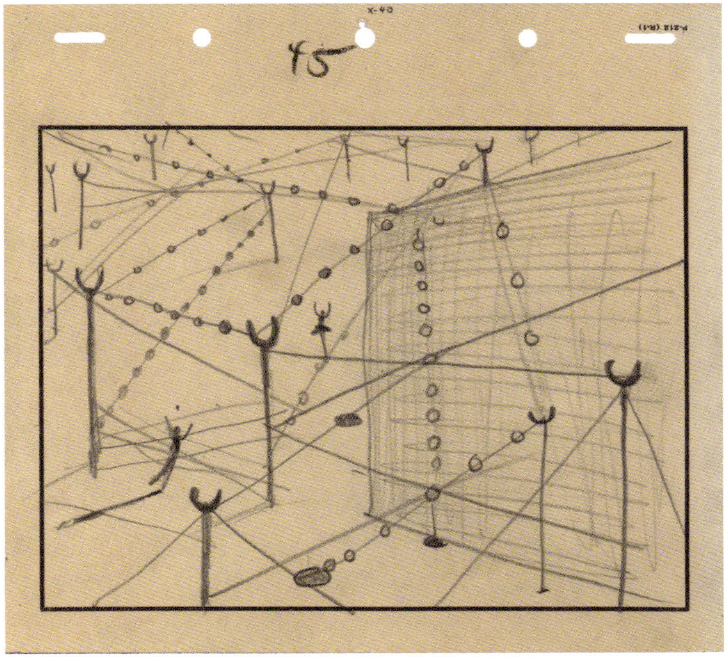

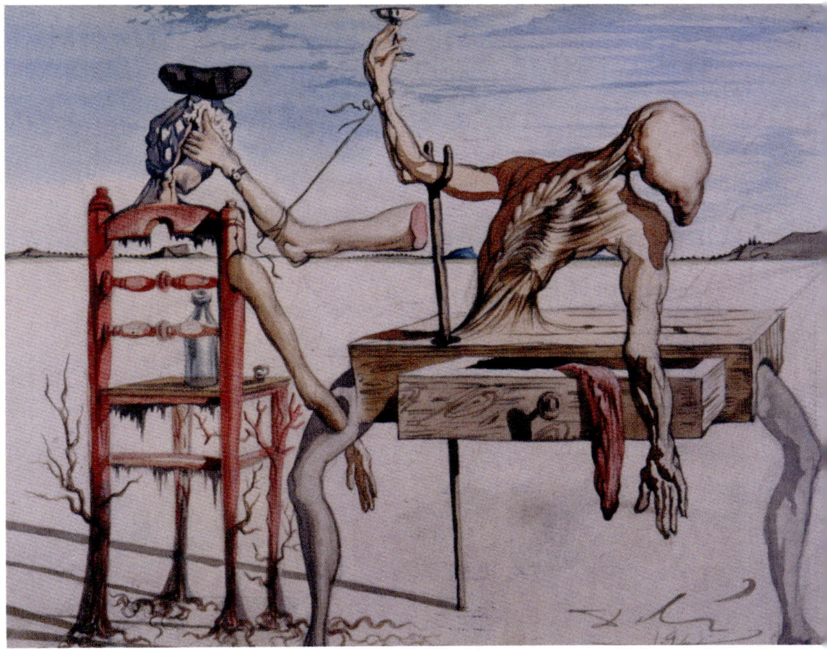

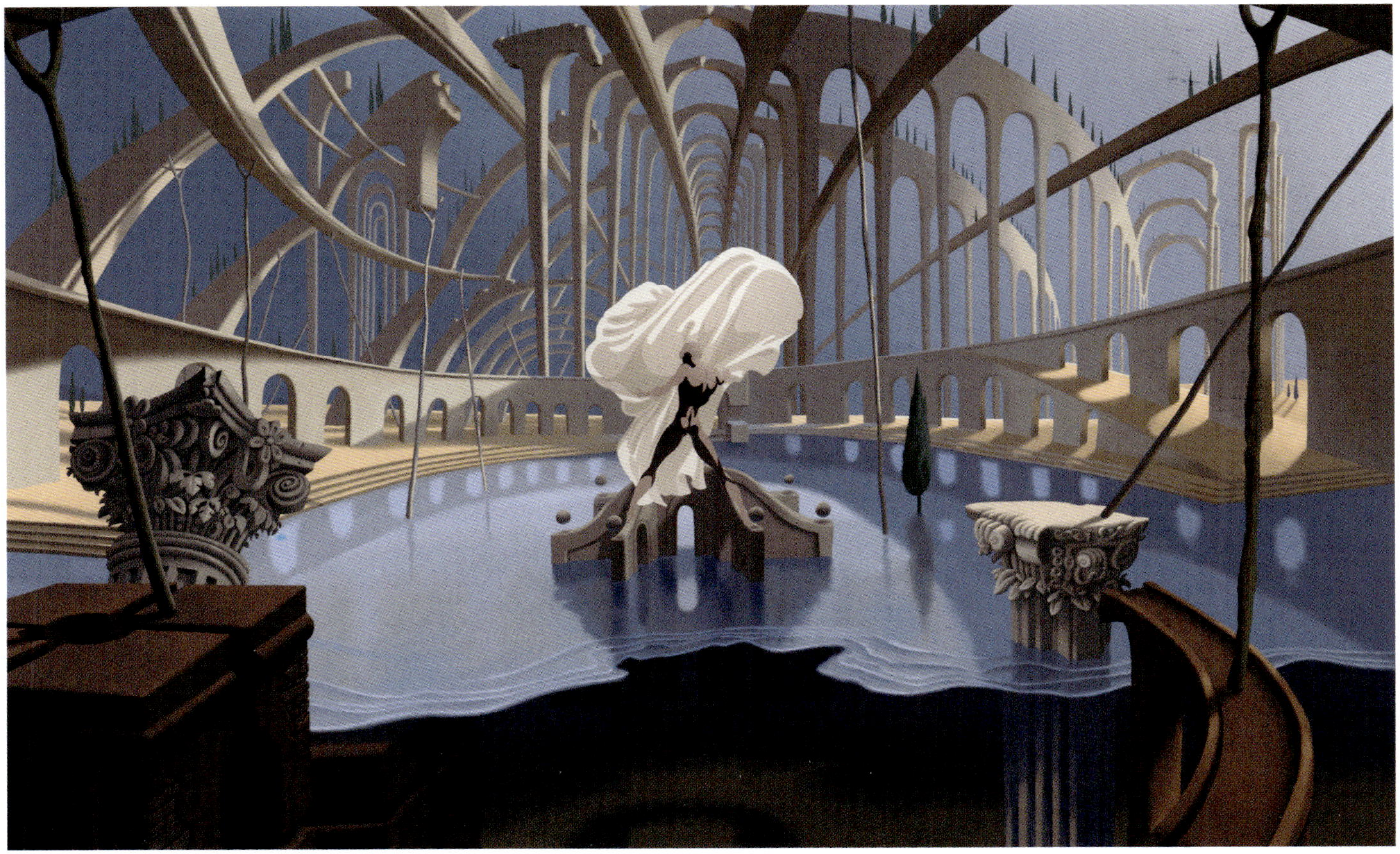

make architectural and durable the fugitive pose of a choreographic leap, to pin the ephemeral butterfly of the dancer with pins that would keep her poised for eternity. Crutches, crutches, crutches, crutches." The artist then later wrote that he had a compulsion to prop up "society people" who had aristocratic attitudes and felt a need to touch "the common base of the world" in order to "maintain their equilibrium."[15]

In *Destino*, however, there is an insect-like quality to the telephone, which appears with spindly legs and an exoskeleton, like a beetle or spider. There are other telephone images that appear toward the end of the film, such as when Chronos hits the baseball and it travels down a long, dreamlike corridor featuring telephone receivers that are in the shape of clouds.

Dalí also put himself into a number of paintings, including *The Great Masturbator* (1929), which has a caricature of his head balancing on his nose. The shape of Dalí's head in this painting appears to be inspired by the rocks of Cap de Creus near his home in Portlligat, another repeating element in his paintings. He also includes himself in one of his most famous paintings, *The Persistence of Memory* (1931), which again features the more literal rocks of Cap de Creus in the distance as well as the now famous soft watches.

Cap de Creus is a rocky peninsula north of Costa Brava; both Portlligat and the town of Cadaqués are nearly in the center of the easternmost part of the peninsula. You can actually walk from Dalí's Portlligat home into what is now the Cap de Creus National Park. The majority of the peninsula is national park land and is a beautiful place to visit.

In *Destino* Dalí uses a more direct caricature of himself and his wife, Gala, for the fate heads, which is the only piece of film that was shot for the Disney short. Dalí painted the heads on acetate cels that were placed on a desolate landscape, painted on Masonite, with a baseball in the center. The two heads come together slowly and form a ballerina within the negative space between the faces as they almost kiss. It was an eighteen-second scene shot by John Hench and screened for Dalí in a theater in Carmel, California.

Hench recalled, "I shot one test; I didn't have an animator available, but I moved everything on cels, shot one little scene I thought would intrigue Walt. It was a marvelous scene. Those two turtles coming together with appendage jewels on their shells; the space in between them formed the female protagonist. She was to step down as an entrance."

Upon further reflection, Hench, in retrospect, added that it's "amazing to see that stuff on the screen. Shot from paintings [Dalí] did, a background limitless plane with a ball on the horizon formed the head of the female. I persuaded him to do the two cels, in oils." Walt was apparently fascinated by it.

Hench went on to recount in an interview with John Canemaker that at the theater in Carmel, at the end of the evening, when the film that was playing ended, the custodian would come in with a giant lightbulb on the end of a stand—a work light. He would stick it on the stage so he could clean up the

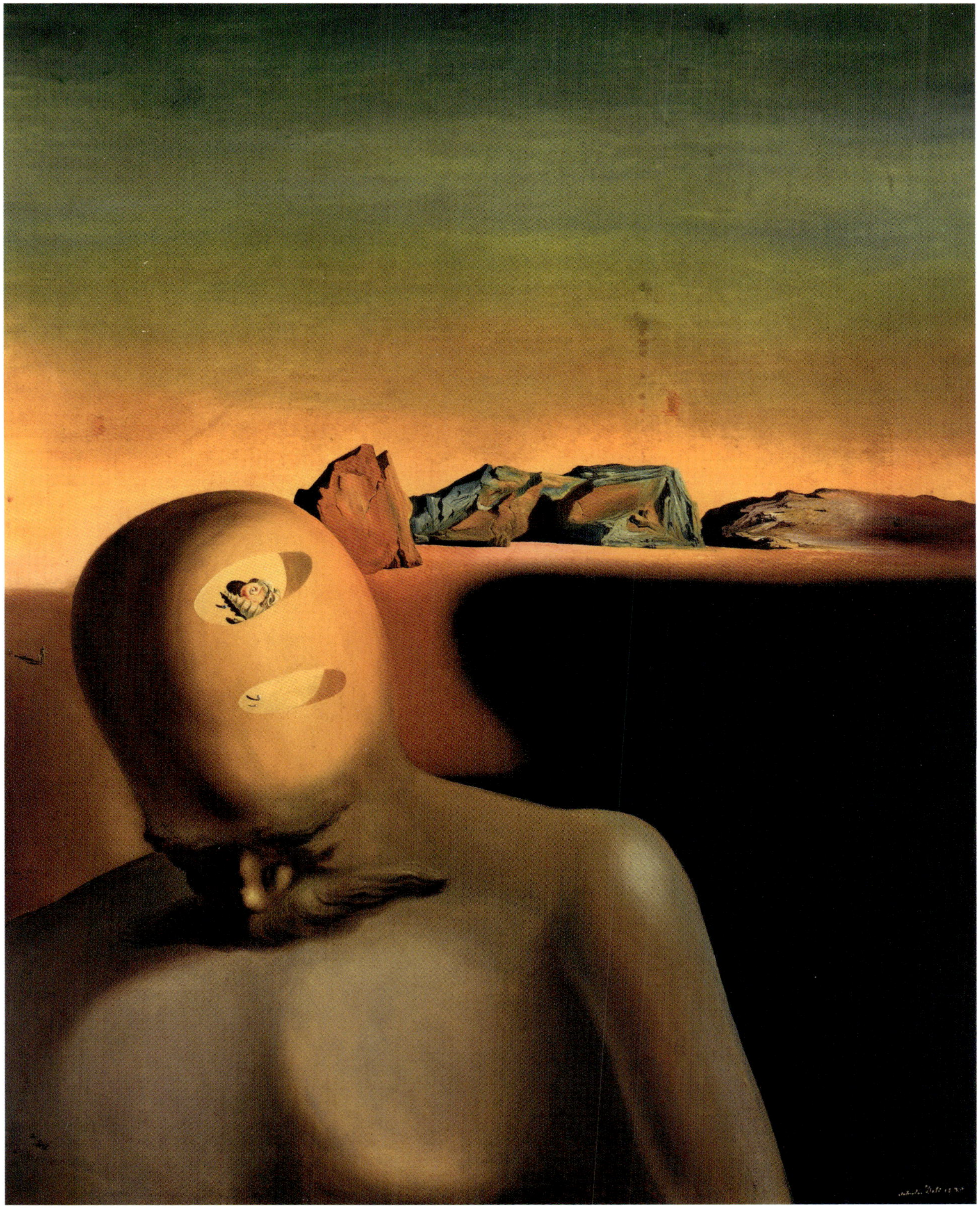

Salvador Dalí's *The Average Bureaucrat*, 1930.
Courtesy of the Salvador Dalí Museum,
St. Petersburg, Florida.

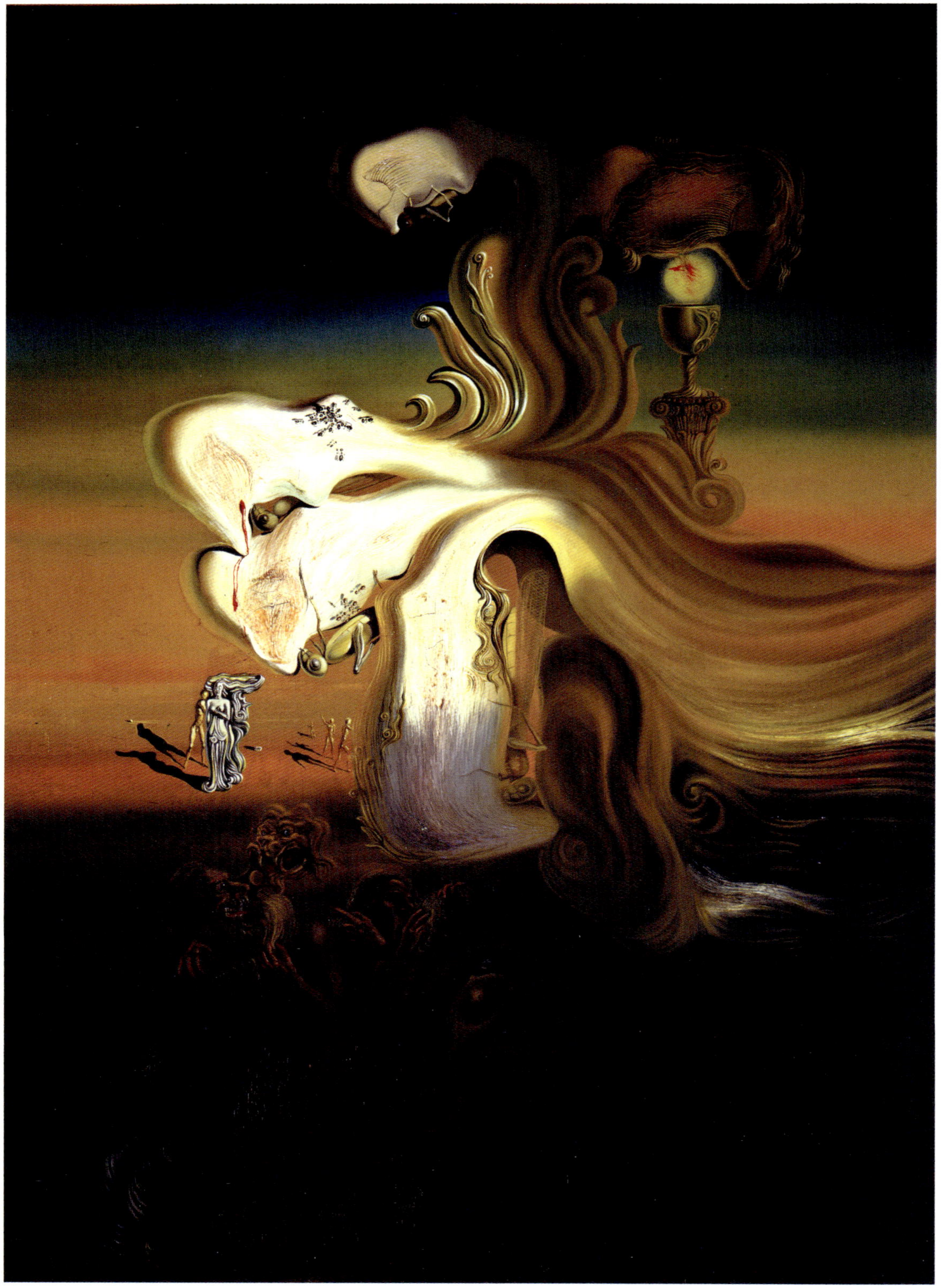

Salvador Dalí's *Profanation of the Host*, 1929. Courtesy of the Dalí Museum, St. Petersburg, Florida.

theater. "Dalí thought that was the most astonishing thing in the world—this old man bringing in this huge light. We had to postpone that and ask the projectionist to run this little piece of film. No sound track, silent.

"The reaction of the manager: 'My God, what was that?'" Hench noted when recapturing the moment in the Canemaker interview years later. "The projectionist had the same opinion: 'What the hell was that?'"[16]

Dalí fulfilled his contract, working on the project at Disney's Burbank studio until April of 1946. He would return for another six weeks in July and August of that year to do some additional work. Then, according to studio documents, Dalí returned one final time, in April 1947, and stayed through early 1948. It is not known whether he was at the Disney Studio continuously or if he had visited several times during that period.

Animators Frank Thomas and Ollie Johnston, authors of *Disney Animation: The Illusion of Life*, wrote, "The picture was not becoming quite what either of them hoped when they started. Towards the end of the film collaboration Walt stopped by to look at the project and was taken aback by the baseball concept being introduced. Walt exclaimed, 'Jesus Christ, $70,000 down the drain!'"[17]

John Hench sent a letter to Salvador and Gala Dalí on January 19, 1949, responding to their inquiry regarding *Destino*. In it, he didn't mince words: "At this moment, as always, the Disney Studio is having a bad time. Truly a state of crisis. Again, how monotonous. Many of the artists and technicians have been terminated, including Bob Cormack, unhappily. Walt has said that there are a great number of persons which are not doing anything or not occupied at the Studio (Gala you have said the same thing)." This is something that plagued the studio for years. (Even when I started at Disney in early 1984, there were many individuals sitting around reading newspapers at all hours of the day. That ended when there was a management change-out later that year.)

The studio was having financial difficulties. Hench revealed, "Thus again, everything depends on the next release[,] *So Dear to My Heart*, which will have its premiere January 16." He went on in the letter that "I confess to be tormented (disturbed) also on the subject of your film. Walt Disney is, at the moment, not able to say how much time is necessary before the commencement of *Destino*. The moment I have anything fixed (or closed or terminated) I will inform you by telegram." That telegram, however, would never be sent.

"Walt thought the market for package films was gone," explained Hench in an interview more than forty years later. "He was an enormously intuitive man; he could look into the future and project a trend. He understood the package concept as communicating a certain kind of thing, and he figured the public needed something else."[18]

Work on the *Destino* film halted in 1948. Audience tastes were changing. Disney's distributor at the time did not want anymore packaged pictures and the Studio was under financial pressure to put out

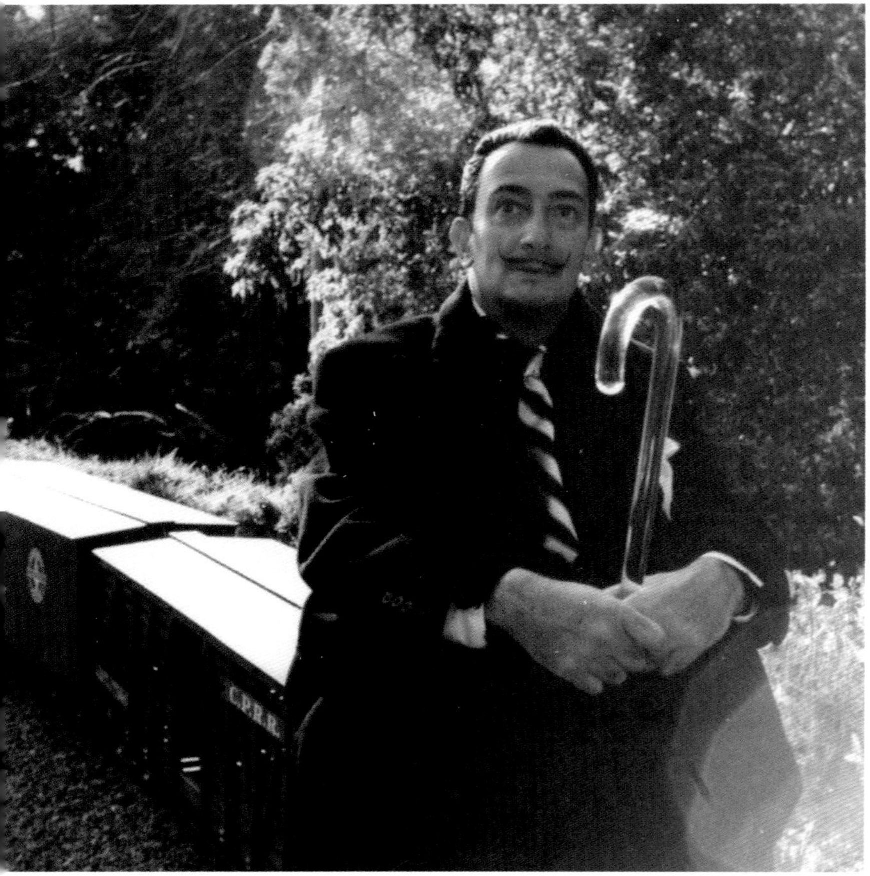

Salvador Dalí rides the miniature train, which was also known as the Carolwood Pacific Railroad, in Walt's backyard in Los Angeles. Courtesy of the Fundació Gala-Salvador Dalí.

feature-length films. According to Hench, "Afterward he [Walt] regretted stopping work on this because it would have been quite a valuable document."

Roy E. Disney reflected: "Walt wanted to be an artist, but he got knocked down by *Fantasia*, and the war [World War II] was brutal. He had to go and make money."[19] *Fantasia*, it has been acknowledged by many, was ahead of its time and was received with mixed reviews. That, coupled with the outbreak of World War II [in 1939], which cut off much of the film distribution to Europe, also reduced the studio's film revenues by at least a third and hobbled the potential success of Fantasia."[19]

There are some that have speculated that the film just developed in a direction that was different from the style of picture being done at the studio during that period. The film had a decidedly Dalí-esque look that overshadowed the Disney house style; it was more Dalí than Disney, and there was a natural concern about that. Commenting on the art style, Roy E. Disney stated, "Can you imagine Disney in 1948 coming out with that!?" It was stylistically different from the work being done on *Cinderella* which represented a transition from the classic style of *Bambi* and *Pinocchio* to a more designed look of the films that came later.

Walt and Dalí nonetheless remained friends throughout the rest of their lives. They traded letters and visited each other when time permitted. On one trip to Hollywood, Dalí even rode the miniature train that Walt had at his home in Holmby Hills. Dalí was so startled by the realistic nature of the precision-scale railroad that it actually frightened him.

In June 1952, Walt sent Dalí a letter electing him vice president of the Carolwood Pacific Railroad, Walt's backyard railroad. He went on to say in the letter, "The only obligation this office entails is, when you're in the vicinity of the 'Fair Weather Route,' that you stop by for a ride and try your hand at the throttle." The letter was accompanied by pass number fourteen, signed in ink by Walt Disney with the printed message, "GOOD UNTIL REVOKED UNLESS OTHERWISE ORDERED."

Right: Letter from Walt Disney to Salvador Dalí dated June 26, 1952, naming Dalí as vice president of the Carolwood Pacific Railroad, which was Walt's miniature backyard train. Courtesy of the Fundació Gala-Salvador Dalí.

Below: Front and back of Salvador Dalí's Carolwood Pacific Rail Road pass, No. 14. Courtesy of the Fundació Gala-Salvador Dalí.

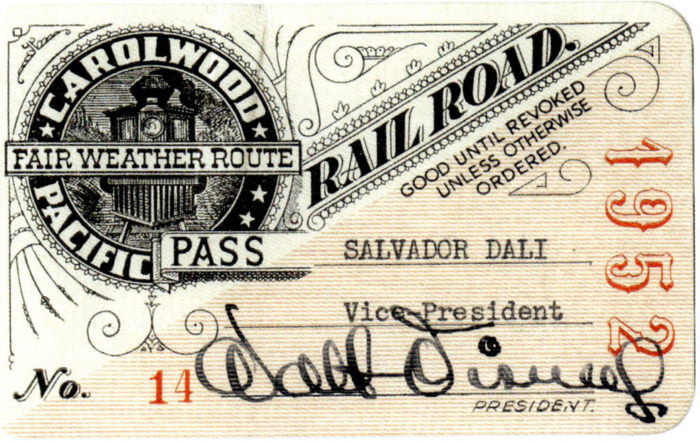

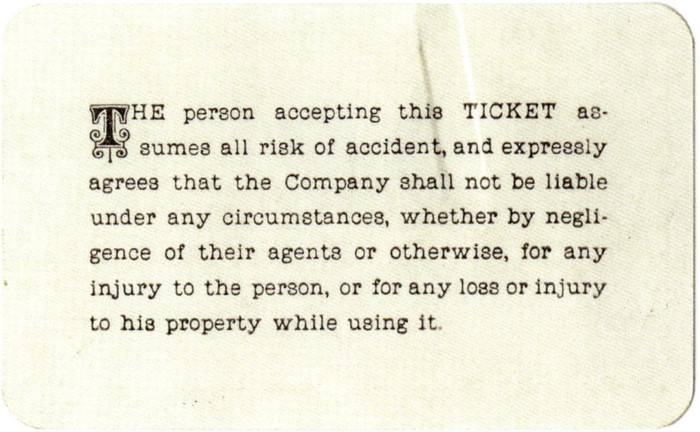

THE person accepting this TICKET assumes all risk of accident, and expressly agrees that the Company shall not be liable under any circumstances, whether by negligence of their agents or otherwise, for any injury to the person, or for any loss or injury to his property while using it.

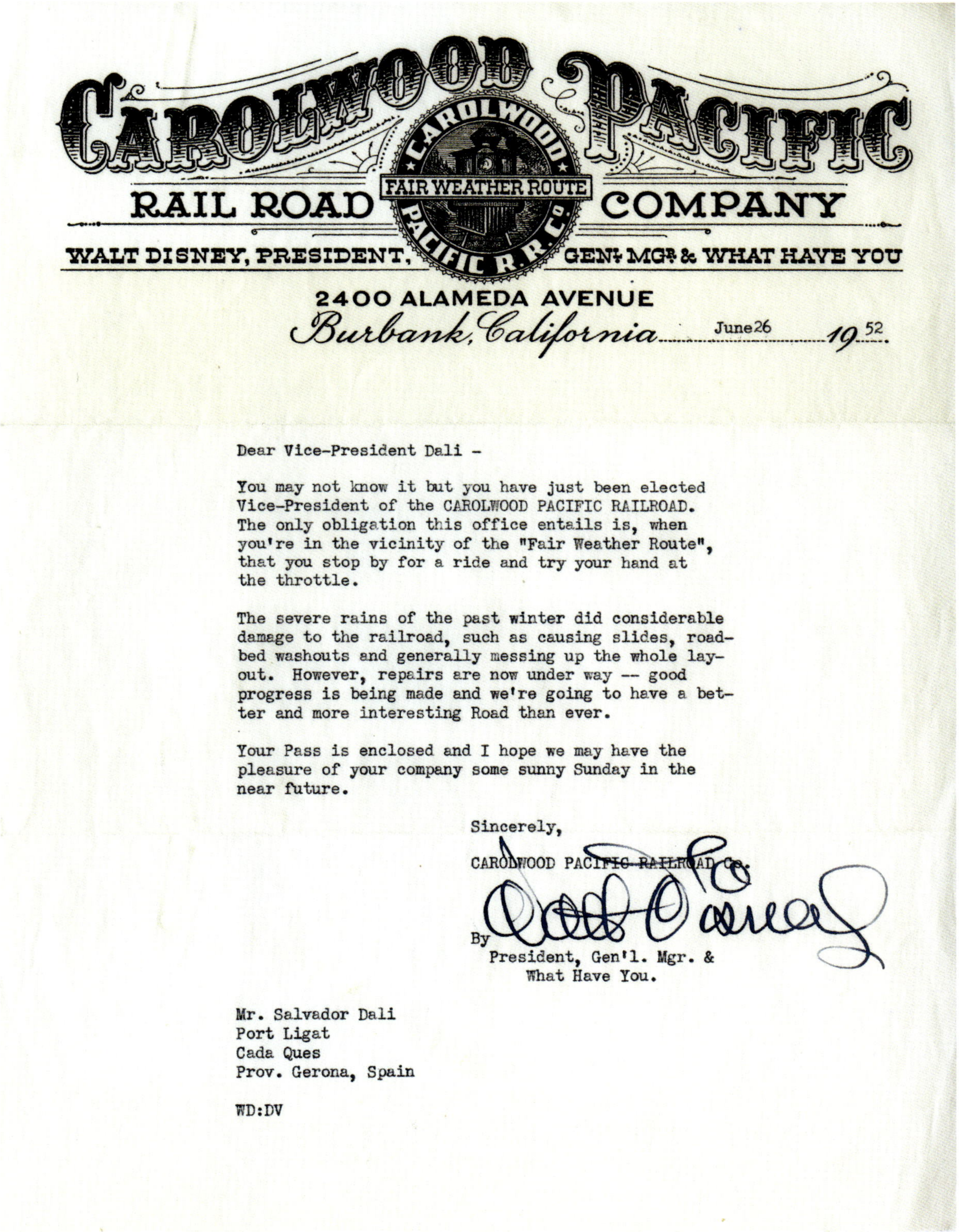

CAROLWOOD PACIFIC RAIL ROAD COMPANY

CAROLWOOD PACIFIC R.R. Co. FAIR WEATHER ROUTE

WALT DISNEY, PRESIDENT, GEN'L MGR. & WHAT HAVE YOU

2400 ALAMEDA AVENUE

Burbank, California June 26 1952

Dear Vice-President Dali -

You may not know it but you have just been elected Vice-President of the CAROLWOOD PACIFIC RAILROAD. The only obligation this office entails is, when you're in the vicinity of the "Fair Weather Route", that you stop by for a ride and try your hand at the throttle.

The severe rains of the past winter did considerable damage to the railroad, such as causing slides, roadbed washouts and generally messing up the whole layout. However, repairs are now under way -- good progress is being made and we're going to have a better and more interesting Road than ever.

Your Pass is enclosed and I hope we may have the pleasure of your company some sunny Sunday in the near future.

Sincerely,

CAROLWOOD PACIFIC RAILROAD Co.

By
President, Gen'l. Mgr. &
What Have You.

Mr. Salvador Dali
Port Ligat
Cada Ques
Prov. Gerona, Spain

WD:DV

Pages 82, 84–85: Salvador and Gala Dalí's visit to the Disney family home in Los Angeles,circa 1952. Courtesy of the Fundació Gala-Salvador Dalí.

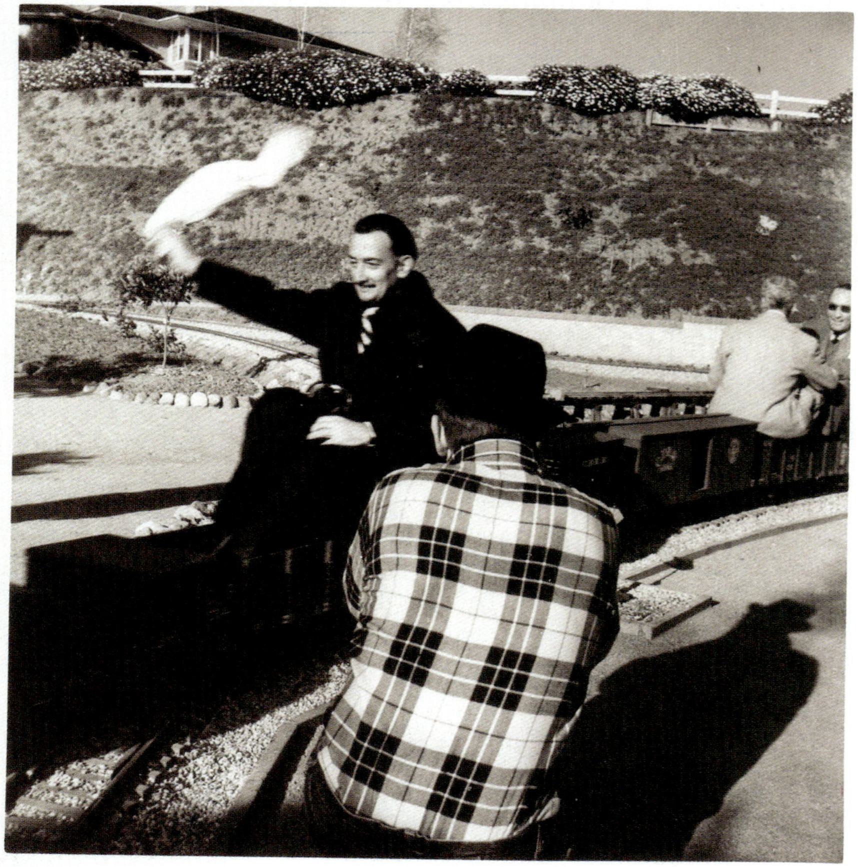

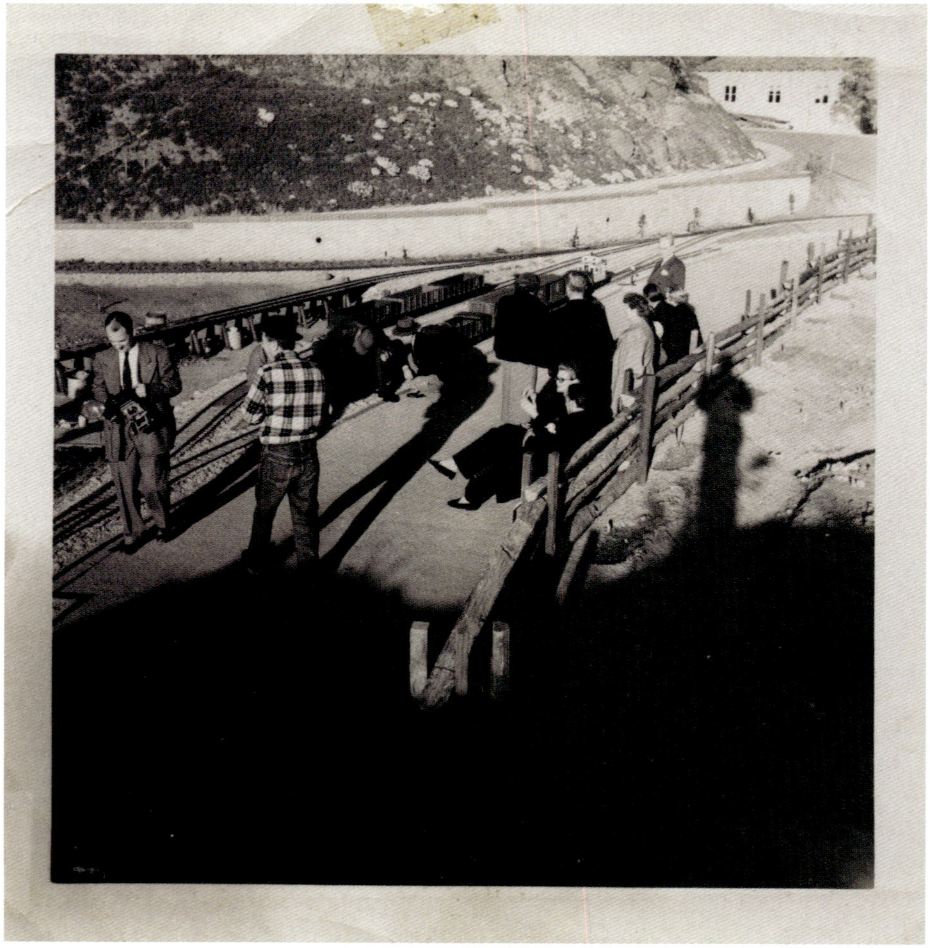

Disney artist Ward Kimball at the throttle of the Fairweather Express train, part of Walt Disney's backyard Carolwood Pacific Railroad, with Gala and Salvador Dalí in tow.

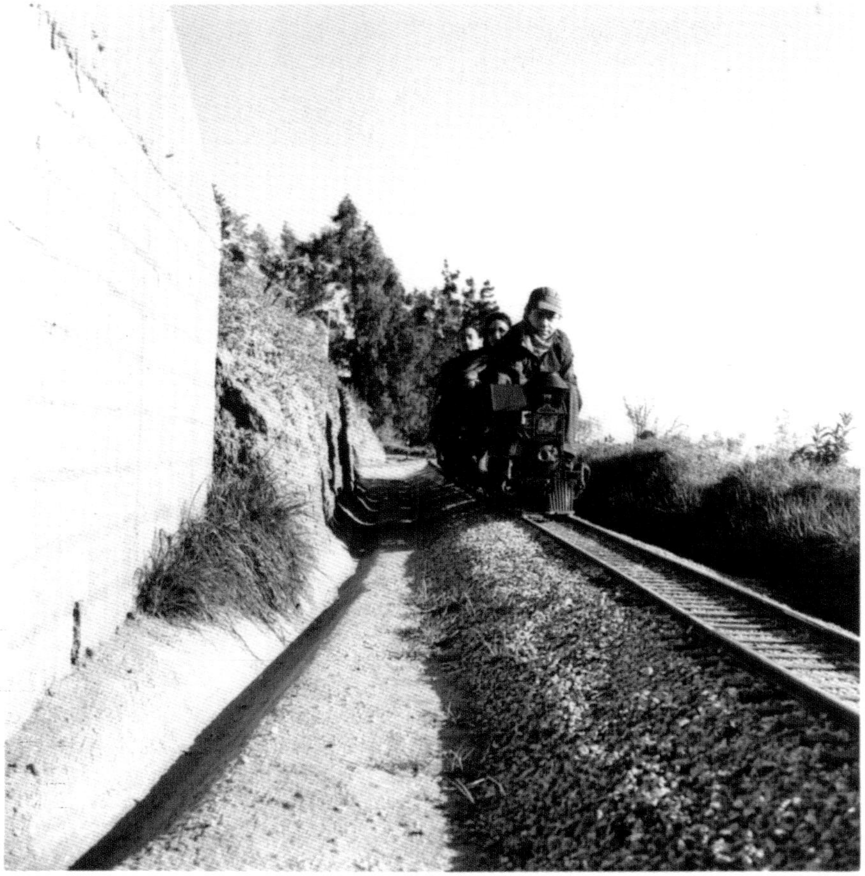

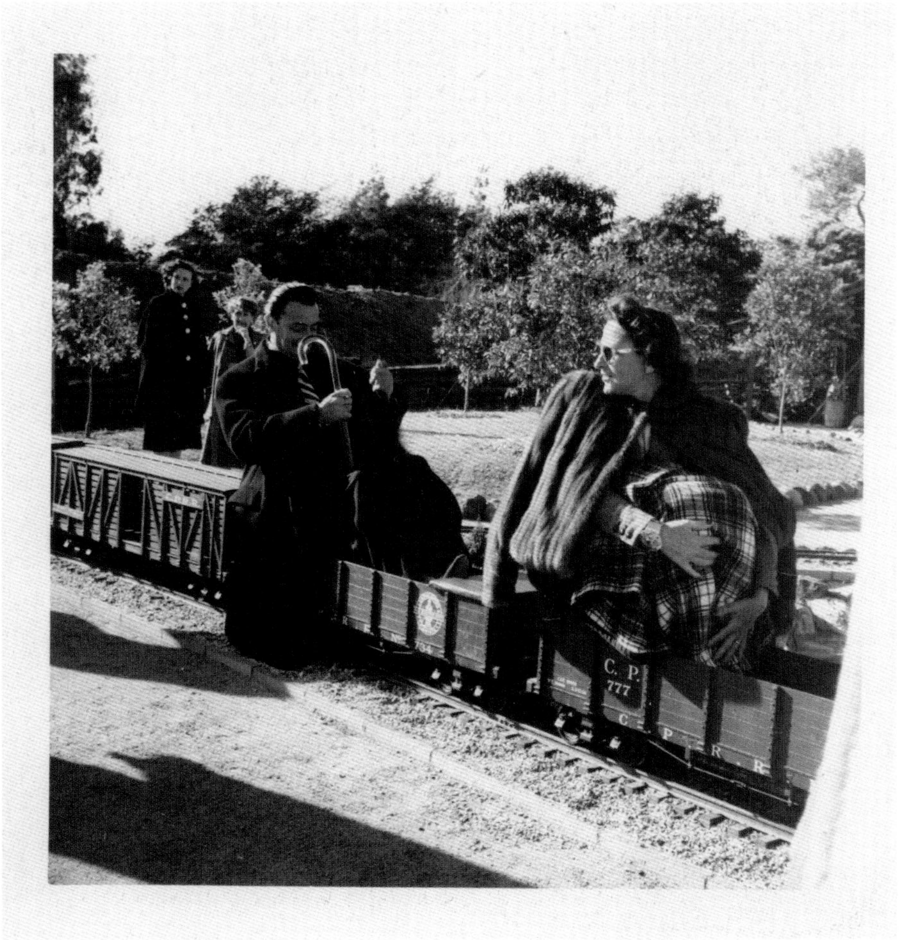

Photograph taken by Gala Dalí, who is photographing Walt Disney taking a photo of Salvador Dalí, speaking with an unidentified woman.

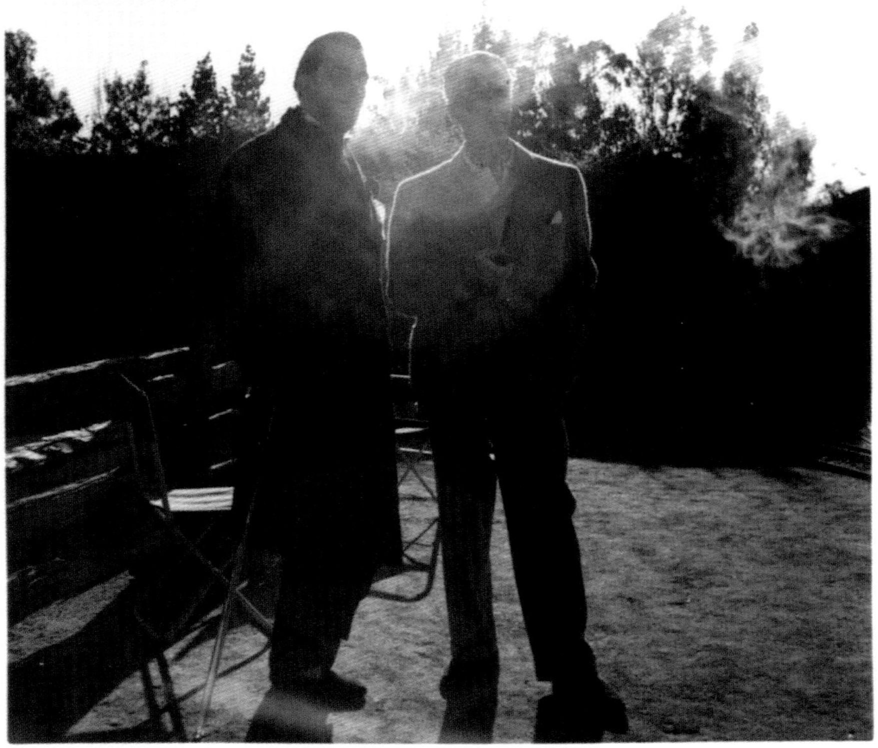

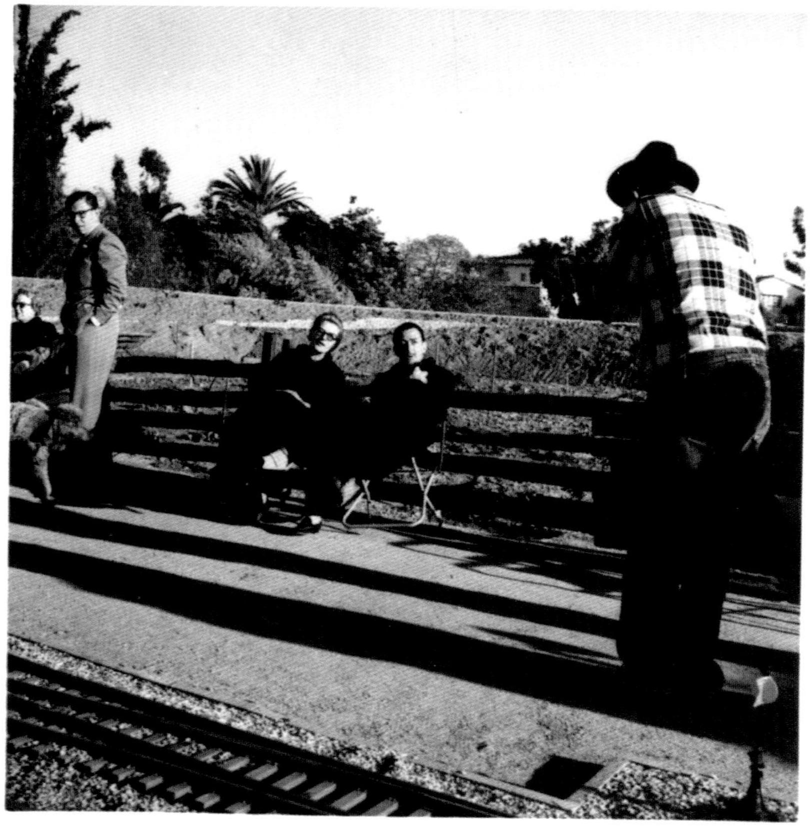

The corresponding photos that Walt took of Dalí sitting on the bench.

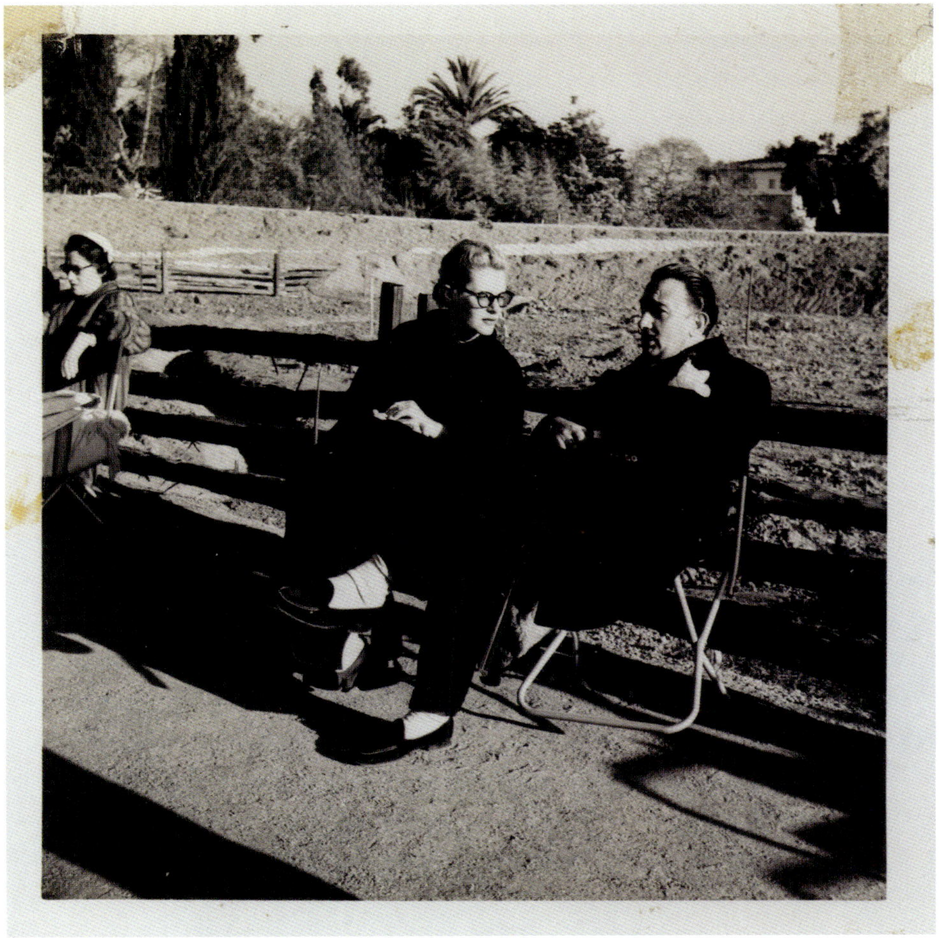

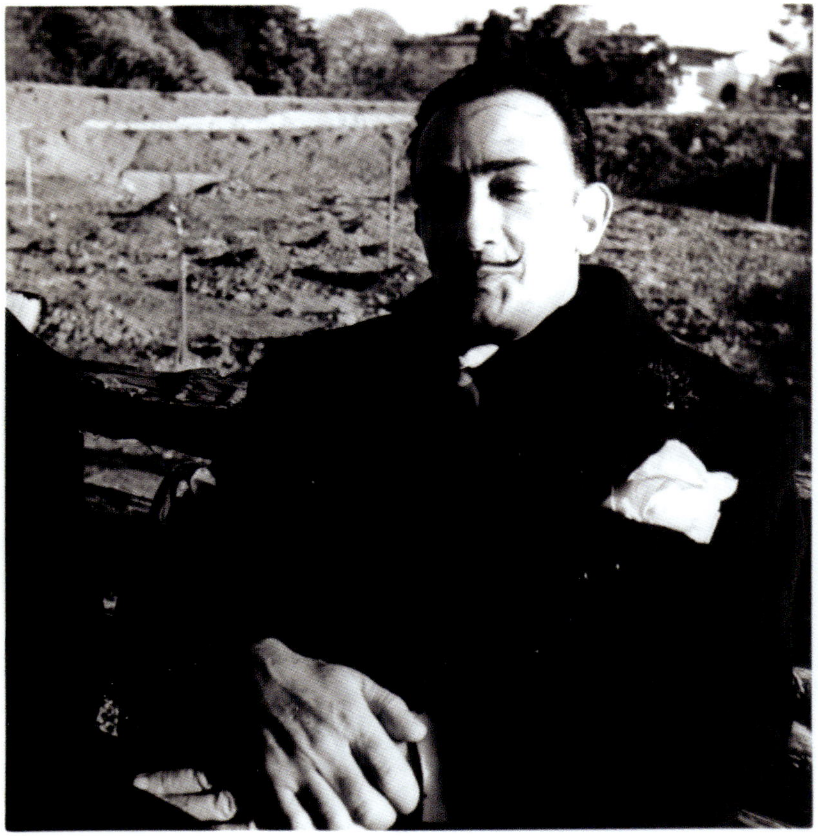

From left to right: Salvador Dalí, Walt Disney, Gala Dalí, and Lillian Disney at the Dalí's home in Portlligat, Spain (circa 1957). Photograph by Josep Postius, courtesy of the Fundació Gala-Salvador Dalí.

Page 89: The Disneys and the Dalís, outside the Dalí home, on the same visit. Photograph by Josep Postius, courtesy of the Fundació Gala-Salvador Dalí.

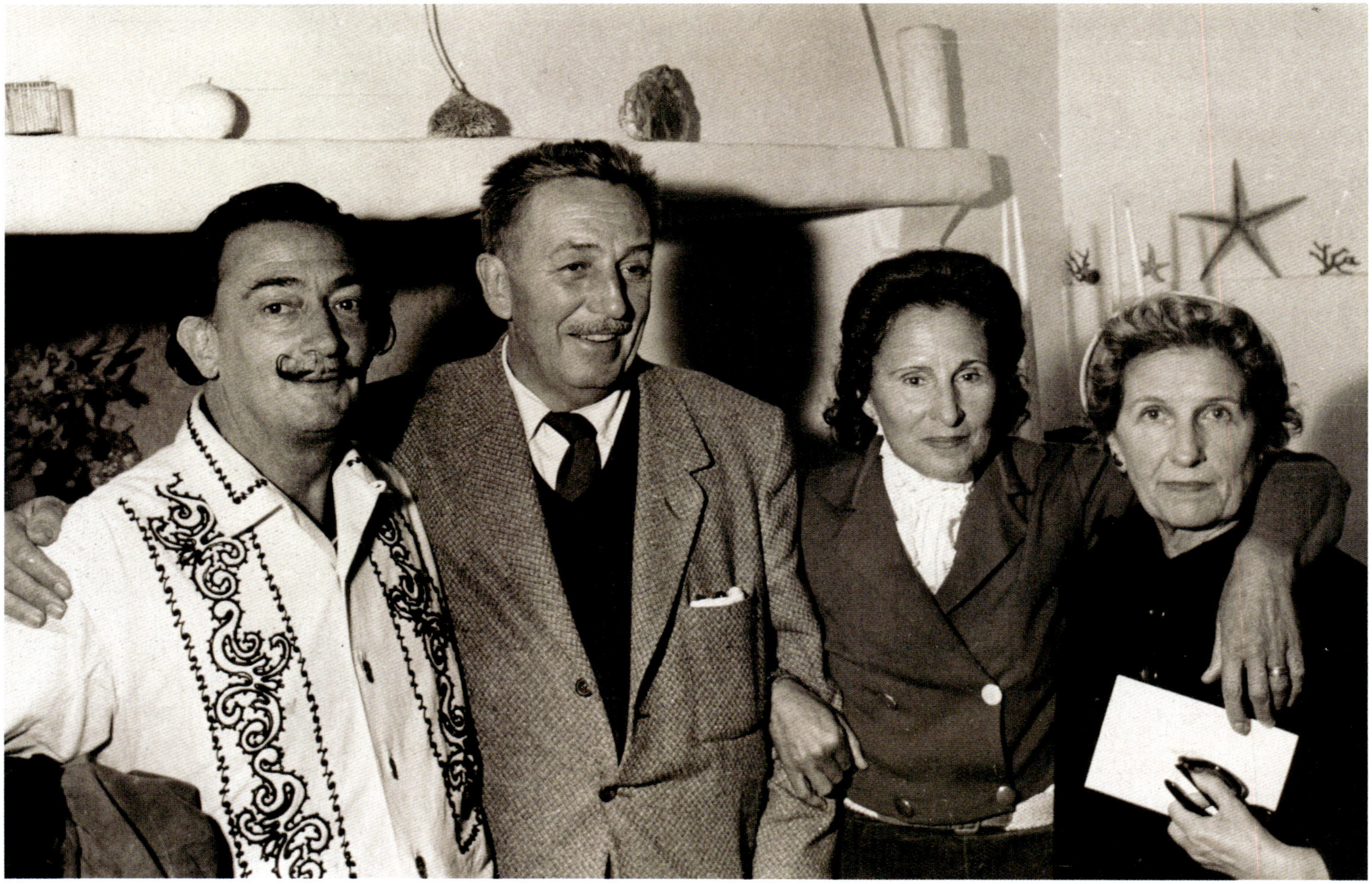

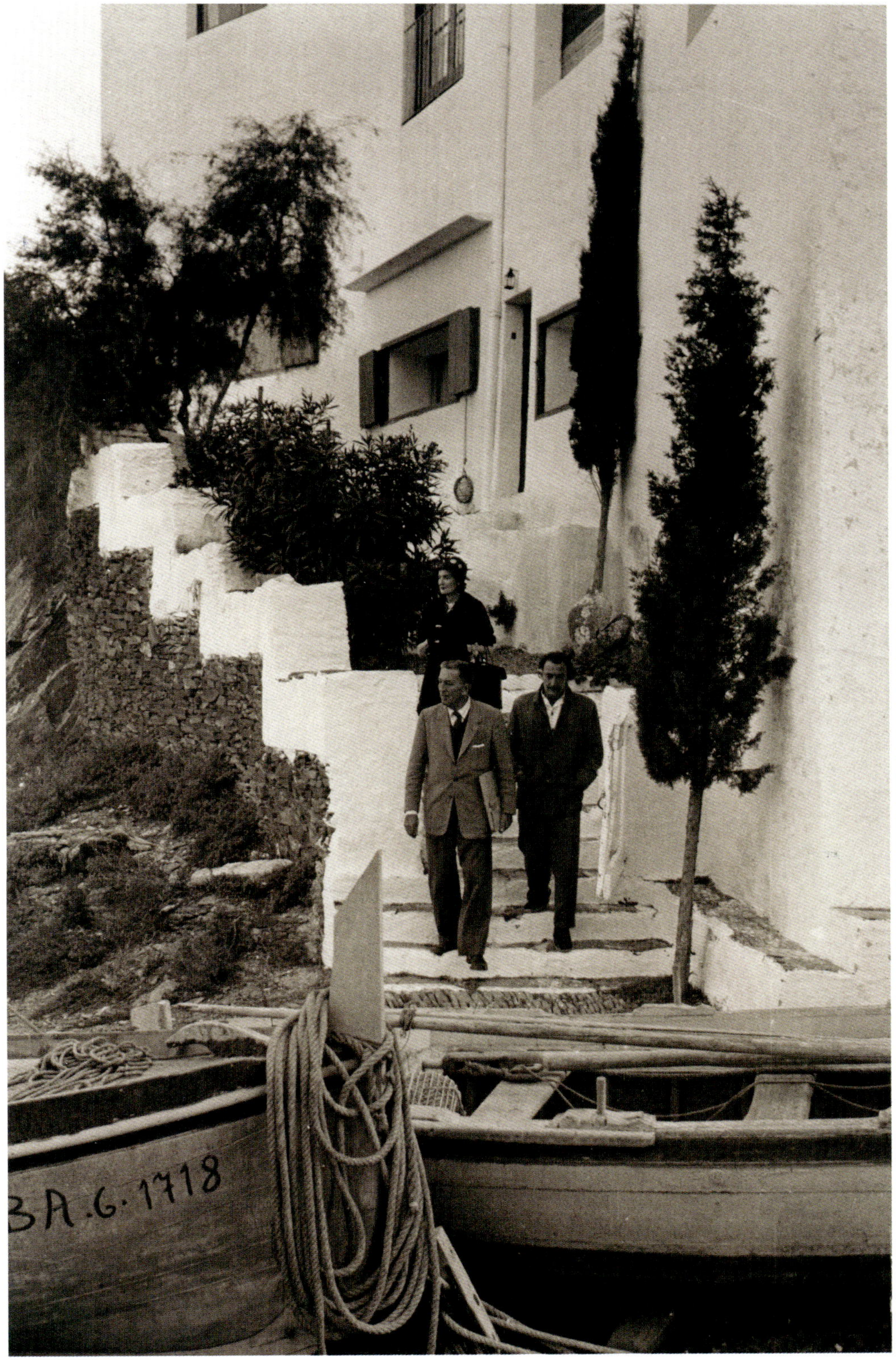

The letter went on to describe some damage done to the scale railroad in the backyard from "the severe rains this past winter," which caused "slides, road-bed [sic] washouts[,] and generally messing up the whole layout." He hoped that Dalí would drop by on "some sunny Sunday in the near future." The letter was sent to Dalí at his home in Portlligat, Spain.

Dalí rode Walt's train, the *Lilly Belle*, and was impressed by the completeness of the detail. He thought, however, it was carried to the extreme. John Hench recalled, "[Dalí] felt it would be dangerous because such perfection of detail would inevitably provoke accidents such as [the ones] real trains have, or even sabotage, like miniature train wreckers! Such perfection did not belong to models."

Walt and Lillian Disney visited Gala and Dalí in Portlligat on at least one occasion over the years. They even discussed developing the Spanish classic *Don Quixote* into an animated picture as well as *El Cid*. Dalí went on to develop various story concepts for *El Cid*, but it never progressed beyond that stage. By then, Walt was preoccupied with building Disneyland and expanding into television production as the company entered a period of growth. Animated shorts production dropped off significantly with the advent of television, and the studio was producing many more live-action feature films, nature films, and TV shows.

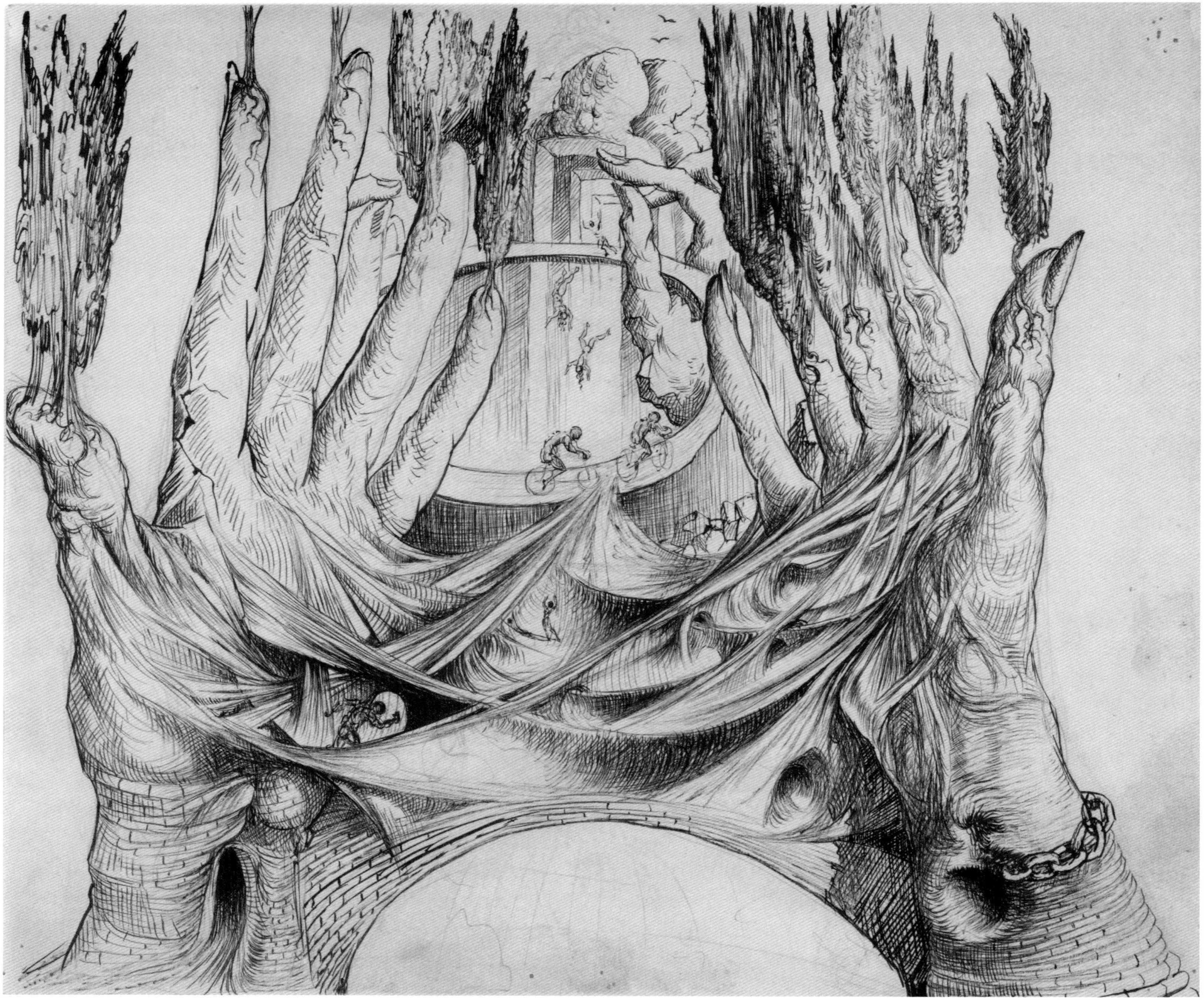

Page 90: Visual development for *Destino* by Salvador Dalí.

Visual development for *Destino* by Dalí using India ink and watercolor.

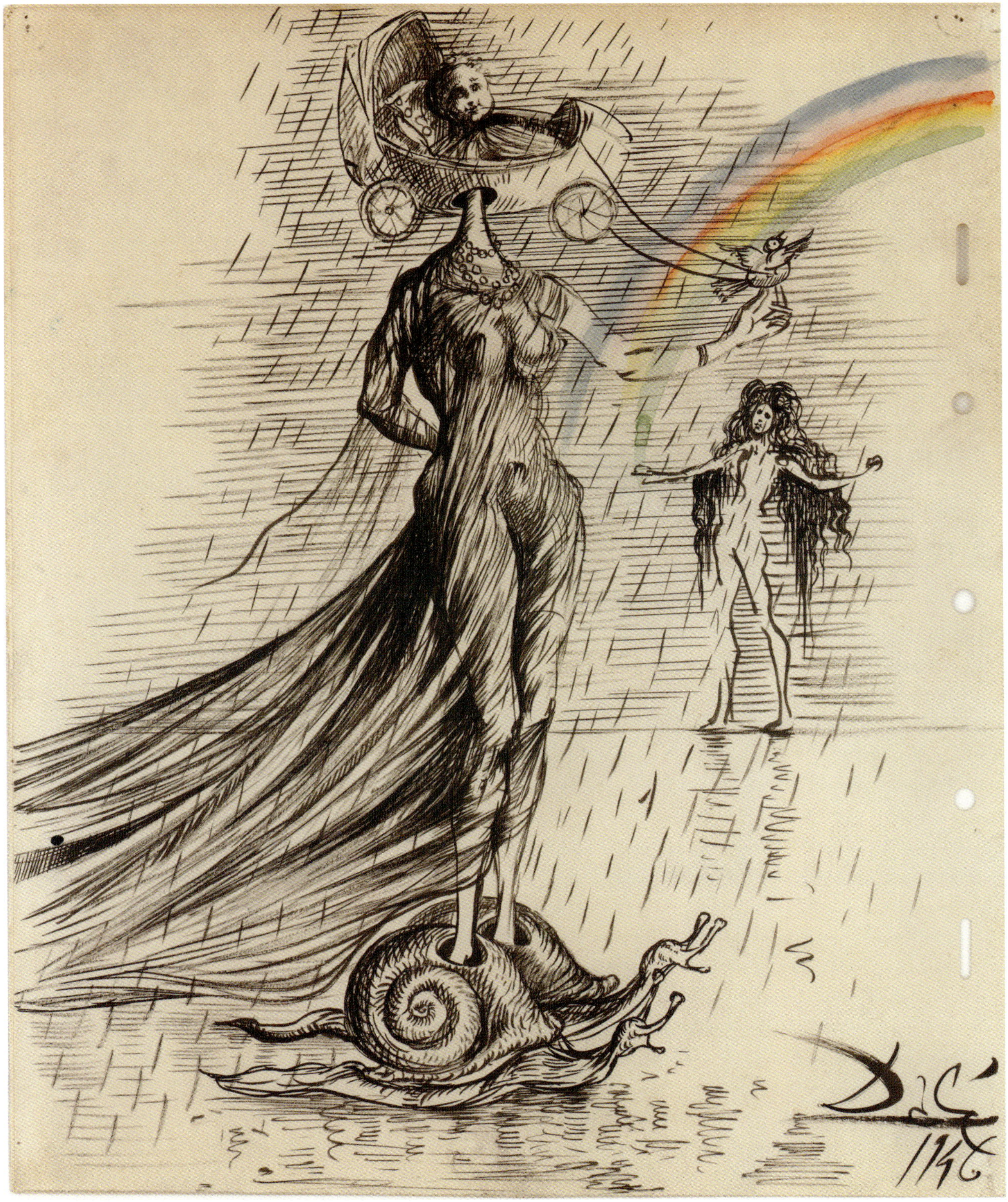

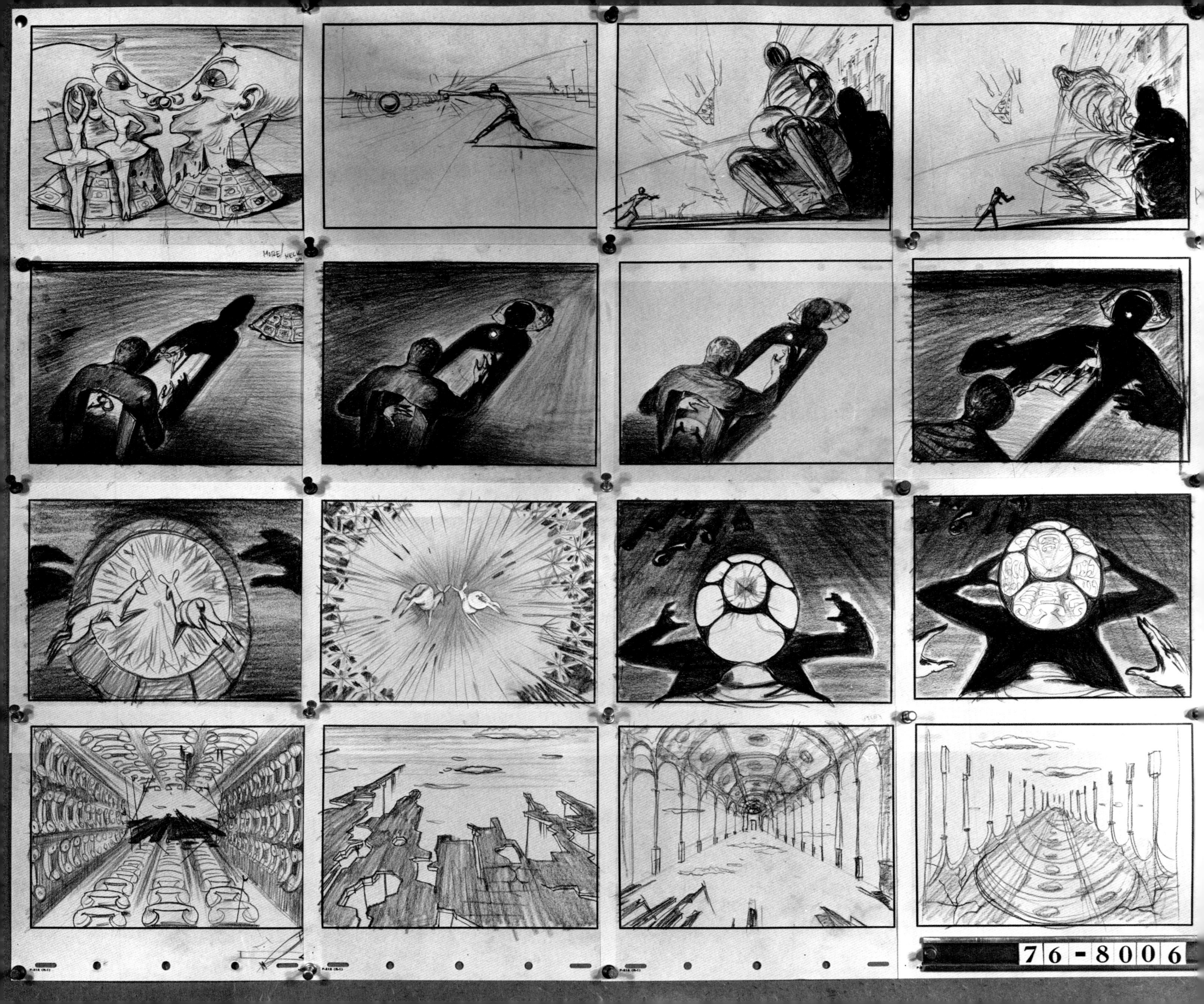

MORE/ NECK ON
76-8006

Page 92: Photostat of storyboard from *Destino*, 1946.

Story sketches by John Hench.

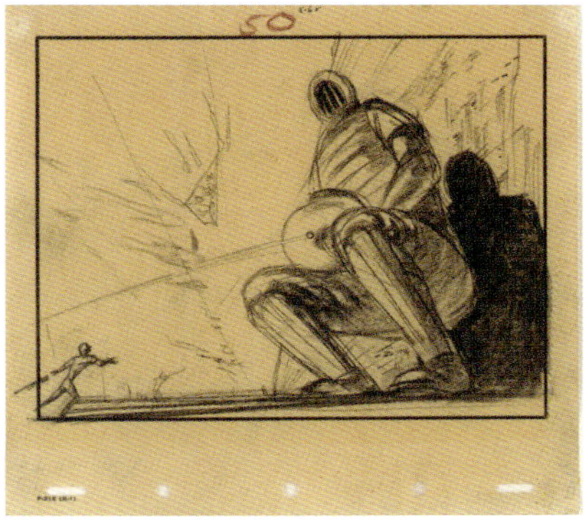

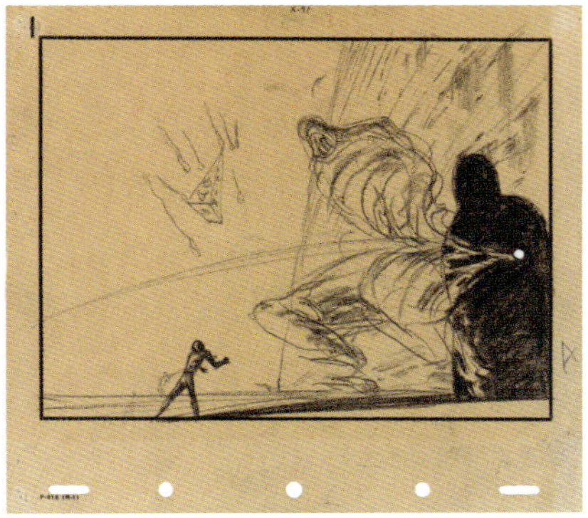

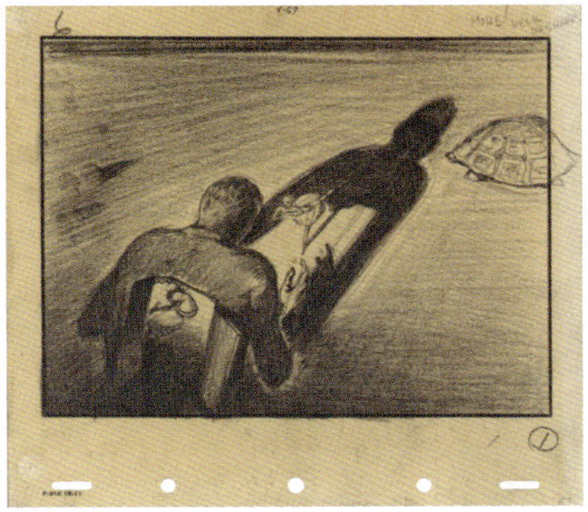

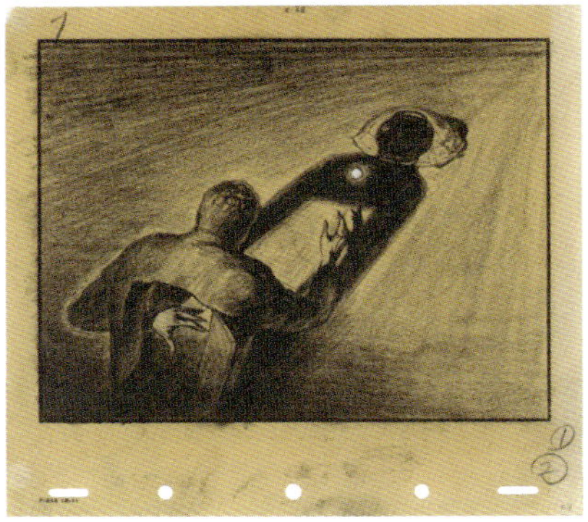

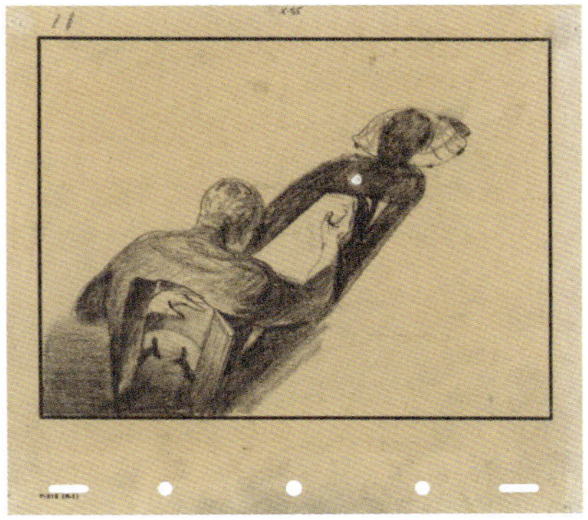

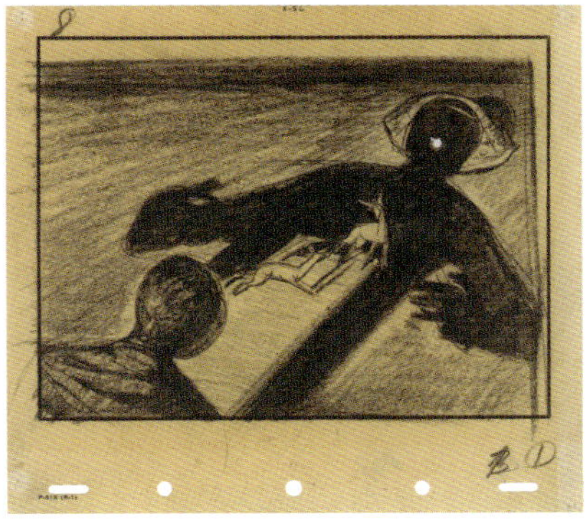

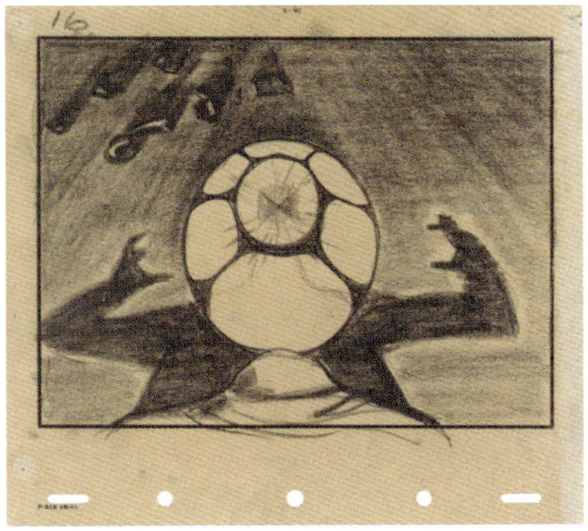

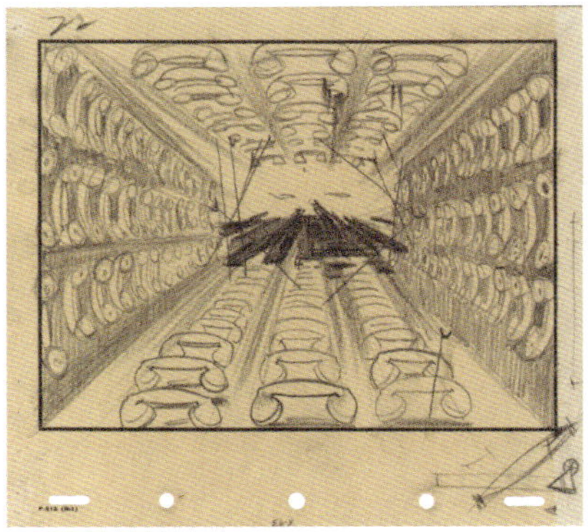

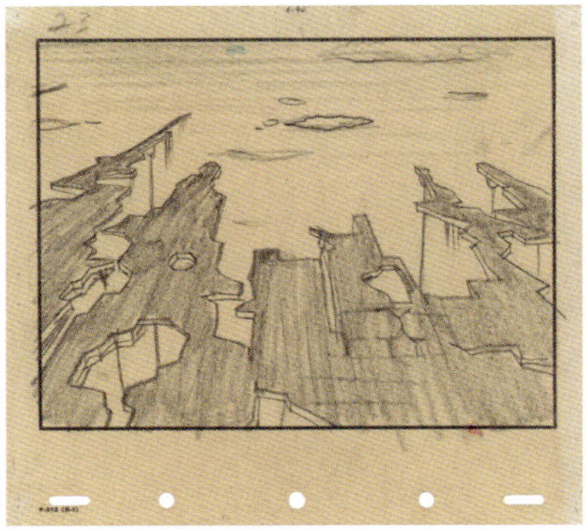

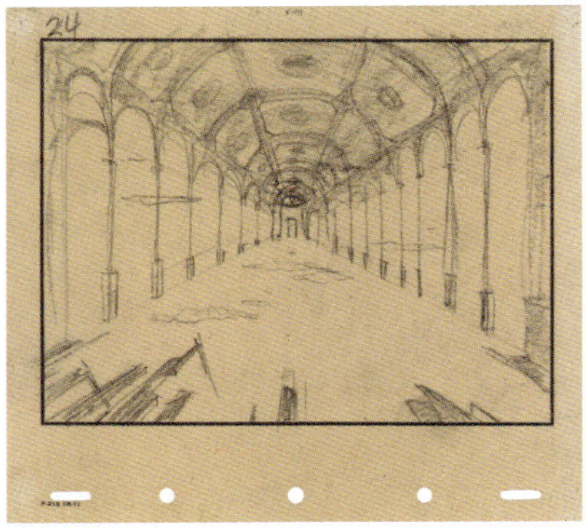

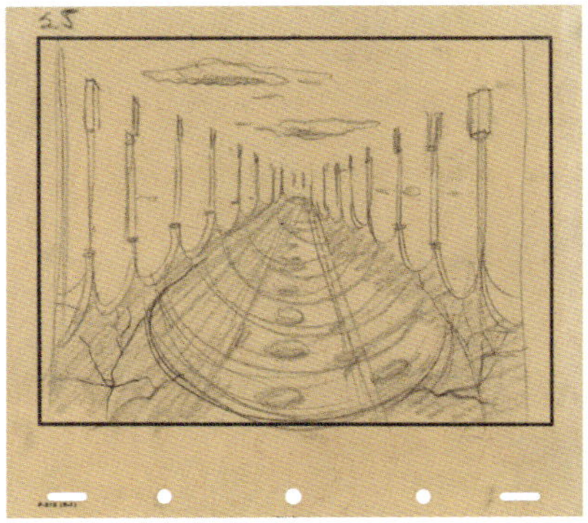

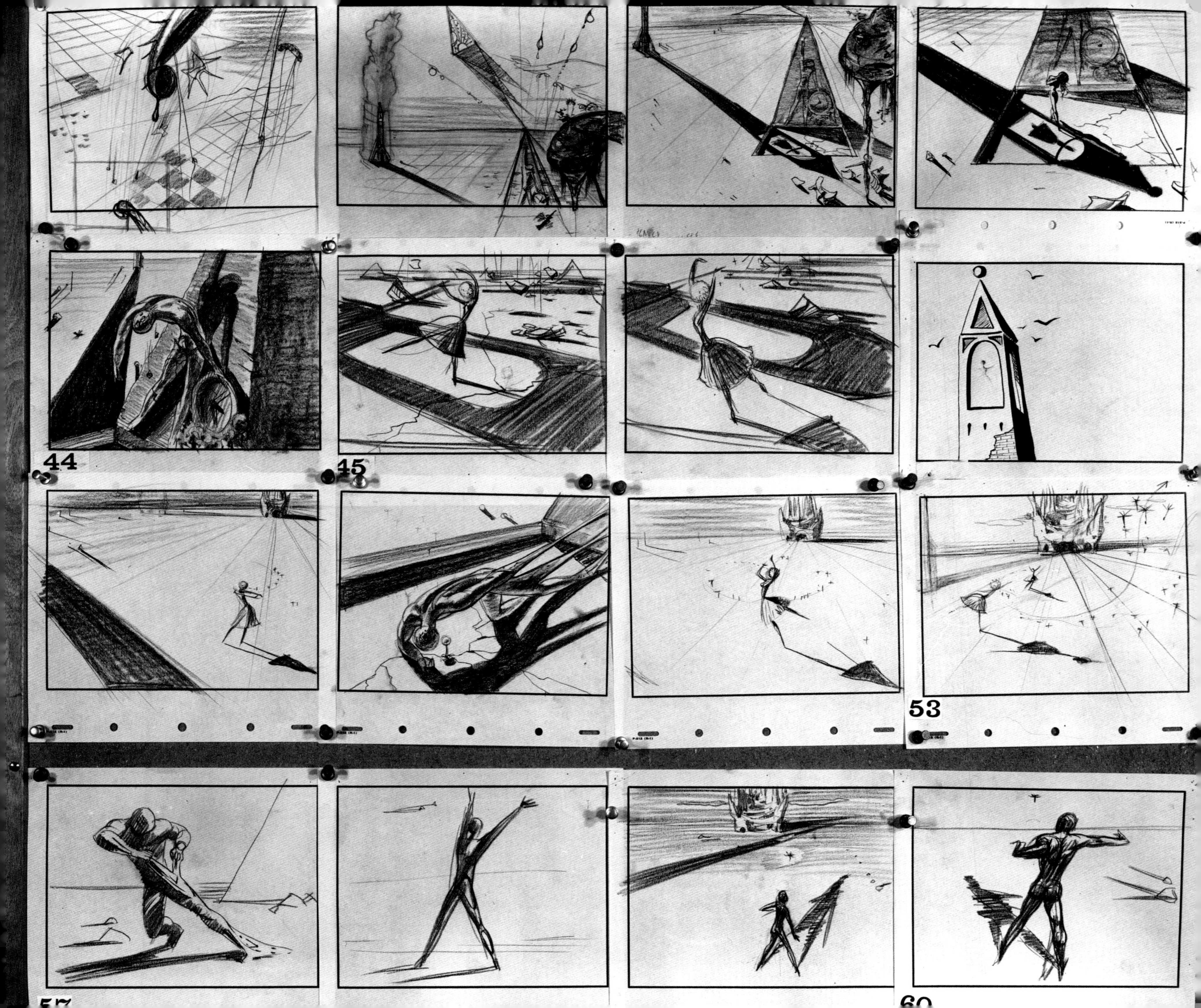
44
45
53

Pages 94–95: Photostat of storyboards from *Destino*, 1946.

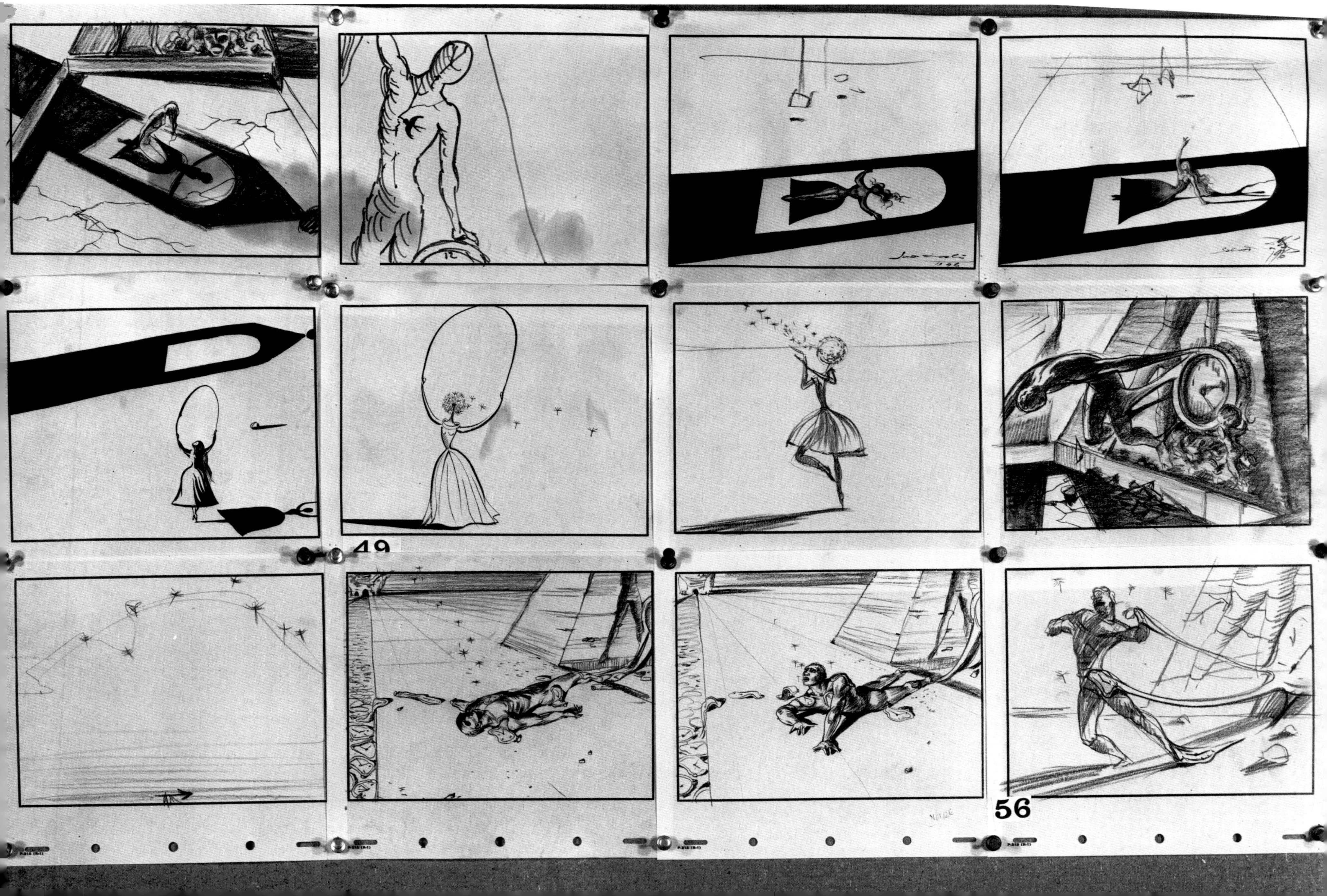

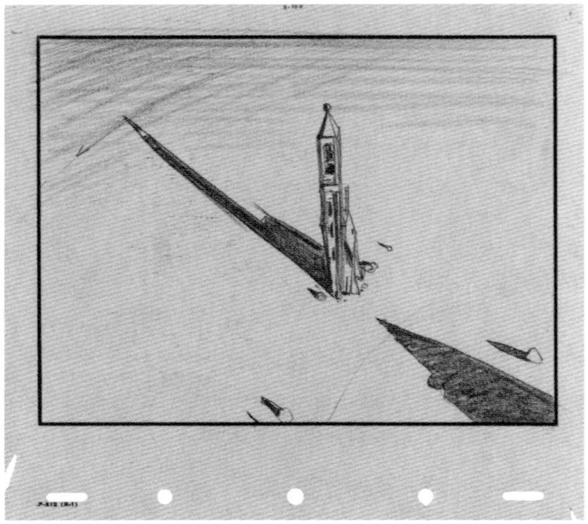
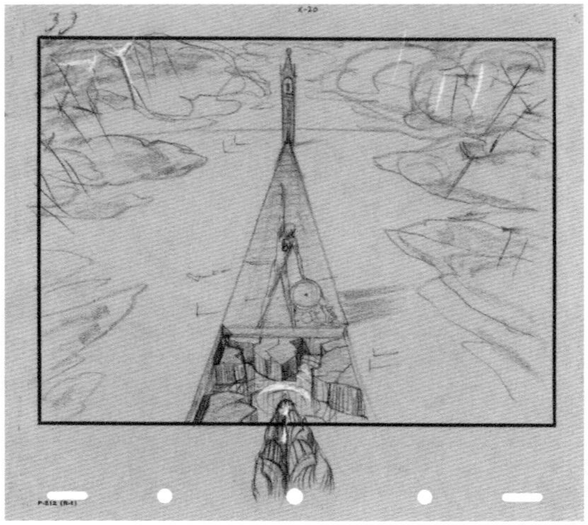
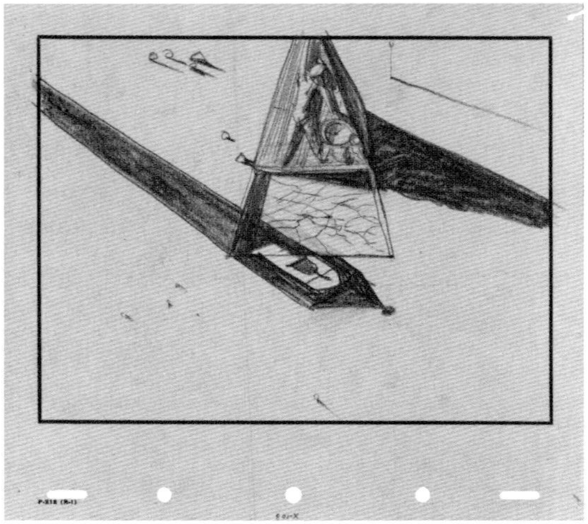
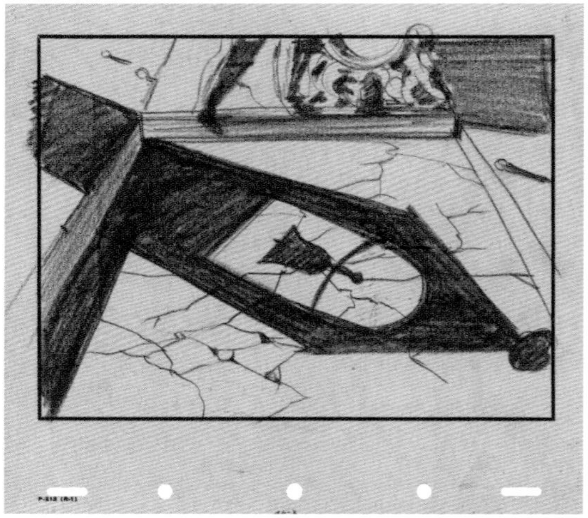
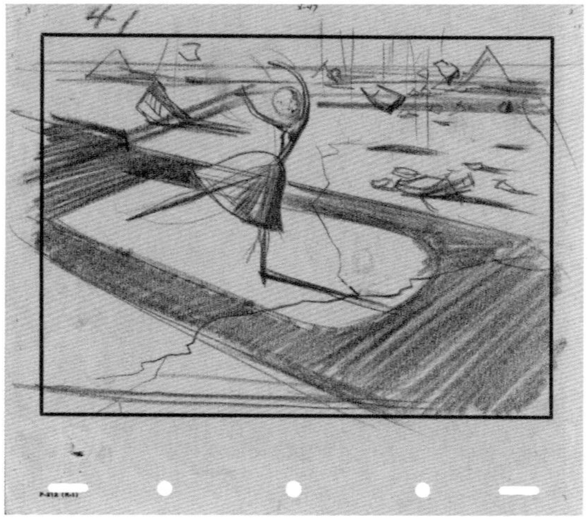
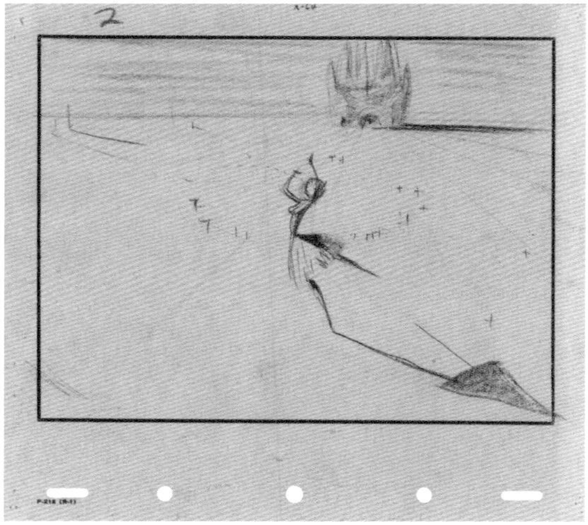
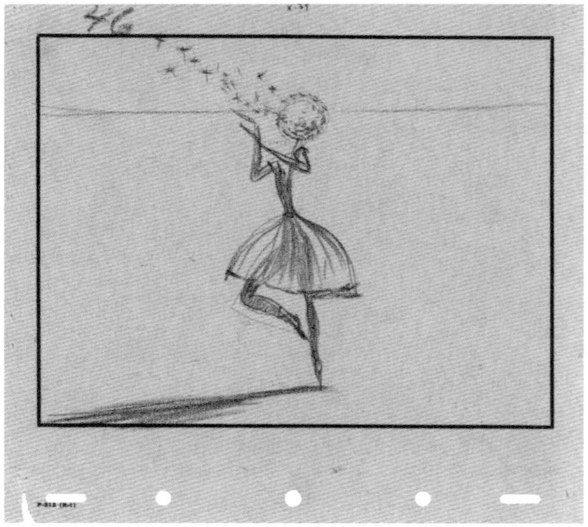
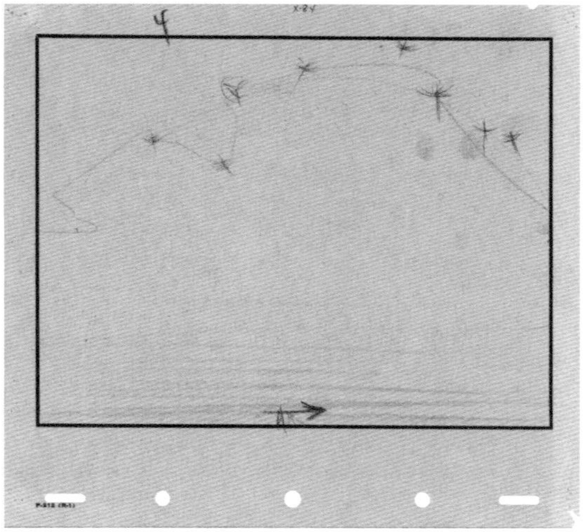
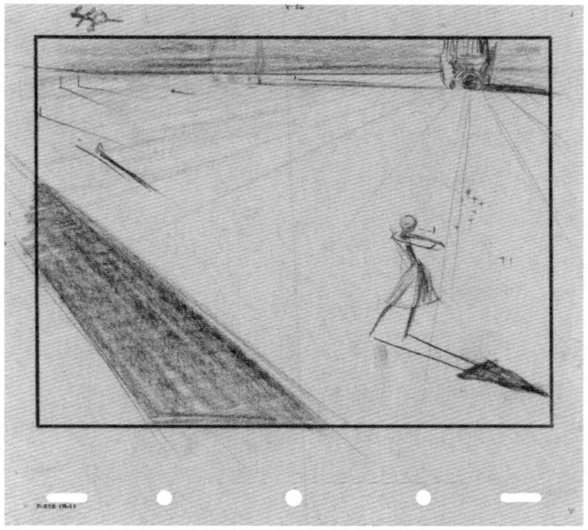

Page 96: Story sketches by John Hench.

Story sketches by Salvador Dalí.

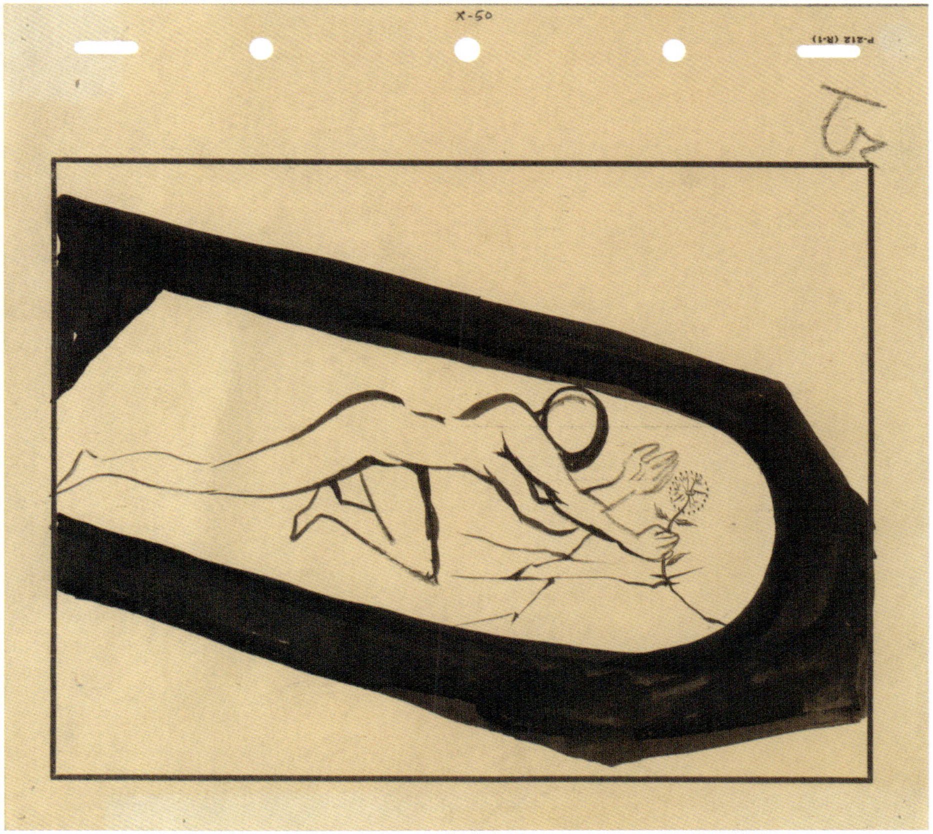

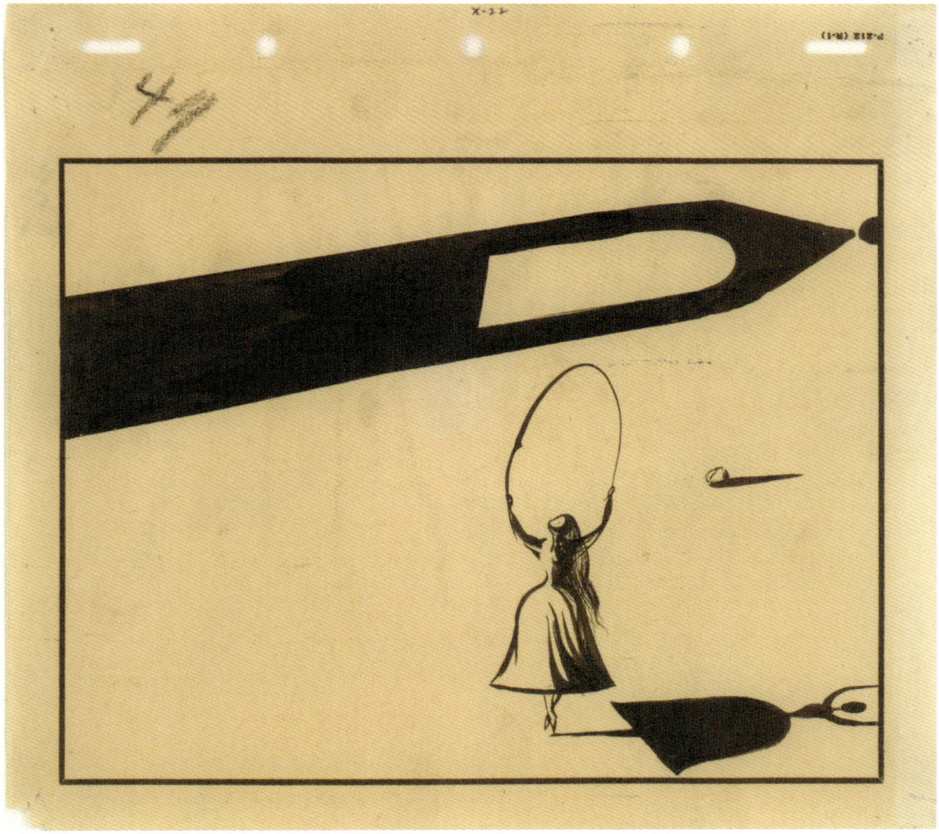

Story sketch and visual development artwork by Salvador Dalí.

Page 99: Image from the film, *Destino*.

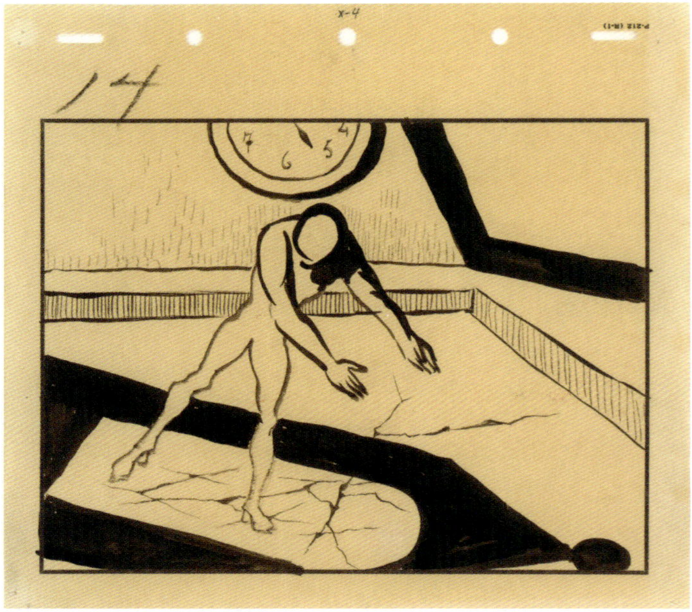

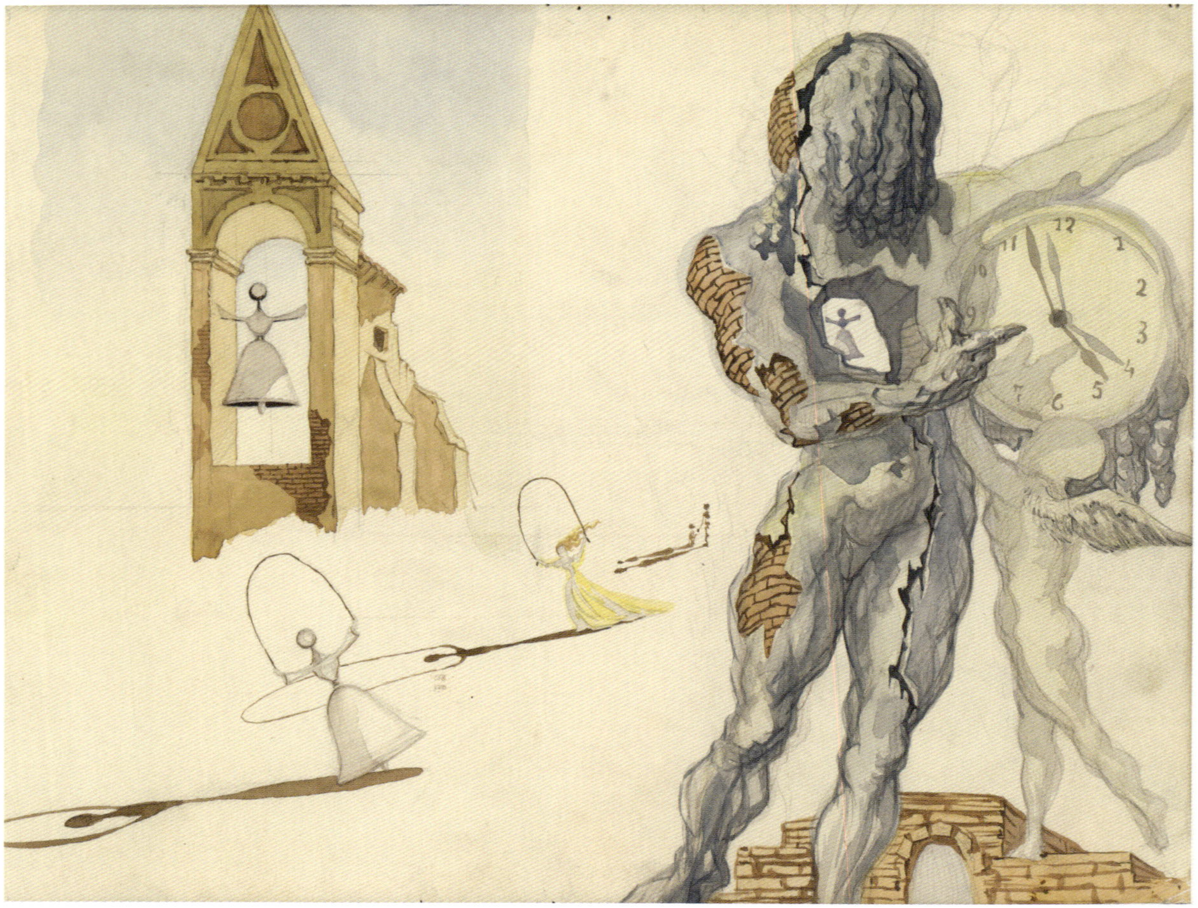

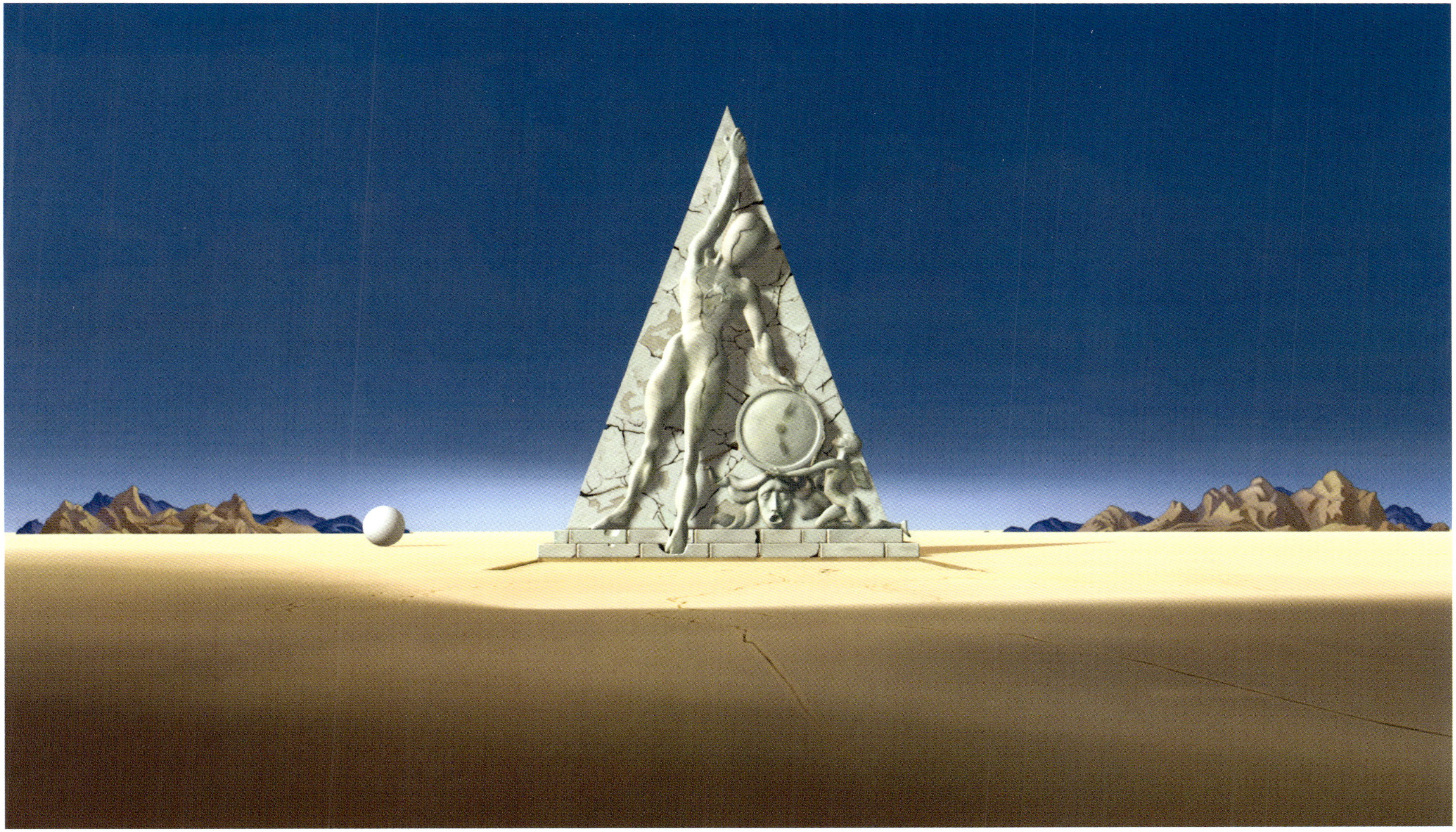

Story sketches by Salvador Dalí exploring the plasticity of time.

Page 101 (top): Photostat of storyboard from *Destino*, 1946.

Page 101 (bottom): Image from the film, *Destino*.

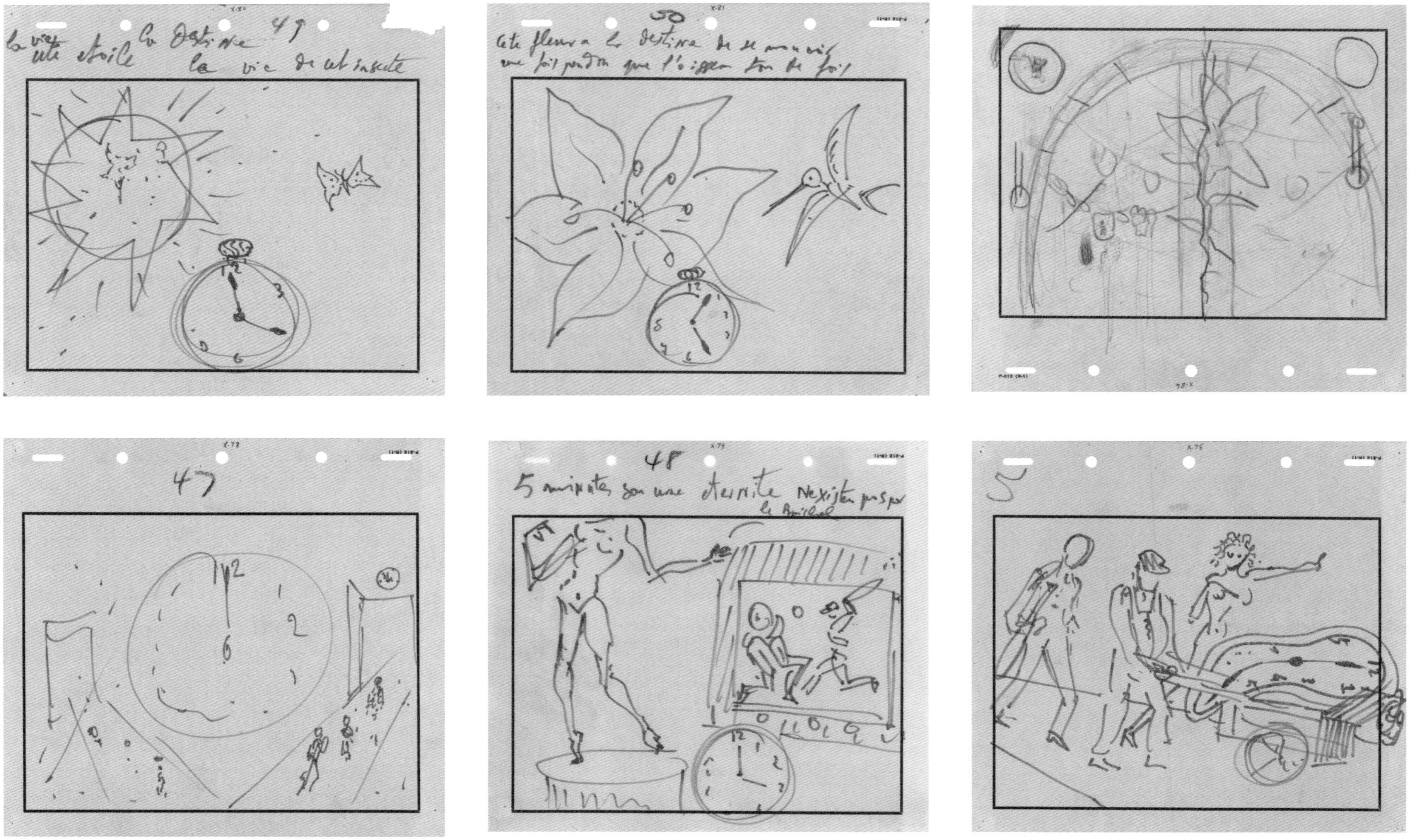

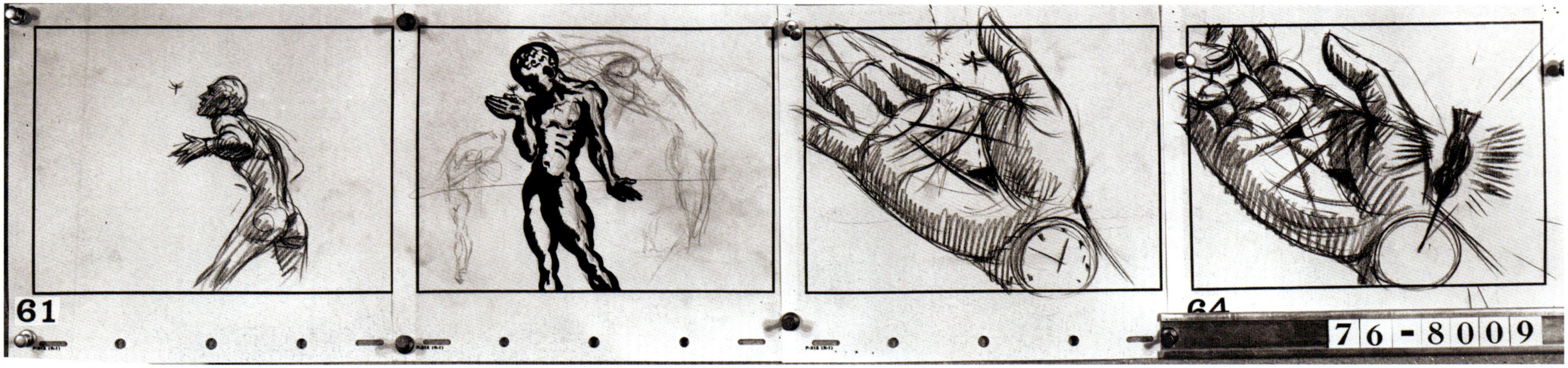
61
64
76-8009

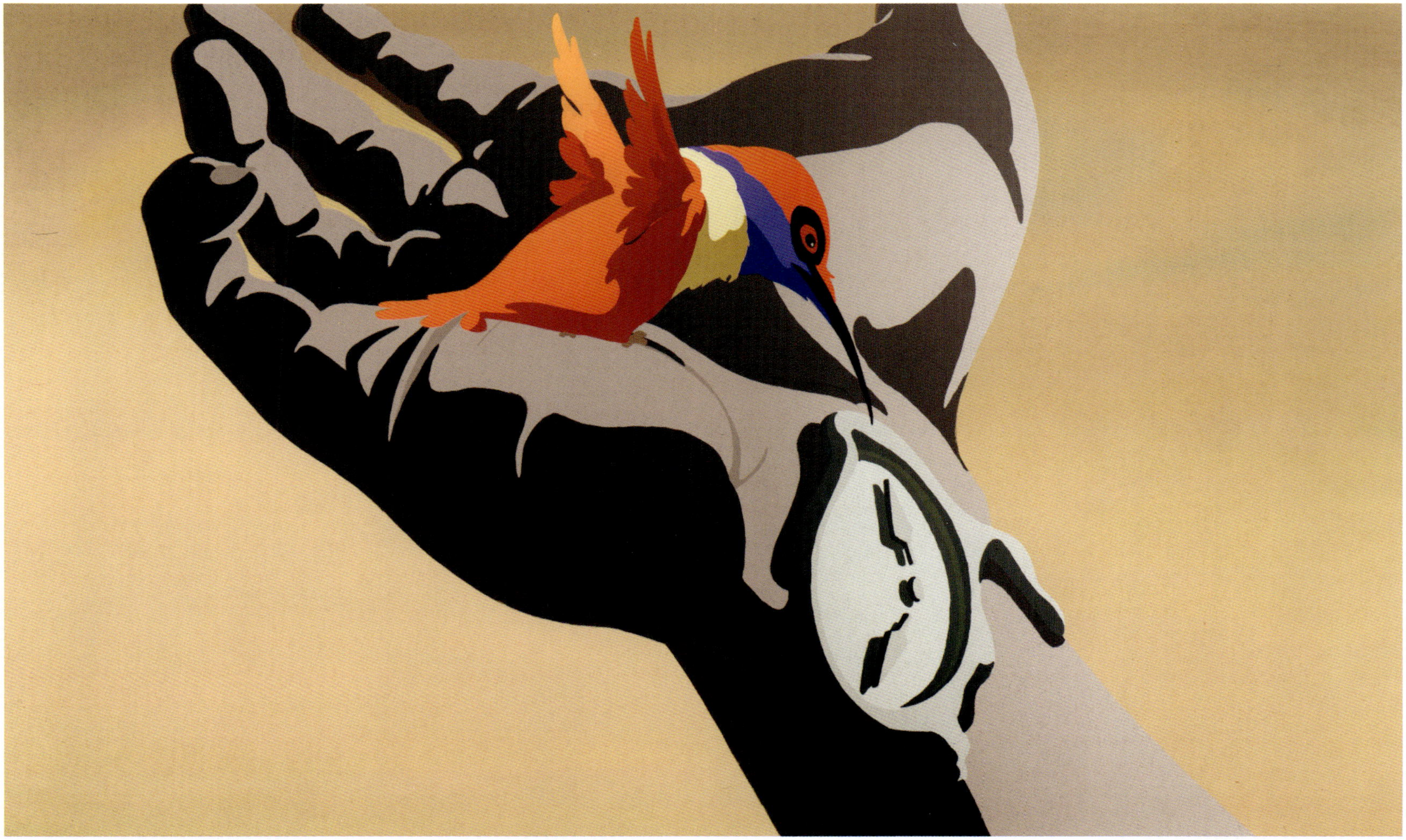

Below left and right: Salvador Dalí, working on a background painting from the film *Destino*; the artist showing the artwork to actor / singer Jean Sablon.

Bottom: Photostat of the formation of the Greek god head through story sketches.

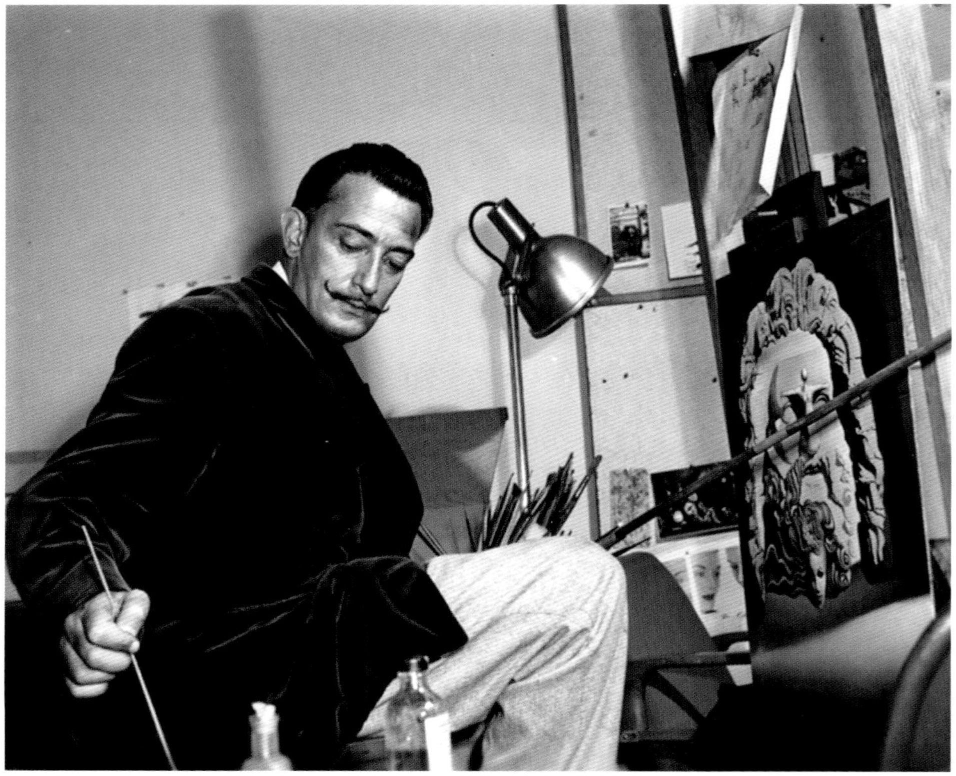

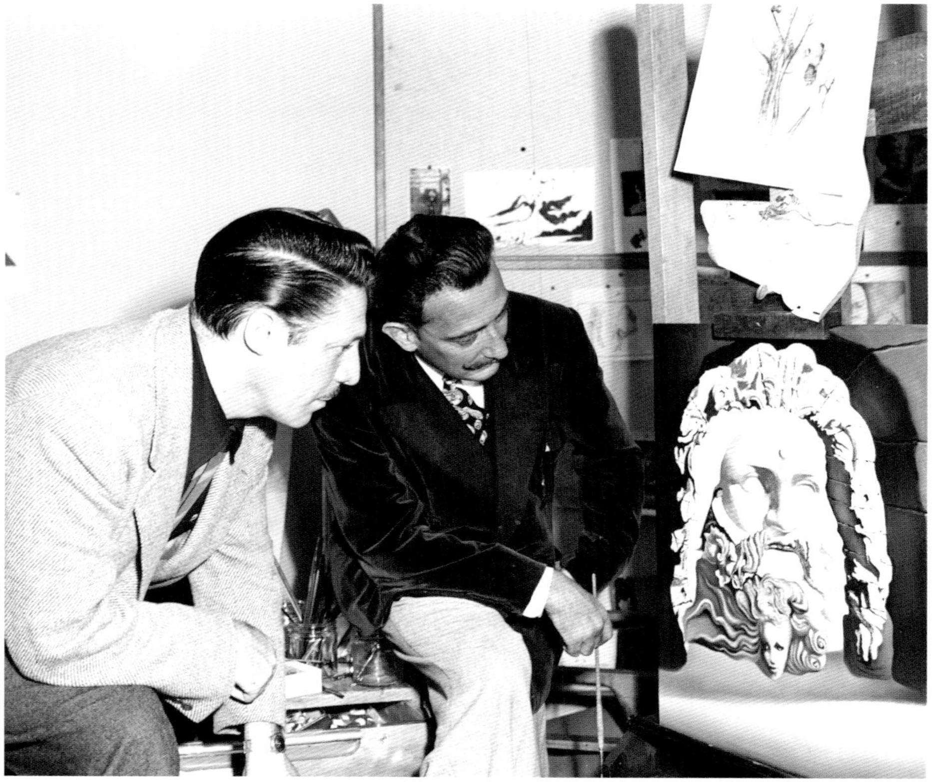

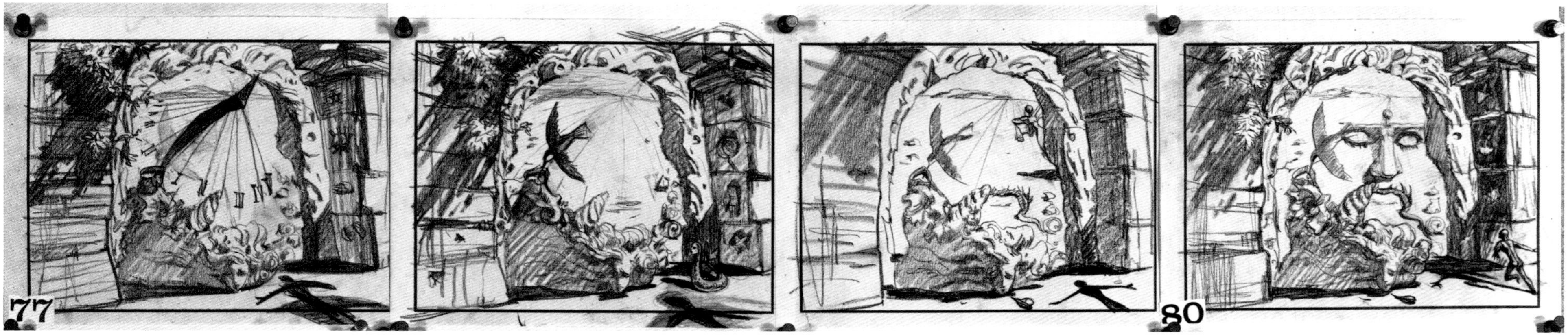

Untitled
Background painting of the large head of Greek god by Dalí.

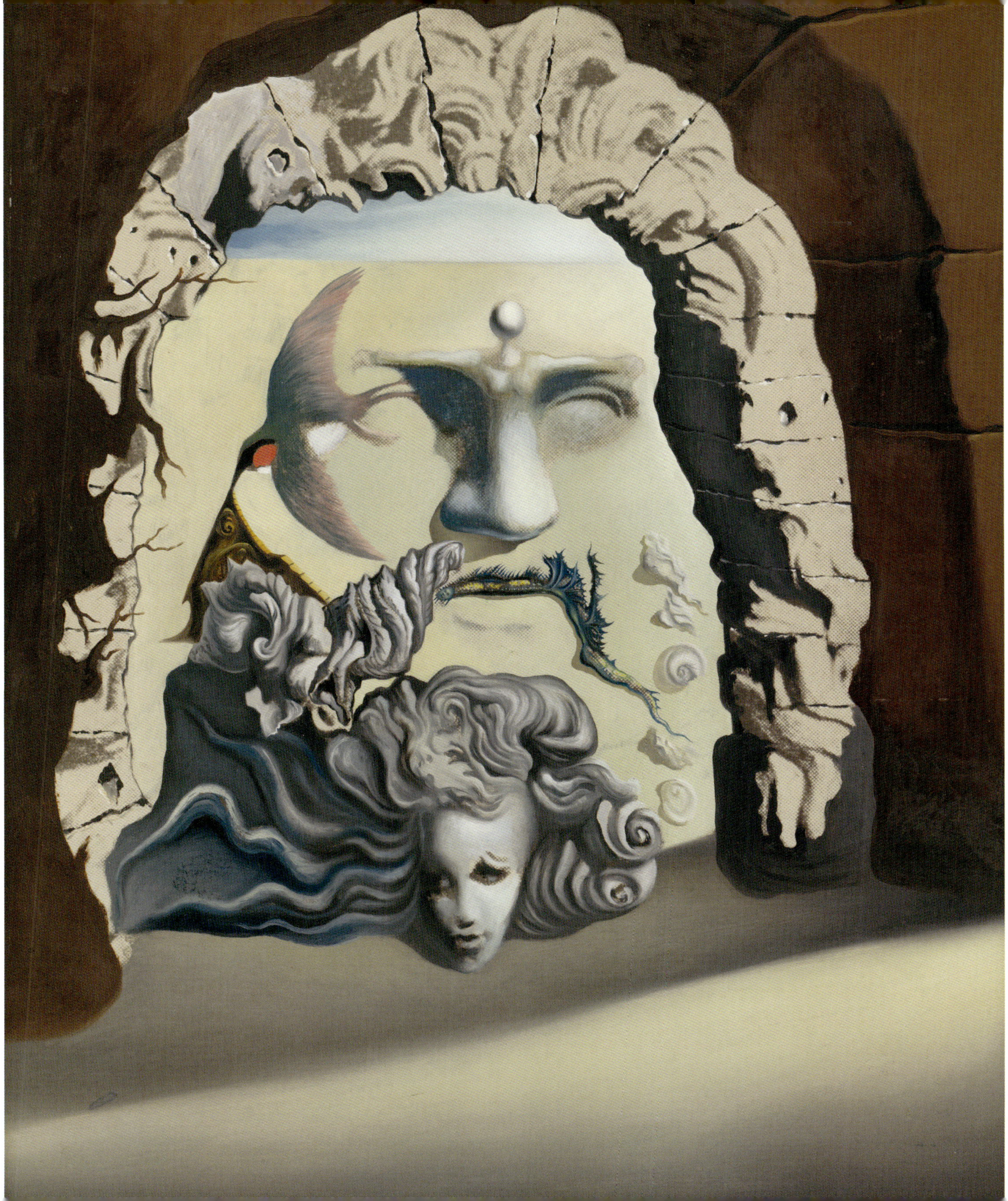

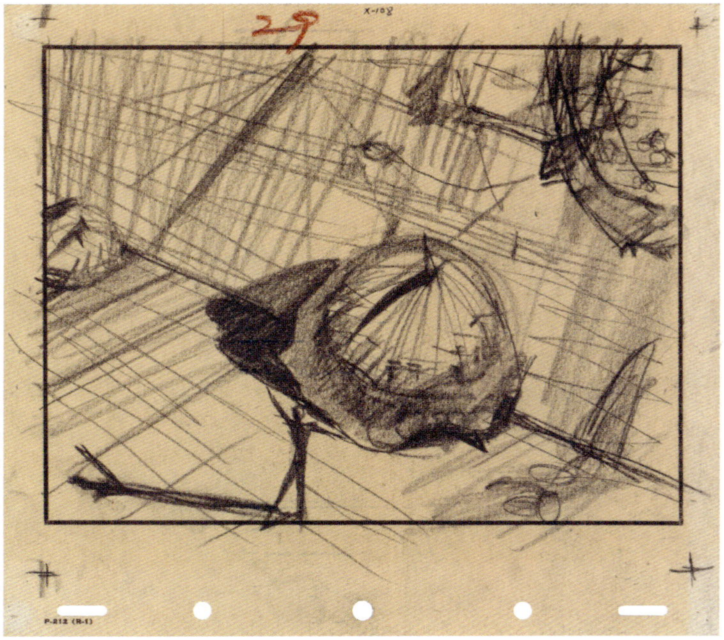

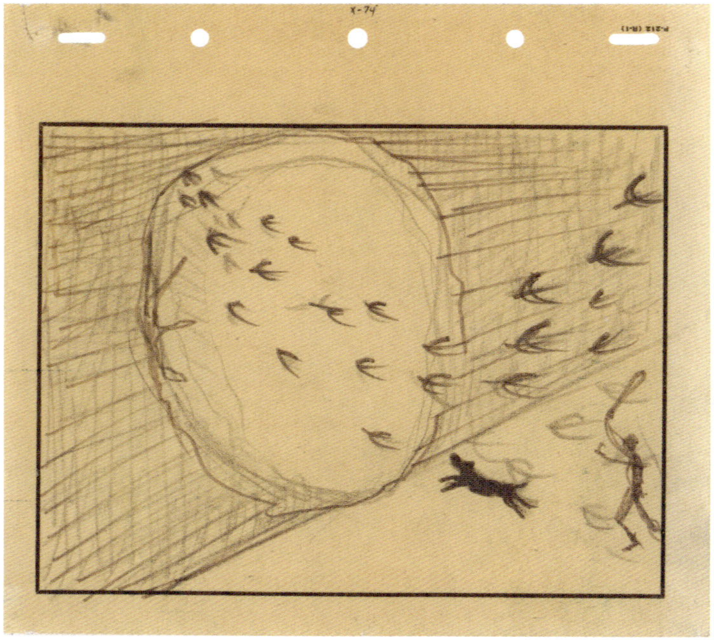

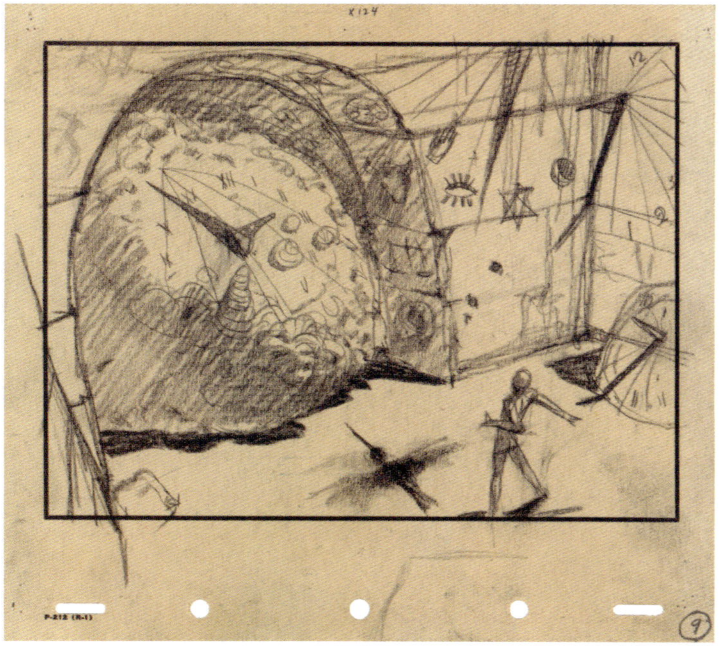

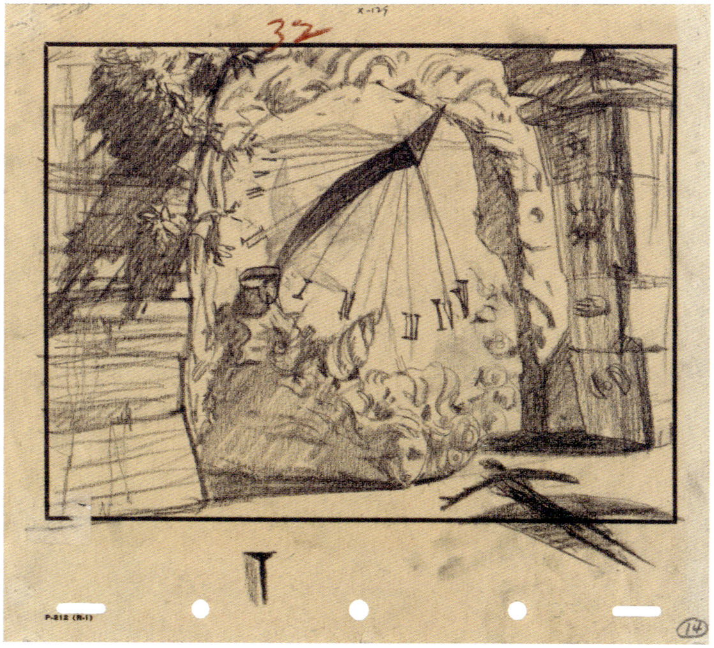

Top left and bottom row: Story sketches by John Hench.

Top right: Story sketch by Salvador Dalí.

Story sketch by Dalí.

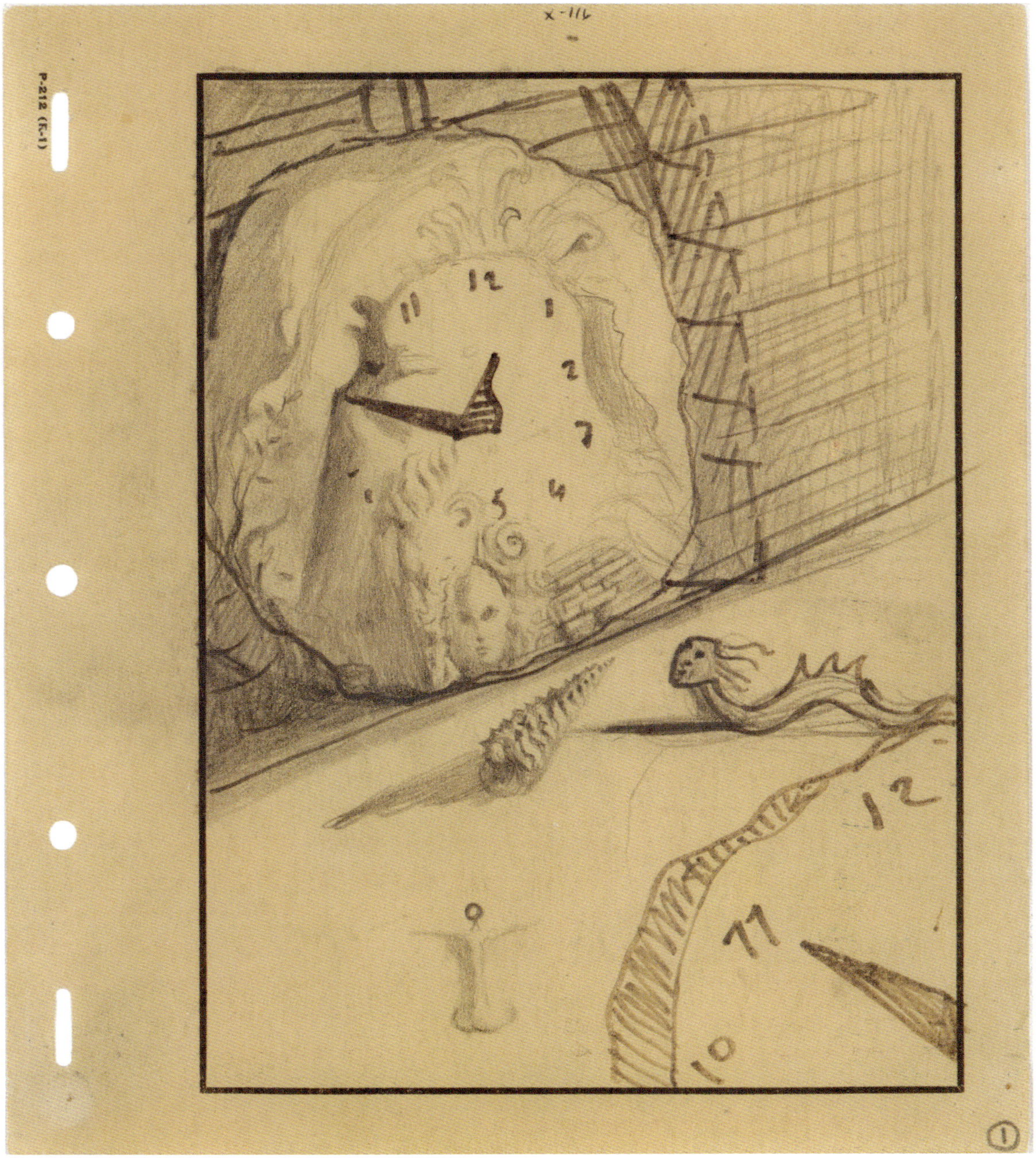

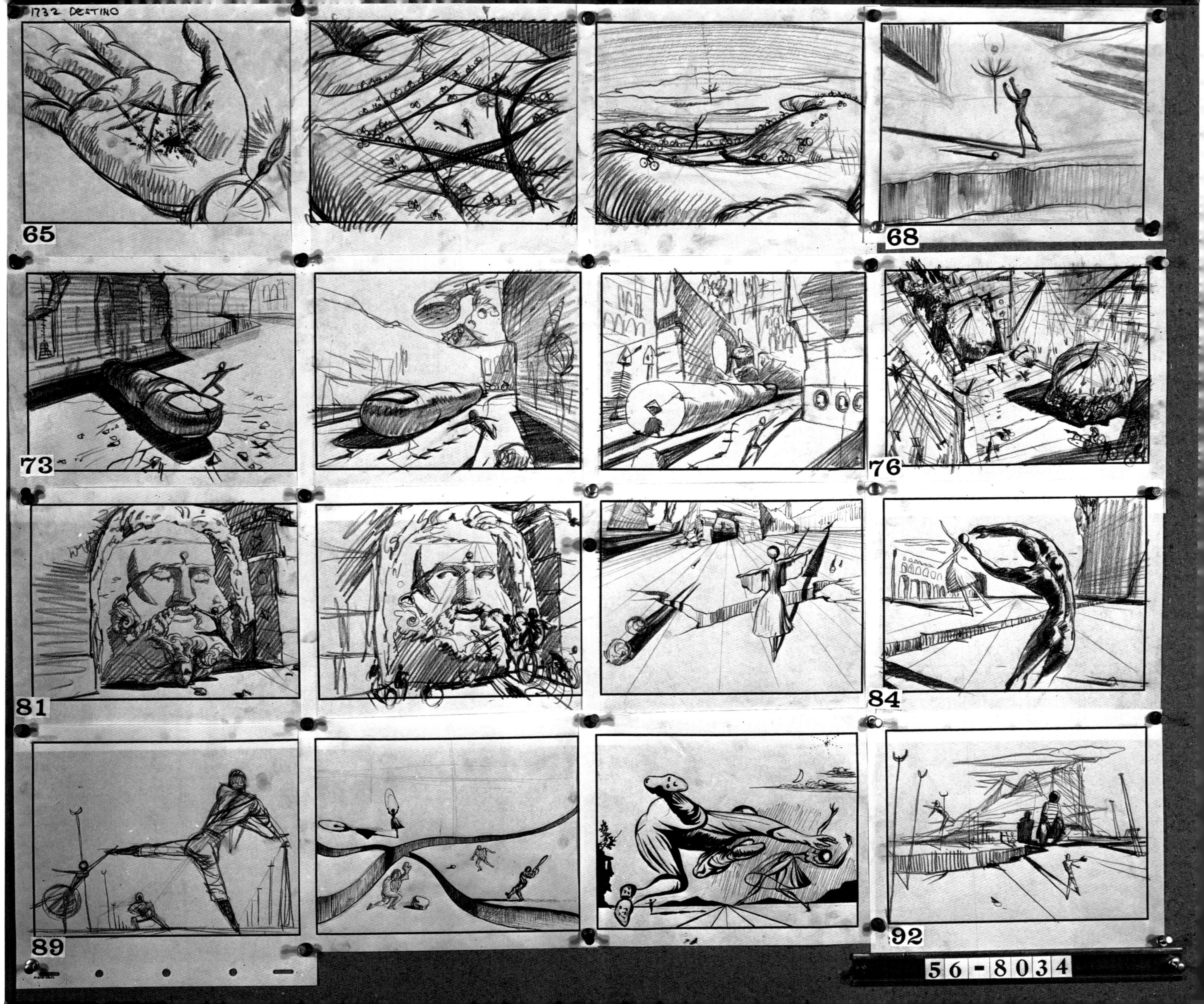
1732 DESTINO
65
68
73
76
81
84
89
92
56-8034

Page 106: Photostat of storyboard from *Destino*, 1946.

Story sketches showing a dismembered finger concept by John Hench that was not used in the film.

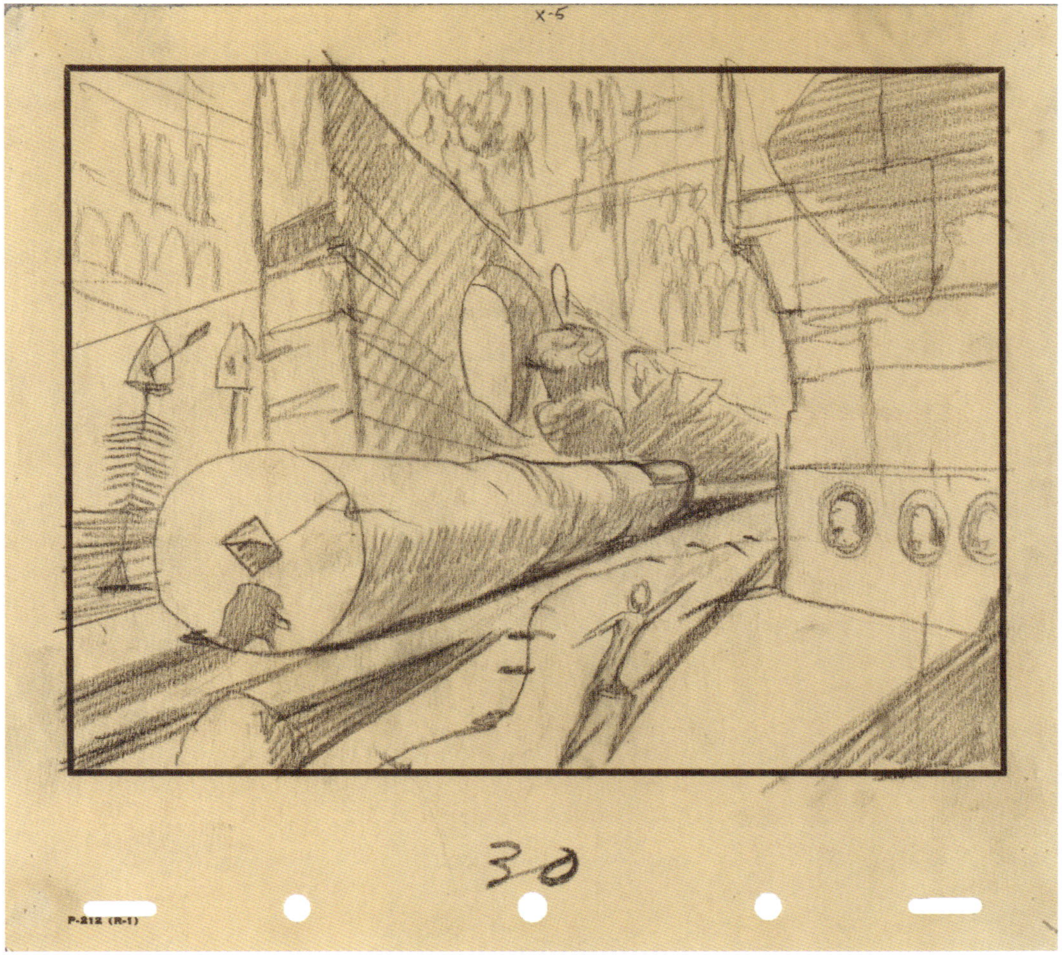

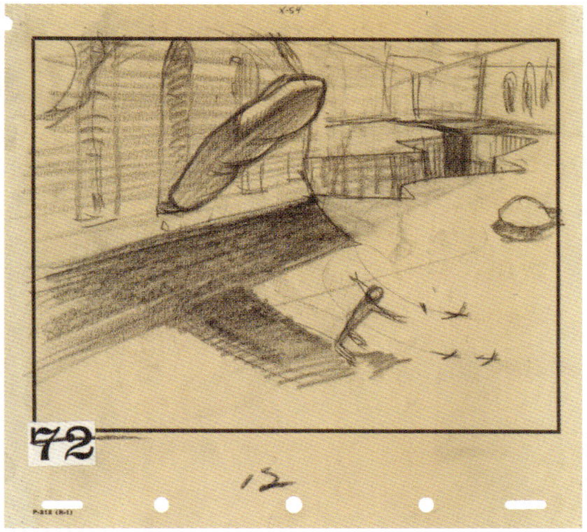

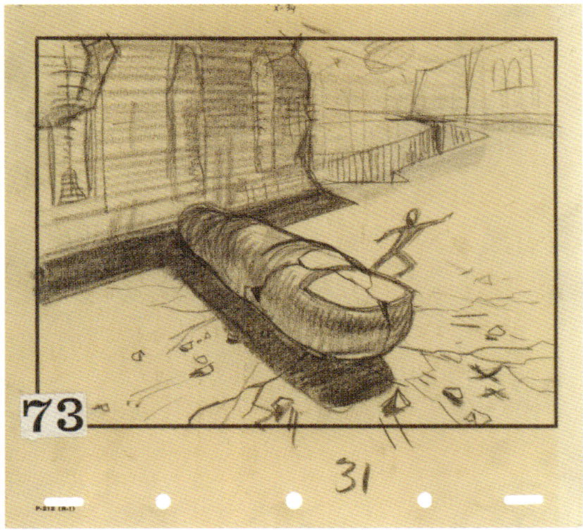

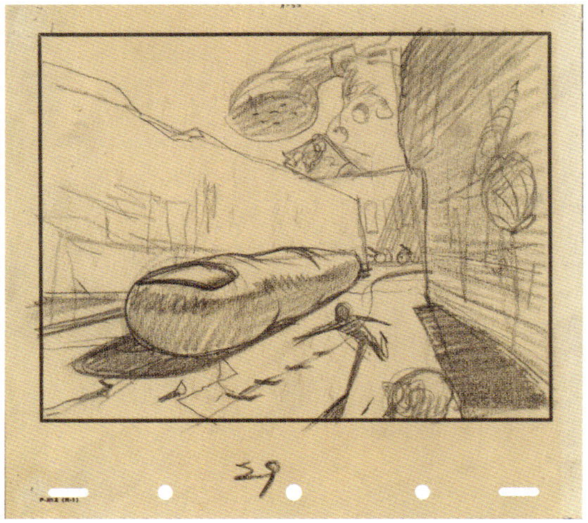

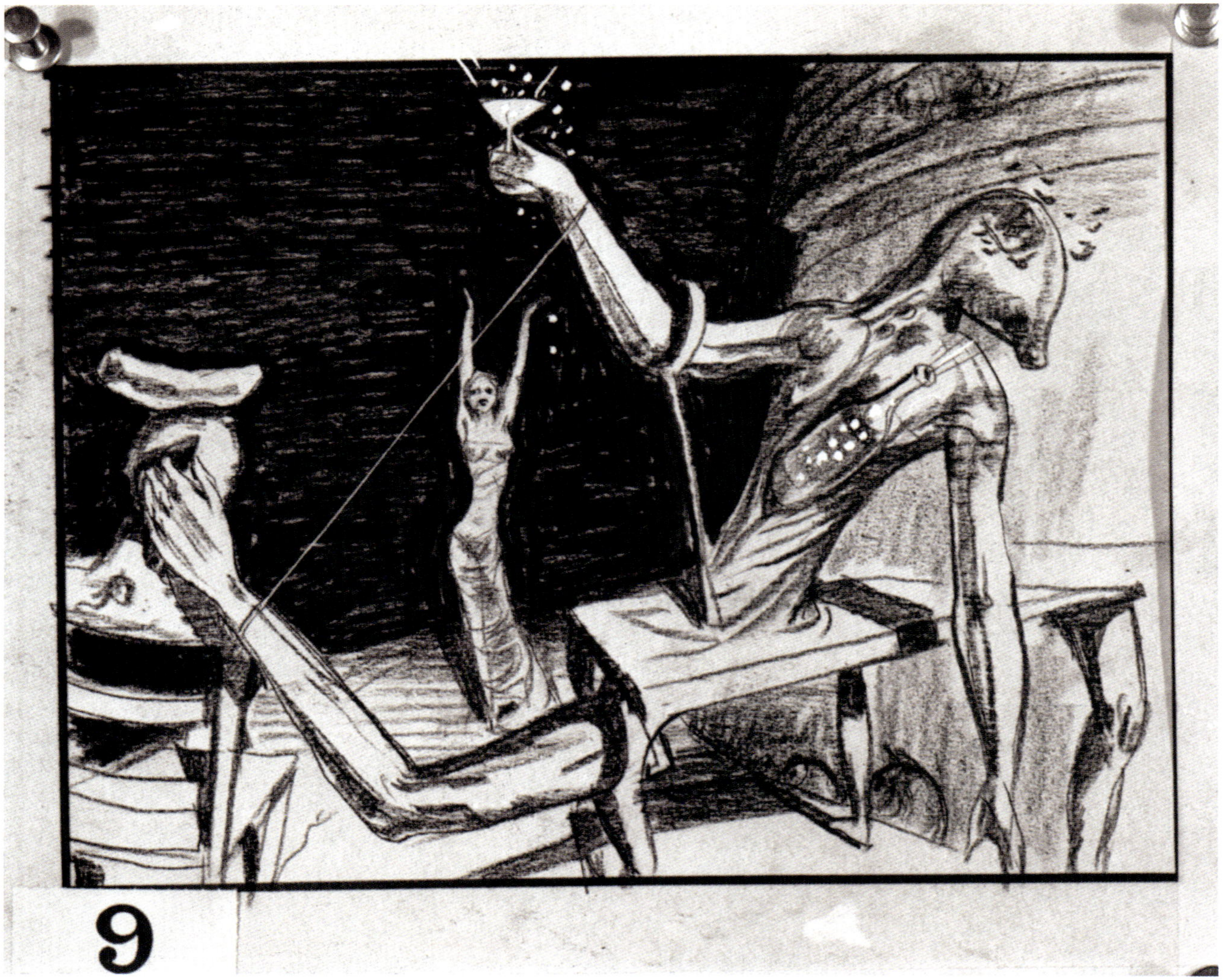

Story sketch from a 1946 photostat.

Page 109: Visual development by Salvador Dalí of the party scene that is similar to an earlier painting by the artist on page 77.

Page 110: Visual development for *Destino* (1946).

Page 111: *Untitled* Background painting by Salvador Dalí (1946).

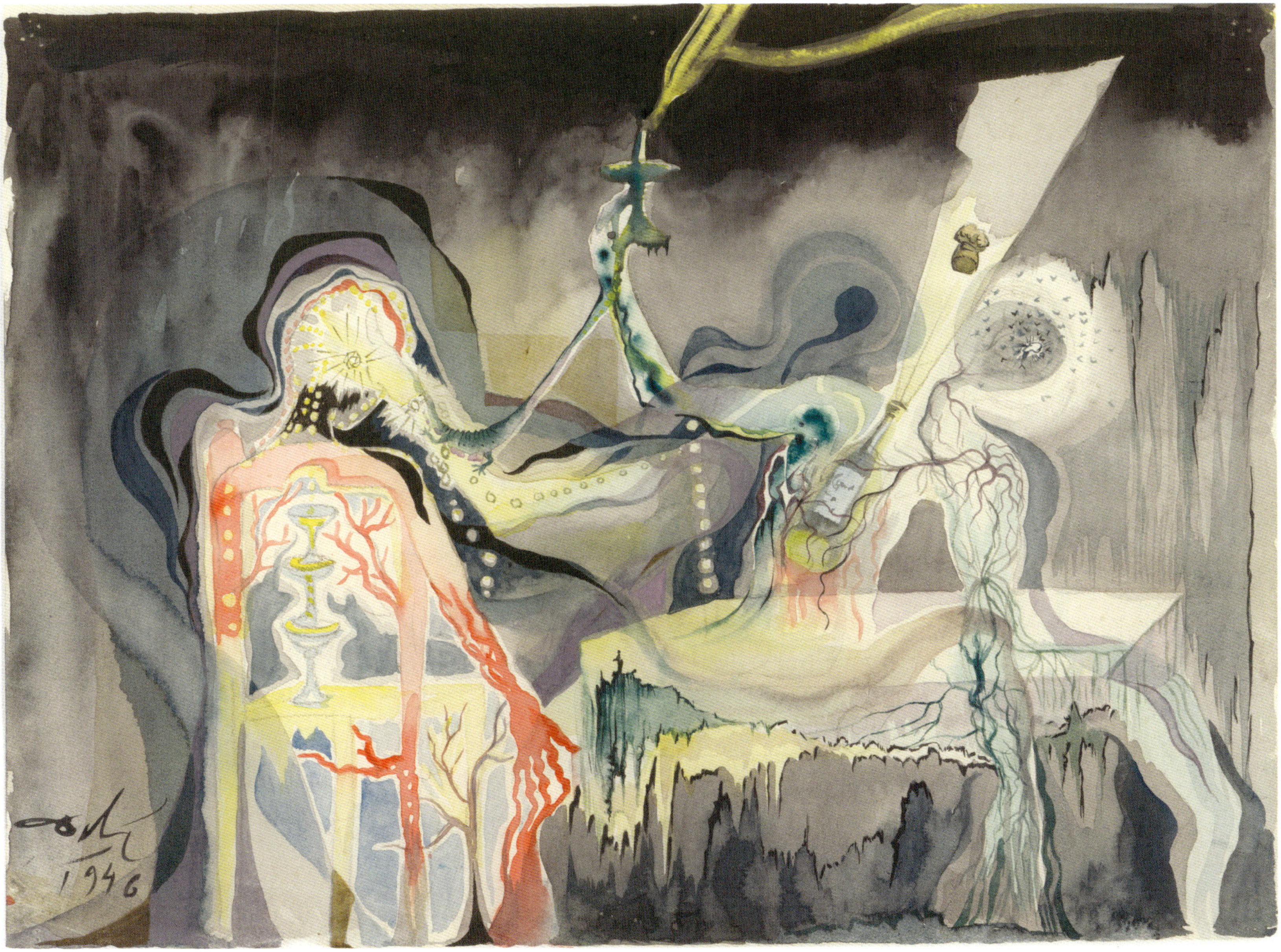

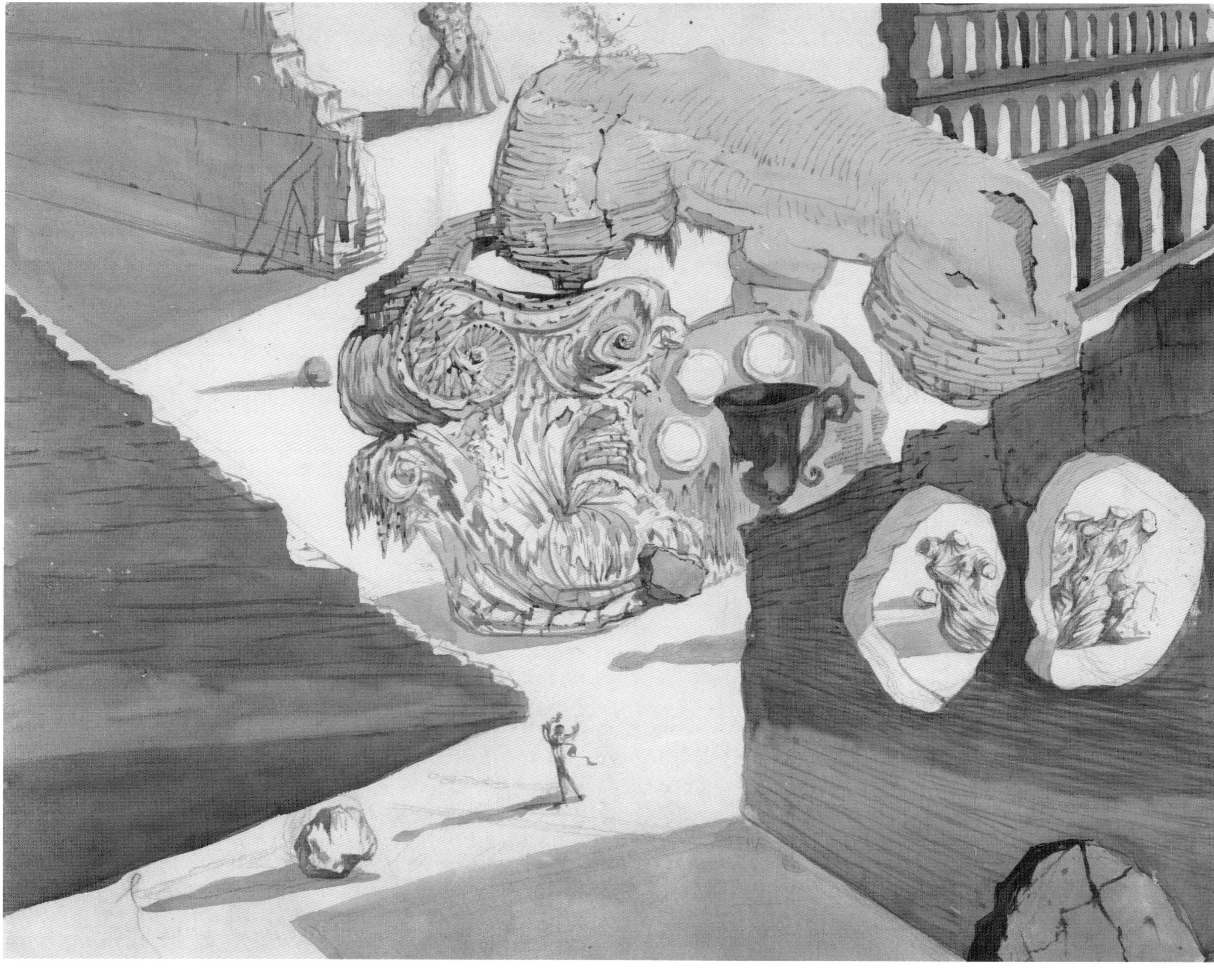

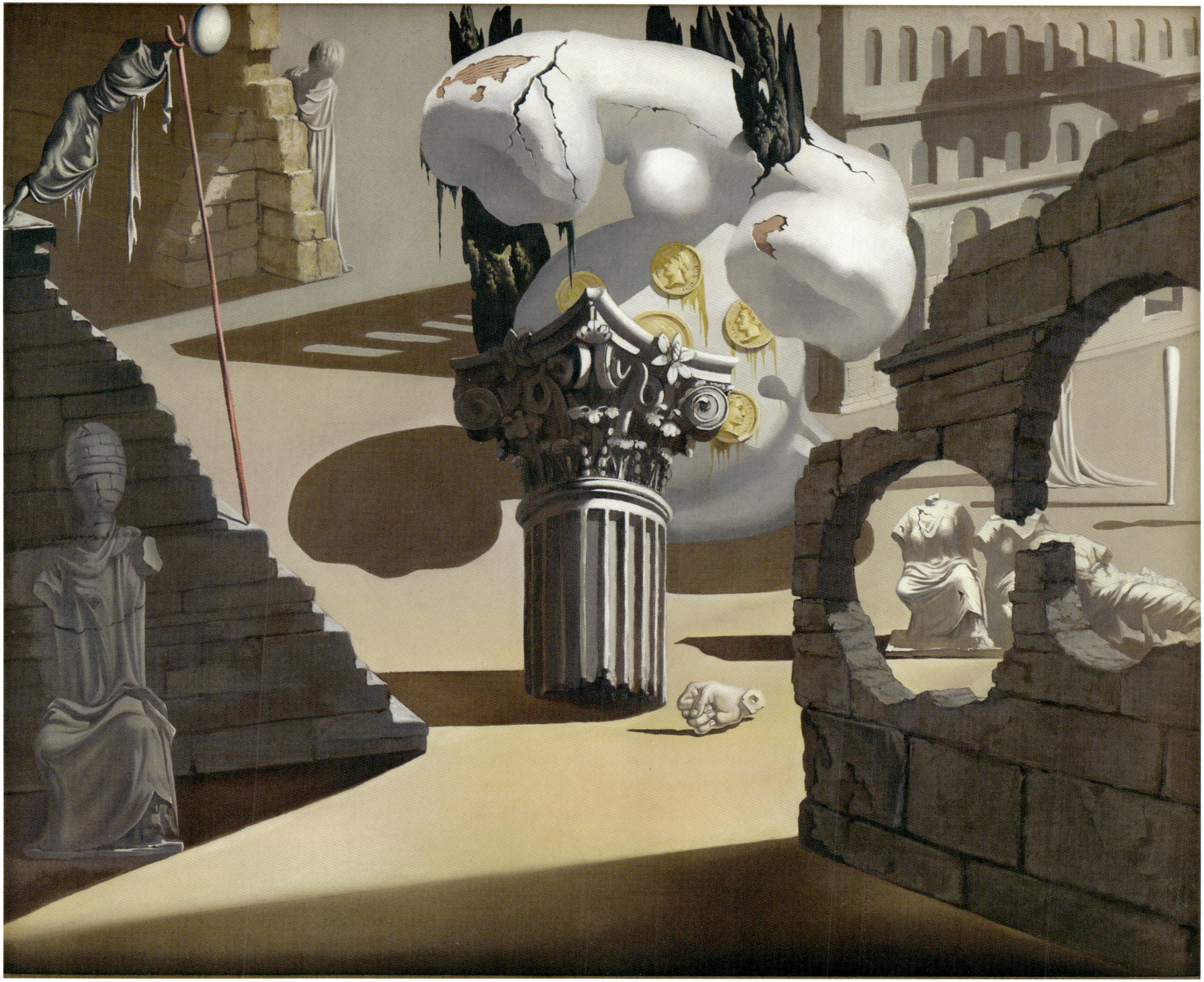

Story sketches by John Hench.

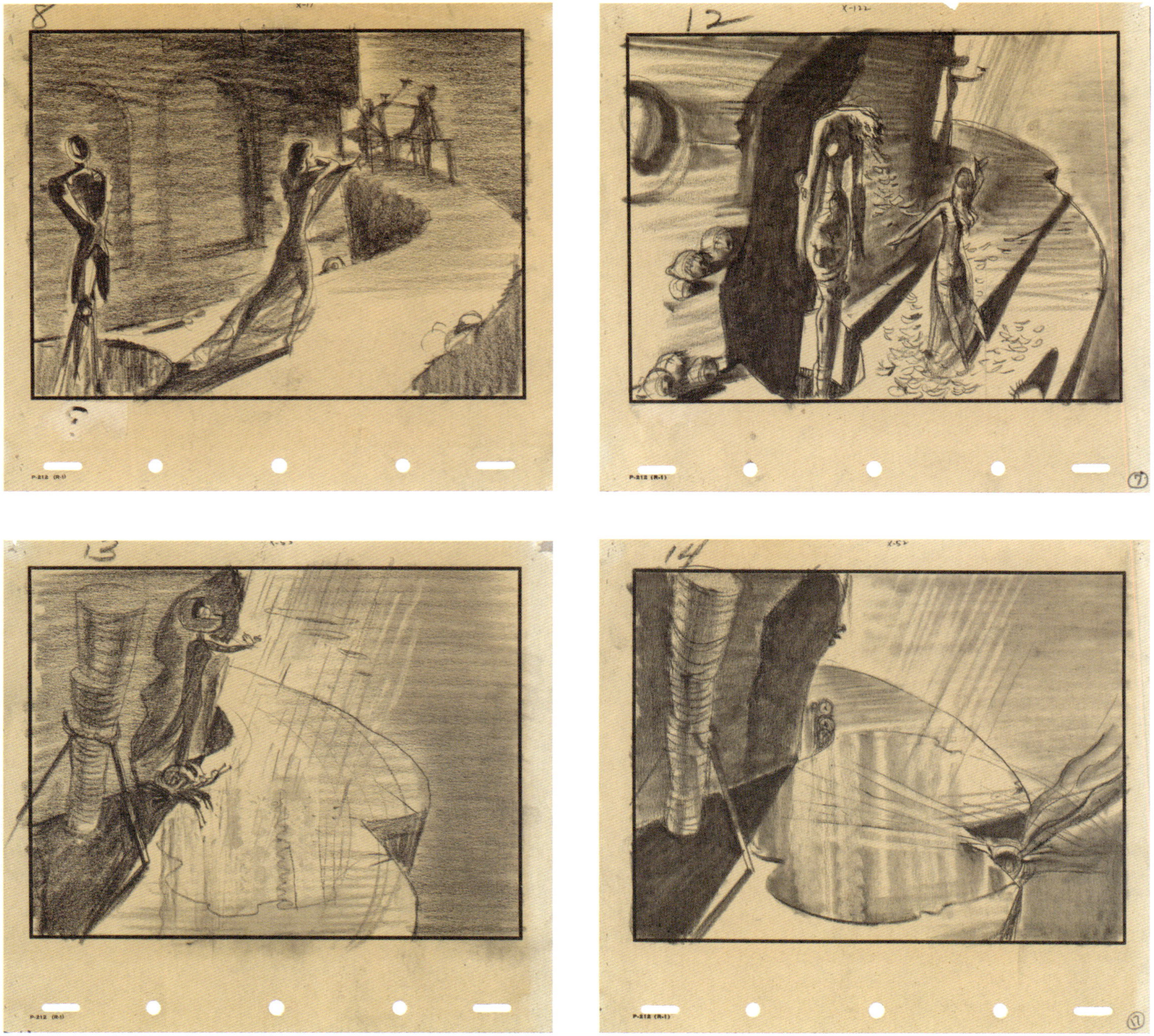

Top row: Story sketches by John Hench.
Bottom row: Story sketches by Salvador Dalí.

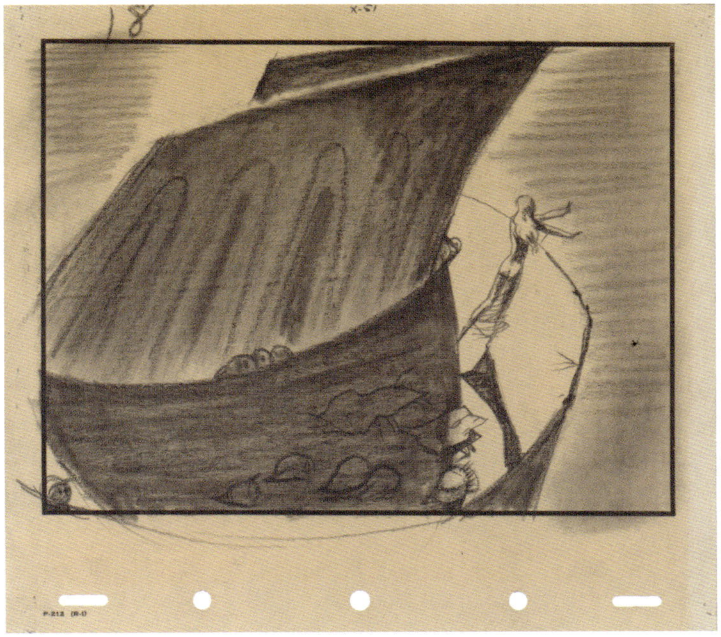

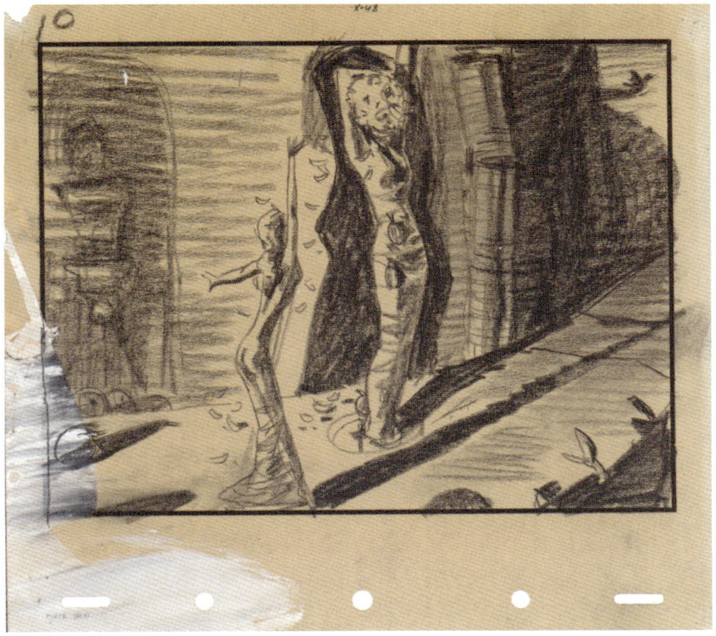

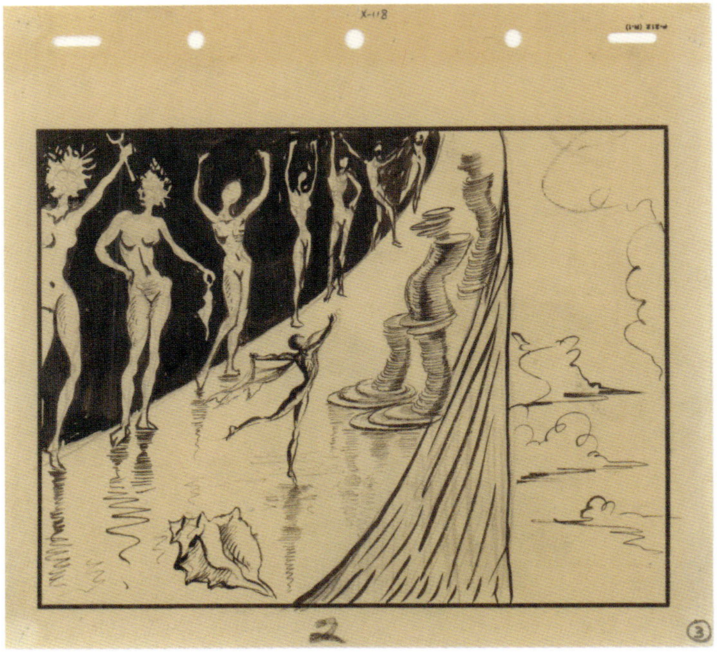

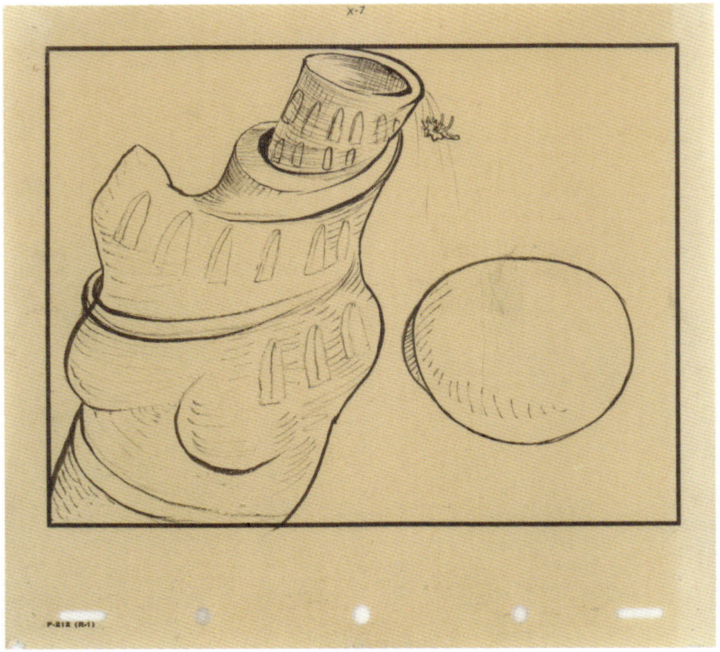

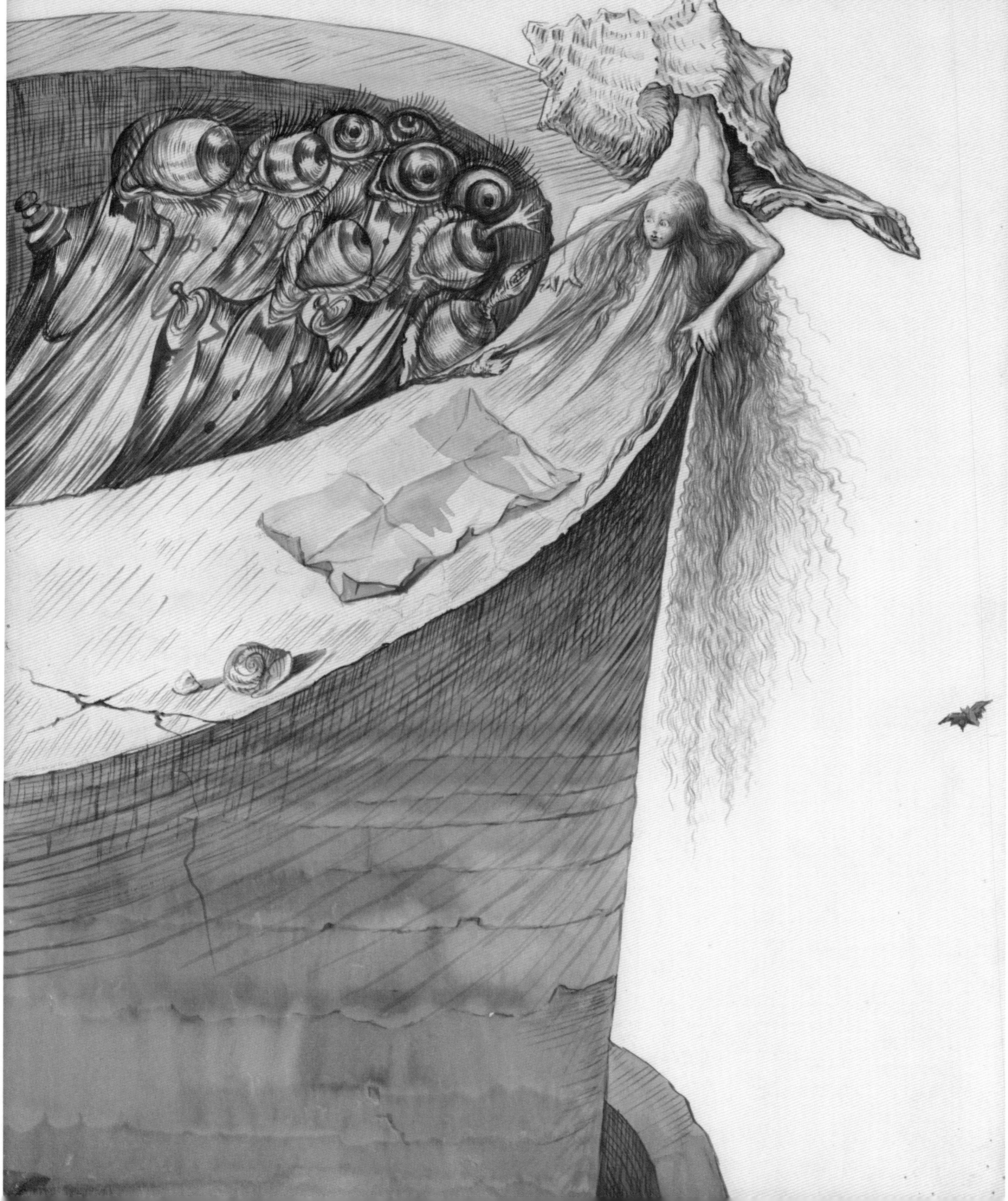

Page 114: Visual development by Salvador Dalí of the girl falling in the conch shell.

Story sketches by Salvador Dalí from the same scene as the one on page 114.

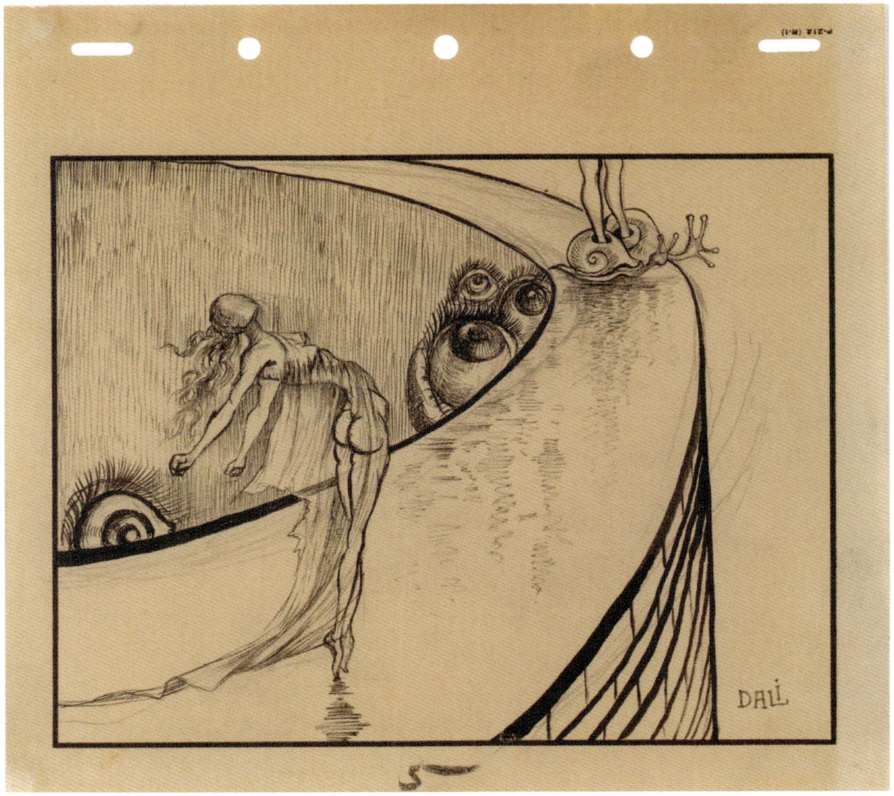

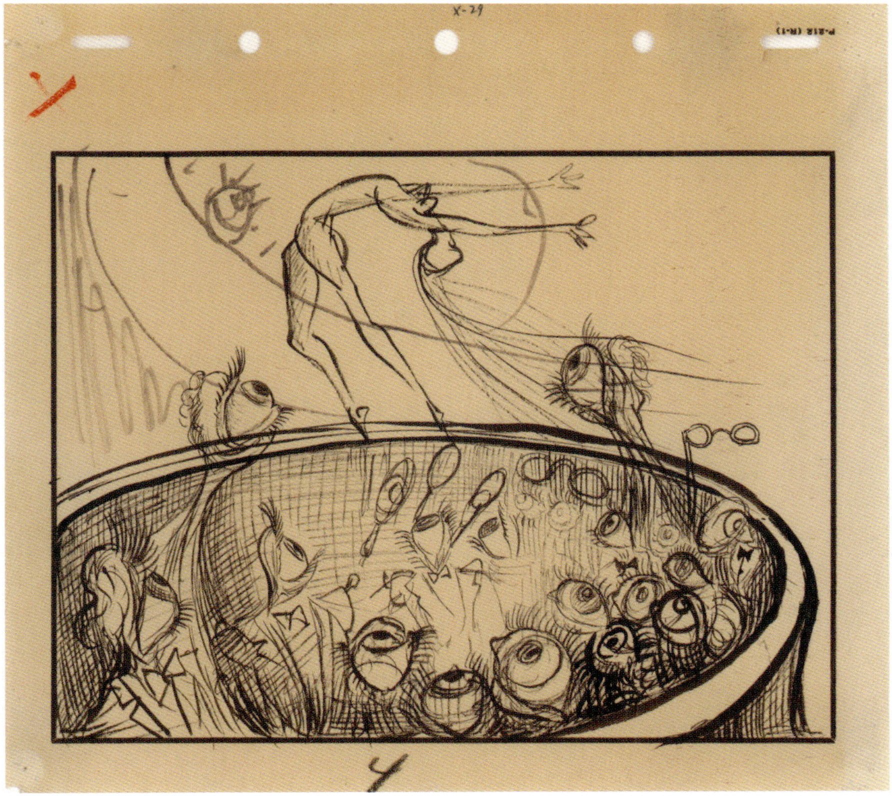

Story sketch by John Hench.

Page 117: *Untitled*
Nude torso on a building on checkerboard study. Background painting for *Destino* by Salvador Dalí (1946).

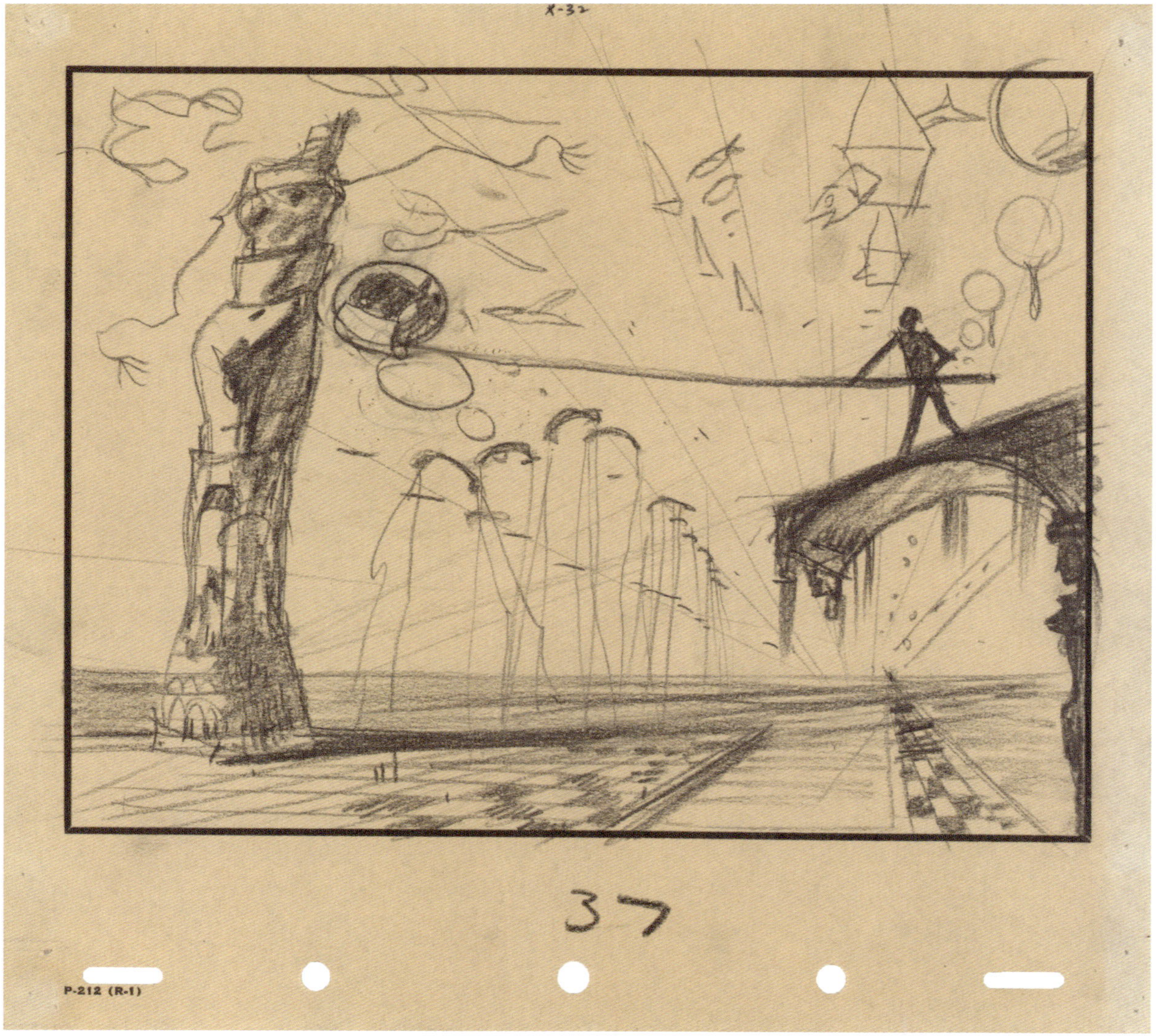

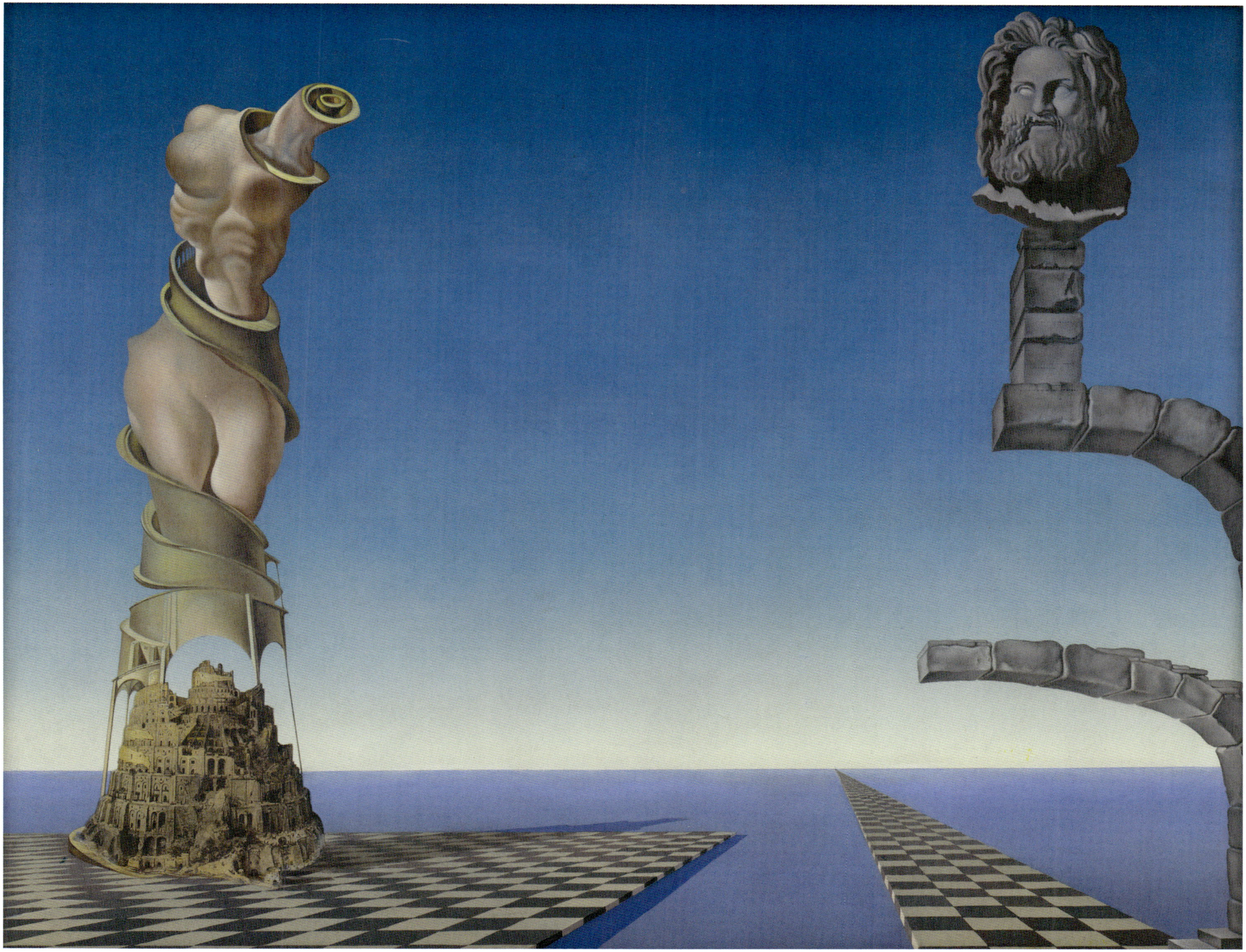

Additional story sketches from concepts that were modified—as well as some that were never used—are shown below through page 123.

Below: Story sketches by John Hench.

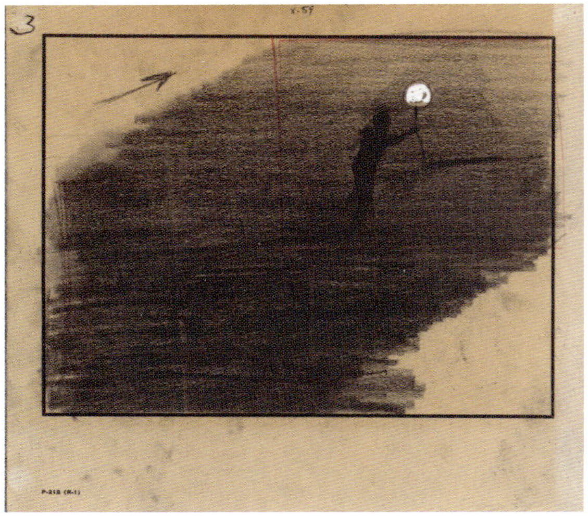

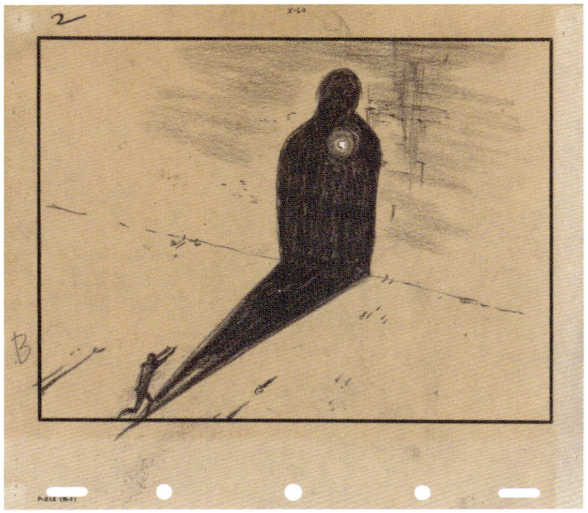

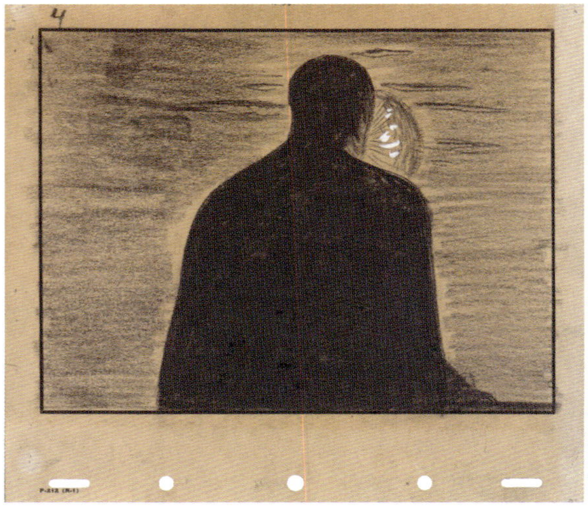

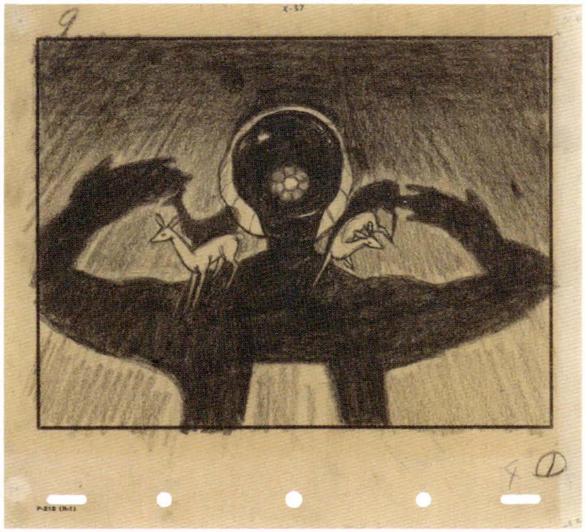

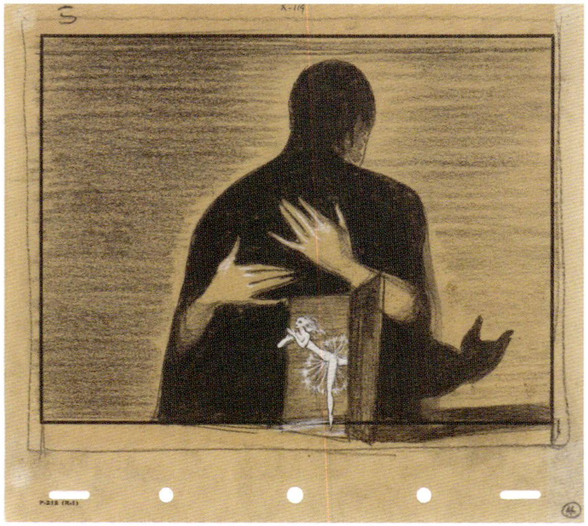

Far left and center: Story sketches by Salvador Dalí.

Far right: Story sketch by John Hench.

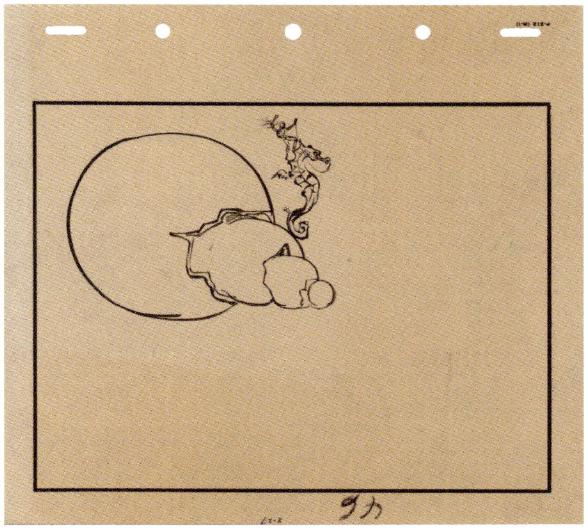

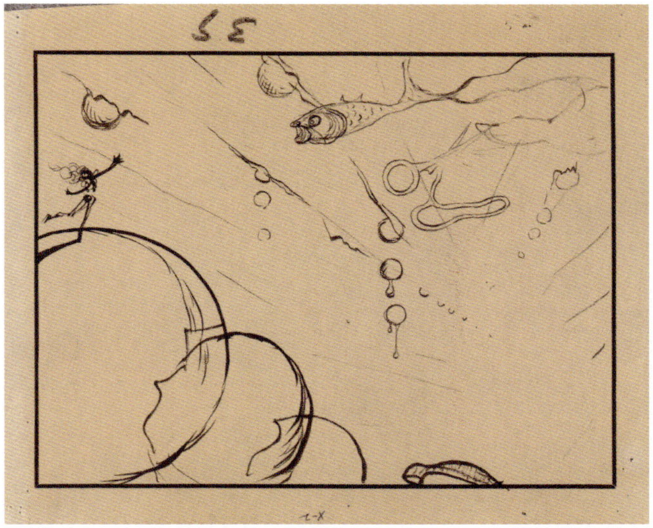

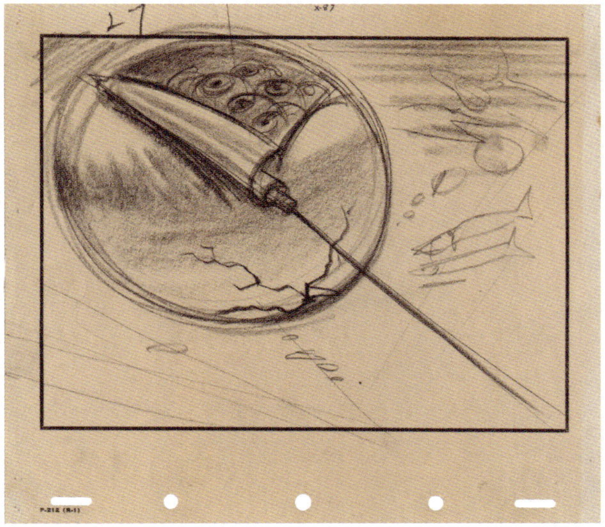

Story sketches by Salvador Dalí.

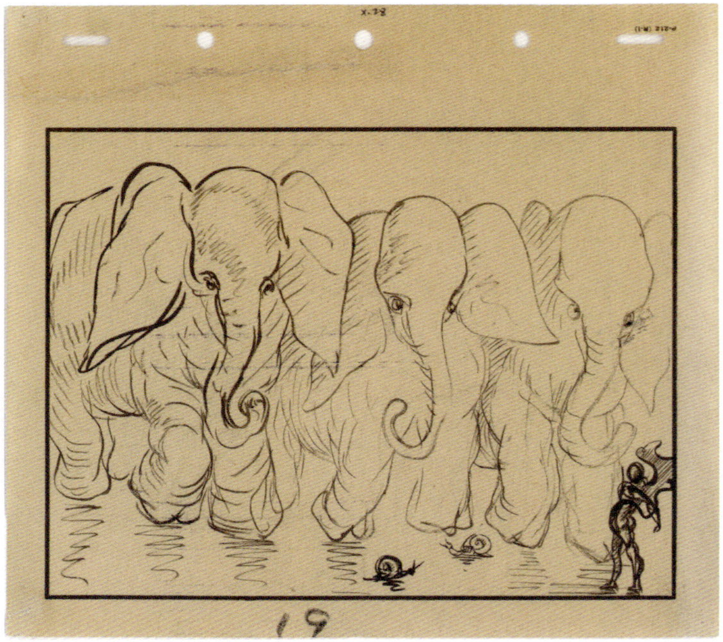

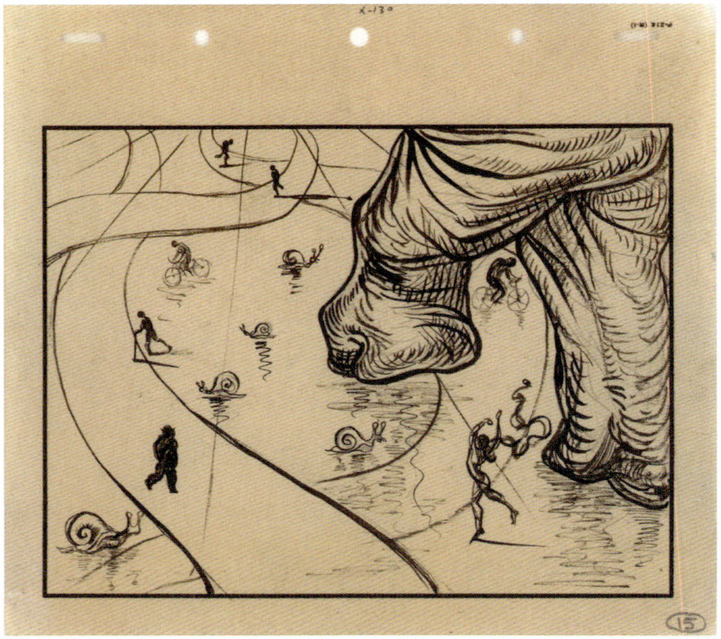

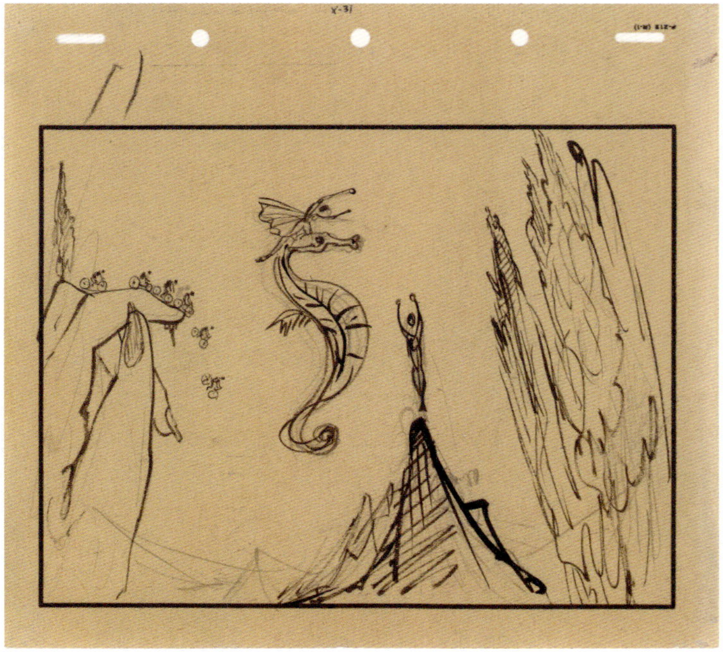

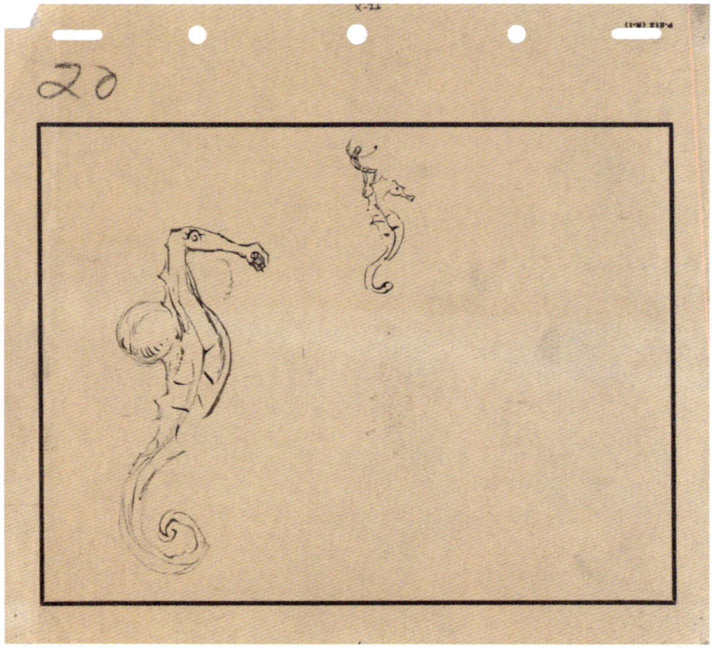

Story sketch by Salvador Dalí.

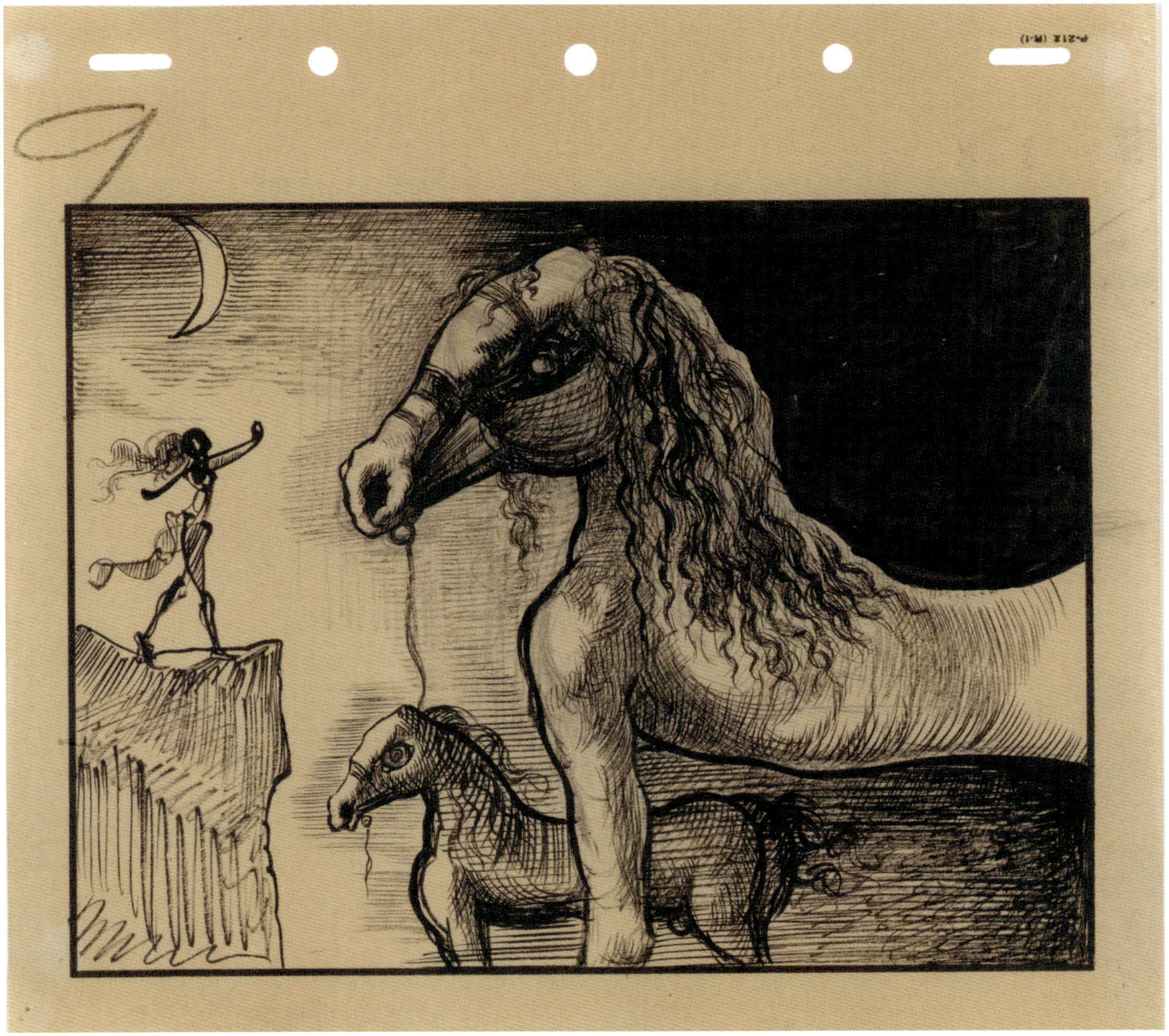

Story sketch by John Hench.

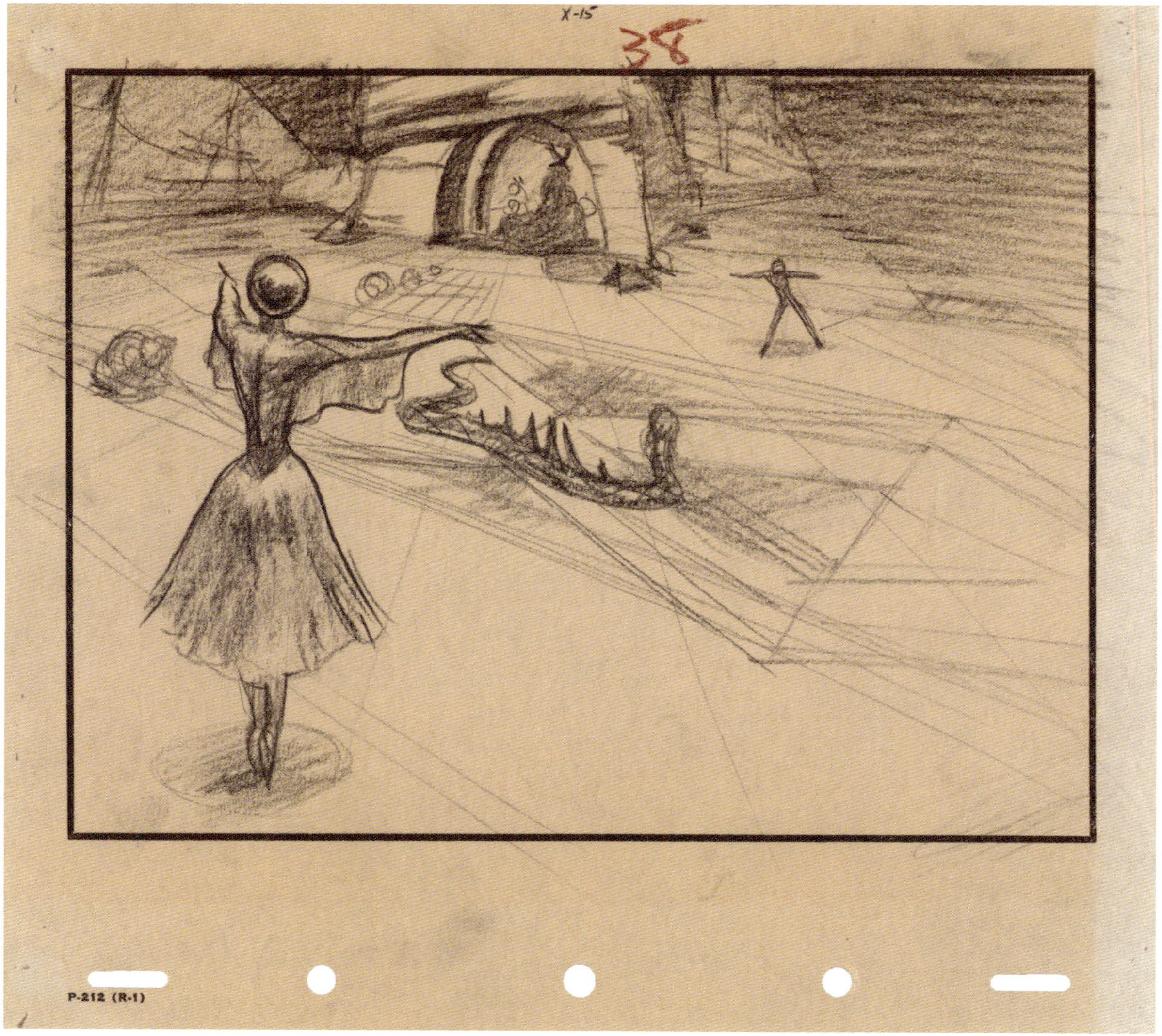

Story sketches by John Hench.

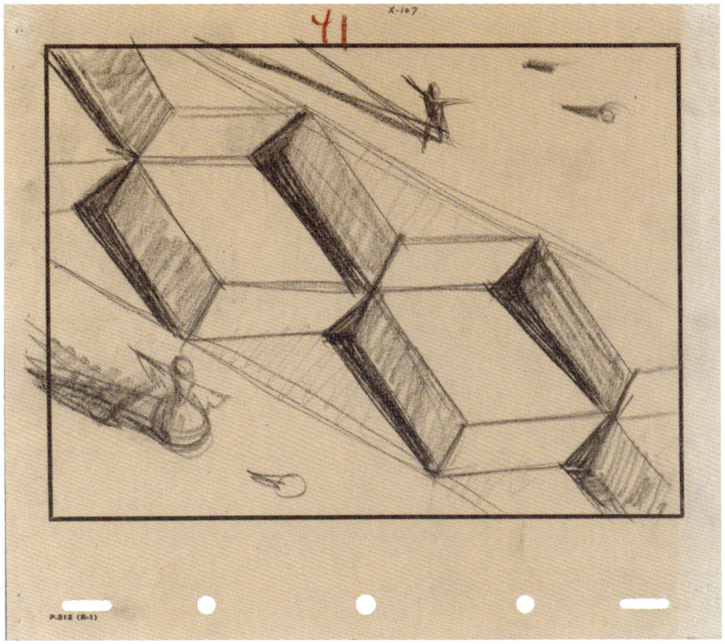

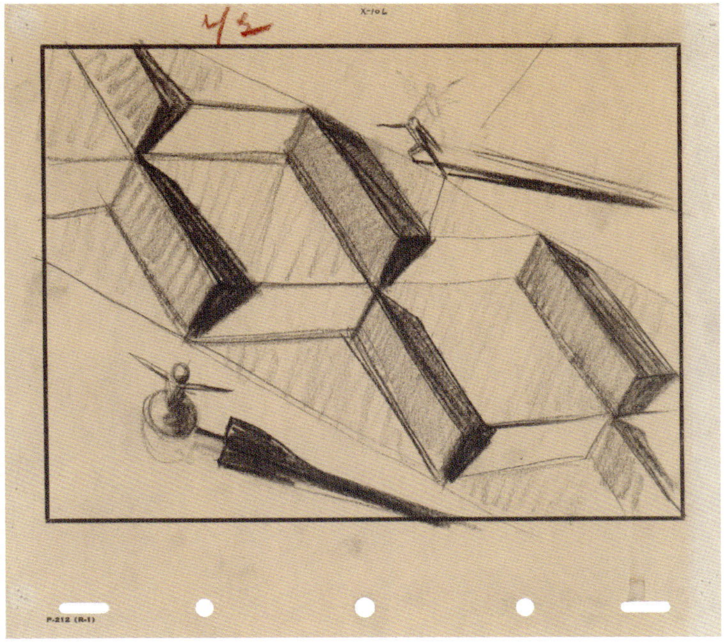

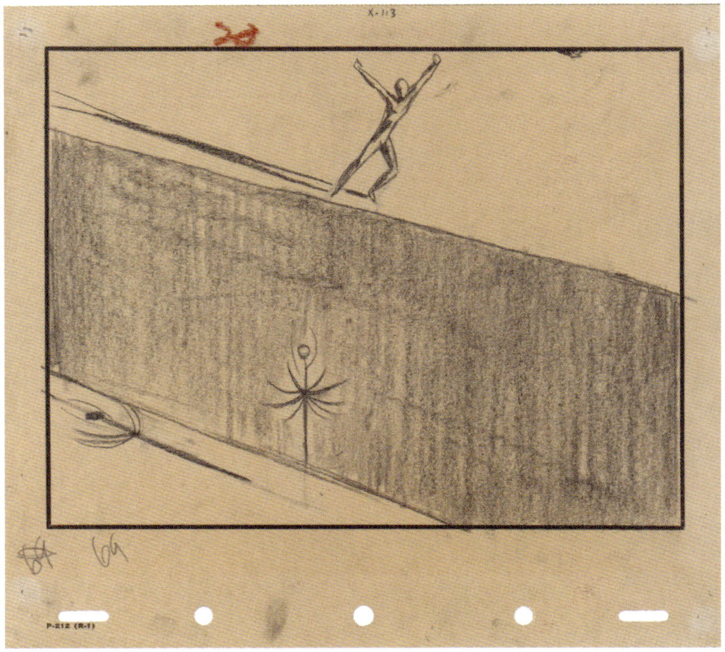

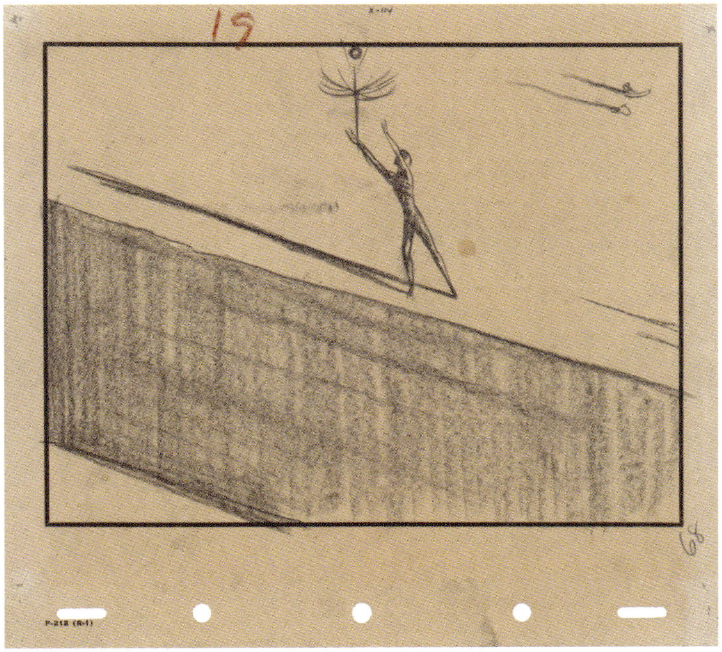

Top row: Story sketches by Salvador Dalí.
Bottom row: Story sketches by John Hench.

Page 125: *Untitled*
Background painting for *Destino* by Salvador Dalí (1946).

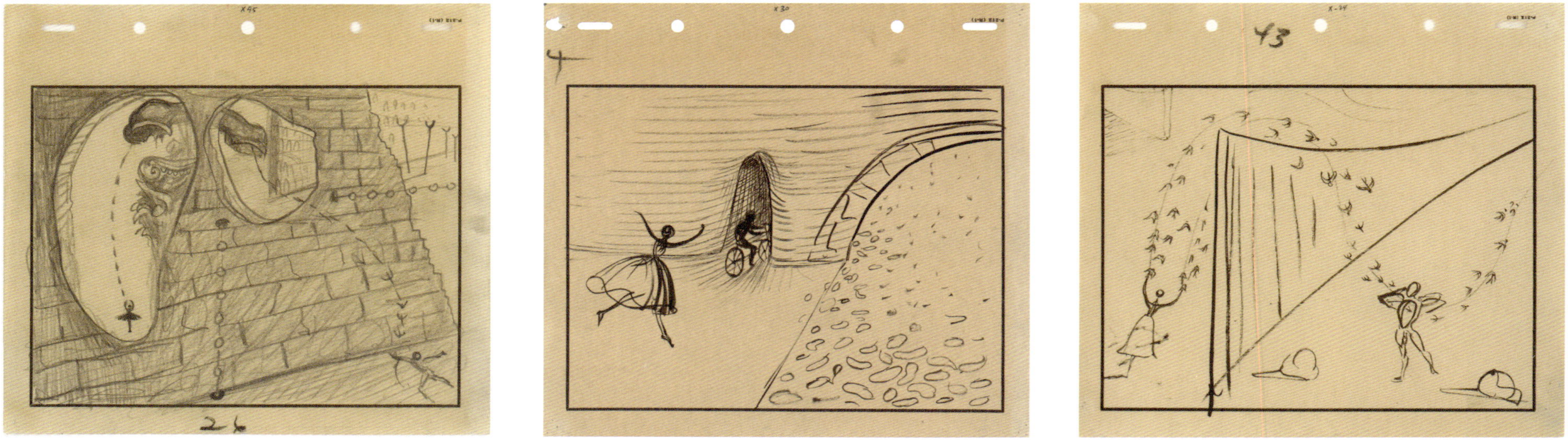

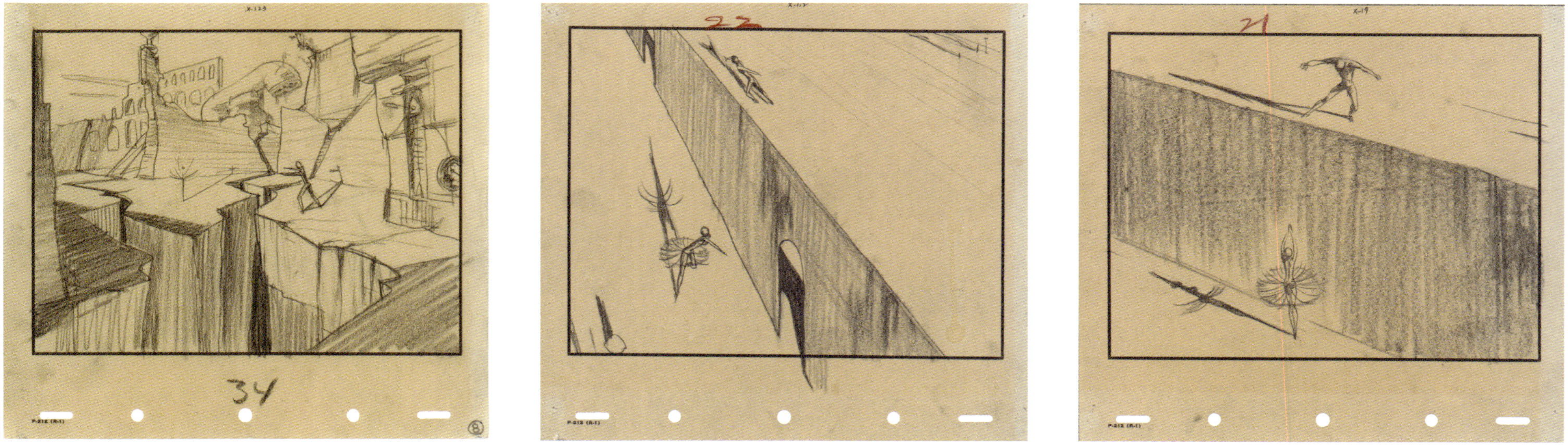

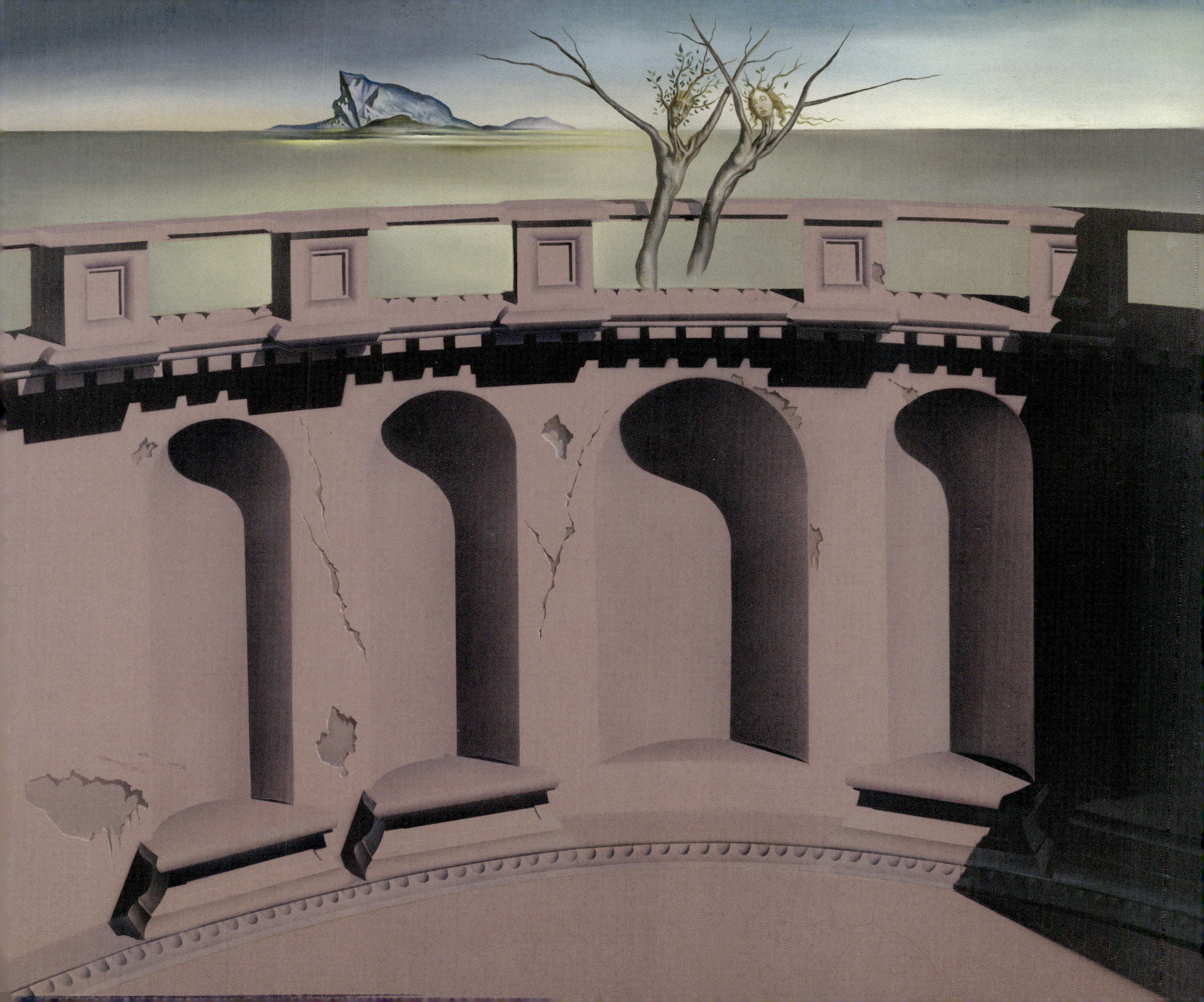

Story sketches by Salvador Dalí, working out the concept of the two fate heads.

Page 127: *Untitled*
Open field with ball in the center and mountains in the rear. Background painting for *Destino* by Salvador Dalí (1946).

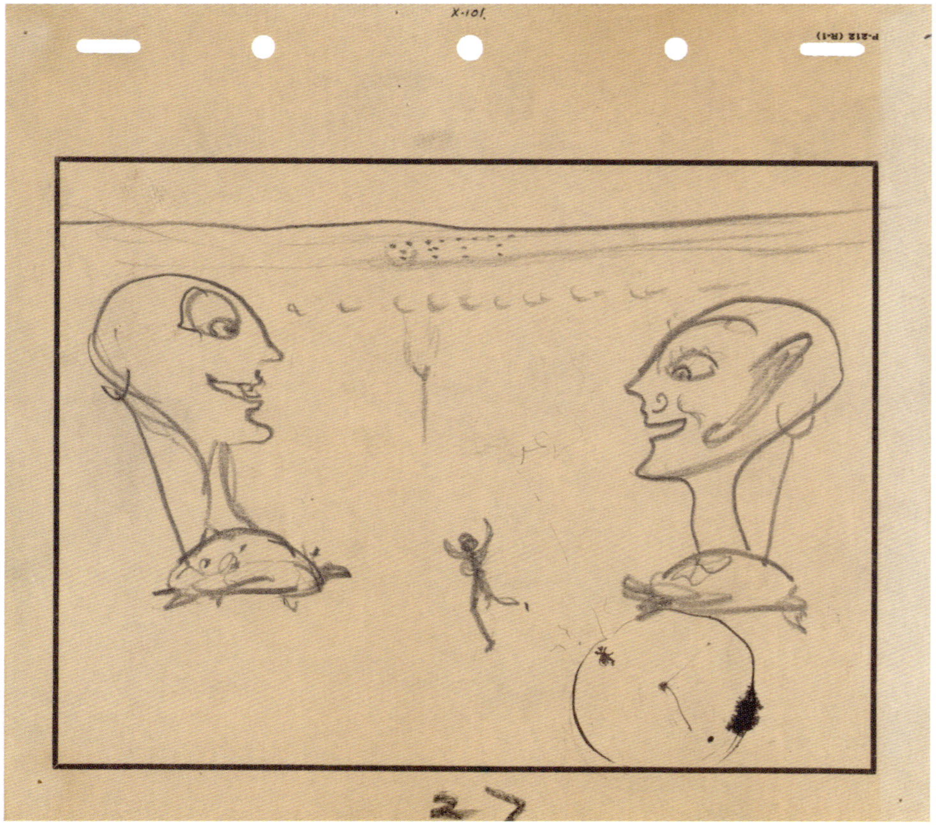

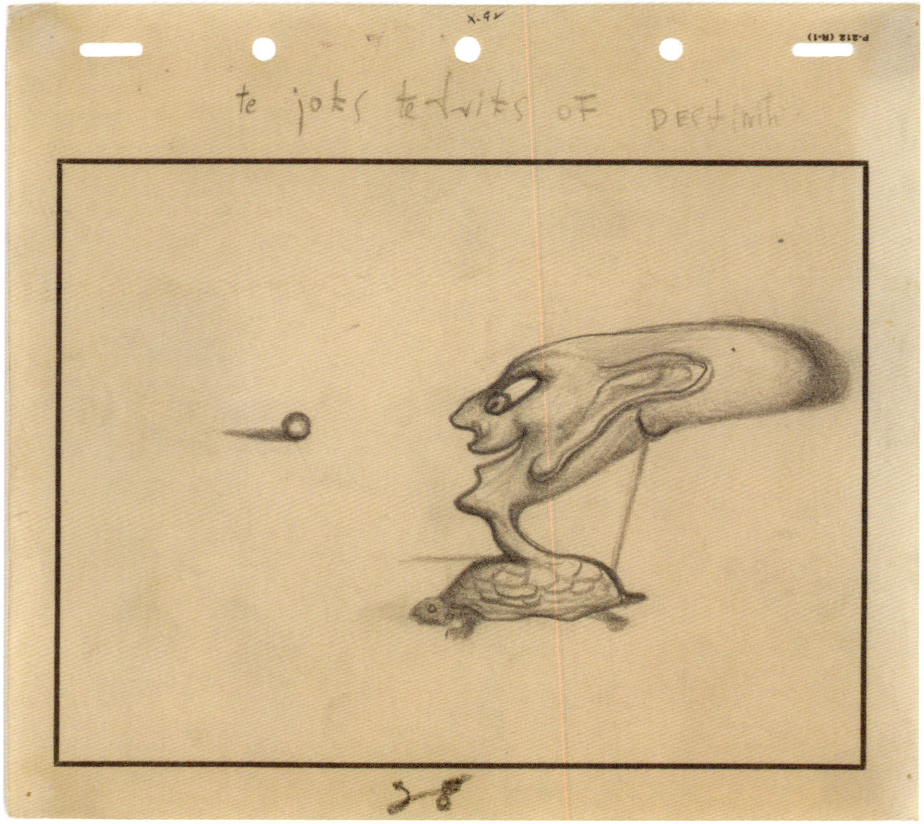

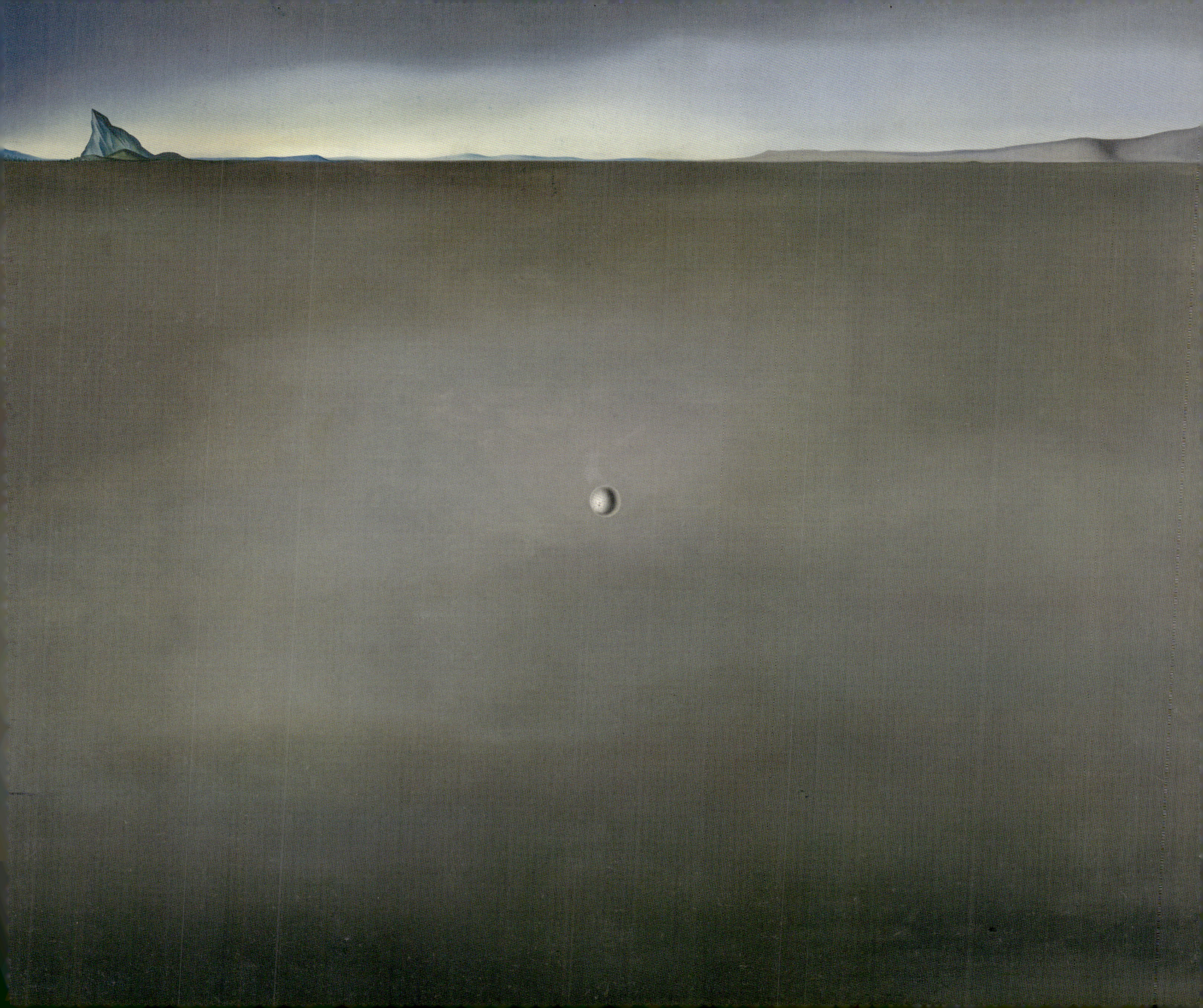

Images of the two fate heads coming together to form the ballerina. This was the only animation test scene that was put to film by John Hench in 1946 and screened for Salvador Dalí, who was staying in Carmel-by-the-Sea, California.

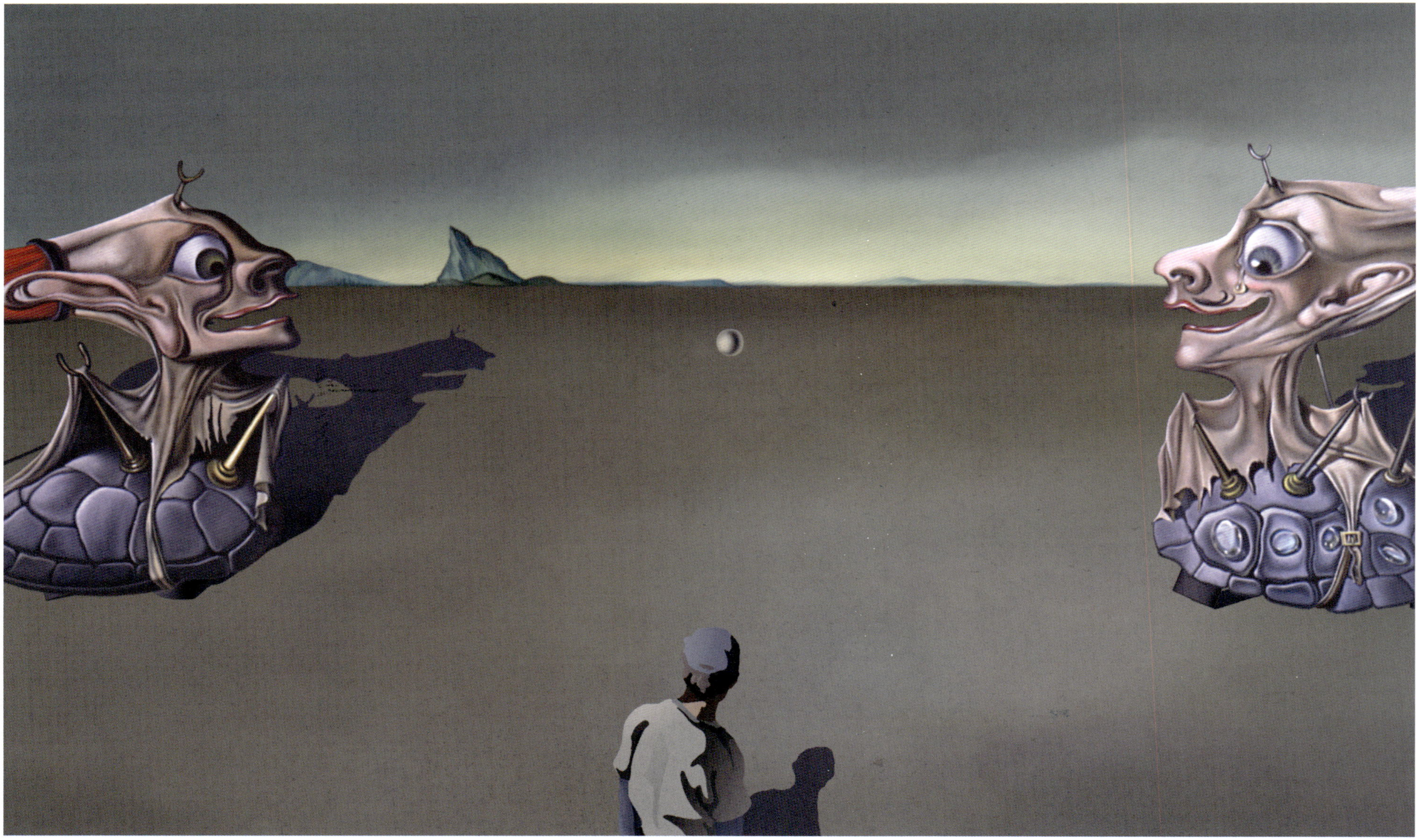

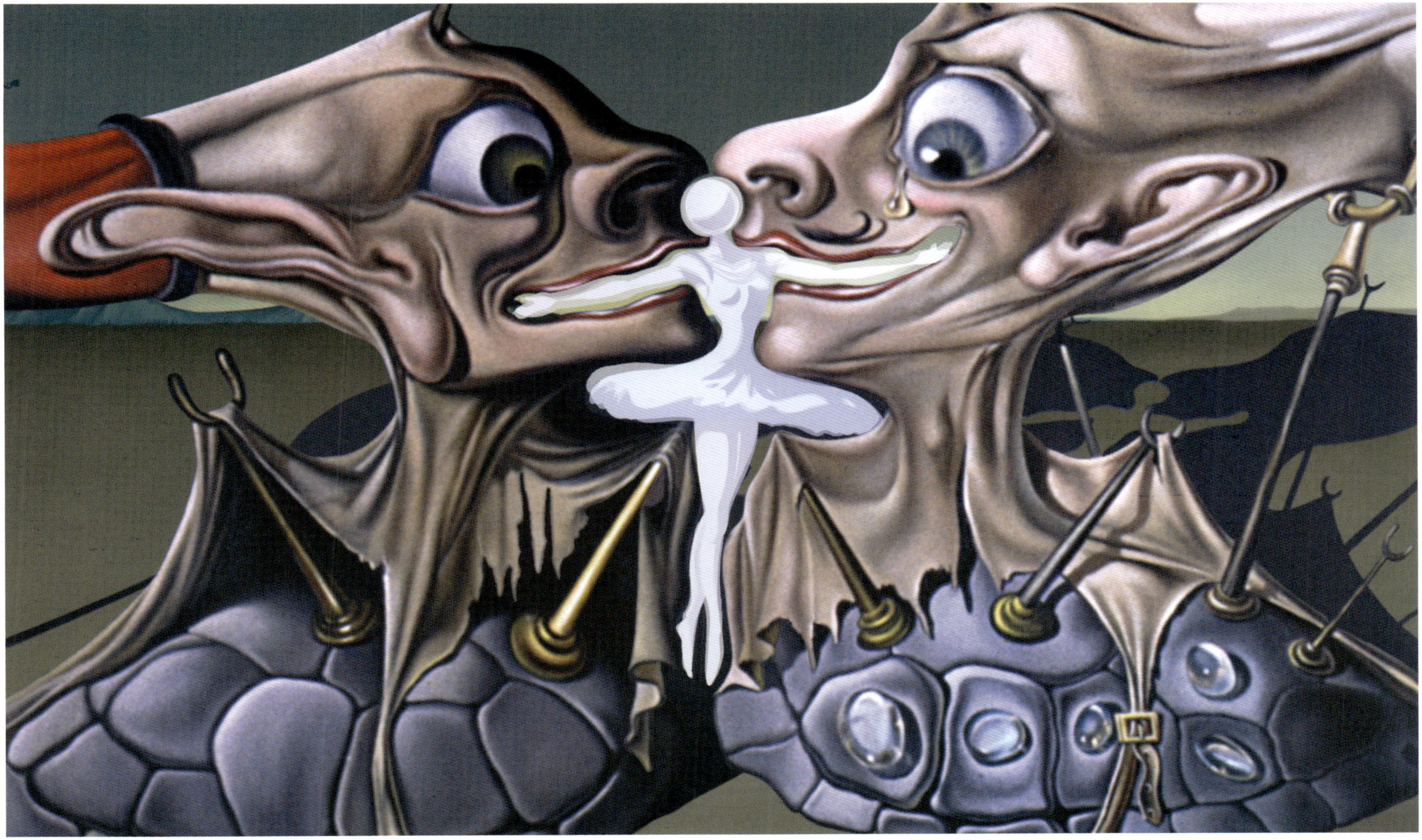

Story sketches by John Hench.

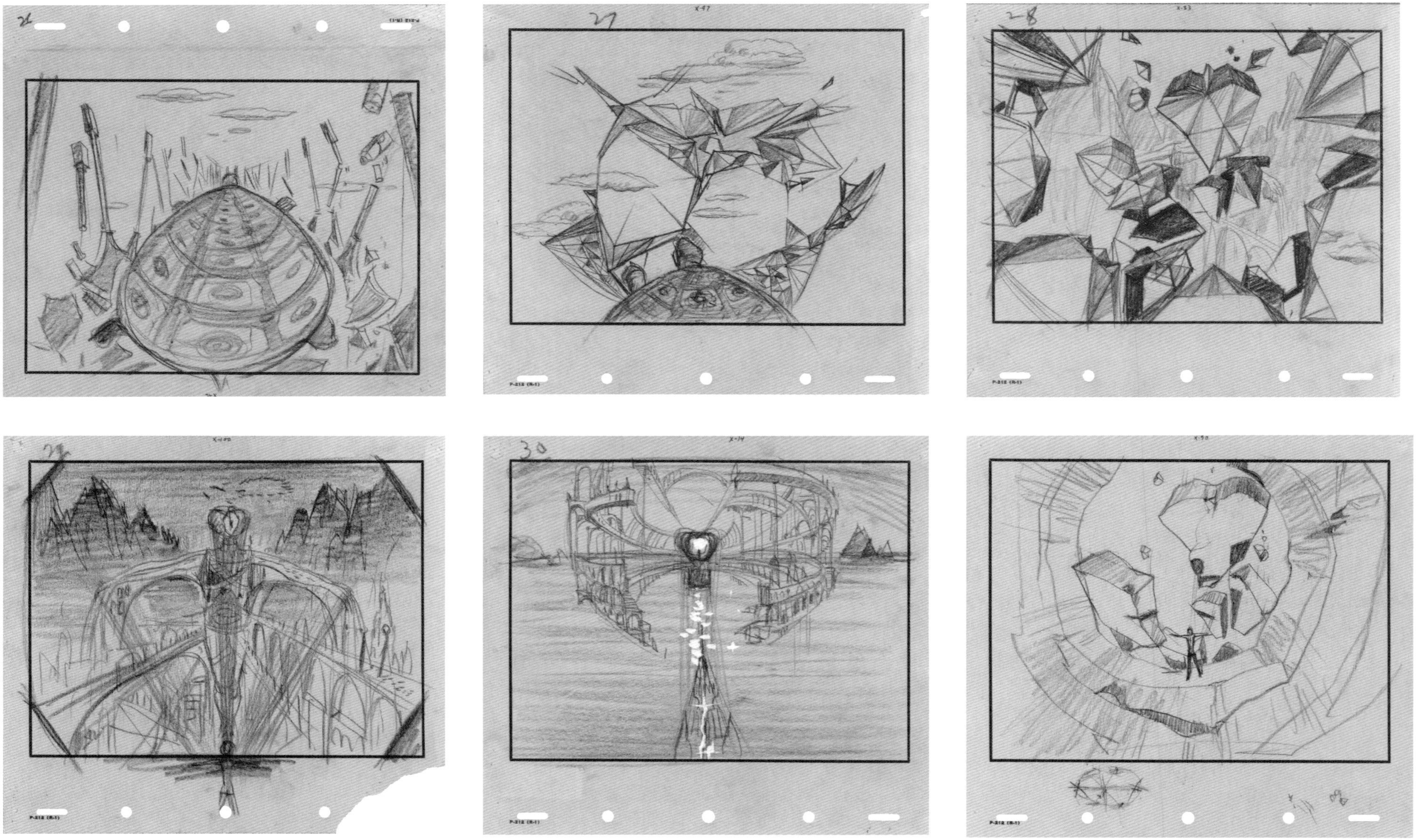

Left: Story sketch by Salvador Dalí.

Right: Story sketch by John Hench.

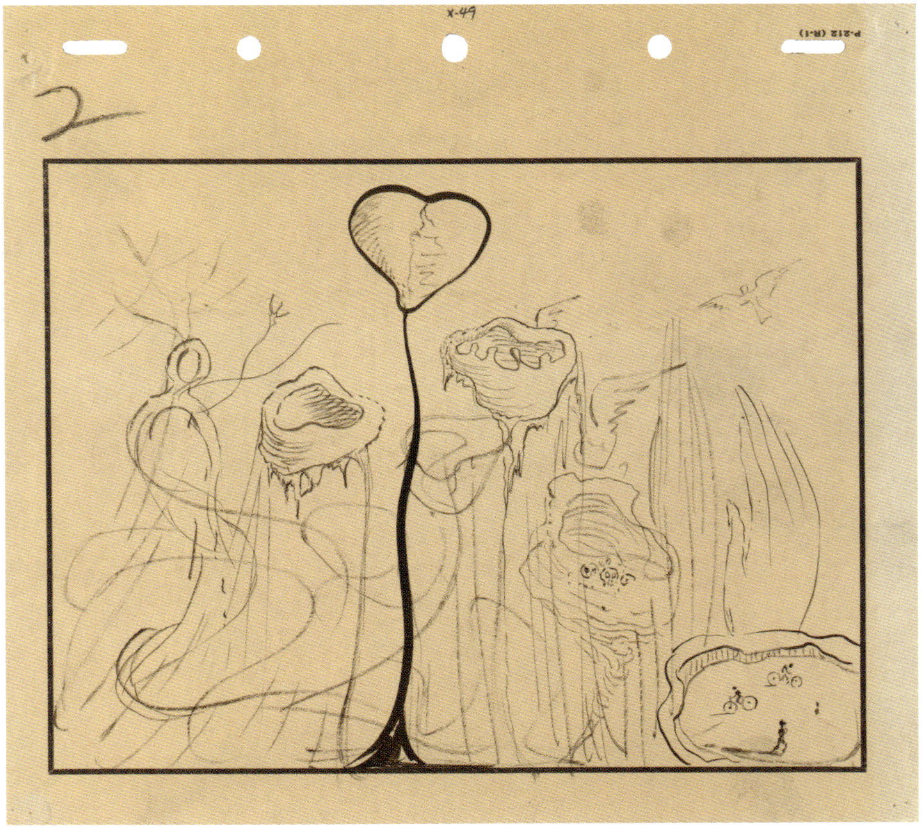

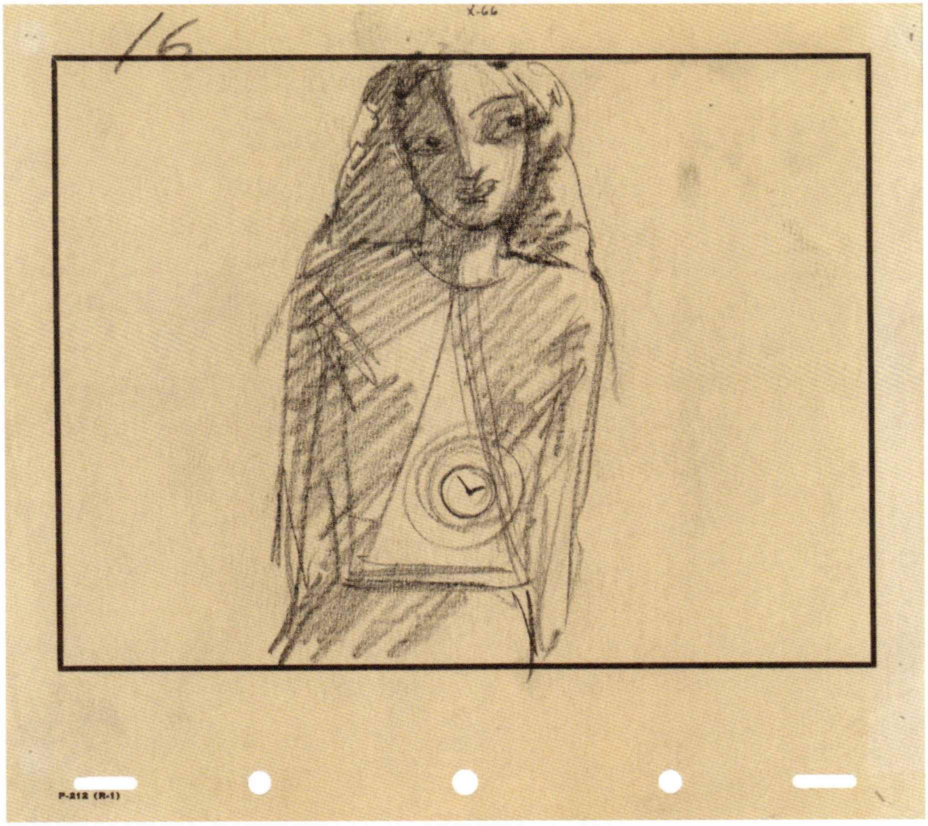

Story sketch by Salvador Dalí.

Page 133 (top): Photostat of storyboard from *Destino*, 1946.

Page 133 (bottom): Image from the film, *Destino.*

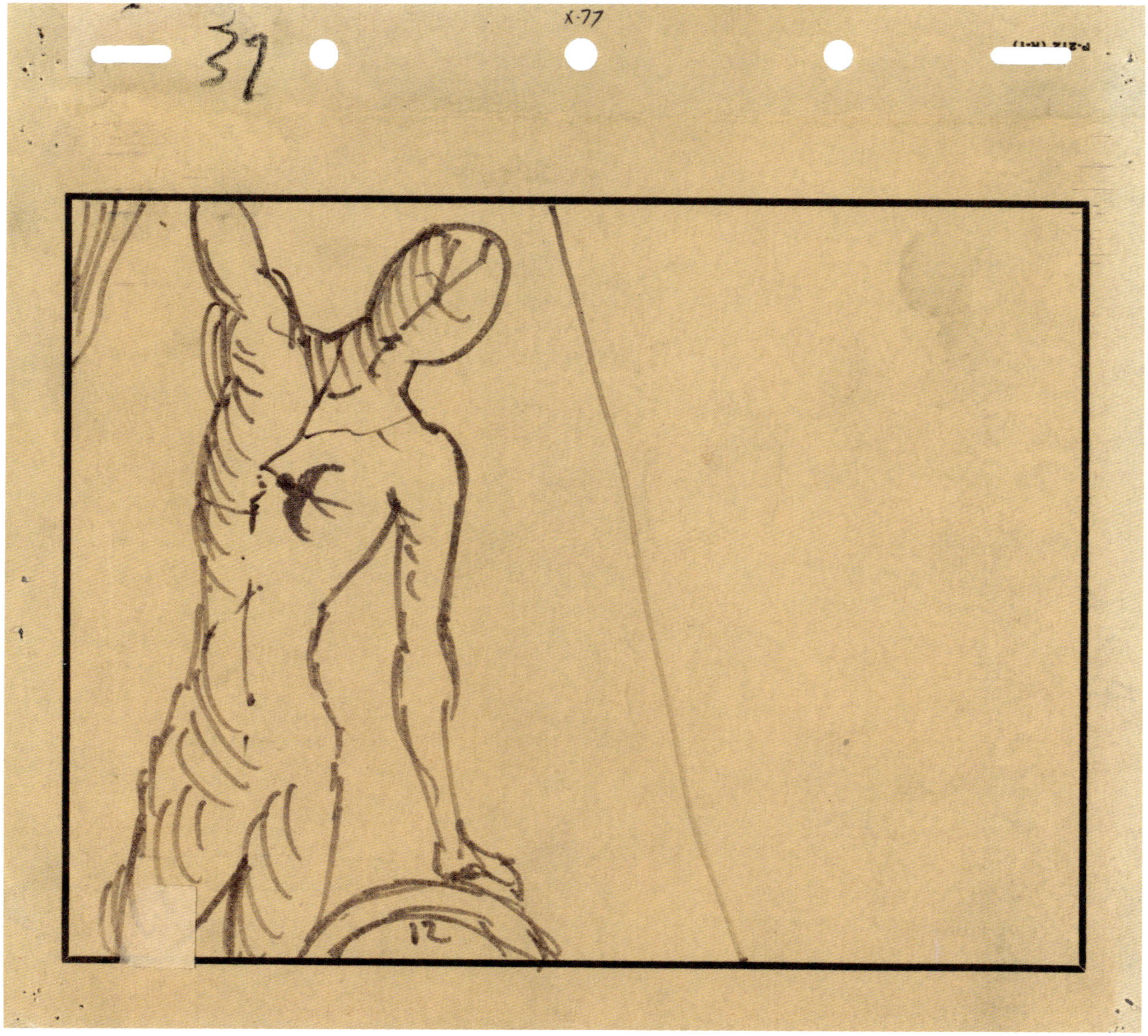

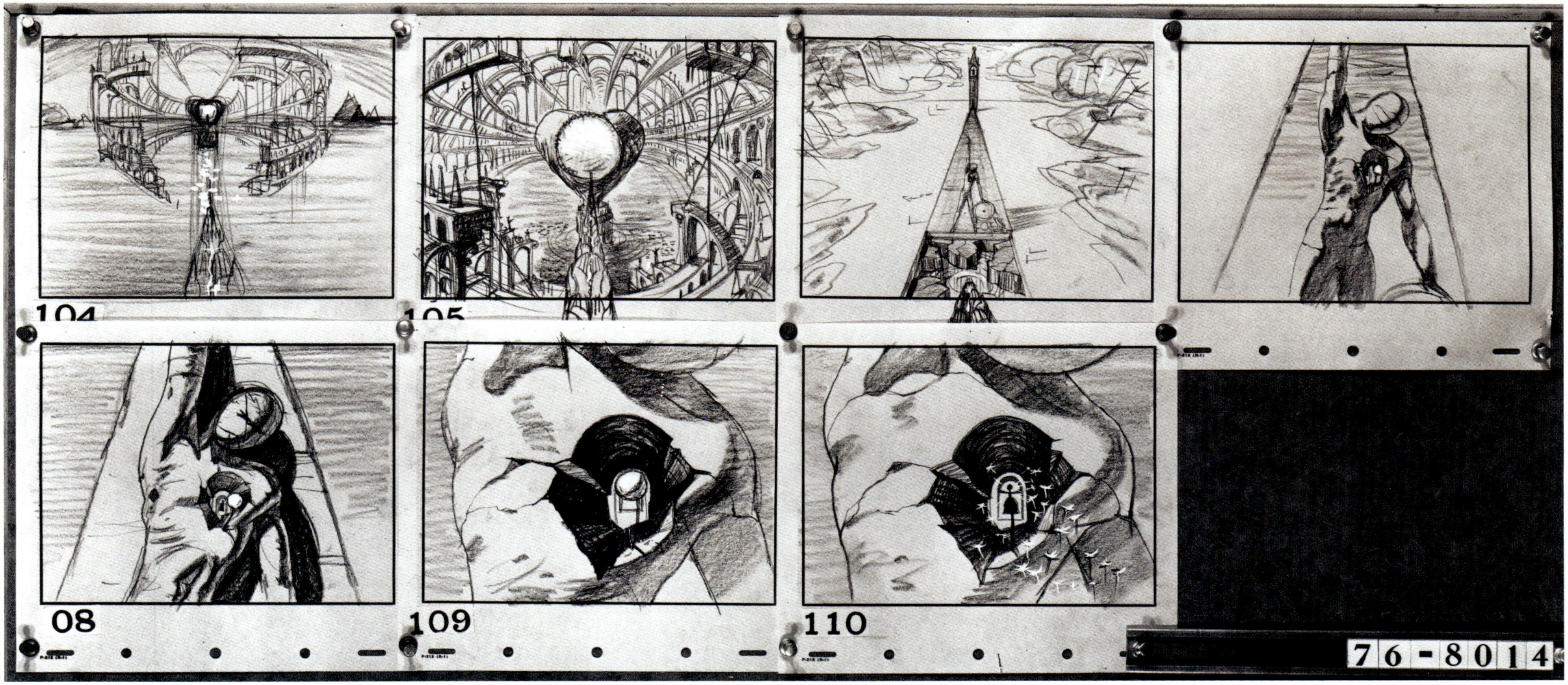
08
109
110
76-8014

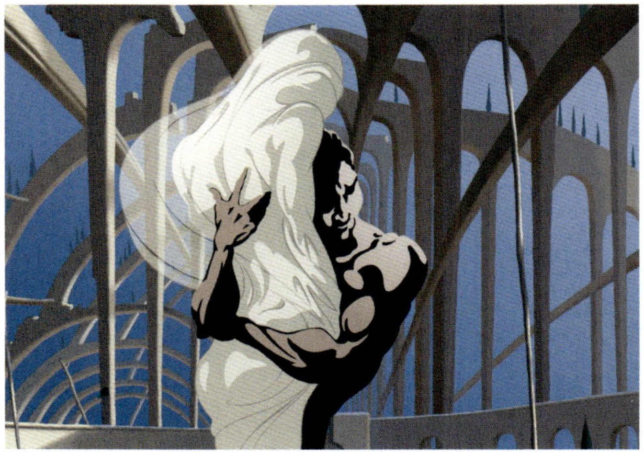

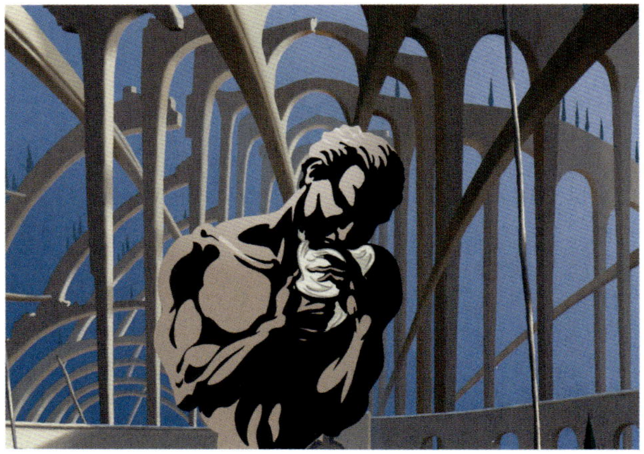

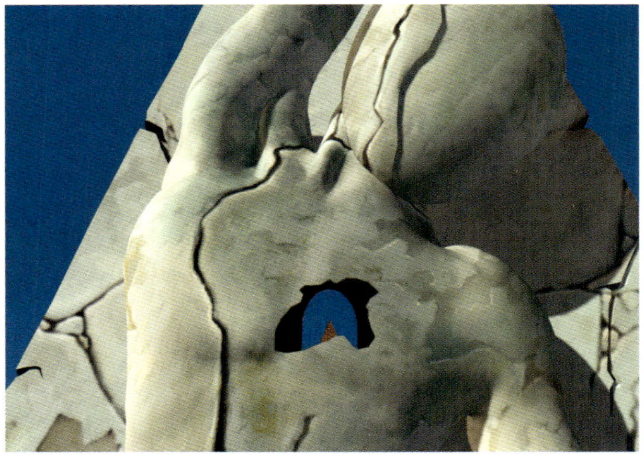

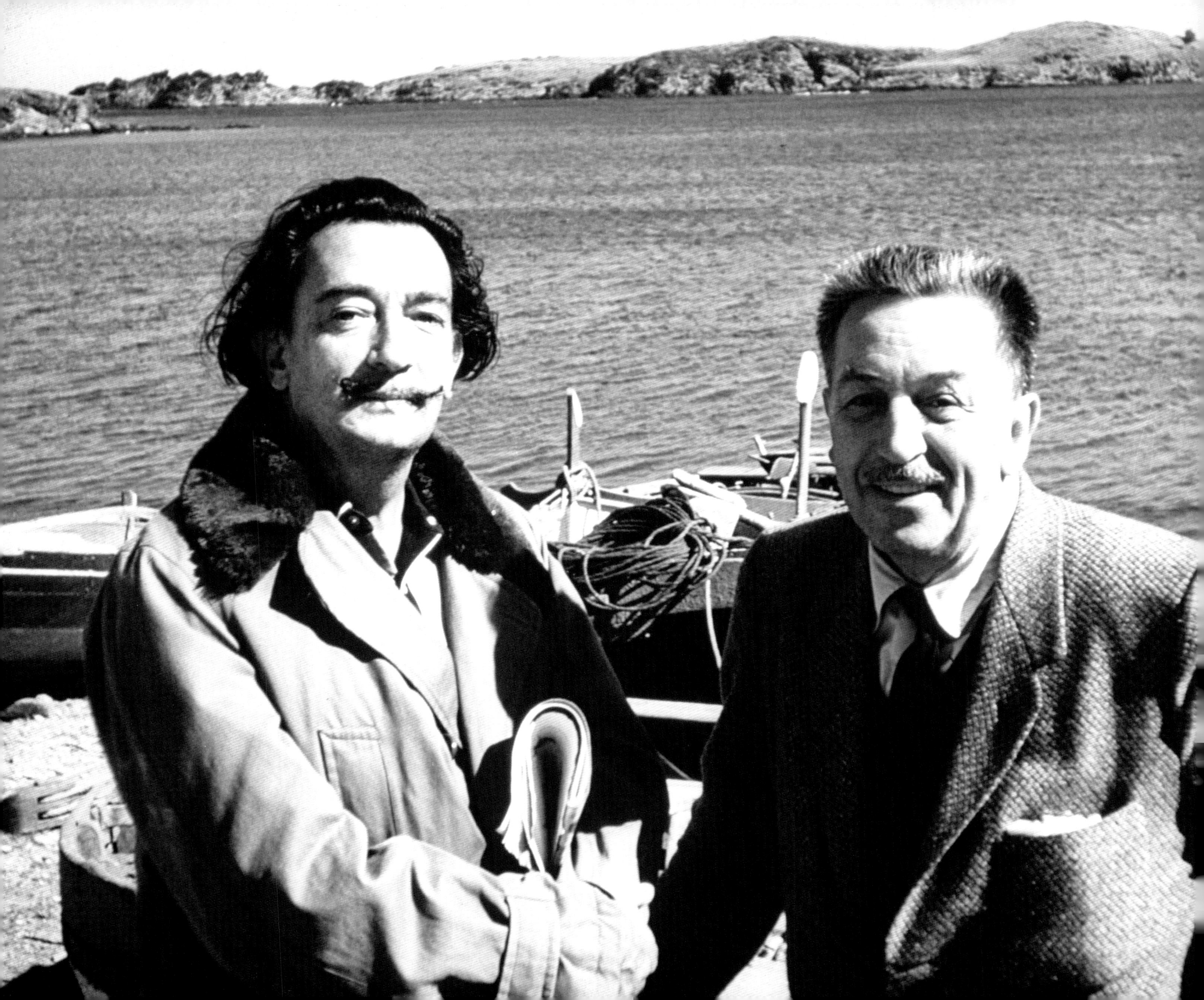

ACT III:
The Completion of the Film

The *Destino* project and the artwork associated with it lay dormant for decades until June 1969. Michael Hughes, who worked in the Art Props department at the Disney Studios, removed without authorization at least 130 *Destino*-related drawings by Salvador Dalí and John Hench. The exact number of stolen pieces is not known, and some of them were never recovered.

Hughes sold part of the cache to Milton Holland and the remainder to a Louis Linetsky, both in the Los Angeles area, for a combined total of $11,500. Eventually Linetsky acquired the group of drawings Holland owned and sold the combined collection of artwork to a gallery in Long Beach, California, for a total purchase price of $20,000, making a handsome profit for himself.

During this time Dalí was living at The St. Regis Hotel in New York City and was approached by an art dealer who asked him to sign the works he had "as a written certification that [he] had created all of the *Destino* artwork in possession of the art dealer" (which included many drawings by Hench as well). Dalí phoned his old friend and collaborator to ask about the artwork, and Hench informed Dalí that the *Destino* artwork had never been sold or given away, and that all the work had been placed in storage at Disney.

Two years had passed by the time the theft was discovered. There was no question that the ownership of the *Destino* artwork belonged to the studio. Disney contacted the gallery in Long Beach with its claim of ownership and sought the return of the stolen *Destino* artwork.

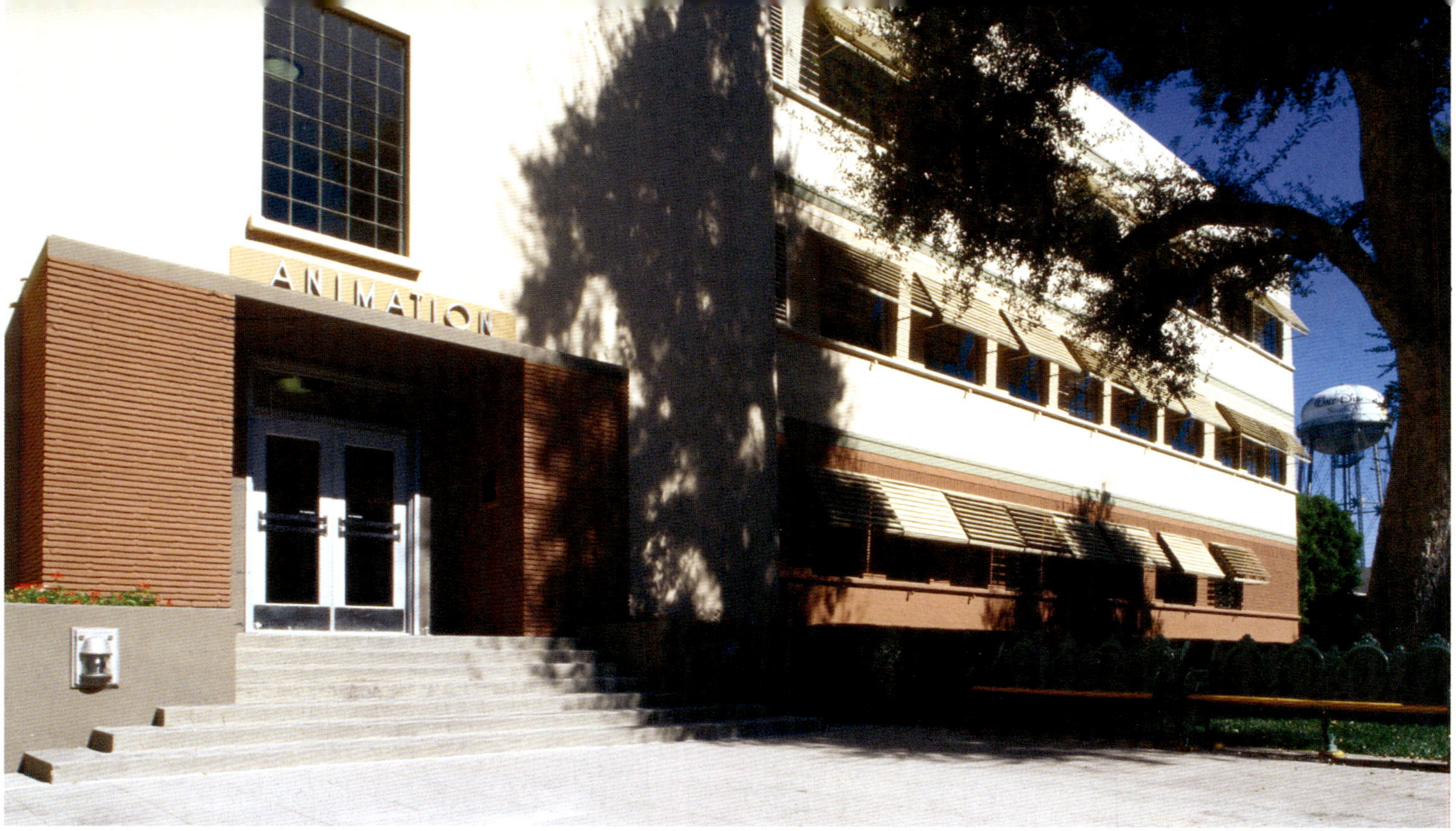

Page 134: Salvador Dalí and Walt Disney in Portlligat, Spain, circa 1957.

Main animation building as it appears today at the Walt Disney Studios in Burbank, California.

In turn, the gallery filed a lawsuit against both Holland and Linetsky on April 21, 1971, and Disney eventually filed suit against the gallery in September 1971. Then on June 5, 1972, all 130 *Destino* drawings that were in the possession of the gallery had been returned to Disney, and the lawsuits were summarily dismissed.

As for Hughes, the Disney employee who had first absconded with the artwork, the statute of limitations had run out on his crime. He had left the company and moved to Connecticut in the ensuing years. Aside from being interviewed about the theft, there were no further recriminations for his actions. The studio had recovered the artwork, and that was truly the most important aspect of the whole episode.

There was a considerable value placed on the artwork during the course of returning it to the studio. While the litigation related to the theft of the *Destino* art unfolded, there was at least one offer of $75,000 made for the entire collection.

The drawings were placed in a safe that was located at the time in office 2E-18 in the main Animation Building on the studio lot in Burbank. They were to be kept in that safe "until some decision is made as to their utilization."[1]

On January 23, 1989, the eighty-four-year-old surrealist painter died in his hometown of Figueres, Spain. He left his entire estate to Spain, which included "fewer than 200 oil paintings" estimated at the time to be worth $300 million.[2]

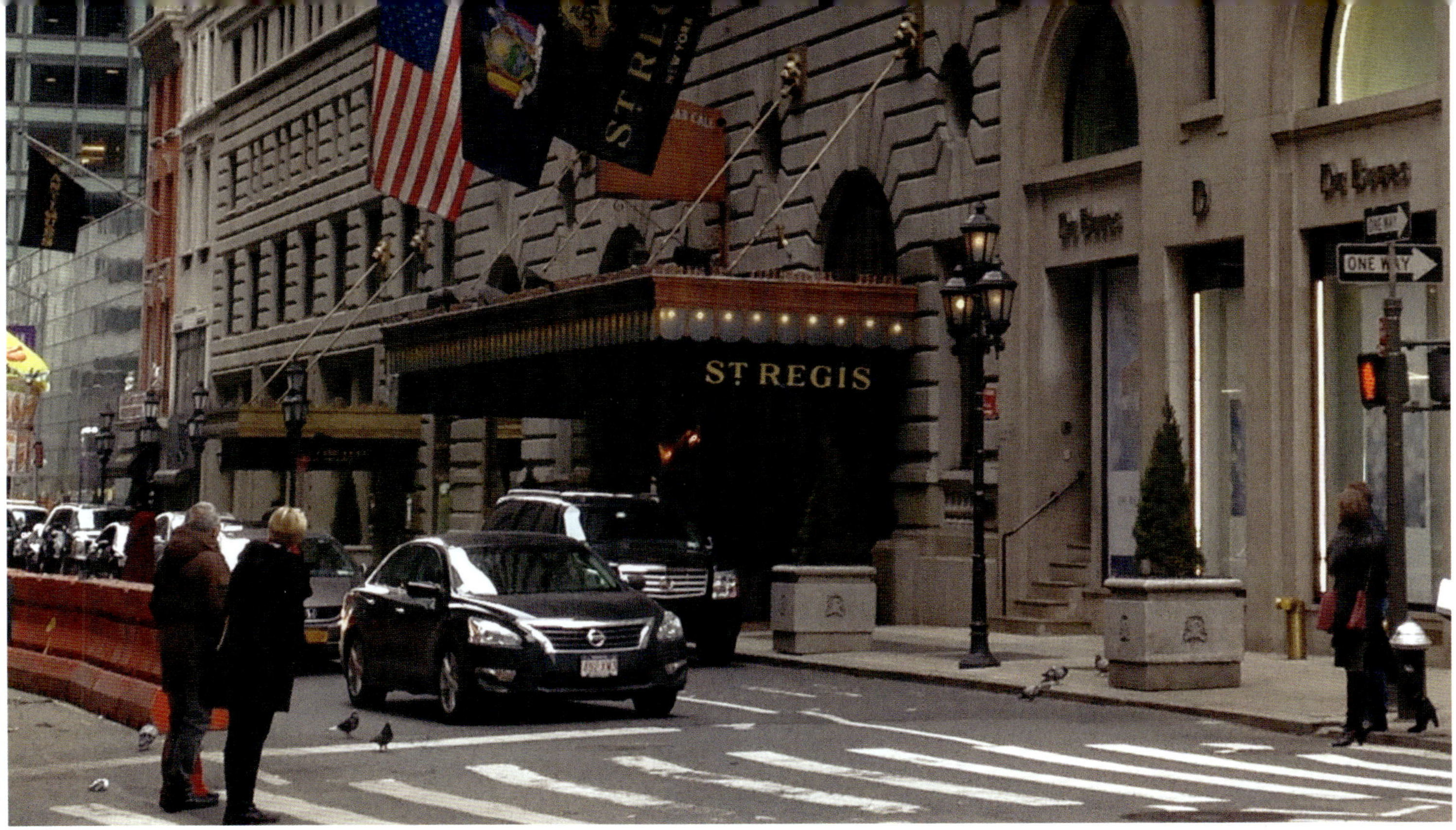

Exterior of The St. Regis Hotel in New York City, where Salvador and Gala Dalí lived on and off during his stay in the United States during World War II, and a few years after the war ended. Photo courtesy of Dave Bossert.

The estate included several thousand drawings, some sculptures, manuscripts, and lavish homes in Cadaqués and Púbol, both in Spain.

Dalí's death prompted several internal memos regarding *Destino*. One memo explained some of the history behind the *Destino* artwork and what happened after the artwork was stolen and recovered. There had been some discussions over the years about possibly donating the artwork to the California Institute of the Arts (CalArts). Sometime prior to Dalí's death, he was living in New York and John Hench contacted him to discuss the possible plan to donate the art to the school.

At one point there was an effort to have Dalí sign the story sketches. Hench had arranged an appointment with Dalí at The St. Regis Hotel where he was staying. When he and others arrived at the hotel for the appointment, Dalí's manager at the time kept them waiting for a very long time, which ultimately resulted in the parties not seeing one another. Ultimately, the *Destino*-related artwork was then placed in the Disney Archives at Walt Disney Imagineering which is where Hench was working during that part of his career.

At that time, there was no formal Animation Research Library. All the animation art resided in the basement of the Ink & Paint building on the main Studio lot and was referred to as the "morgue". The animation art was in folders stacked on rows of shelves behind a chicken-wire partition and gate.

Letter to Salvador Dalí from Jack Warner. Courtesy of the Fundació Gala-Salvador Dalí.

CABLE ADDRESS
"WANEWAR"

TELEPHONE
HOLLYWOOD 1251

WARNER BROS.
PICTURES, INC.
WEST COAST STUDIOS
BURBANK, CALIFORNIA

March 18th, 1947.

Mr. Salvador Dali,
St. Regis Hotel,
Fifth Avenue at 55th Street,
New York, New York.

Dear Salvador:

I was happy to receive your recent letter and want to apologize for not answering sooner but I have really been very busy since my return to California.

I appreciate your suggestion about making a picture based upon the book you are writing and will look forward to receiving the table of contents. You know I will give it every consideration as soon as I hear further from you.

Hope this finds you and Gala in excellent health and spirits, and wish that we can all get together again soon whether it's in Los Angeles, Delmonte, or New York City.

Always your friend,

Jack

WB

VITAPHONE
REG'D TRADE MARK

TWENTIETH ANNIVERSARY OF TALKING PICTURES
Warners

Letter from John Hench planning for the 1964–65 New York World's Fair. Courtesy of the Fundació Gala-Salvador Dalí.

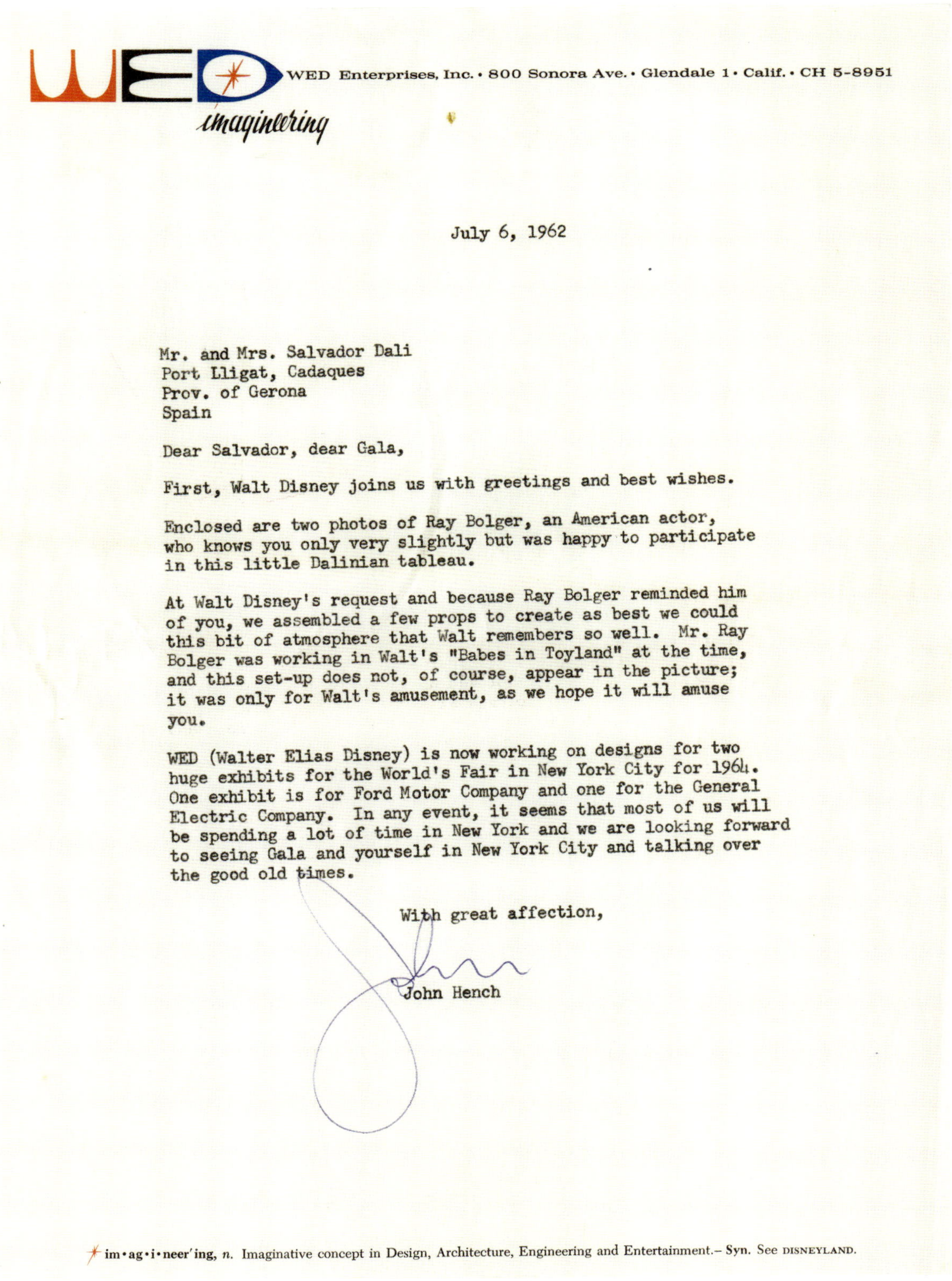

WED imagineering

WED Enterprises, Inc. • 800 Sonora Ave. • Glendale 1 • Calif. • CH 5-8951

July 6, 1962

Mr. and Mrs. Salvador Dali
Port Lligat, Cadaques
Prov. of Gerona
Spain

Dear Salvador, dear Gala,

First, Walt Disney joins us with greetings and best wishes.

Enclosed are two photos of Ray Bolger, an American actor, who knows you only very slightly but was happy to participate in this little Dalinian tableau.

At Walt Disney's request and because Ray Bolger reminded him of you, we assembled a few props to create as best we could this bit of atmosphere that Walt remembers so well. Mr. Ray Bolger was working in Walt's "Babes in Toyland" at the time, and this set-up does not, of course, appear in the picture; it was only for Walt's amusement, as we hope it will amuse you.

WED (Walter Elias Disney) is now working on designs for two huge exhibits for the World's Fair in New York City for 1964. One exhibit is for Ford Motor Company and one for the General Electric Company. In any event, it seems that most of us will be spending a lot of time in New York and we are looking forward to seeing Gala and yourself in New York City and talking over the good old times.

With great affection,

John

John Hench

im•ag•i•neer'ing, *n.* Imaginative concept in Design, Architecture, Engineering and Entertainment.– Syn. See DISNEYLAND.

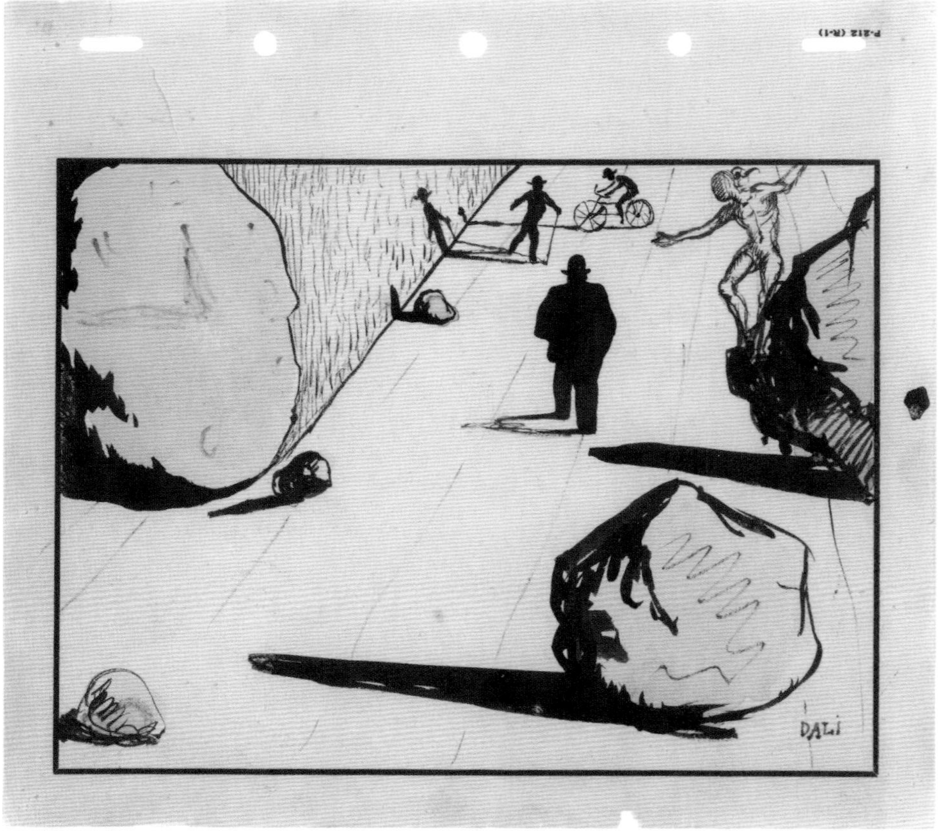

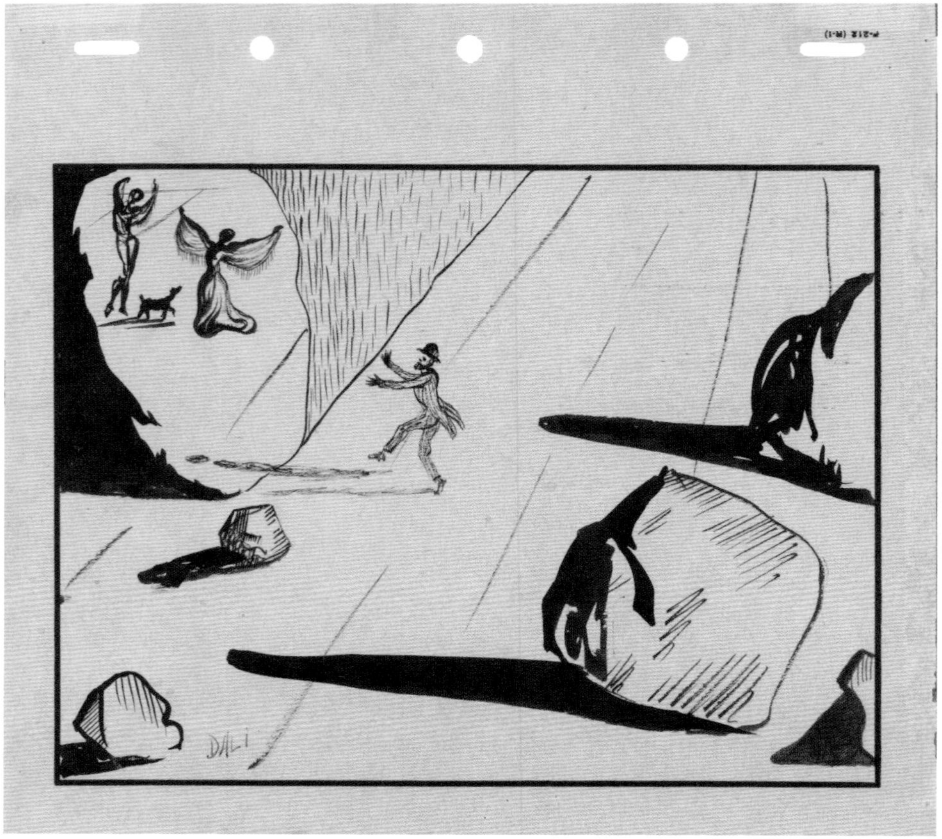

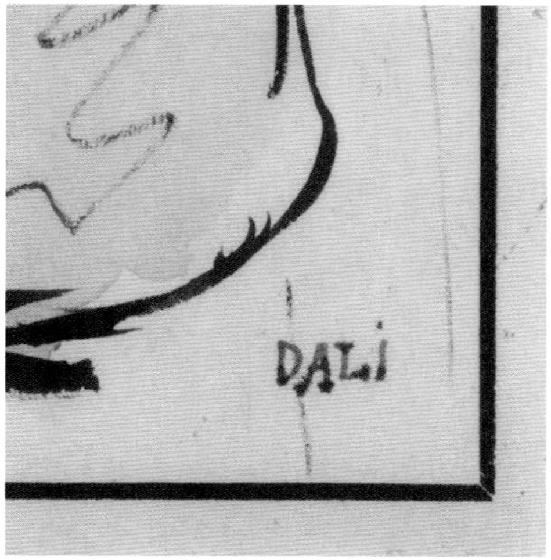

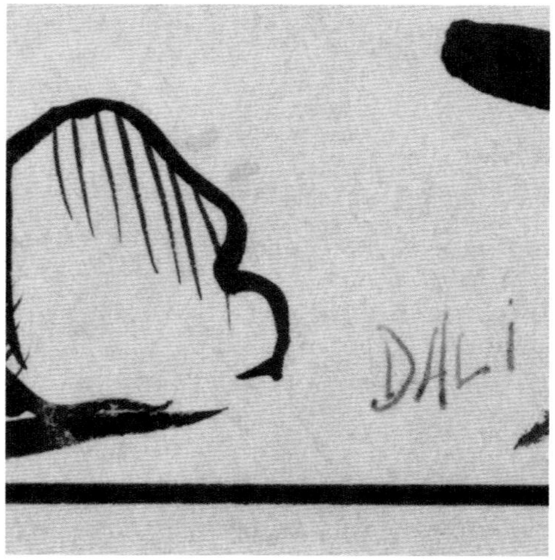

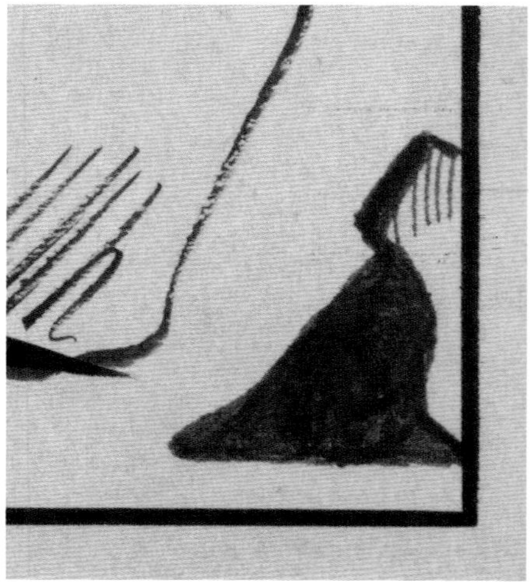

Original production story sketches by Salvador Dalí for *Destino*, which were stolen and later recovered with a forged signature added. Far right image shows the botched forgery inked over. Story sketches courtesy of the Walt Disney Animation Research Library.

When it rained heavily there was usually a leak or flooding that would damage or destroy some of the art. At the time, it was not the place to put the *Destino* artwork.

Two additional *Destino* drawings, *Dancers* and *Promenade*, surfaced in April 1989, with a Los Angeles-area art dealer named T. R. Rogers. Both pieces were identified by John Hench as original *Destino* drawings, though both were altered with the addition of a forged Dalí signature. The *Dancers* piece also had the addition of a shadow at the lower right corner, "the supposed purpose of which is to conceal an unsatisfactory, forged signature of Dalí," Hench stated after the pieces were recovered. Rogers claimed to have legitimately purchased the drawings from a third party. The drawings were seized by the Los Angeles County Sheriff's Department as part of an ownership dispute between Rogers and an art collector. Both pieces were returned to The Walt Disney Company.

The death of Dalí in 1989, along with the surfacing of the additional two *Destino* drawings, would again rekindle interest in the array of artwork associated with the *Destino* project. Several years earlier, Michael Eisner and Frank Wells had joined the company in a sweeping management change engineered by Roy E. Disney, the nephew and son, respectively, of its founders, Walt and older brother Roy O. Disney.

The new management team of Eisner and Wells were in the process of waking a sleeping giant and reenergizing the Disney brand. In doing so, they were combing through the entire company to squeeze out inefficiencies and uncover underutilized assets with hidden value. The Dalí/Hench artwork created decades earlier for *Destino* certainly constituted a valuable hidden asset and there was a flurry of inquiries about the actual value of that artwork. CEO Michael Eisner considered selling the *Destino* artwork and acquiring other works for the new corporate headquarters, the Team Disney Building, being constructed on the Burbank lot. The iconic Disney corporate headquarters building would not be completed until 1991, so there was time to sell the *Destino* artwork at that point. The company considered what was necessary to sell the artwork, but concluded that it should do something significant with the works as originally envisioned by Walt Disney and Salvador Dalí.

Among the options considered were: (1) a "Destino" section for a revised and theatrical rerelease of *Fantasia*; (2) a stand-alone animated motion picture based on the Dalí works to be released as a featurette theatrically; or (3) a limited animation cartoon television program.

But, as before, none of these plans in 1989, nor a later query by a publishing company as to whether Disney would allow the artwork to be used in a book, came to fruition.

In March 1991, there was also an inquiry about the artwork being used in a book being considered by a venerable publishing house. This and other discussions were not acted on primarily because the company was continuing to formulate plans for use of the *Destino* artwork. During this time, the Disney Consumer Products division was examining if they

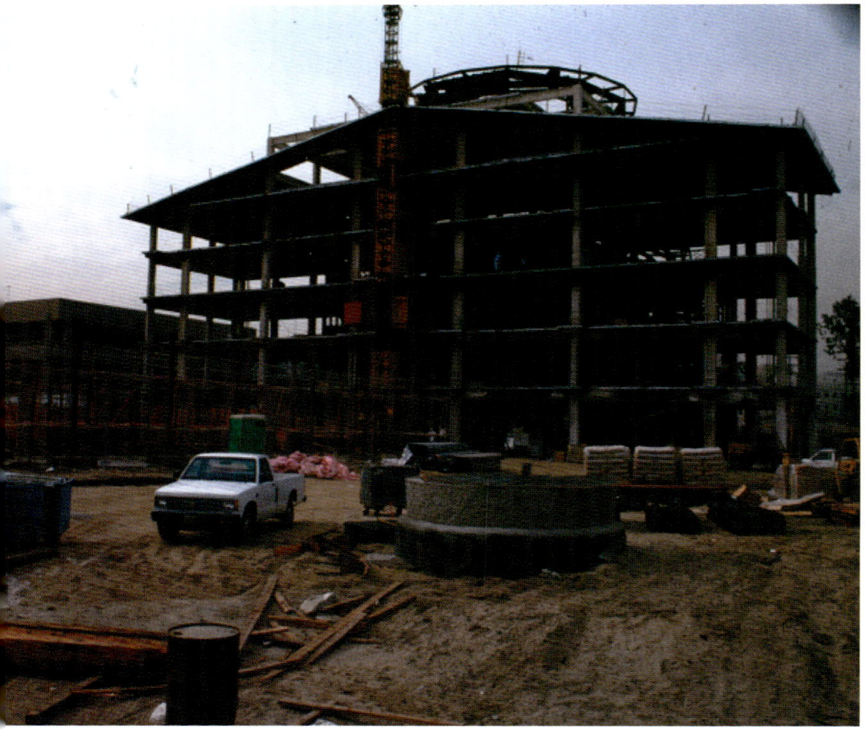

Construction of the Team Disney Building, circa 1990.

could exploit the artwork in some way. But once again it was put aside, likely because it was a one-off project.

The *Destino* artwork continued to lay dormant for much of the 1990s. It did, however, eventually become the subject of renewed interest in 1998 when *Fantasia/2000* was in full production, specifically during a discussion about the movie's interstitials, the live-action segments between the animation sequences. This time the *Destino* artwork was brought up by Roy E. Disney. Having grown up on the Studio lot, Walt's nephew recalled Salvador Dalí working there and felt that his art would make for an interesting inclusion in one of the interstitials.

The interstitial in discussion revolved around the theme of the Disney "that never was": those film projects developed at Disney over the years that were never made. Roy went on to describe *Destino*, the short film he remembered his uncle Walt and Dalí working on, as a segment for a *Fantasia*-like packaged picture. He suggested that some of the *Destino* art be used for illustration-project purposes in the movie that was in the process of being developed, but had not been completed at the time.

Several of the *Destino* art images ultimately were used in *Fantasia/2000* as part of the interstitial that starred Bette Midler. During the segment, Midler explains that at Disney there are many projects that have been developed over the years that never make it to the big screen. For whatever rationale, a project might start development but is then scrapped for various reasons: the project may not have been working from a story standpoint, the subject matter might not resonate with audiences, or it just simply didn't garner positive feedback on a number of levels.

According to Ed Nowak, deputy general counsel for The Walt Disney Company, "The first time I think I can remember [this attention to *Destino*] coming up with Roy was as a result of Frank Wells's interest in the fact that the new management in the late 1980s had found out that there was this treasure trove of Dalí art."

Nowak explained that senior management wanted a valuation of the artwork to understand what the company had as an asset. He said, ". . . and then the conversation went dormant for some period of time. There were these initial conversations, and

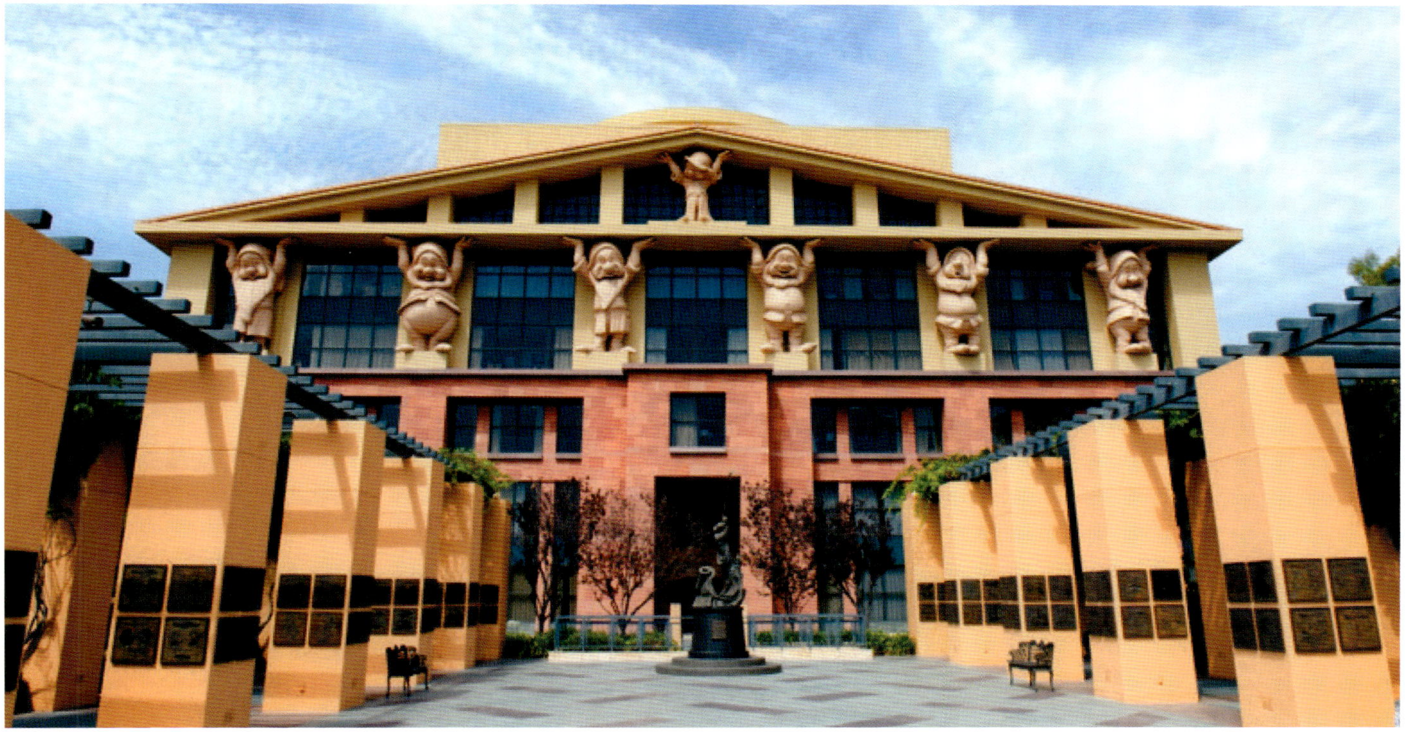

The Team Disney Building today, showcasing the Legends Plaza in the foreground.

then one day I get a call from Roy, which was a real event because I'm not sure I had ever talked to him before, or talked to him at any length about anything before." He recounts Roy telling him, "I'd like to make that movie."[3]

Ultimately, Nowak was deemed a key player in finally moving the project forward. When Roy E. Disney told the story, he basically said that if it weren't for Ed Nowak, *Destino* might never have gotten made. "Ed was the one guy at the studio who doggedly went through all of the associated paperwork and cleared up any internal matters that might have been a stumbling block to completing the movie." Making the short would also fulfill Disney's goal of putting the *Destino* artwork to use in a production.[4]

All the delays worked out well for this author. I had started with Disney in 1984, and by 1998 I was the artistic coordinator and visual effects supervisor on *Fantasia/2000*. I was going to be part of the *Destino* team along with a group of talented artists in Burbank and Paris. With a go-ahead to make the short, one of the first things we did was to pull out all of the Dalí and John Hench artwork that had been created in 1946.

The artwork was transported from the Walt Disney Imagineering Art Library in Glendale to our facility in Burbank, which was then known as the Northside Building. It was there that we had a special high-end digital scanning camera that looked very much like an animation down-shooter camera complete with a glass platen that allowed artwork to be pressed completely flat before being scanned. To scan the Dalí/Hench artwork, the platen was actually removed from this camera stand so that the artwork would not be damaged in any way during the scanning process.

The filmmakers wanted to be able to use the original art not only as reference but also as the original story sketches in the reconstruction of the story reels for the film. Scanning and making printed copies of that art was an efficient way to achieve this and allowed us to handle the originals only once. The original artwork was then transported to its new home at the Walt Disney Animation Studios' Animation Research Library for preservation care and proper archival storage.

While we were in the process of scanning all the *Destino* art, we invited many of the animators who were working in the Northside Building at the time to come down and see it. Colleagues from various disciplines made their way to the scanning room throughout the day, and we had laid out many of the paintings and visual development pieces for easy viewing. It was a private exhibition of sorts, which was appreciated since much of the artwork had never been seen by this generation of Disney artists.

The way Disney makes its animated films today is by numbering sequentially all the story sketches so that pinning them up on boards can be done easily and in the correct order. As we started to review the artwork from Dalí, however, the production team realized that the *Destino* story sketches were not numbered, making it very difficult to figure out the correct order in which to hang up the panels. Typically story sketches are pinned up on four-by-eight-foot horizontal boards with story panels in horizontal rows starting at the top in successive order across forming a row. The images are pinned up one next to another from the left side of the board across to the right side; we then drop down and start the next row of images on the left side of the board, continuing to the right and so on until the storyboard is filled. Once a board is completely filled, the next successive panel is started at the top left of the next storyboard and so on.

According to Hench, though, Dalí was not interested in, nor thought it important to have, continuity with one sequence after another in a linear, storytelling fashion. This goes back to the origins of surrealism, which is defined as an "avant-garde movement in art and literature that sought to release the creative potential of the unconscious mind, for example by the irrational juxtaposition of images."[5]

That "irrational juxtaposition of images" was counter to the fundamental continuity component of Disney storytelling. Disney animated films are generally told in a linear way—a great story featuring endearing characters who encounter some conflict or obstacle that the character(s) must overcome and that transforms them; they need to grow or change in some way. All of this takes place in a fantastic world or environment that the audience will enjoy viewing and spending time in.

It was Don Ernst, the producer of *Fantasia/2000*, who figured out the correct sequence of the *Destino* story sketches. Instead of running in succession

Top: *Destino*'s director, Dominique Monfery, and Executive Producer Roy E. Disney review scenes from the film.

Bottom: Dominique and Roy review a scene with Art Director Thierry Fournier at the studio in Paris.

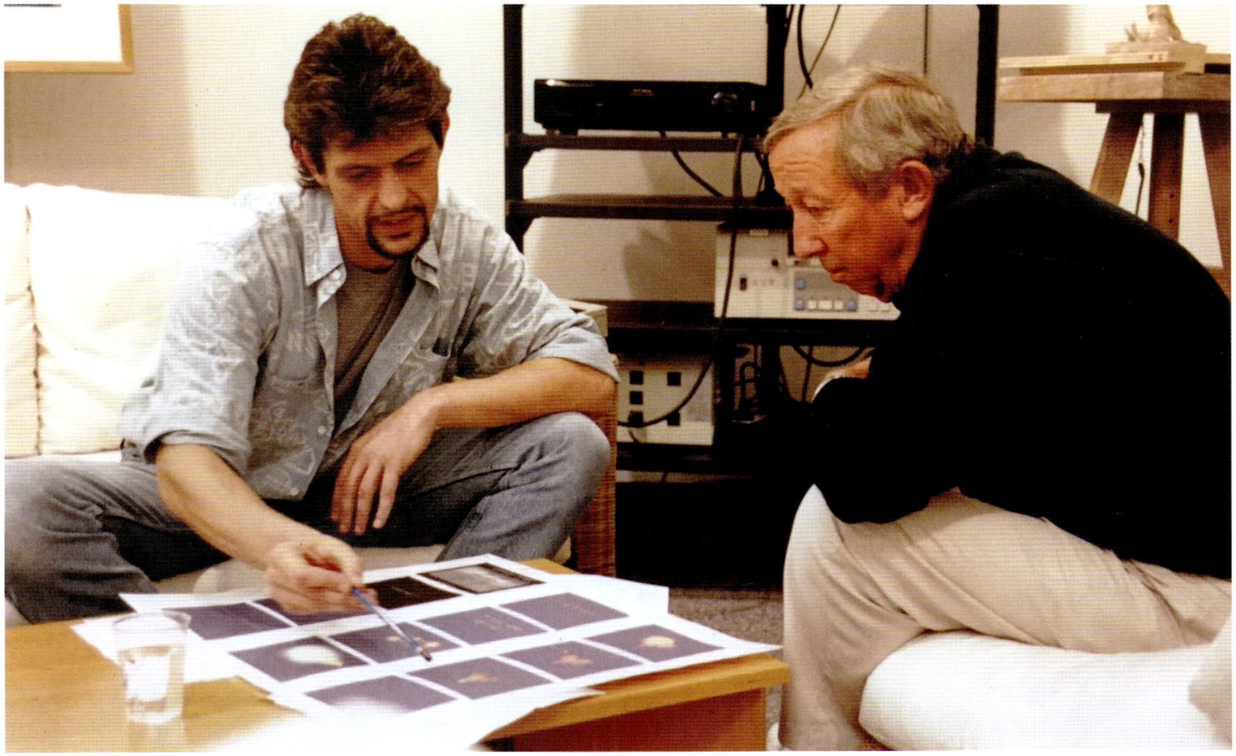

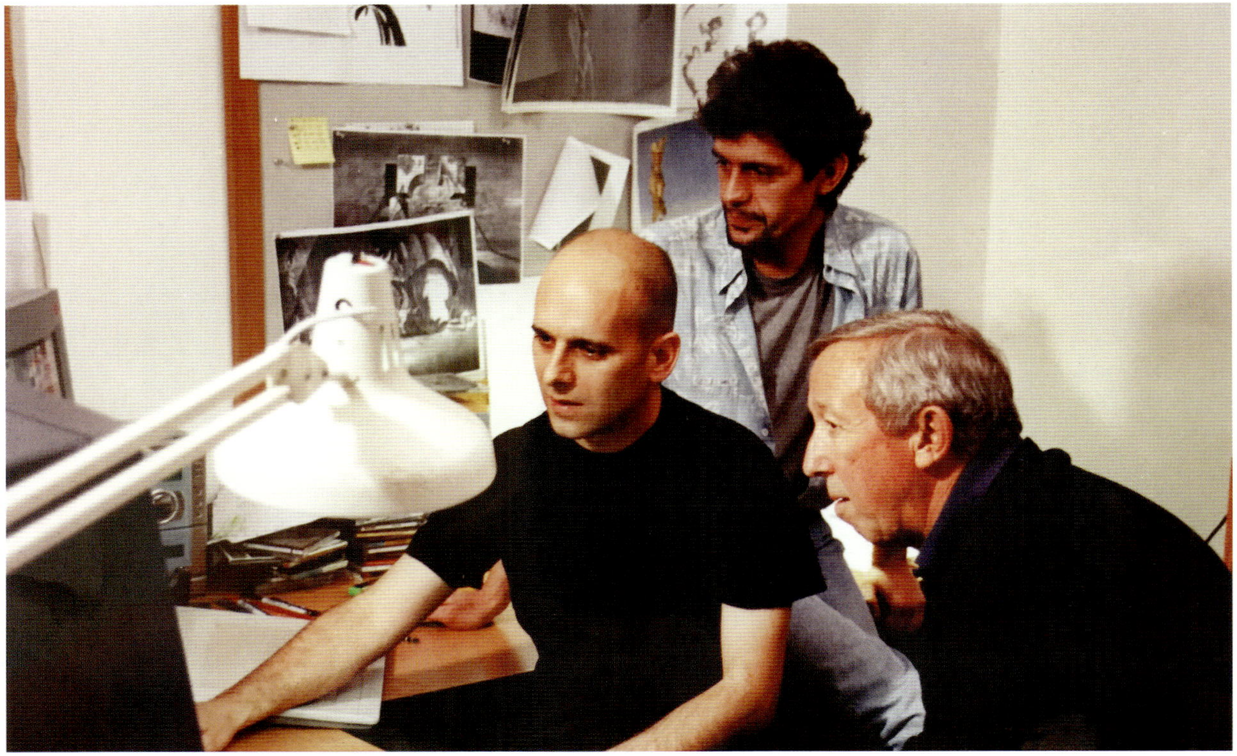

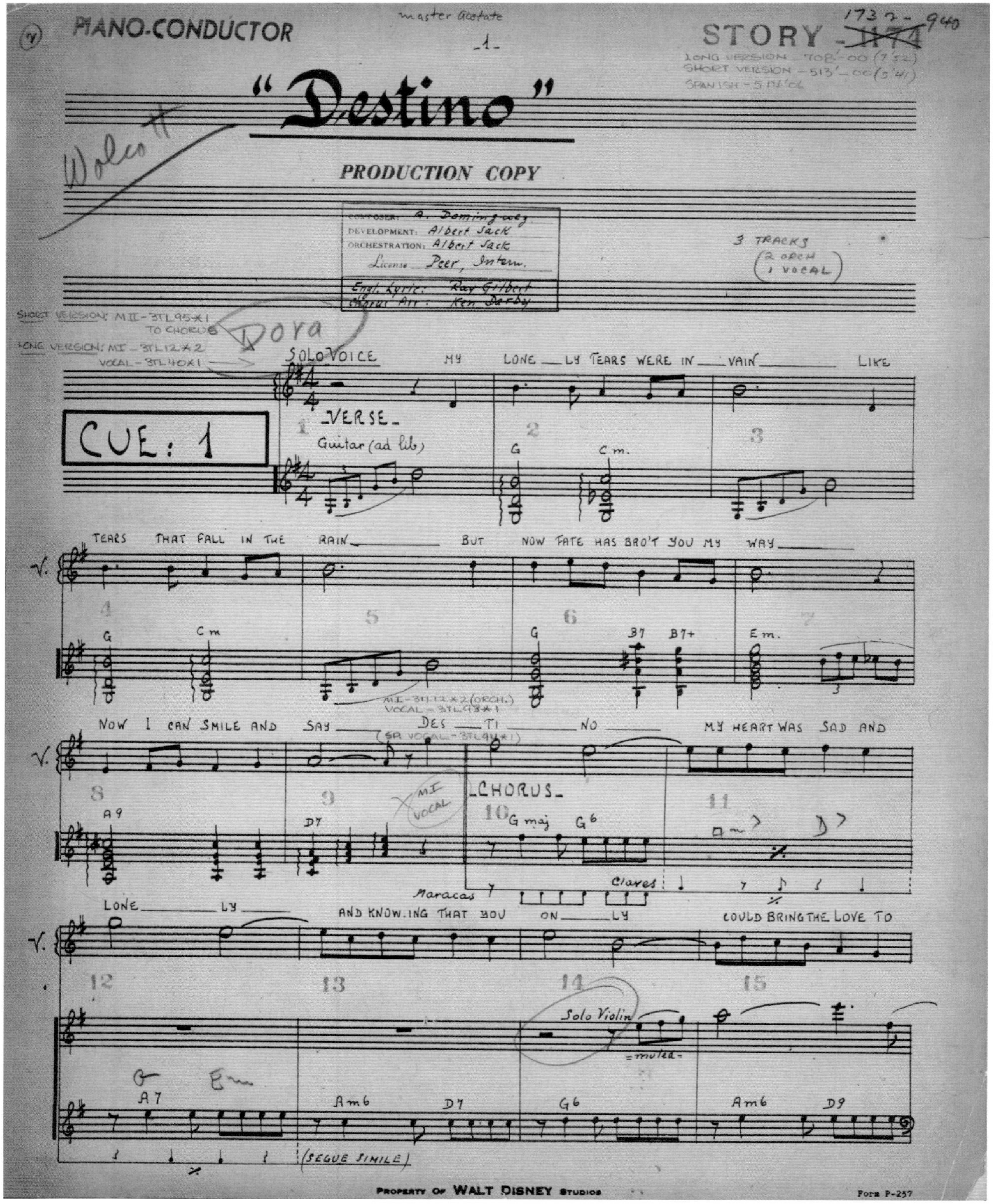

Sheet music from the introduction of *Destino*.

on one storyboard and then going to the next, the *Destino* sketches actually ran horizontally across two storyboards side by side. Once this was verified by John Hench, the original story line fell into place and made sense, or at least as much sense as *Destino* can make.

At the time, Hench was in his nineties, but he was still coming to work every day at Walt Disney Imagineering. In the 1950s, Walt Disney had selected Hench to be one of a number of select artists who helped to start WED Enterprises, which would eventually become known as Walt Disney Imagineering (WDI), the group that would design Disneyland and all the other Disney theme parks. Hench was the expert consultant on *Destino* and came in for reviews and screenings throughout the production process.

Chief Archivist Emeritus Dave Smith brought out all the artwork and photographs of the original storyboards to show to Roy and other members of the *Fantasia*/2000 animation team. Dave had inventoried the *Destino* art in the early seventies and worked with Hench to identify which drawings were his and which were done by Dalí. Once the order of the story sketches was determined, they were then built into a story reel with the original Dora Luz recording of *Destino* as the sound track. It became evident after viewing the story reel that some amount of additional orchestration would be needed for the head titles and the end credits. That new orchestral score for *Destino* was written by Michael Starobin. A needle-drop sound effect was added at the head of the sound track so that the new orchestral music could be properly integrated into the vintage recording. This added a sense of authenticity to the entire recording by seamlessly blending the Starobin score material with the original recording.

Executive Producer Roy E. Disney and Producer Baker Bloodworth then flew to Paris and met with Dominique Monfery about directing the short. Roy explained the project to the prospective director, who was flattered and proud to be offered this assignment. He became very anxious, however, because the film had originated with Salvador Dalí and Walt Disney; it made him quite uneasy, at least initially, to follow in their footsteps heading up the completion of *Destino*.

Monfery was an animator at the Disney Animation Paris Studio, which at the time had been doing sequences for some of the Disney animated pictures in the 1990s, including *The Hunchback of Notre Dame* and *Tarzan*. He was a very talented animator and had the visual sensibilities of a European artist. The choice of a European artist made a lot of sense on many levels, including the ability to get into the head of Dalí, also a European artist, and more fully understand the thought process behind *Destino*.

That may be a stretch, but there is a different cultural sensibility related to art between America and Europe; besides, Disney had a group of artists that were on downtime in Paris!

As noted, Monfery was openly apprehensive about taking on the project—at least initially. He felt that it was too abstract from a story and visual standpoint, and that he was not the right person for

Scene from the *Destino* workbook of Chronos breaking free.

Page 149: Story sketches from the same scene by Dominque Monfrey for the 2003 production of *Destino*.

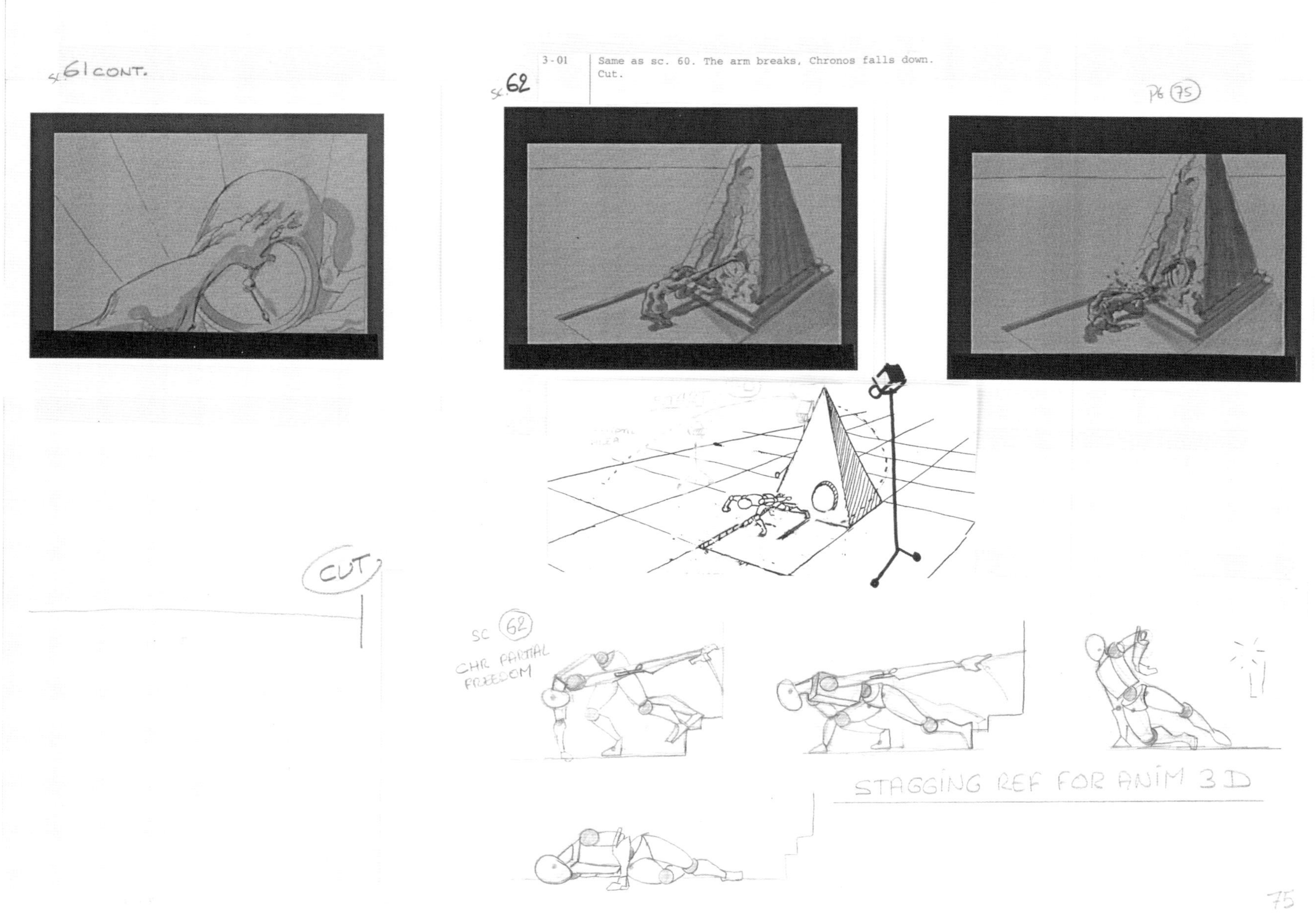

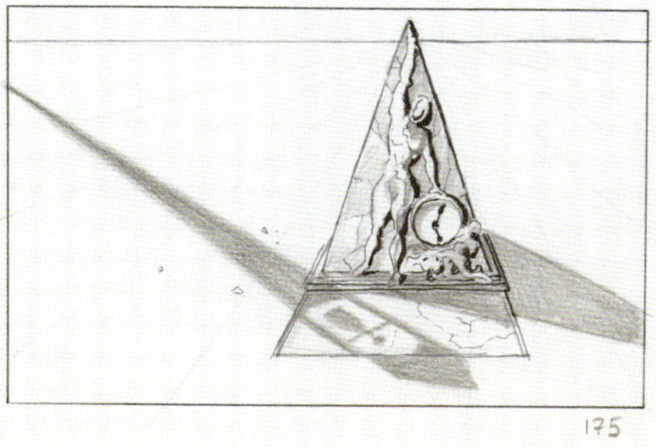
175

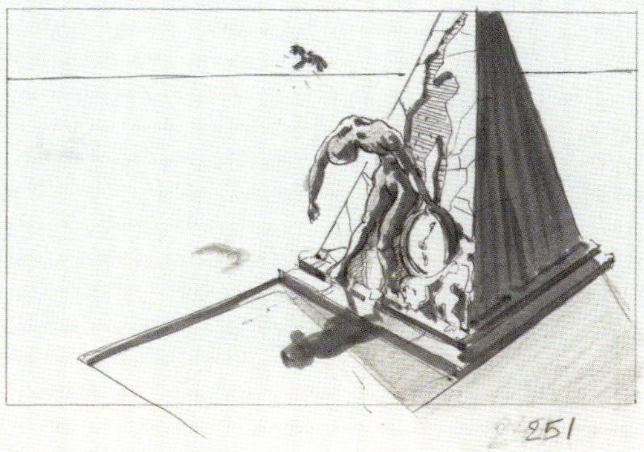
251

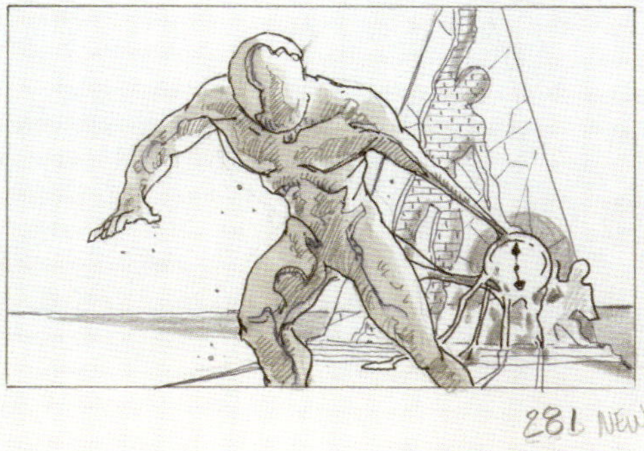
281 NEW

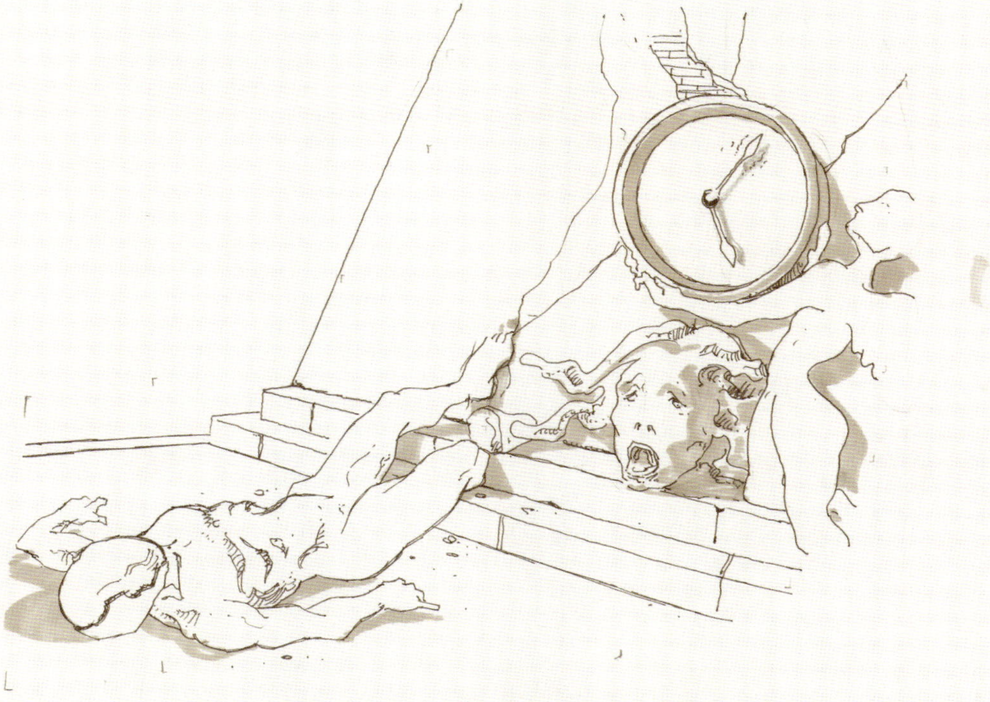
261

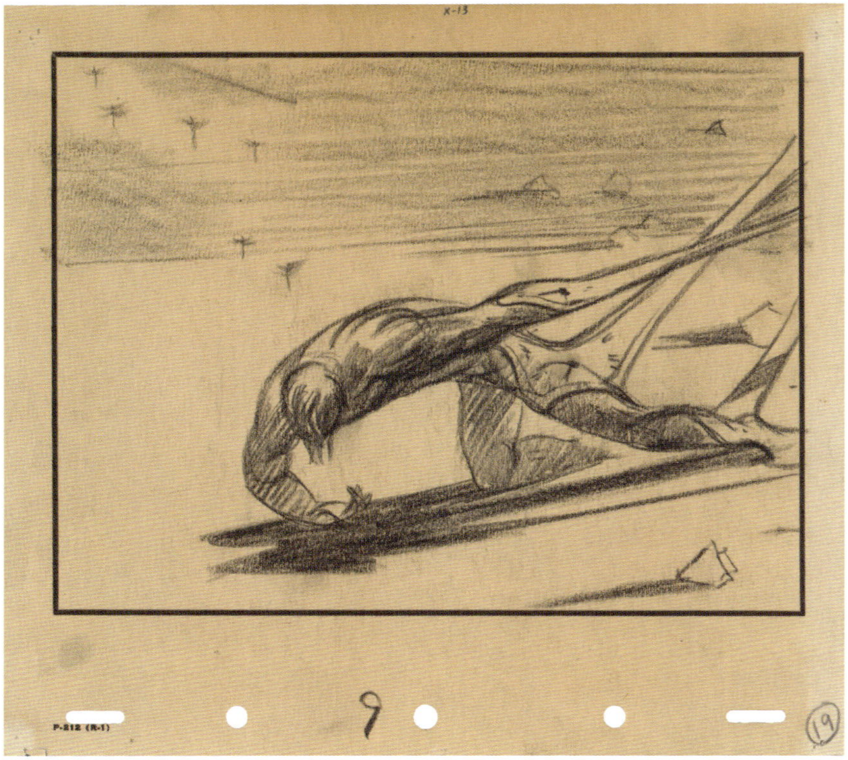
X-13
P-212 (R-1)
9
19

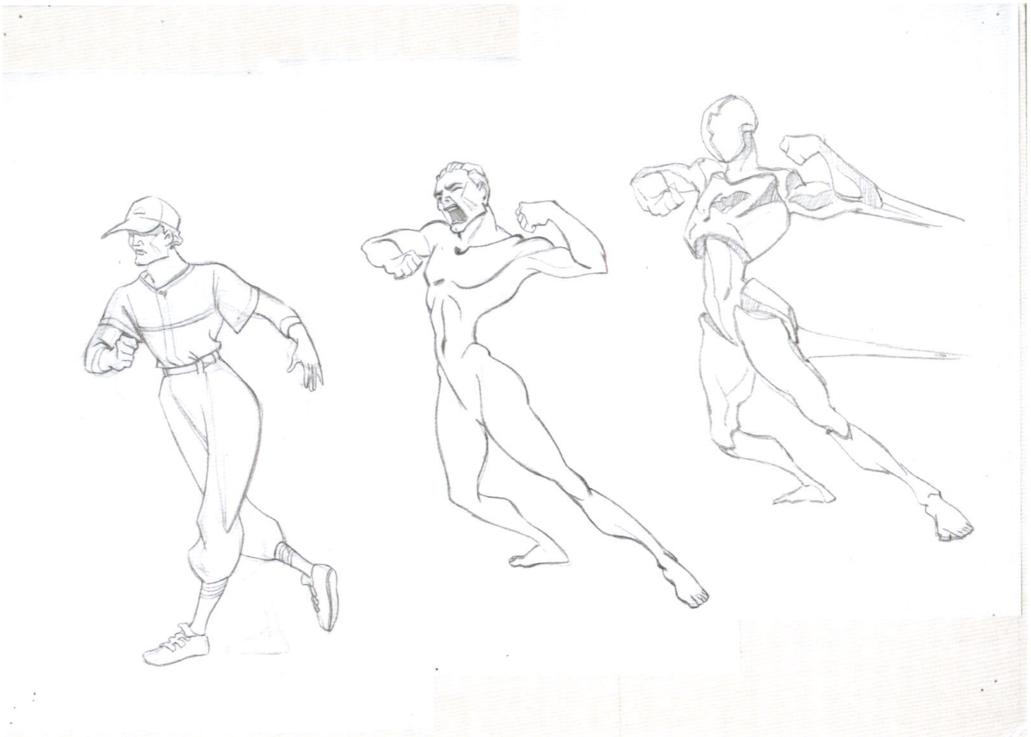

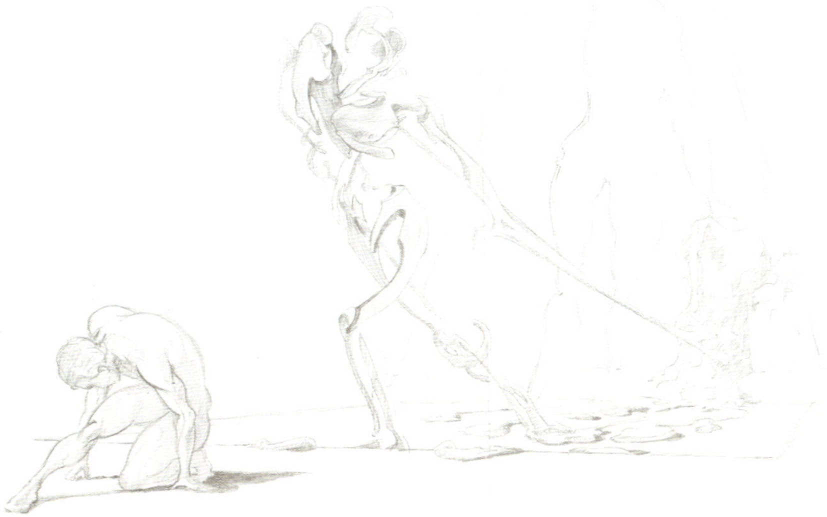

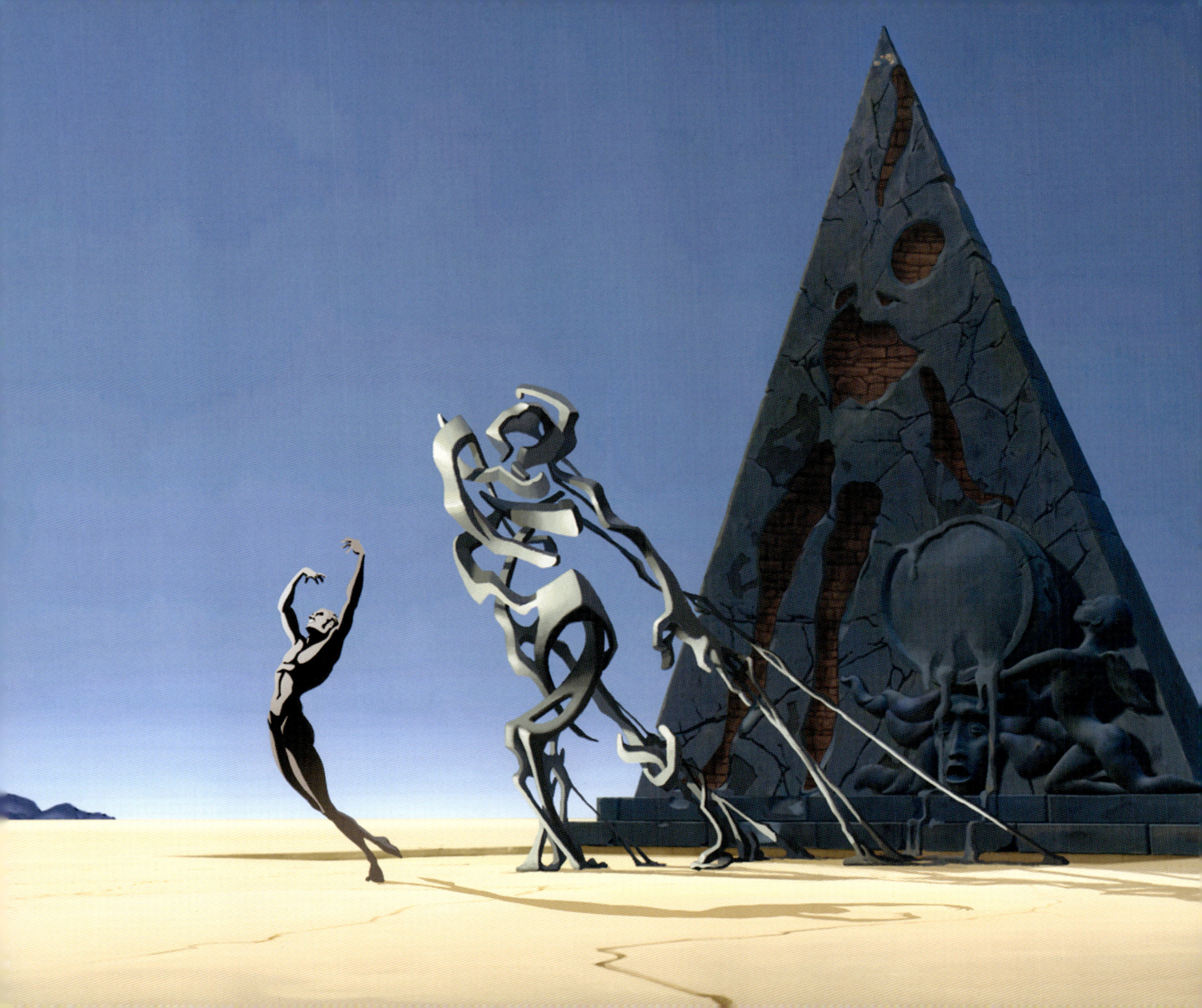

the job. Again, the story was different and certainly out of the comfort zone of any Disney artist, let alone a first-time director. His inclination initially was to respectfully decline the offer to direct the project. However, as he thought about it over a few weeks, he grew more secure with the idea of directing it and realized that the project would be a challenging opportunity.

"I wasn't really familiar with surrealism. This weakness became a strength later on because I could make sure the project became a lot more readable at the narrative level," Monfery recalled. One of the first things the new director did was delve deeply into Dalí and his surrealist paintings. He studied Dalí's artworks to get "inside the artist's head" and to understand, as much as he could about what made Dalí's paintings—well, Dalí-esque.

He studied the way Dalí created and painted light on the characters in his paintings, how there was often a main light, or key light, that generated the shadows—and how within those shadows there was a secondary light or what would be seen as a fill light. Examples of this type of lighting are evident in numerous paintings, including *The Face of War* (1940), *The Great Masturbator* (1929), *Geopoliticus Child Watching the Birth of the New Man* (1943), and other works.

Monfery spent a lot of time exploring the design of the central female character of the film. In the original Dalí/Hench drawings and paintings from 1946, there are a variety of designs of the heroine, verification that they were trying different looks for the woman. Ultimately Monfery came up with a character that represented the essence of what Dalí and Hench were originally developing. The French director was able to merge all those ideas and distill out of the original artwork the final design of the female lead that would be animated in the final version of the film.

Based on this study of Dalí's art and the work created in the development of *Destino* with John Hench, Monfery and art director Thierry Fournier developed a visual style for the film that paid homage to the original intent of the project, but made it so that it could be animated. They wanted to maintain the Dalí look but also wanted to instill the Disney animation style into the project so that it was a creation out of the minds of both these great artists.

To do so, they created the animation characters with no outlines; in other words: self-colored lines. This allowed for sharp contrasts of color to define the character along with the animated movement, which gave a sense of volume to the figures. "The only problem is, how do you make a drawing look like a painting," commented Cleanup Supervisor Jeroen Dejonckheere. "We always had to think, where does the light come from?"

The process involved using a cleanup level of the character and second level that was a "tone matte" or shadow level. Those, coupled with the self-color ink lines, gave the impression that the character was made up of just patches of color and no actual line work. According to Monfery, "So, we are revealing the volume of the characters through their movement by

Page 150 (left): Story sketch by John Hench (1946).

Page 150 (right, top and bottom): Development artwork of Chronos breaking free from time by Dominque Monfrey (2003).

Page 151: Image from the film, *Destino*.

Page 153 (left): Color model showing color separation lines.

Page 153 (right): The corresponding image from the film, *Destino*.

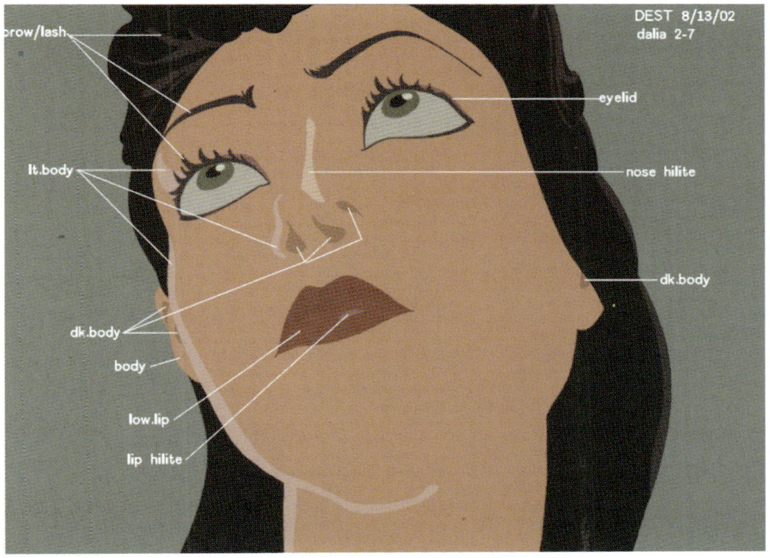

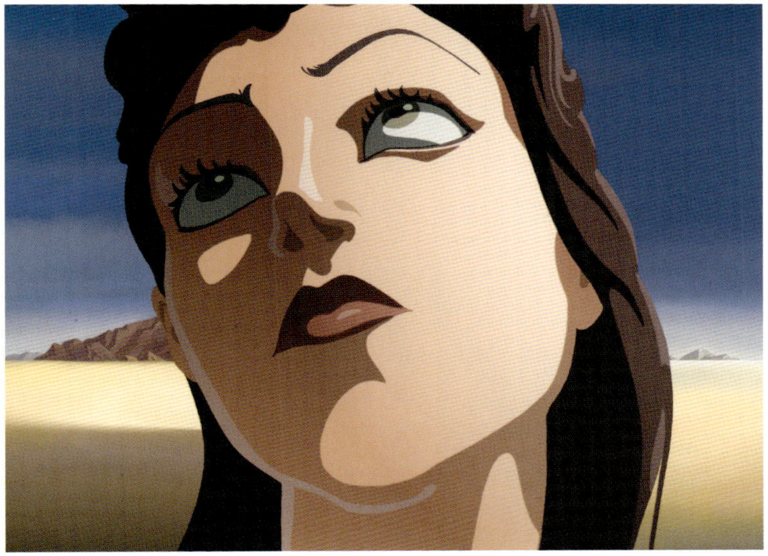

generating a light and a shadow. It was our decision to create these types of images in order to stick to the way Dalí was painting."

The filmmakers stuck with, as closely as possible, the strong, stark elements found throughout Dalí's visual development sketches done in India ink and watercolors, plus the final background paintings done for the project, while bringing in the graceful, elegant movement of the Disney animation style. It was a careful balancing act, though the film is certainly reflective of Salvador Dalí's vision and style for *Destino*.

The production planning started in late 2001 with scheduling, Computer Animation Production System (CAPS) disc space allocation, and the review of the workbook. The workbook is basically the storyboards put together into a book form with about four story panels per page. Space was allotted under each story panel for notations regarding how scenes would be handled in production as well as planning out the overall complexity of the project.

In January 2002, I wrote an e-mail to one of the production managers in Paris explaining the importance of the complexity review early in production:

> I can appreciate that Dominique's time is focused on preparing for the Roy [E. Disney] update, but I do feel that we need to do this review sooner rather than later. It will allow us to have a better handle on the overall scope of the project. We usually do these types of complexity overviews at the very start of a film. These documents are fluid, to some degree, and do get changed and updated as the production progresses. I think if we can get together for an hour on the CLI [command-line interface] we can do a loose pass on rating all the scenes on a 1 to 5 scale[,] as well as an A, B, and C rating. I believe that Dominique, Thierry[,] and I can do this rating pass even if the department heads are not up to speed or [are] unavailable.

It was important enough that our producer Baker Bloodworth was willing to reschedule the update with Roy E. Disney to facilitate the completion of the complexity document. It truly is a road map to understanding the time and resources needed in getting a project done.

Each of the scenes in the film were reviewed by the various animation production departments, including layout, scene planning, background, special effects, animation, cleanup, and digital production, and given a complexity rating. This rating system allowed us to have a better handle on the overall scope of the project so that the project could stay within budget and schedule guidelines. These documents were generally fluid, to some degree, and did get changed and updated as the production progressed.

By February 2002, the production was in full swing with the bulk of the animation being done at the Disney Animation facility in Paris and the postproduction being handled in Burbank. The entire film was color modeled in Disney's proprietary CAPS system between the Paris and Burbank facilities. There was a relatively easy flow of work back and forth from the two studio locations: between overnight package delivery services, videoconferencing, and regular phone calls, the production flow was seamless.

Much of the digital preproduction was also done in Burbank as well with David Mooy doing the CG modeling for the Tower of Babel and the Partygoers segments featured in the film. The models were based on maquettes made by the Paris team, which were referencing some of the original visual-development art. These were built as CG elements within the MAYA software program being used at the time.

The models were designed to be rendered as elements within MAYA as well for the final production. These elements would then be outputted as image files and imported into the CAPS system for final compositing with the hand-drawn animation elements and respective backgrounds.

Film tests were also generated in Burbank to test color as well as the cross-dissolving animation technique. This essentially is a camera technique which allows for an overlap of one image to fade out while another, slightly different image fades in creating a change of location or mood, or, in this use, provides the illusion of motion. Cross-dissolving was originally explored as a way to save money but quickly became the preferred method for the film as this was a technique that was explored during the early production stage with Dalí and Hench.

Coincidentally, while at the Disney Studio, Dalí invented a new cross-dissolve technique. John Hench noted in 1968 that the dissolve was so carefully done that the audience was not aware of it and only became conscious of it when the camera pulled back. At that point it was a "terrible surprise; suddenly you were in a new scene entirely. One thing had become quite another." Dalí's cross-dissolve technique was more complex and subtle than what was eventually used in the final film. The technique employed in

Page 155, top left (clockwise from left): Roy E. Disney is shown meeting with Raphaëlle Preynat (marketing), Dominique Monfery, David Berthier (animation).

Top right: Cent Alantar (layout) at his table.

Bottom left: Dominique Monfery (left) and EFX artist Ivan Kassabov.

Bottom right: Roy E. Disney and Sylvie Bennett-Fauqué, looking at color models of Dahlia.

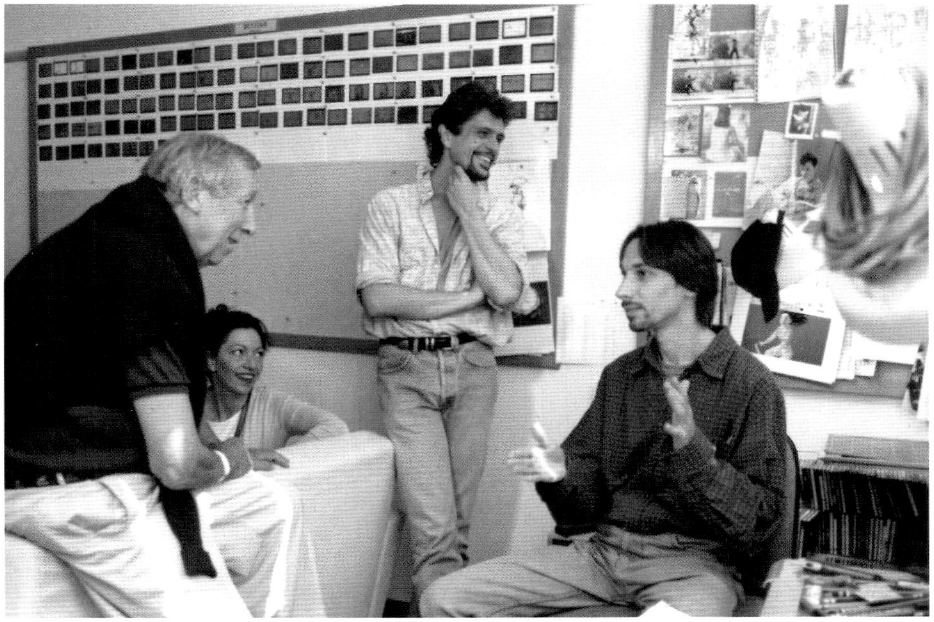

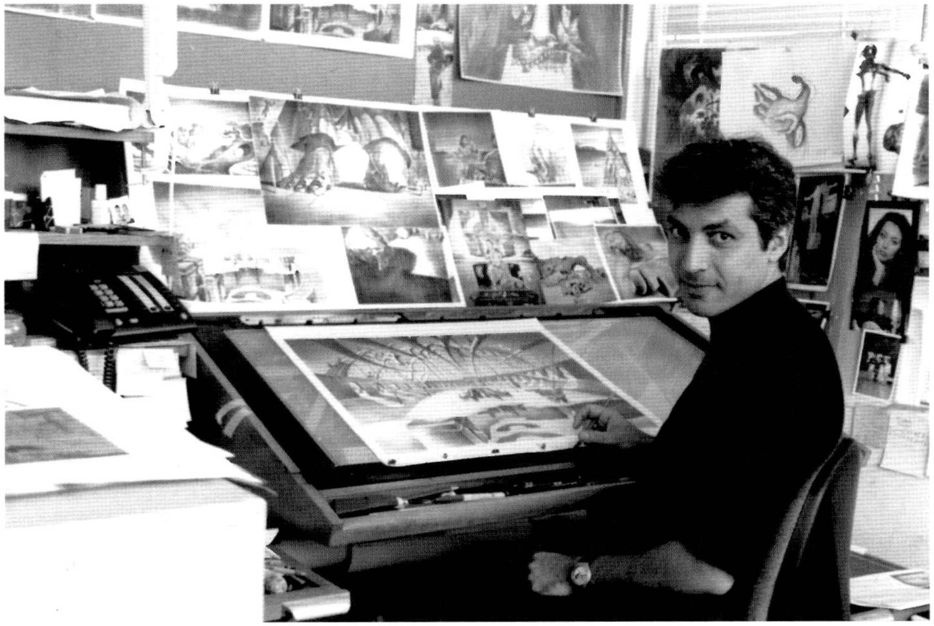

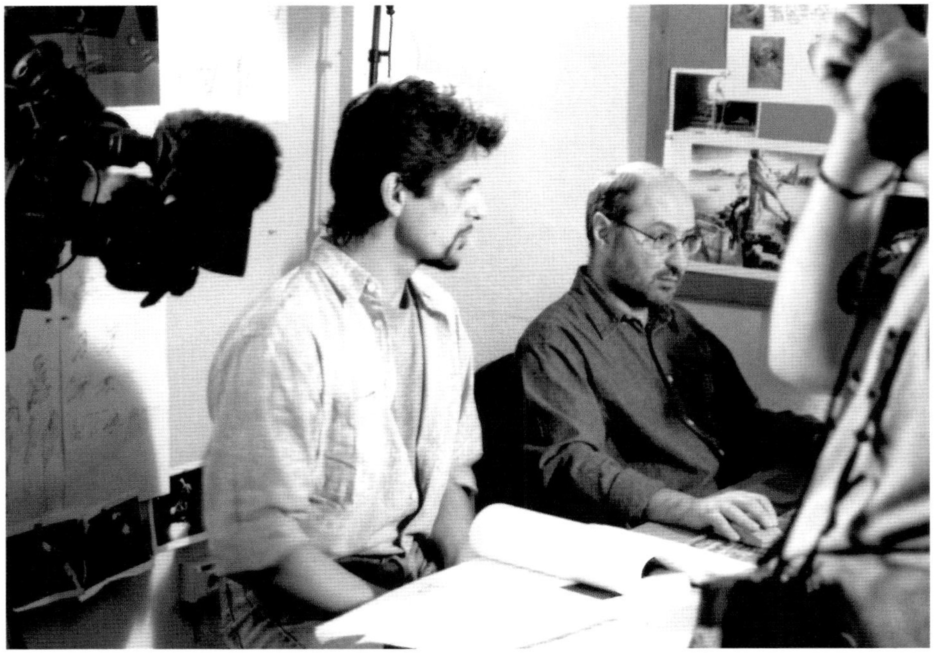

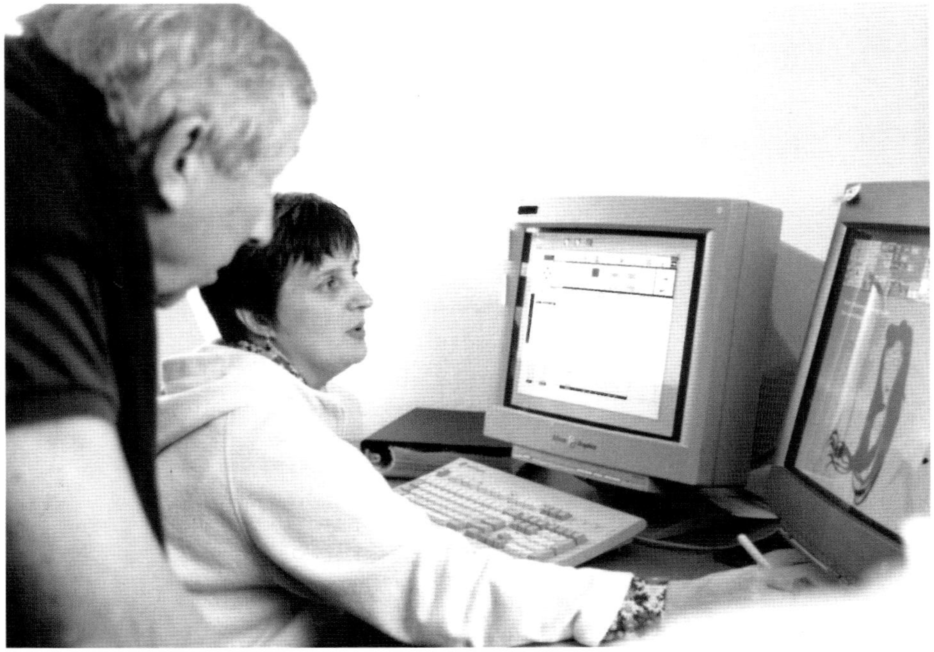

the film was a simpler cross-dissolve that helped to contribute to the dreamlike quality of the animation and enhanced the storytelling.

In late March 2002, the original piece of film that John Hench had shot of the two fate heads coming together was located in the Disney Studio film library. Years earlier the eighteen-second color negative of the animation test had been discovered by Chief Archivist Emeritus Dave Smith. In 1993 a print of that negative had undergone a photochemical restoration, and this would be the element that we would use for the current production.

Although the desolate background with the baseball painted in the middle was still in the archives, the two cels with the fate heads were missing. It is presumed that the two fate heads, which Dalí had painted in oil on cels, were part of the artwork stolen in 1969 but never recovered.

In May 2002 that piece of the Hench *Destino* film test was digitally scanned so that we could separate the individual elements into eight separate levels. Using mattes generated in the Matador software package, we were able to separate the painted heads from the background. The Matador was a popular digital paint application at the time that allowed for the creation of mattes or masks that would either clip out or cover a designated area. It gave us the ability to separate the fate heads off of the stark background in the surviving film test.

An extensive digital restoration was performed once those elements were separated. These levels were cleaned to remove any dust, dirt, cel scratches, cel reflections, and other artifacts that were captured on film when it was first shot on the animation camera in 1946. The movement of the turtle legs and cloth were added to the scene so that it would fit seamlessly into the film. All of these elements—the traditionally drawn animation of the turtle legs and the CG manipulated cloth—came together in the CAPS system.

Roy E. Disney was involved throughout the entire production and was reviewing the progress every step of the way, even when he was traveling. In early April, he wrote:

> Believe it or not, the fedex [sic] package arrived today. It is a holiday here, but I guess not for them . . .anyway, I got the tape, and have only a very few thoughts:
>
> 1. I think it all looks terrific, very stylish (and I agree with the simplifications that were done) and in the few instances when we saw everything composited, very Dalí-esque, I think.
>
> 2. Of course it's pretty hard to get a sense of the real colors from the video, but if I had to make a comment, it would be that maybe things are a little less bright than I would prefer. In Dalí's material[,] the colors are pretty basic and strong—out of the can, not very subtle. There are also a lot of fussy details here and there, but the big flat planes of color, at first glance, make everything look very "designy," so I would tell Dominique [Monfery] not to be afraid of brightness.
>
> 3. The characters looked wonderful to me, and the nice thing is that I felt

Page 157: Image from the final film, *Destino*, incorporating Salvador Dalí's background painting on page 117.

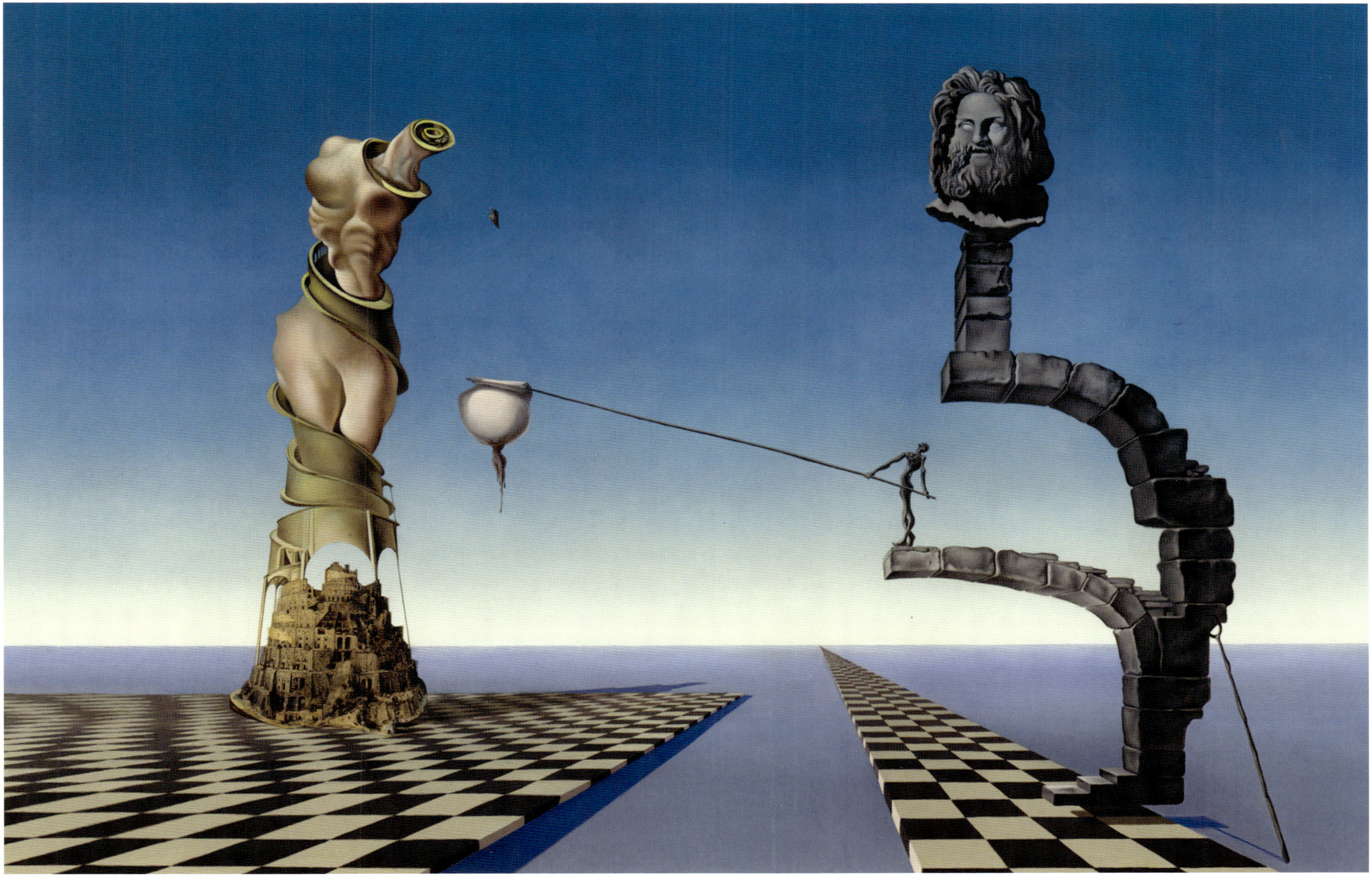

they would look very organic with the backgrounds, not pasted on at all . . .

4. The one item I questioned in the color sketches was the string of phones (the ones she falls onto from the tower) being painted white. Were they not black phones in the story boards [sic]? Black phones were far and away the most common in the [']40s[;] I'm not sure they'd even invented white ones yet . . . and anyway, black, to me, is more menacing, or subversive, more Dalí-esque. The other ones, in the "time tunnel" (or whatever it is) near the end, are okay, I think . . . as the meaning is a bit different.

So that's all I have. Looking great! I'm off line [sic] now until early next week, but Monica [Elsbury, Roy's assistant] can reach me if there's something desperate . . .

Best, Roy

The production continued on schedule throughout the summer and fall of 2002. The usual types of technical issues would crop up, such as large file sizes, which were difficult at that time to transfer back and forth easily between Paris and Burbank. There were not enough computers at the Paris studio to accommodate the production, so four additional Octane computers were leased for a period of time to help alleviate the impact on production and allow for the project to stay on schedule. By today's standards, the file sizes of *Destino* may not be an issue, but in the early 2000s it was a constant concern in managing data properly.

Each scene in the film had to progress through a series of departments as in a regular full-length feature production. Once the animation and special effects were completed, the scene would go through animation check. This is where each frame of the scene is checked and set up as it would be in the final color frame. This was done to see if there were any technical issues such as registration mistakes or misalignment of drawing or other elements.

We would be reviewing the film weekly and looking at completed scenes in film on a daily basis. Roy was at some of those sessions if he was in town. If not we sent him a tape or DVD to review, and he would send notes regularly.

"Are we still going to add some in-betweens on the girl's cross-dissolve to the guy who dissolves? This is still herky jerky [sic] to me," Roy wrote in March 2003 while work on *Destino* was proceeding. "I've looked at it again and it still seems jerky. Is it just me? Nobody else seems to be bothered . . . if I'm alone in this, let's just let it go as is."

Once through animation check, the scene would move to the Color Model Department. This is where key frames from the scene would have color added to determine how the entire scene would have each cel painted. This step involved the color model stylist and the art director working together to get the look just right, and then the director would have the final approval.

From color models, the scene went into the digital Ink and Paint Department where, following the color callouts from the Color Model

From left to right: *Destino* producer Baker Bloodworth, Executive Producer Roy E. Disney, and Director Dominique Monfery.

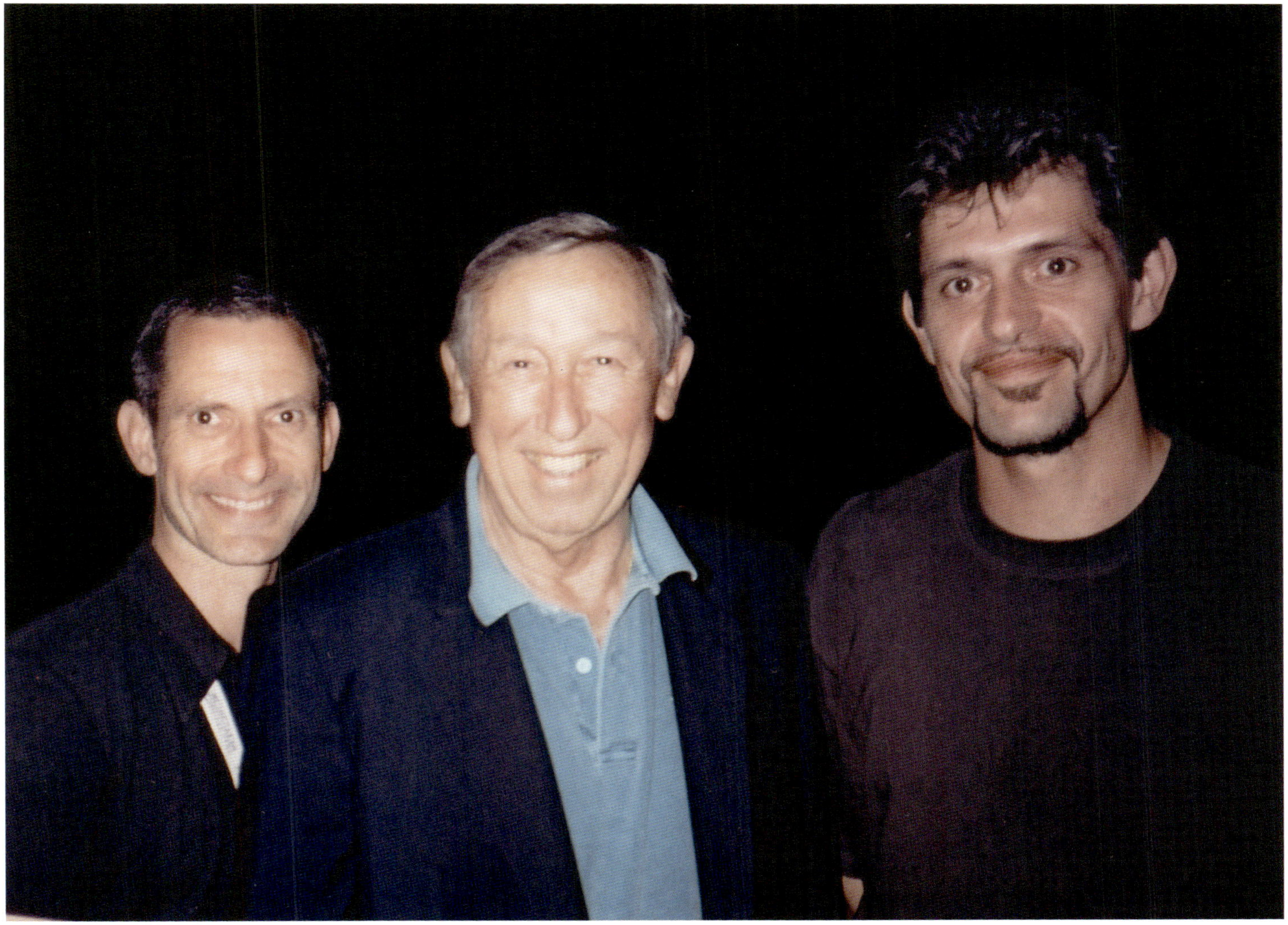

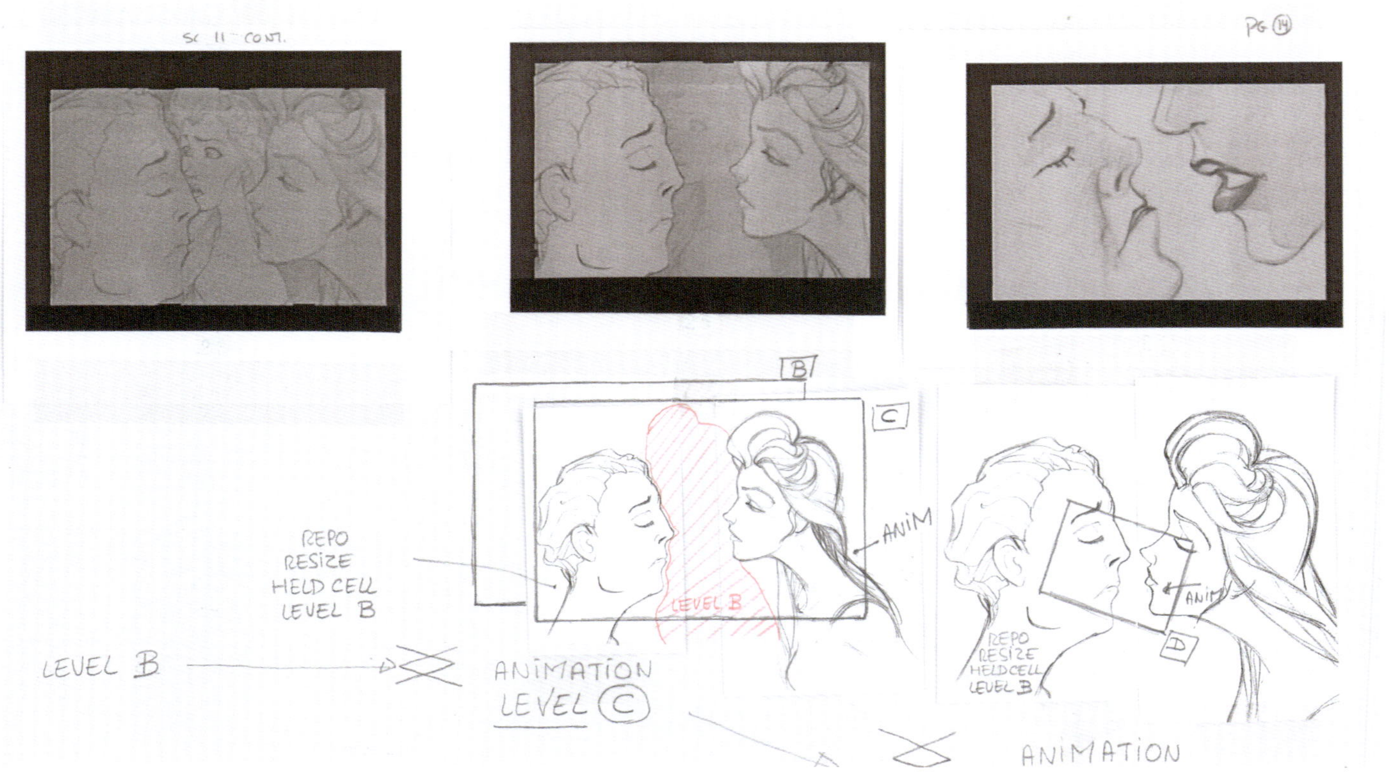

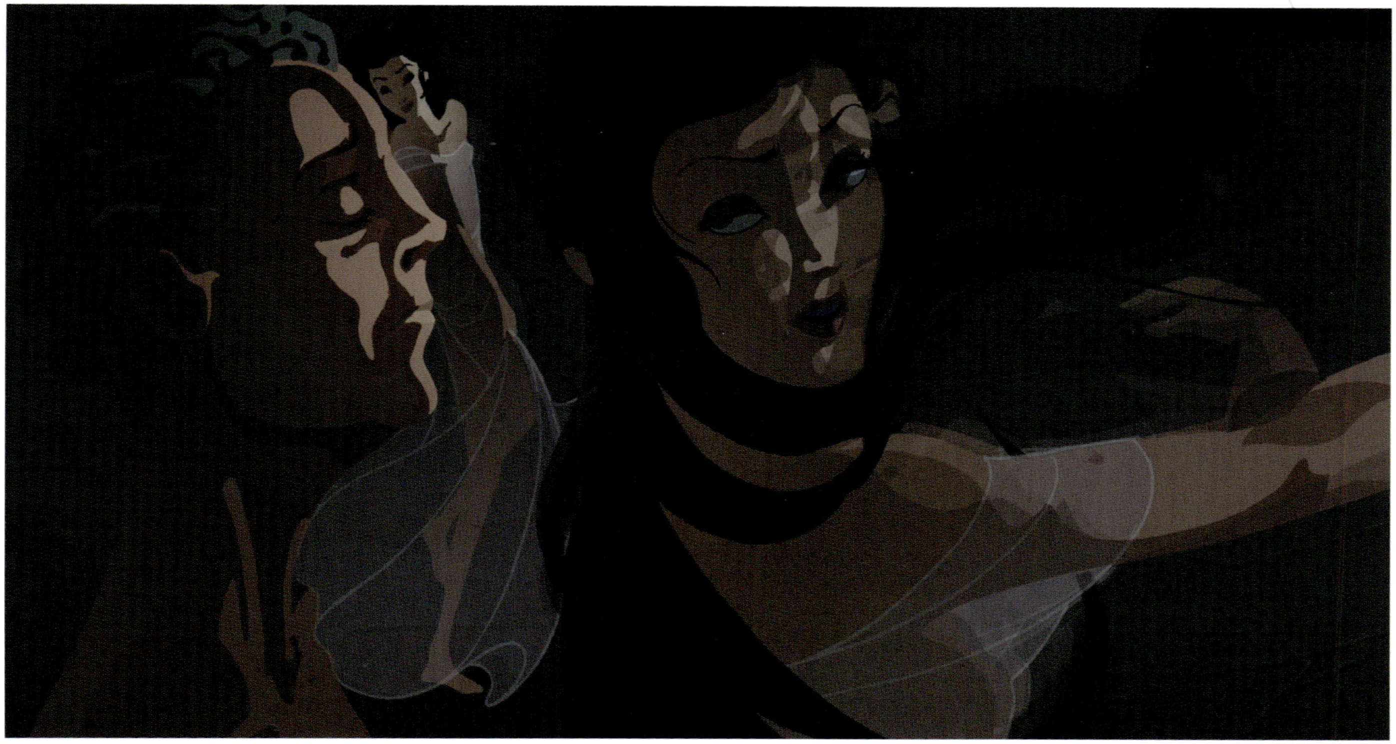

Top: A page from the *Destino* workbook.

Bottom: Film image from sequence 2, scene 11 of *Destino*.

Page 161: Story sketches by Dominique Monfery from the 2003 production of *Destino*.

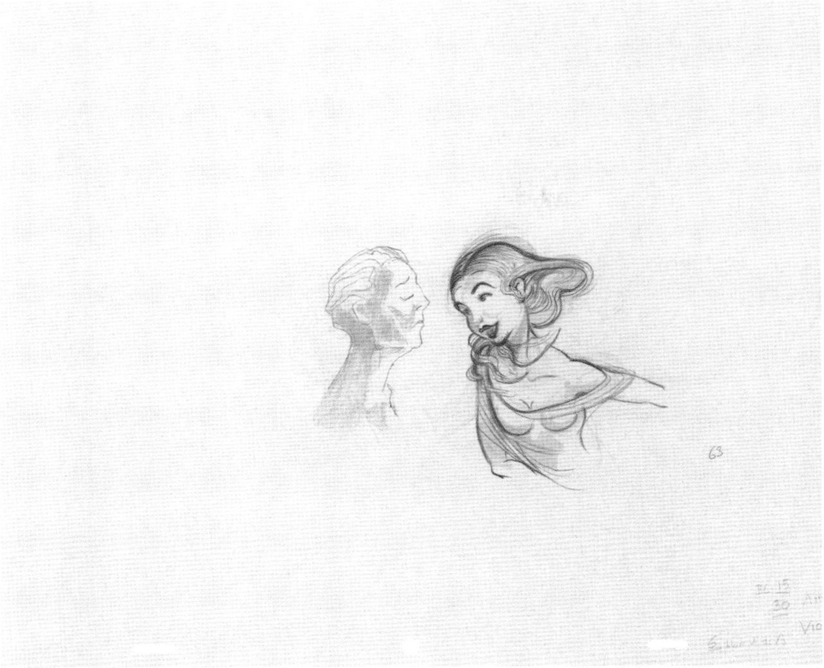

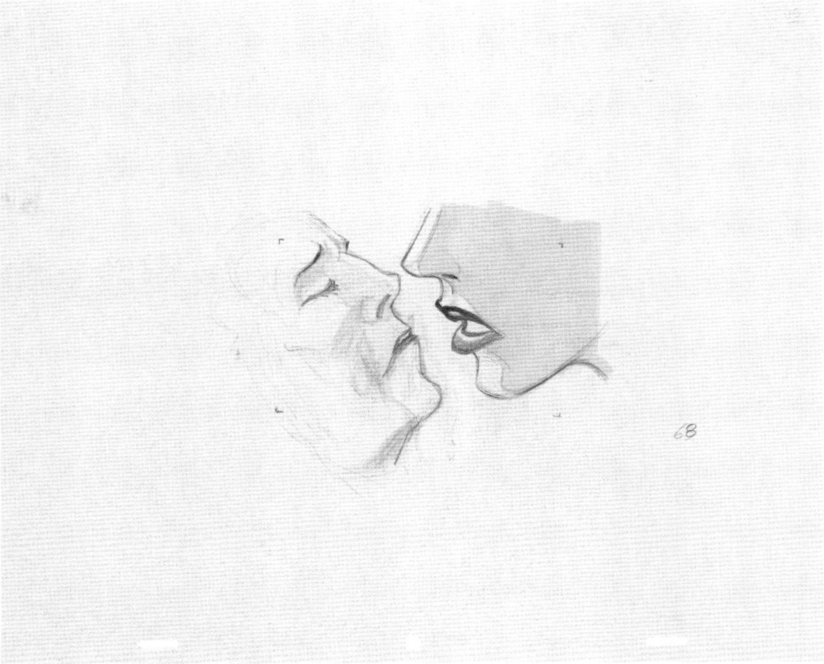

Department, every individual drawing or cel was painted. This was usually achieved rapidly by parceling out the scene to a group of painters and then reassembling it when all the cels were painted.

Final color shots were starting to be outputted to film beginning in September 2002; that continued into early 2003. These color shots would be reviewed in what have long been called "sweatbox" sessions. The name derives from the early days at the studio when a bunch of people were crammed in a small screening room to review film tests. (Such screenings continue today but are in nicely appointed, air-conditioned theaters or editorial suits.)

During these sweatbox sessions the filmmaking team would review each shot and either issue a note to fix something or approve it to DCI (daily cut in), meaning that the shot was a final color-approved scene and it was completed. A typical note might read: "DEST 2.0/11 Test ID #12—there may be some flickering in this scene around 4-10. Dave Bossert will check it in CAPS in the morning."

In early 2003, we started designing the titles for the film. The actual font for the word "Destino" was designed by the studio's marketing department. They created the look based on design elements found within Dalí's own handwriting style. That "Destino" logo actually now appears at the end of the film before the film credits start.

At the head of the film a card was added in English and French. The choice of French was a nod to the animation team in France, and because the surrealism art movement was founded in Paris. The card simply reads:

In 1946, two legendary artists began collaboration on a short film.
More than half a century later, their creation has finally been completed.

En 1946, deux artists légendaires ont commencérent a collaborere sur un court-métrage. Plus d'un demi slècle après, leur création a finalment été achevée.

IN 1946, TWO LEGENDARY ARTISTS BEGAN COLLABORATION ON A SHORT FILM. MORE THAN HALF A CENTURY LATER, THEIR CREATION HAS FINALLY BEEN COMPLETED.

EN 1946, DEUX ARTISTS LÉGENDAIRES ONT COMMENCÉRENT A COLLABORERE SUR UN COURT-MÉTRAGE. PLUS D'UN DEMI SIÈCLE APRÈS, LEUR CRÉATION A FINALMENT ÉTÉ ACHEVÉE.

We also wanted to have Walt Disney's and Salvador Dalí's names represented in the titles and opted to use their actual signatures. In the case of Walt, we used his full name, Walter Elias Disney, which was scanned from an early company stock certificate. Dalí's signature was scanned off the contract that he signed with Disney for the project. Both signatures would animate on the screen as if being written on with a pen.

By March 2003 we were in the process of building the credits for the film and were pushing to get it all completed so that the film could be screened at Annecy, the big annual animation festival held every June in France. The credits are almost always difficult, as invariably someone gets left out, a name is misspelled, someone complains about their placement, or for several other reasons too numerous to list.

And, as it turned out, there were two versions for the film initially: a long and short credit version. Even that would prove to be a bone of contention years later when there was some confusion about which version of the film was to be shown at a museum screening.

The final high-resolution images were then outputted by the digital film recorders to film in the Camera Department located on the lower level of the Walt Disney Animation Studios Building in Burbank. The images were shot to 35mm Kodak EK film, which was the standard practice at the time.

The film with the long version of the credits was then sent to the Annecy International Animation Film Festival in June 2003. Ultimately the official version of the film had the short version of the credits, and that is what was released on DVD/Blu-ray and shown in museums around the world in associated exhibitions.

"Though *everything* was conspiring against us in getting the image to the paper and in getting a print of *Destino* to Annecy, I am happy to say that even with multiple French strikes and technical difficulties, we have the goods," wrote producer Baker Bloodworth the morning of the *Destino* premiere. "Thanks for all your help this weekend. The press is *very* excited about the surprise news that *Destino* will [be] screened tonight at the opening." Bloodworth's note alluded to us going down to the wire to get the movie completed and outputted to film—and getting a copy to him in France. It was a nail-biter!

Director Dominique Monfery sent an e-mail from Annecy, France, on the evening of Monday, June 2, 2003, to the entire *Destino* production team describing the premiere of the film:

> Roy is very warmly welcomed on stage and introduces *Destino*. He briefly explains how and why this project came about. The lights dim . . . music starts . . . two names appear on screen [sic]. . . you know what happens next. Throughout the piece the auditorium is silent, even during the part with the ants and baseball player no one speaks. The title appears and the audience (about 1,000 people) applauds during the entire length of the credits (the applause are [sic] so loud I cannot hear the music). What else to say? You, we, they can all be proud. CONGRATULATIONS.

That was the first public presentation of the completed film and the beginning of a whirlwind of festival screenings.

It was wonderful to get the film out into the festival circuit for audiences to enjoy, but it was even more thrilling when the film started to win awards. In 2003 *Destino* won Best Animated Short at the Rhode Island International Film Festival; the Jury Award of Merit at the Palm Springs International ShortFest; the Grand Prix at the Melbourne International Film Festival; and a Certificate of Merit at the Chicago International Film Festival. The film also was a special selection at the 2003 Venice Film Festival, 2003 Telluride International Film Festival, 2003 New York Film Festival, 2003 Montreal International Festival of New Cinema, 2003 AFI Los Angeles International Film Festival, and 2004 Sundance International Film Festival.[6]

Screenings of *Destino* at this time were not only reserved for film festivals. It was also screened at the

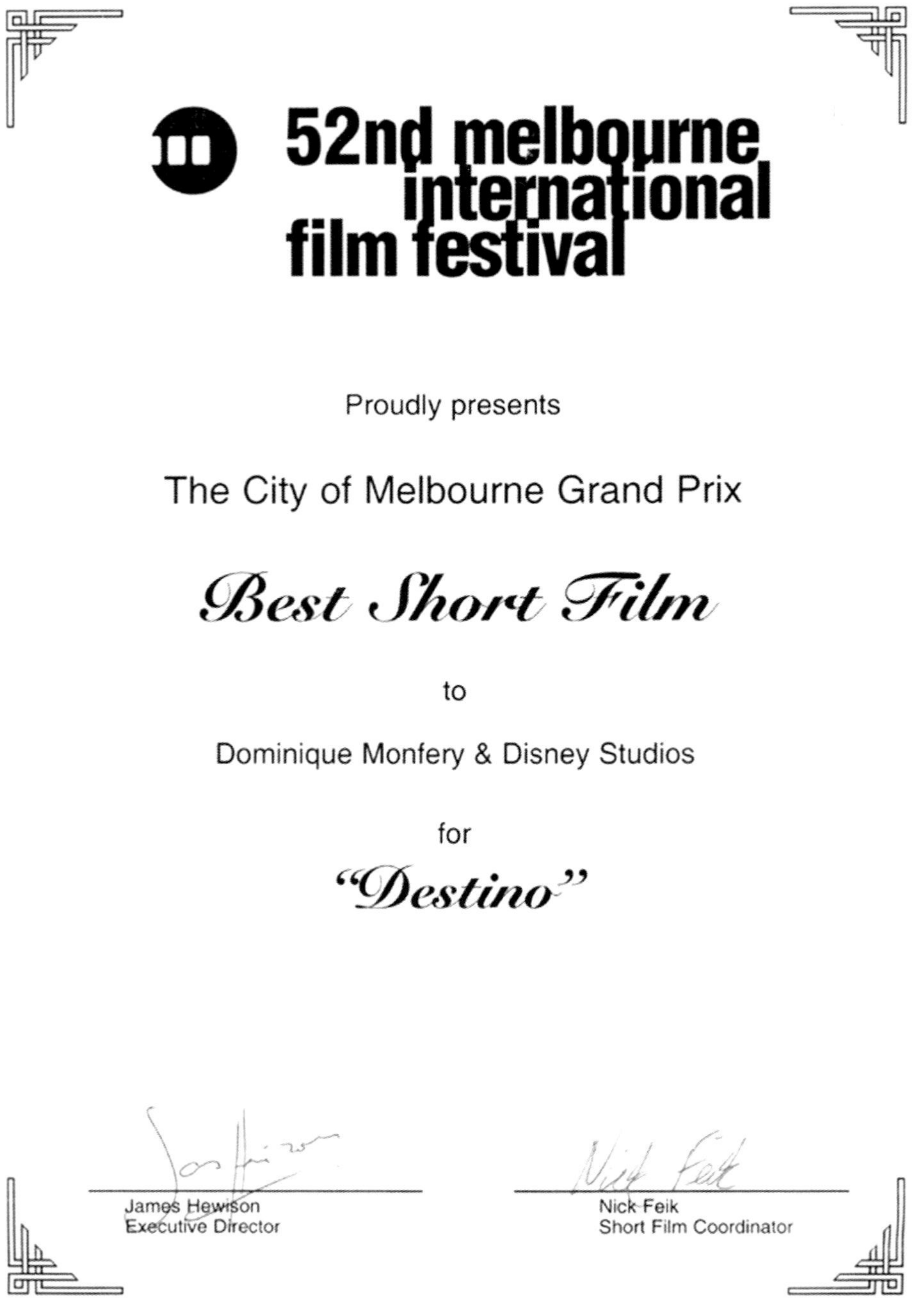
52nd melbourne international film festival

Proudly presents

The City of Melbourne Grand Prix

Best Short Film

to

Dominique Monfery & Disney Studios

for

"Destino"

James Hewison
Executive Director

Nick Feik
Short Film Coordinator

Page 164: *Destino*, which was selected from 922 entries and eighty-eight finalists, won Best Short Film at the Melbourne (Australia) International Film Festival in 2003. Courtesy Dave Bossert.

Certificate of Nomination for Best Animated Short Film by the Motion Picture Academy of Arts and Sciences. Courtesy of Dave Bossert.

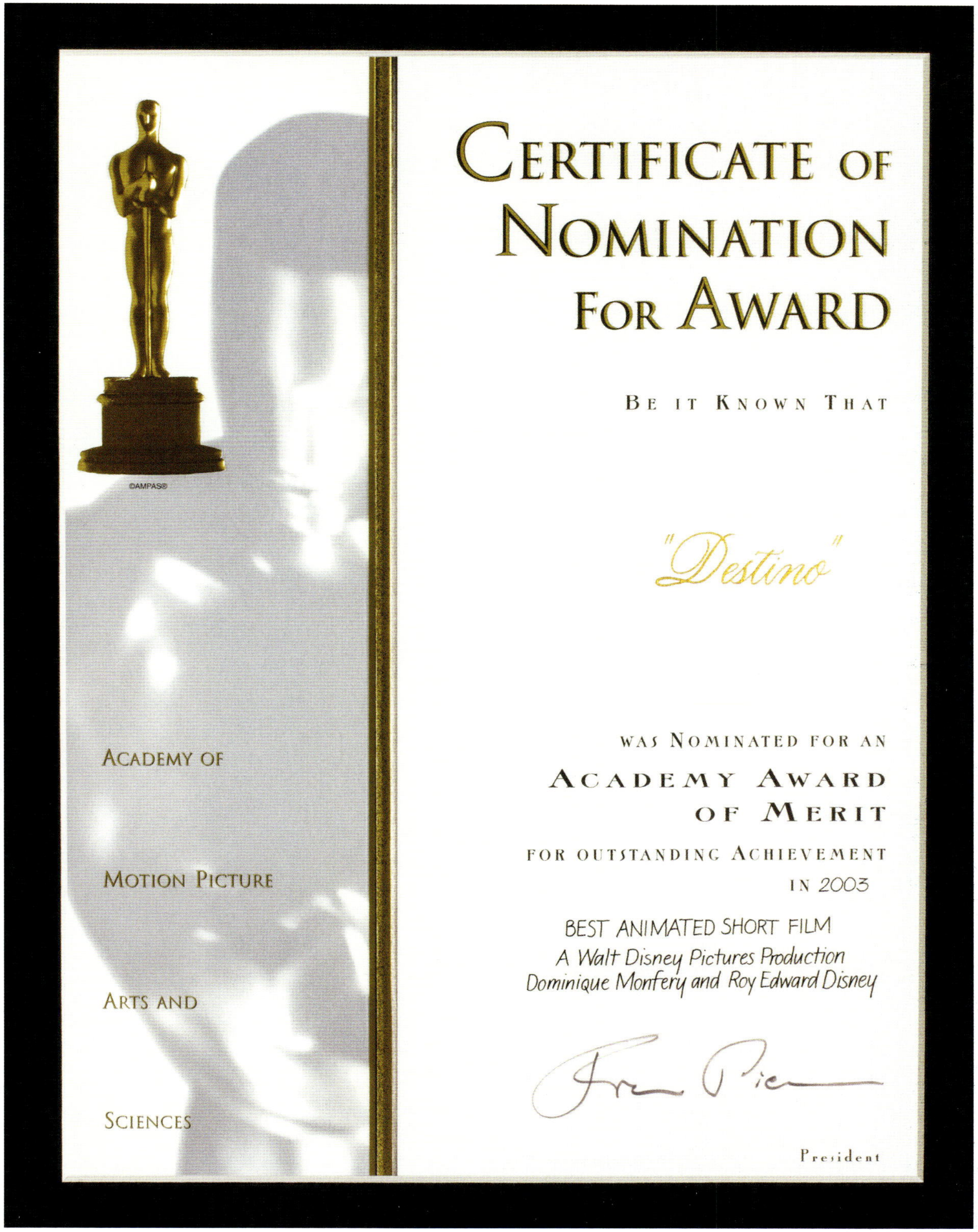

grand opening of the Dalí-2004 Mass Media and Culture Exhibition in Barcelona, Spain, on February 5, 2004. Sadly, however, that same day we learned that John Hench had passed away. John, then ninety-five, had still been coming to work at his Walt Disney Imagineering office. He died from complications he suffered from a simple fall outside his office two weeks prior to his passing.

"[Hench] has been such a tremendous source of inspiration for this project, it is somewhat beautiful that at ninety-five years old, he should die on the day that we celebrate the art of the film in the homeland of Dalí," stated Bloodworth in an e-mail.

We were all so glad that we had been able to screen the completed film for Hench in the theater at the Animation Building. He was thrilled with how it had turned out and felt that we had captured the essence of what he and Dalí had worked on between 1946 and 1948.

In early 2004, *Destino* won a Special Citation at the Los Angeles Film Critics Association Awards. This was followed by a nomination for an Annie Award, which is an animation award given out annually by the International Animated Film Society, ASIFA- Hollywood. And then the ultimate nod came when *Destino* was nominated for an Academy Awards Oscar by the Motion Picture Academy of Arts and Sciences.[7]

We were overjoyed. Roy E. Disney and Dominique Monfery were the two nominees designated for the award. Roy was immensely proud of the fact that we completed the film started by his uncle Walt. It was something that was very important to him in chronicling and documenting his family's business. The fact that it was also nominated for the most prestigious film award in the world was the icing on the cake.

The Seventy-Sixth Annual Academy Awards show was on February 29, 2004. Arrangements were made for Roy and Patty (his wife); one of the film's producers, Baker Bloodworth; Dominique Monfery, the director; and my wife, Nancy, and me for a car to take us to the live ceremony, which was being aired worldwide.

We all met at Roy and Patty's house in Toluca Lake (just outside Los Angeles). From there we headed in a limo together to Tinseltown, specifically Hollywood and Highland, the location of the then-named Kodak Theatre, where the Academy Awards ceremeny was being held (and where we would exit the limousine to walk the famed red carpet).

In the weeks leading up to the awards ceremony, I had put together ten matted images of the two fate heads coming together from the film along with a copy of the additional orchestration sheet music for *Destino* signed by Michael Starobin. I brought those to Roy and Patty's home that evening for Roy, Dominique, Baker, and me to sign. We each kept one for ourselves. The others were given out as gifts to a select group, including one to Ed Nowak. The matted images were accompanied with a gift note.

The left side of the set is the top sheet from the new orchestral score for *Destino* written and signed by the composer, Michael Starobin.

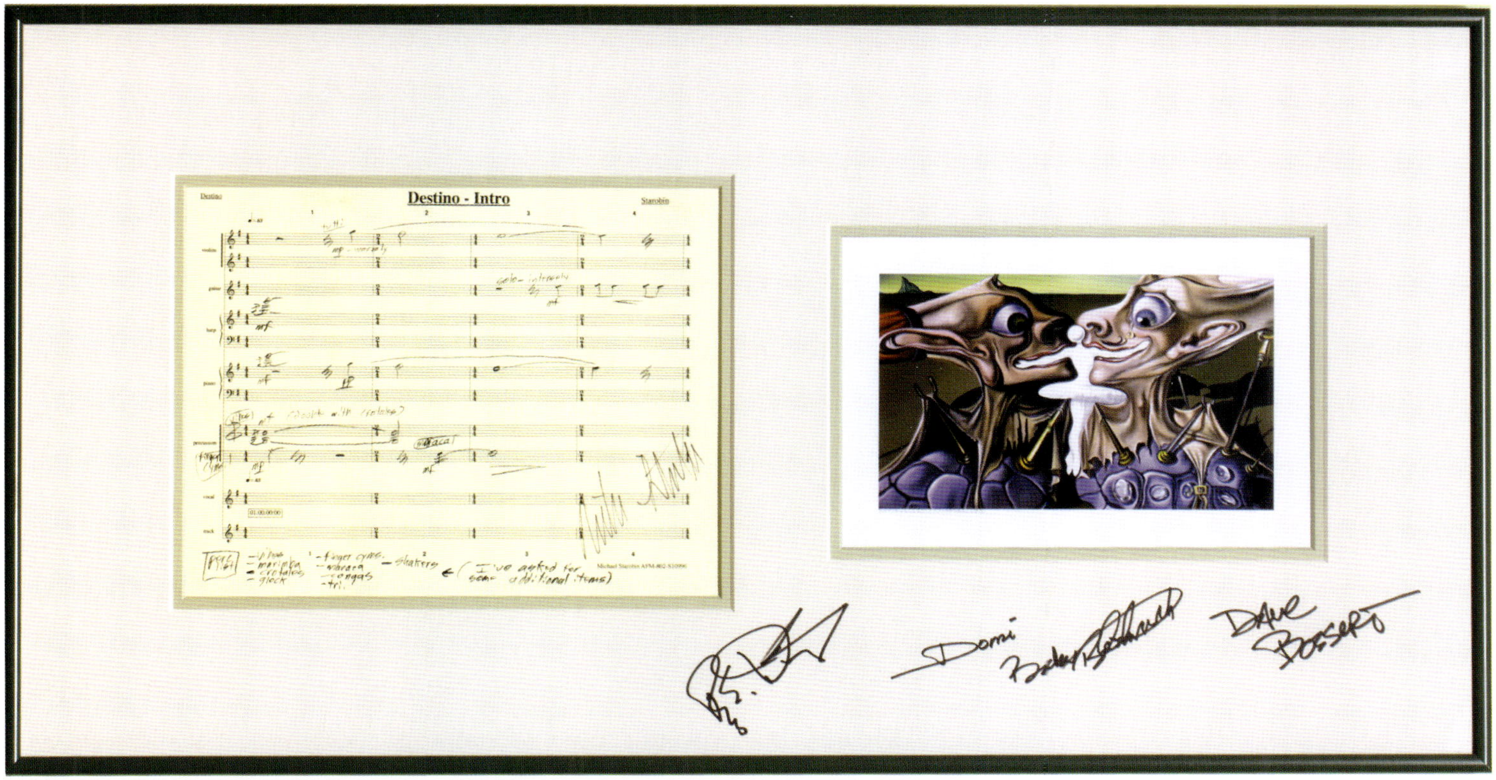

Commemorative set with a fine art reproduction print of the score and a final film image from *Destino*, created February 26, 2004. This set is No. 4 of an edition of 10 framed prints, and hangs in the author's office.

The right side of the set is an iris print of a final frame from *Destino*. This particular frame includes an original Dalí background combined with overlays from an original film test done in 1946.

Since Roy and Dominique were the nominees, they would be seated in the orchestra section of the Kodak Theatre with their respective guests throughout the ceremony. Nancy and I would be in the first balcony area looking down on them. When we parted ways as we entered the theater, we had all agreed to meet up in the main lobby at the end of the show regardless of the outcome. That way we would figure out what the rest of the evening's plans would be.

At that year's Academy Awards show, there were five films nominated in the Best Animated Short category: *Destino*, *Bounding*, *Gone Nutty*, *Nibbles*, and *Harvey Krumpet*. All of these shorts had merit and had done well in the previous year's festival circuit. But the two front-runners were *Destino* and *Bounding*. So, we were all shocked when the winner was announced: *Harvey Krumpet*, a stop-motion film from Australia.

Roy told me later that as the envelope was opened and the name was being read onstage, he actually grabbed the armrests of his seat as if to get up. When he realized that *Destino* wasn't the winner, he sunk back into his seat and told me he was really disappointed. We were all let down not just for losing out on an Academy Award, but also on the missed opportunity to hear Roy's acceptance speech, which no doubt would have been elegant. There was also a special congratulatory trade ad created by the studio's marketing department that would have appeared in the trade papers had *Destino* won.

There was great disappointment, not just because you want your film to win but also because there was a sea of change happening in the animation industry during that period. Disney itself was in the process of shifting from 2-D hand-drawn animation to 3-D computer-generated animation, and *Destino* was predominately hand animated. There was great anticipation that had *Destino* won, Roy would have made reference to that, among other things, during his acceptance speech.

When the awards show ended, we made our way to the main lobby. The crowd was starting to thin—with some guests holding Academy Governors Ball tickets heading to the grand ballroom for the main after-party. All nominees, presenters, and the usual VIPs get tickets to the Governors Ball. Roy and Dominique, along with their guests, had them.

Roy still asked the question that was on everyone's mind: "What do you want to do?" No one really said anything. So Roy turned to Patty and said; "What do you want to do?" Patty promptly replied that she would like to get out of the theater and go to In-N-Out for some burgers and fries. That answer provoked an outburst of laughter, and everyone loved the plan.

We all headed down to the location where the event organizers had designated the limo pickup area to have our car notified to come get us. It took a while, but eventually our car came around and we all piled in to head out for burgers.

When we pulled into In-N-Out Burger, we discovered that the drive-through lane would not accommodate our stretch limo. Our driver didn't realize that initially, and he spent several minutes trying to back out of the lane. While he was working the car out of the tight spot, some of us got out of the car in the parking lot and went inside to place our order.

Food in hand, we headed for Roy and Patty's home next in Toluca Lake. The burgers and fries were distributed around the dining room. Patty made sure that we all had whatever we needed: ketchup, utensils, water, and glasses. Roy broke out a magnum of red wine that happened to be from John Lasseter's family winery. We ate and drank and enjoyed some great conversations until the early hours of the next morning.

The story of *Destino* is not over yet. There is still artwork from the 1969 theft missing, including the two fate heads painted by Dalí in oil on acetate cel. This and a number of other drawings have never been recovered. Hopefully someday that artwork will be found and repatriated to the Walt Disney Animation Research Library for generations to enjoy and to appreciate one fascinating part of The Walt Disney Company history.

For me, the song sung by Dora Luz grew on me over time. With all the digital restoration that was done to the recording, it actually sounded pretty

From left to right: Dominique Monfery, Roy E. Disney, and Patty Disney during arrivals on the red carpet before the 2004 Oscar Awards.

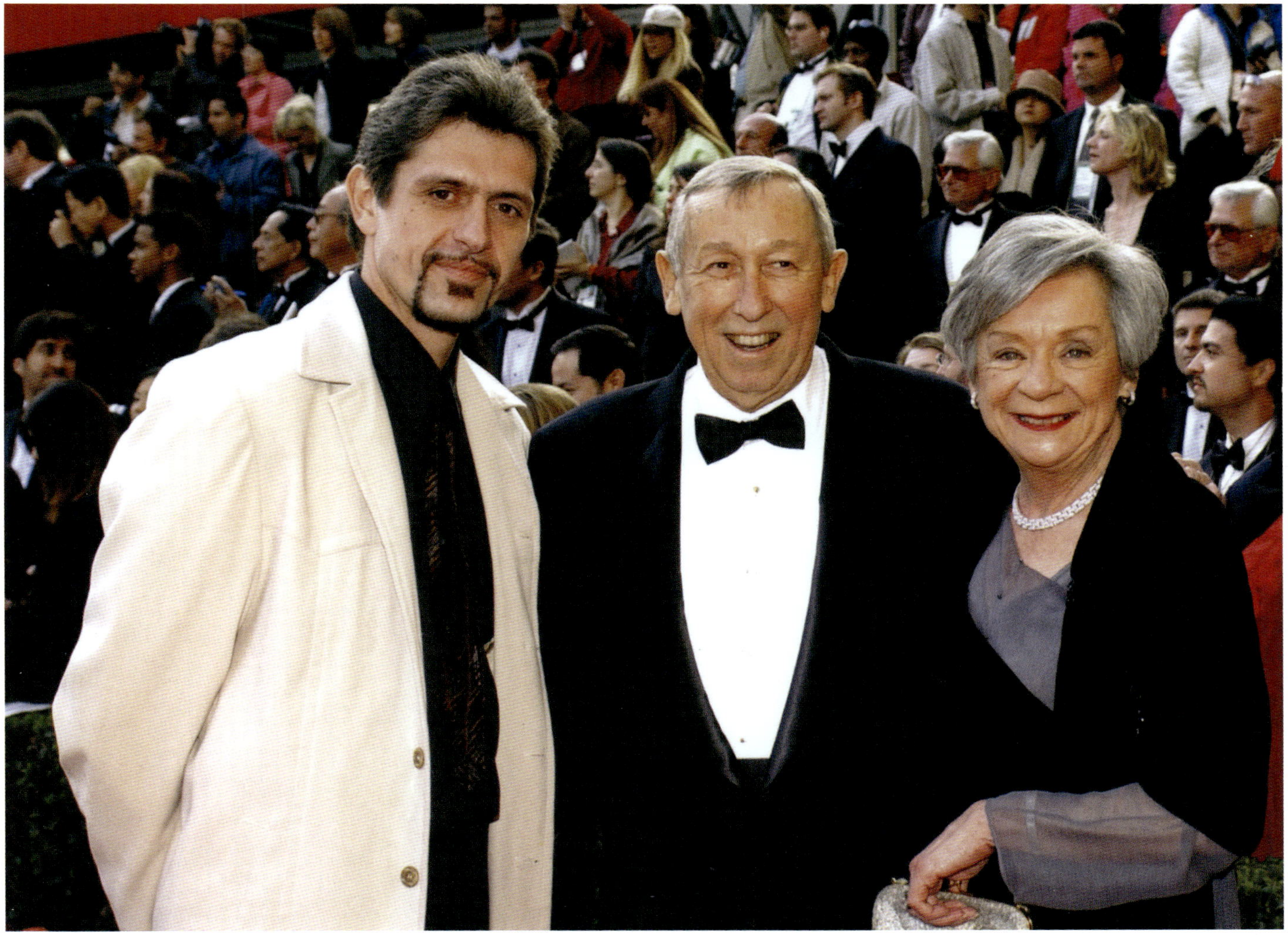

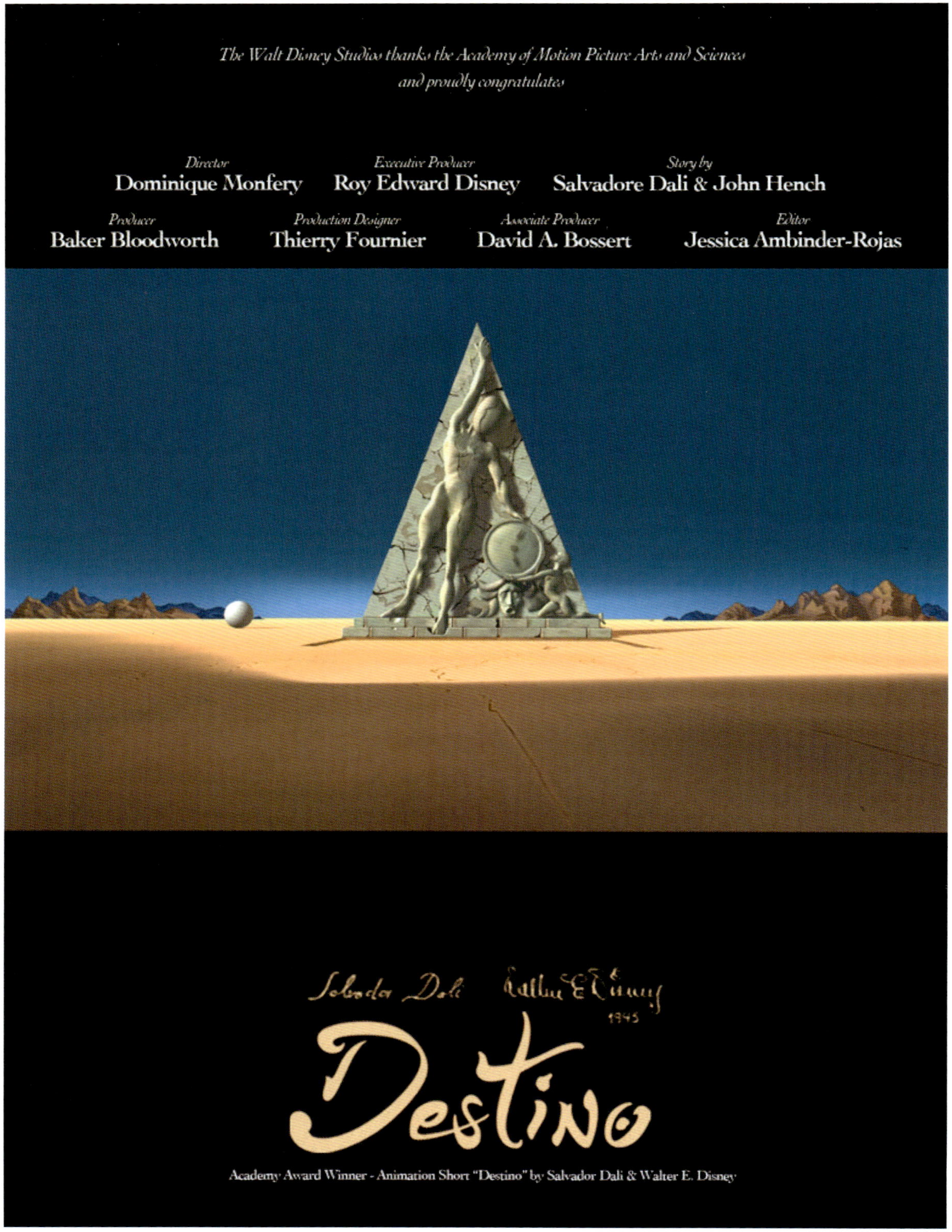

This was the ad designed to run in the trades the day after the Oscars, if *Destino* had won the Academy Award in its category. Unfortunately, the film did not win, so this ad was never seen.

Visual development of Chronos by Dominique Monfery from the 2003 production of *Destino*.

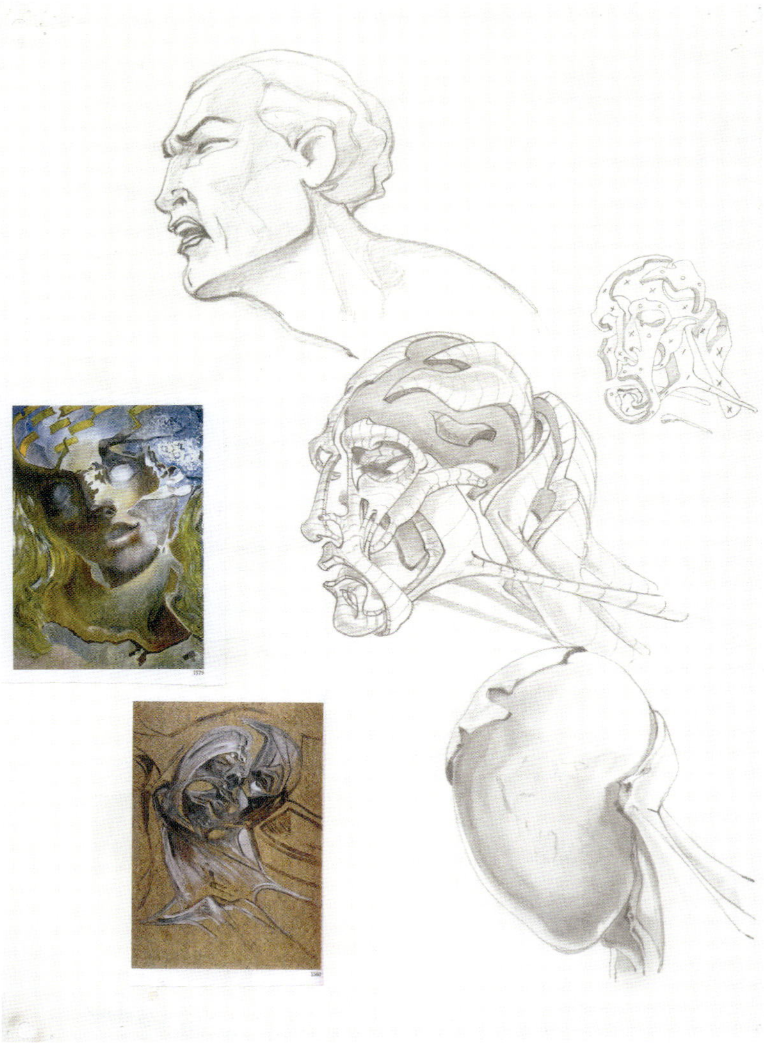

good by the time the film was completed. Now, when I listen to *My Destiny of Love* it evokes many fond memories of an incredibly special film that started with a chance meeting by two artists. I am so proud to have been a part of it and that meeting that happened during a bygone era.

"When I think about *Destino*, I think about Roy [E.] Disney's passion to make it," reminisces Tom Schumacher, former president of Walt Disney Animation Studios and current president of Disney Theatrical Productions. "Because my contact with the project was all in the early days of finishing the production and verifying which art was Salvador Dalí's, and which art was John Hench's. What was the story intended to be," Schumacher remembers thinking at the time while "watching it get pinned up on the wall, and how valiantly Roy fought to actually get the thing made, "My recollection was that nobody wanted *Destino* made; they didn't understand why this would be restored, and this assemblage would be done," Schumacher adds. "I think Roy wanted it because it was extraordinary art by extraordinary artists, that without being made into a film it was never going to be seen and appreciated. For Roy, it was about documenting the family business. It was always so important to Roy that stuff be seen, that people know it was there."

Roy E. Disney commented in an interview in 2003 that he thought it was important to complete *Destino* from a historical standpoint. "I think history is important. I really do," he said. "You need to know where you came from. This is a little piece of our history that has kind of a, I started to say quaintness, but also a ring of what our roots really are. Our roots are in art, in that side of the world rather [than] the commercial side. It's important that we keep remembering that." ■

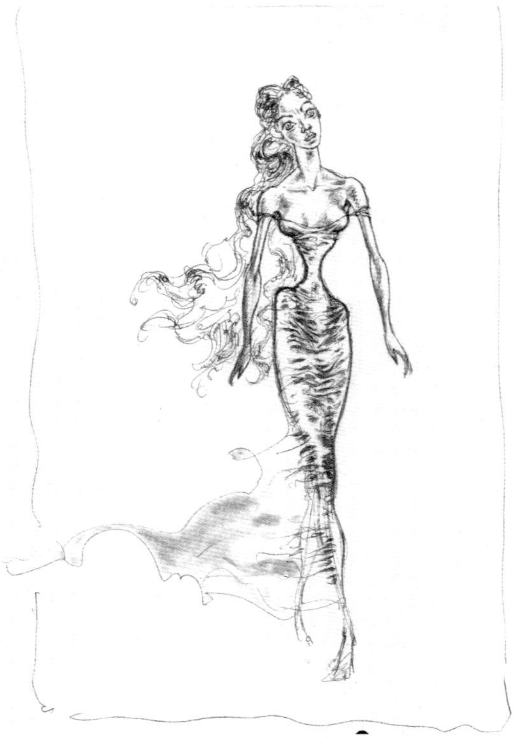

Visual development of Dahlia by Dominique Monfery from the 2003 production of *Destino*.

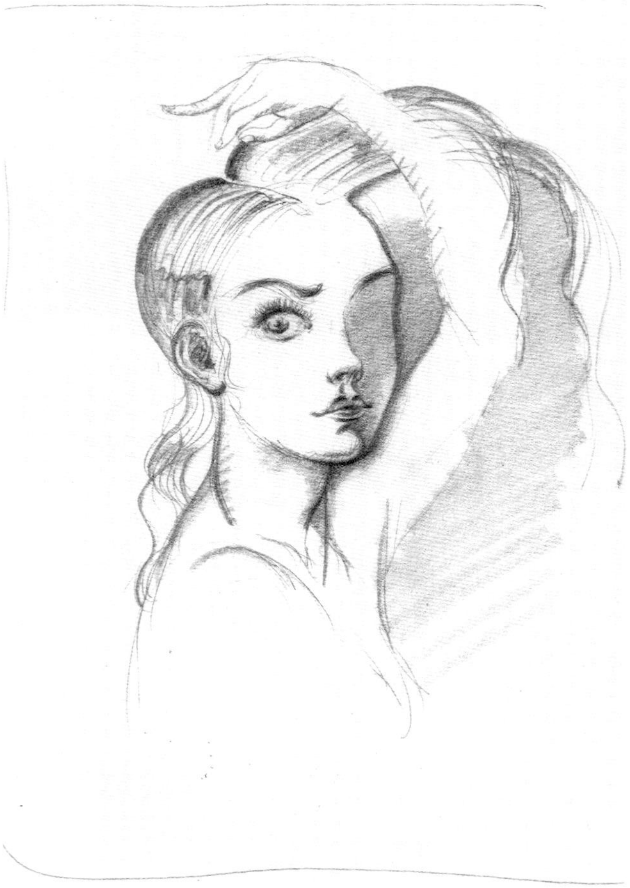

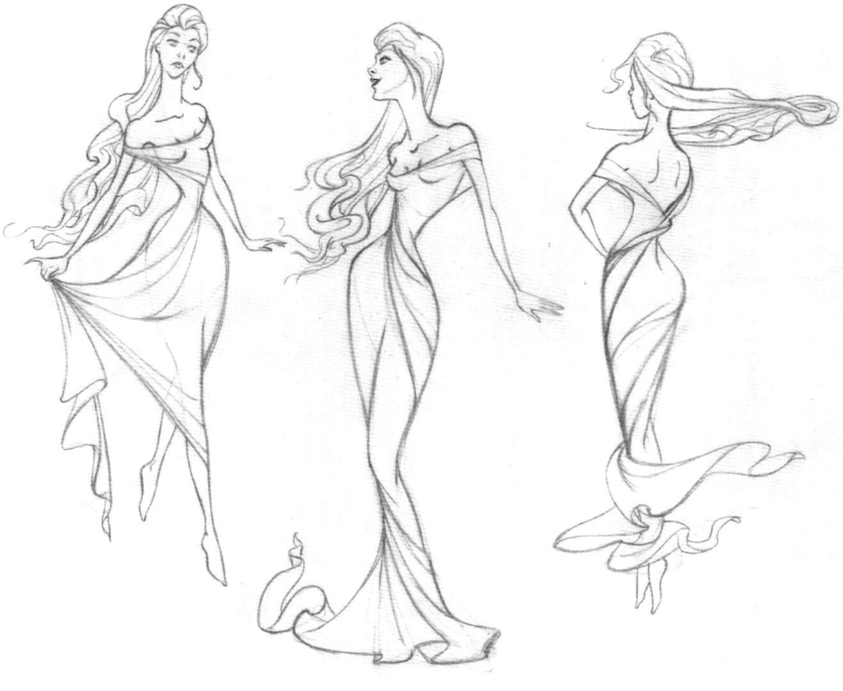

Visual development of Chronos by Dominique Monfery from the 2003 production of *Destino*.

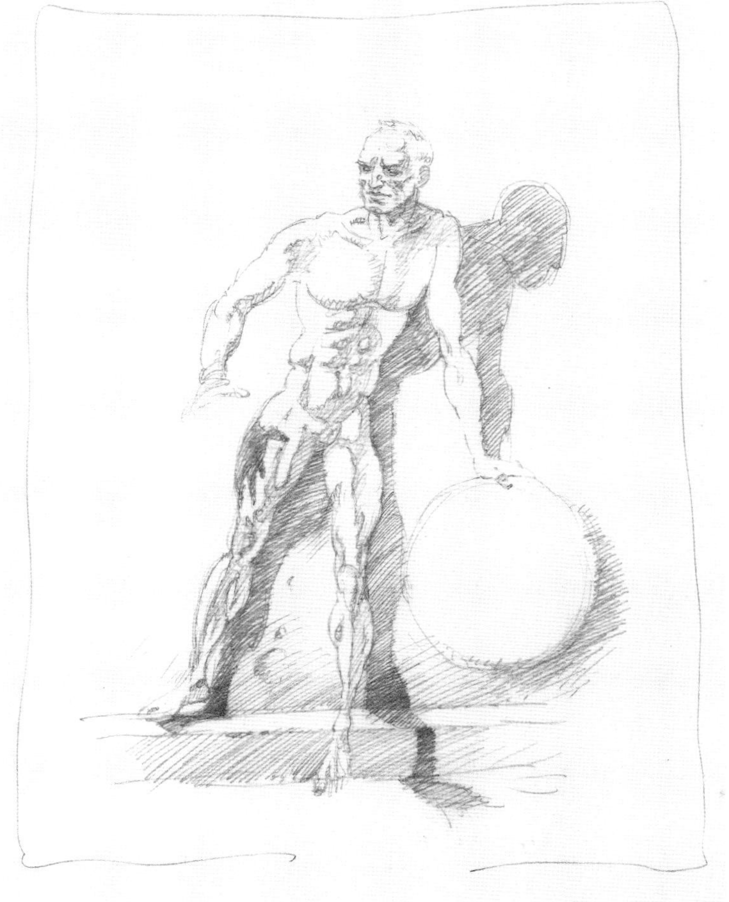

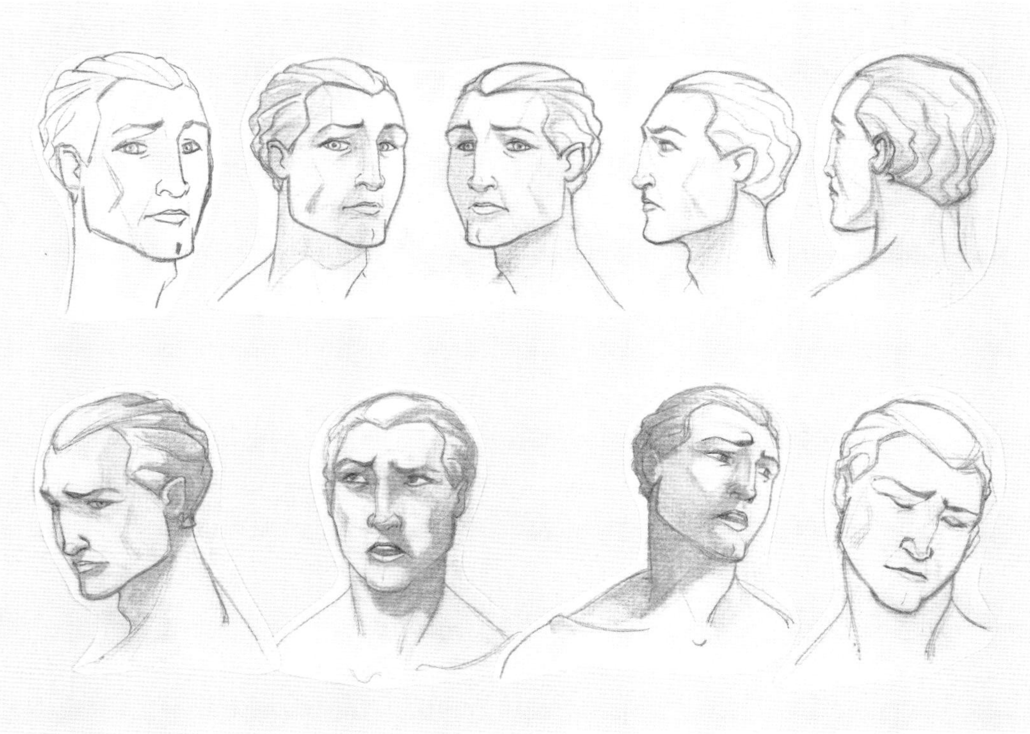

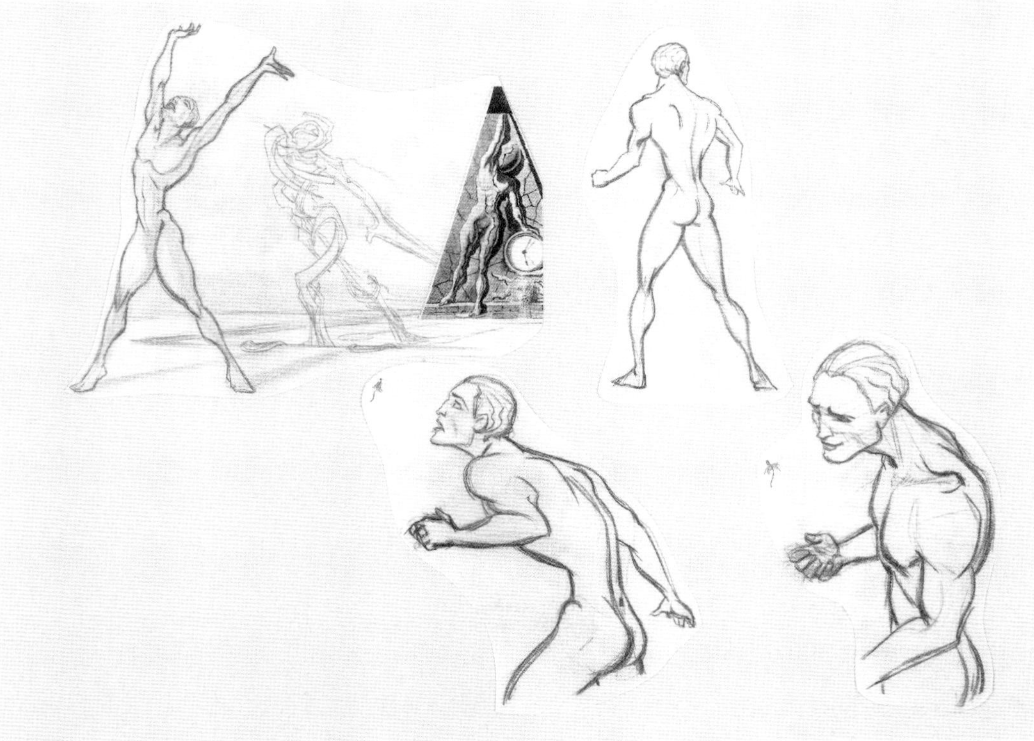

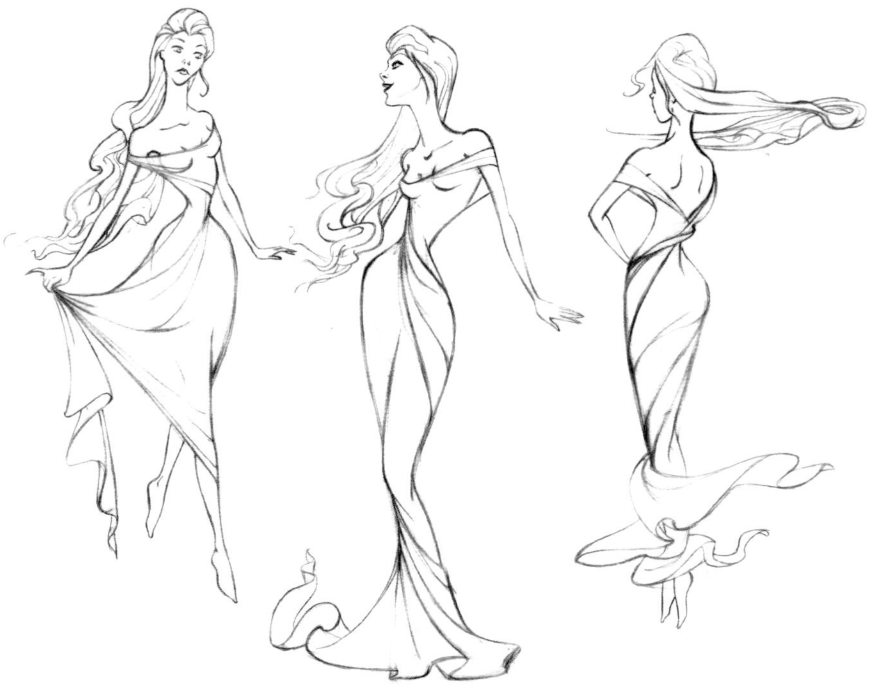

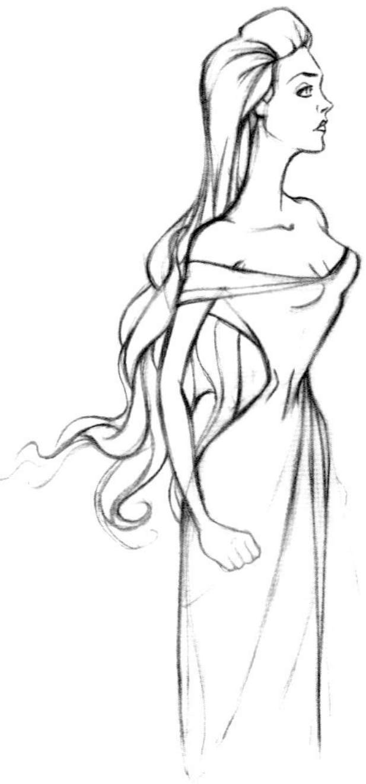

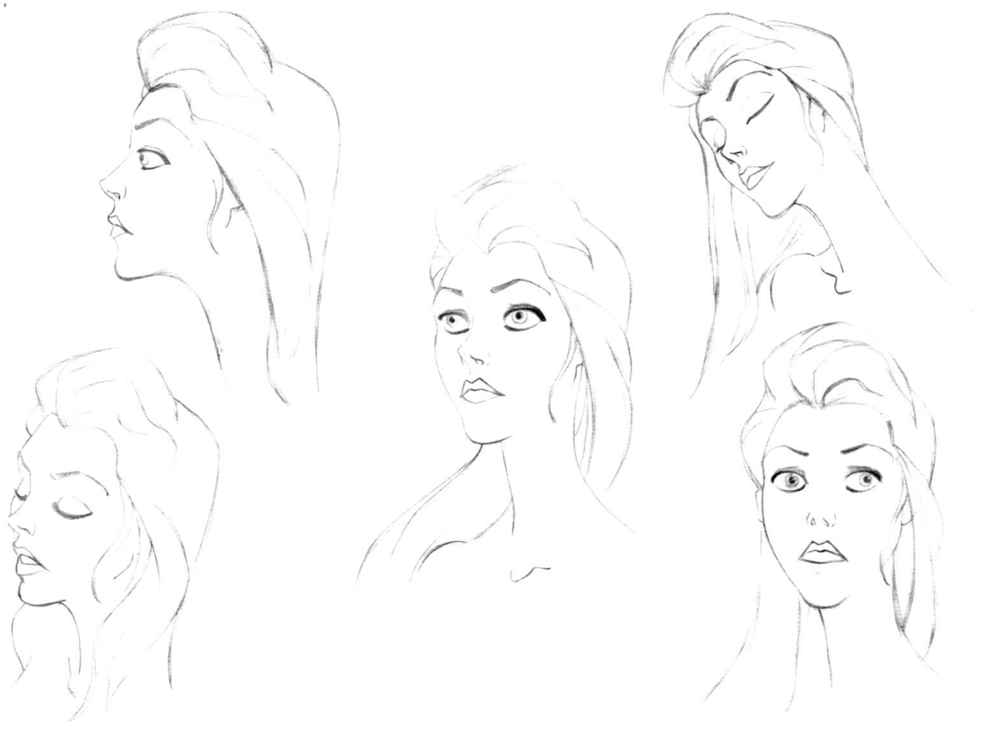

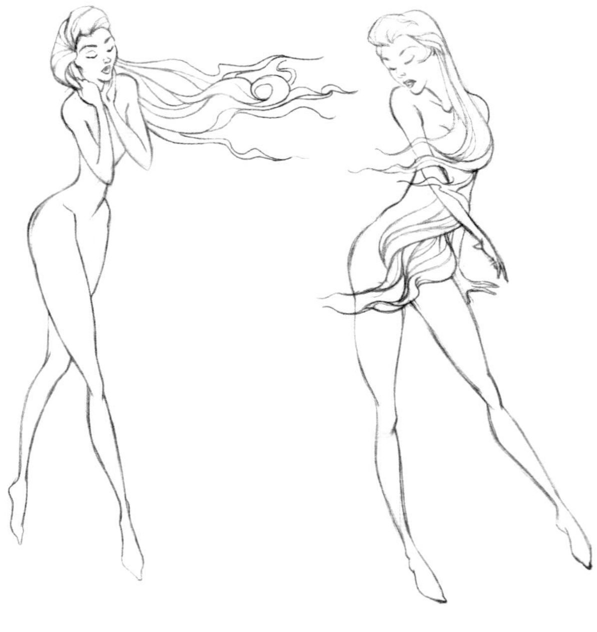

Page 174: Several studies of Dahlia by Dominique Monfery.

The filmmakers were conscious to not portray the female character, Dahlia, as overtly sexy, but to appear like a real woman, the way Salvador Dalí would have painted her, as seen in these final images from the film, *Destino*.

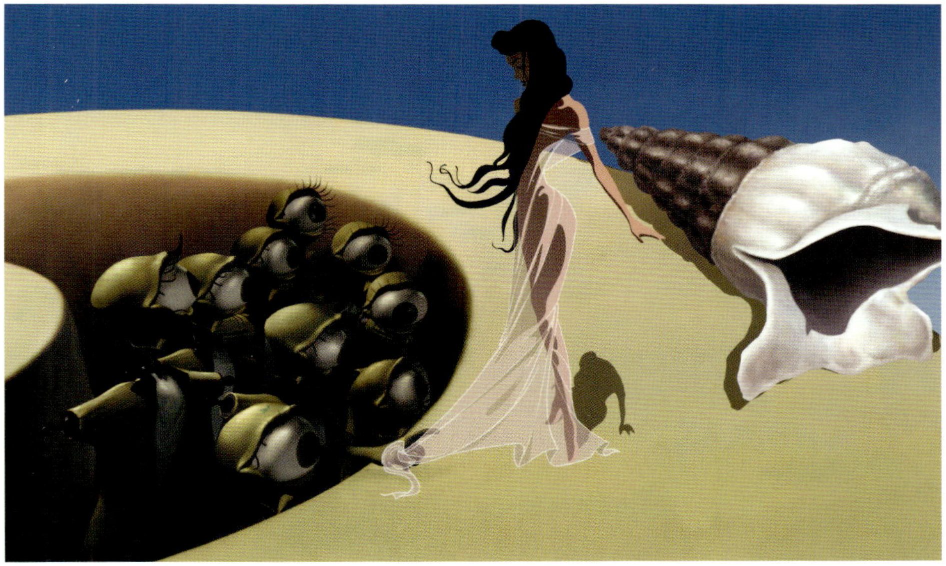
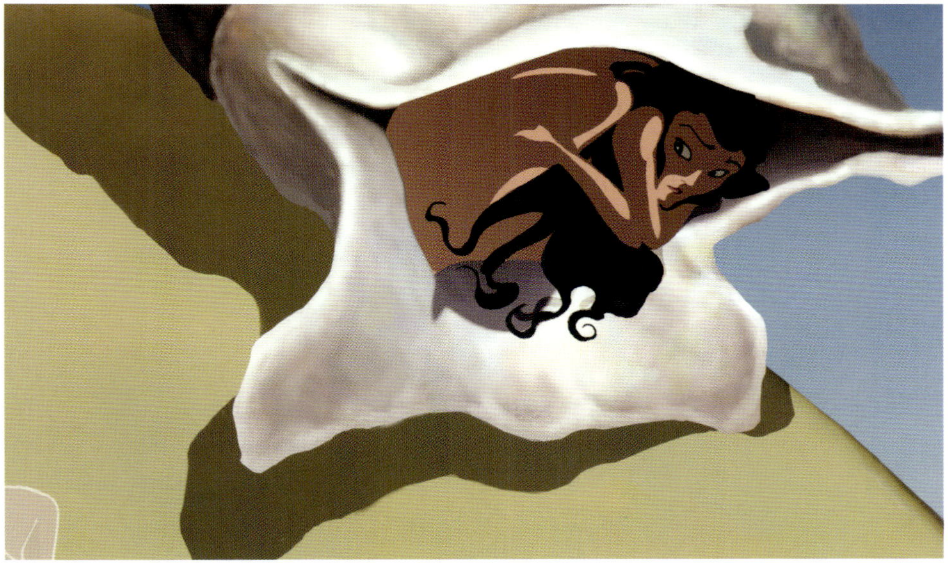
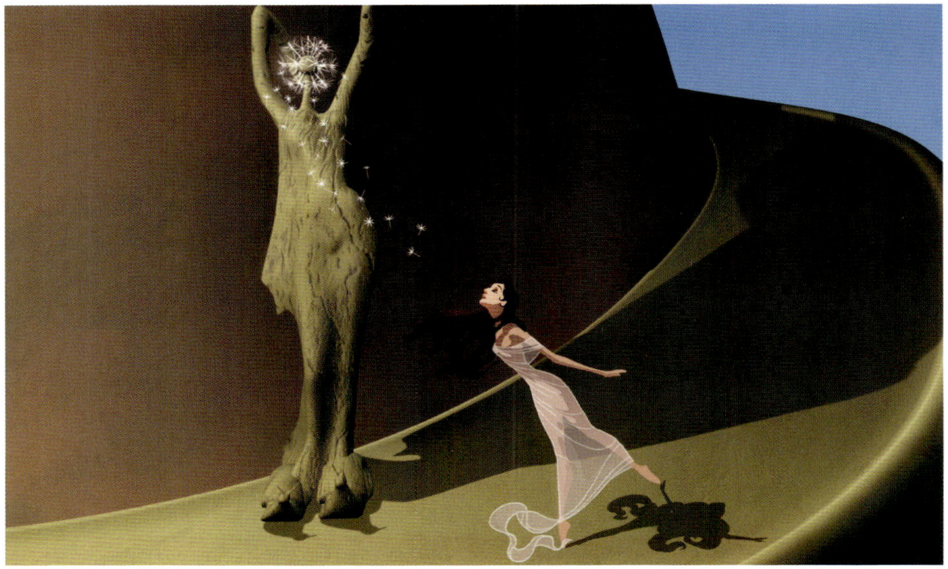
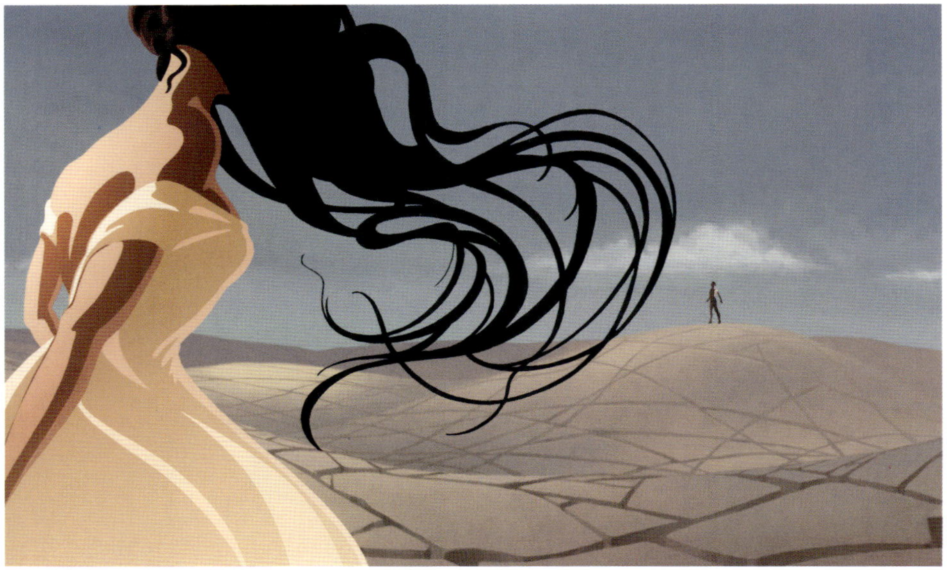

Visual development drawing of Dahlia from the 2003 production of *Destino* by Dominique Monfery.

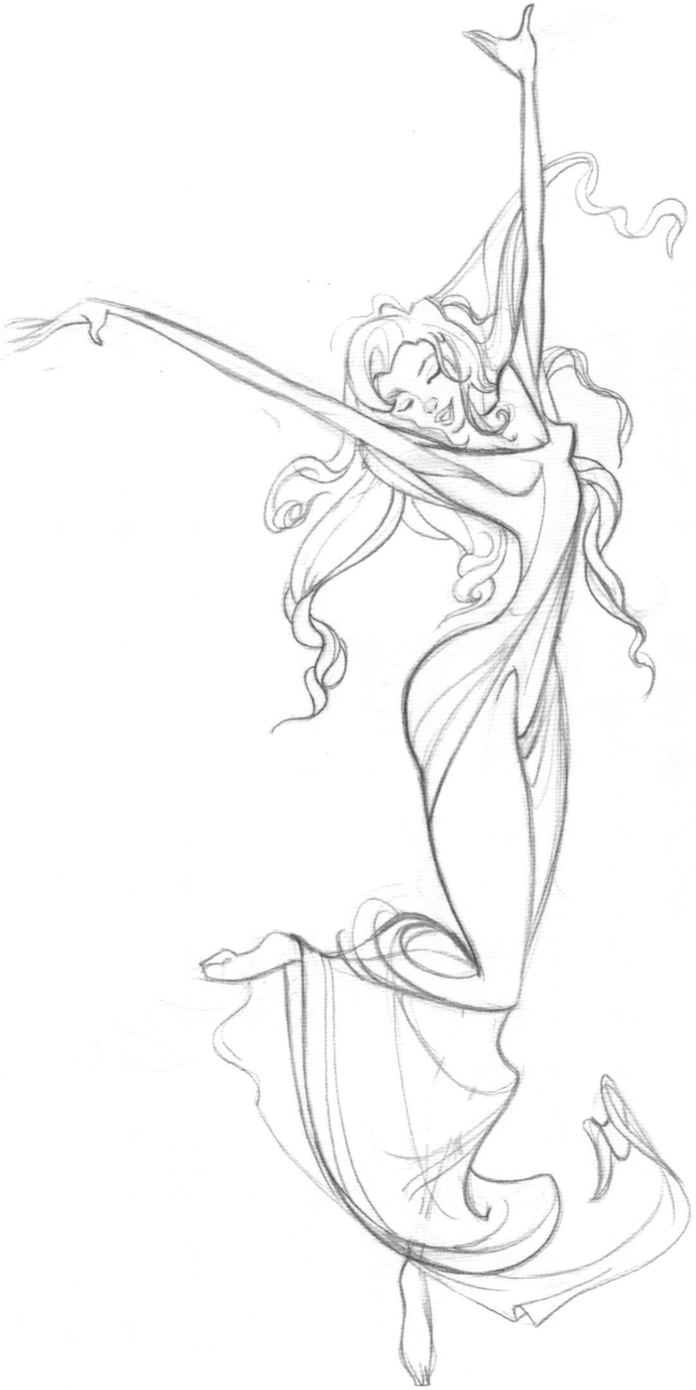

Top: Rough animation drawing of Dahlia from the 2003 production of *Destino* by Dominique Monfery.

Bottom: Image from the final film, *Destino*.

Page 178: Story sketch from the 2003 production of *Destino*.

Page 179: Image from the final film, *Destino*.

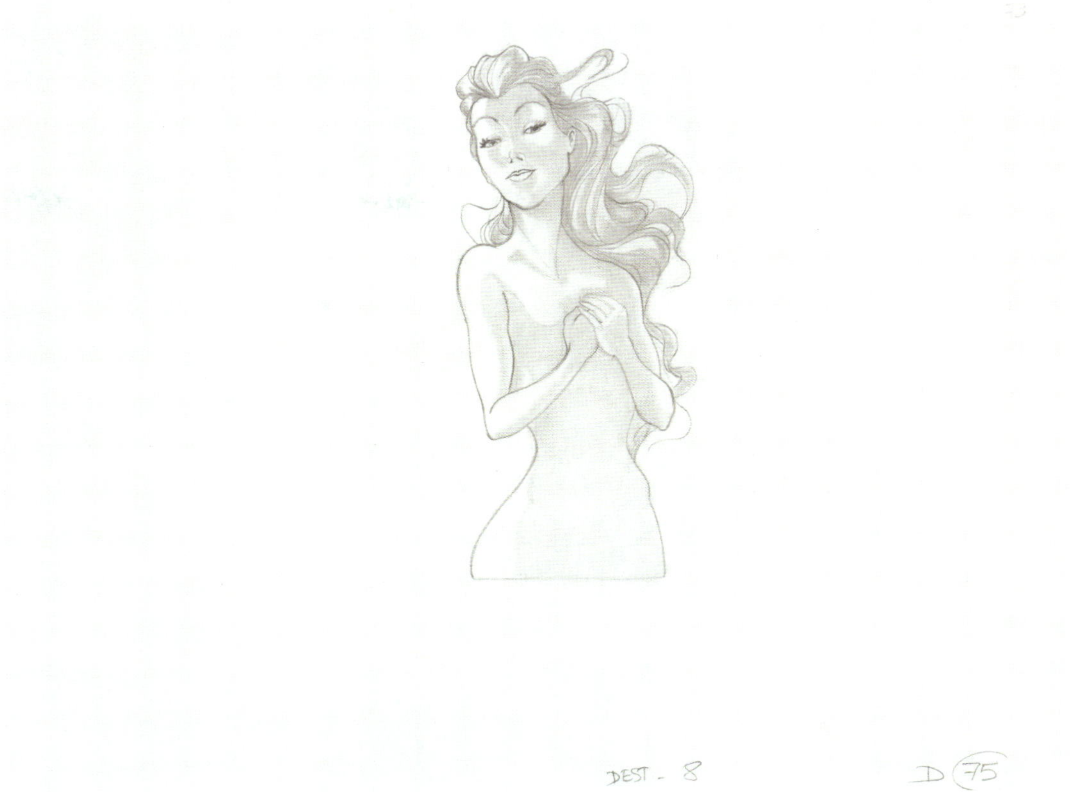

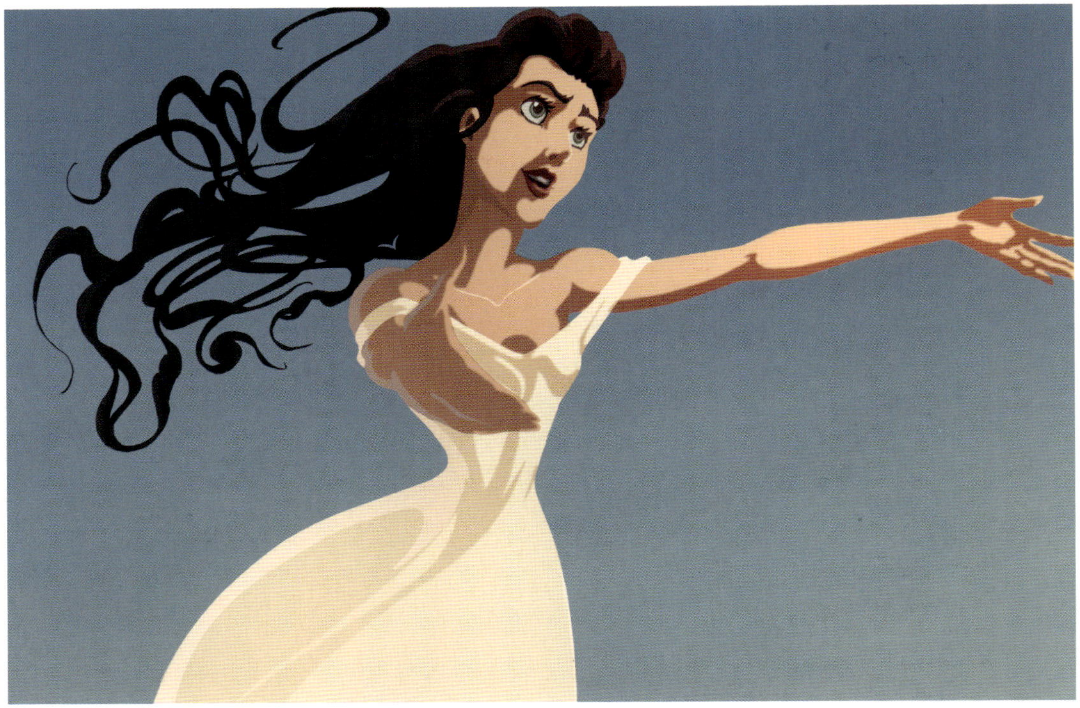

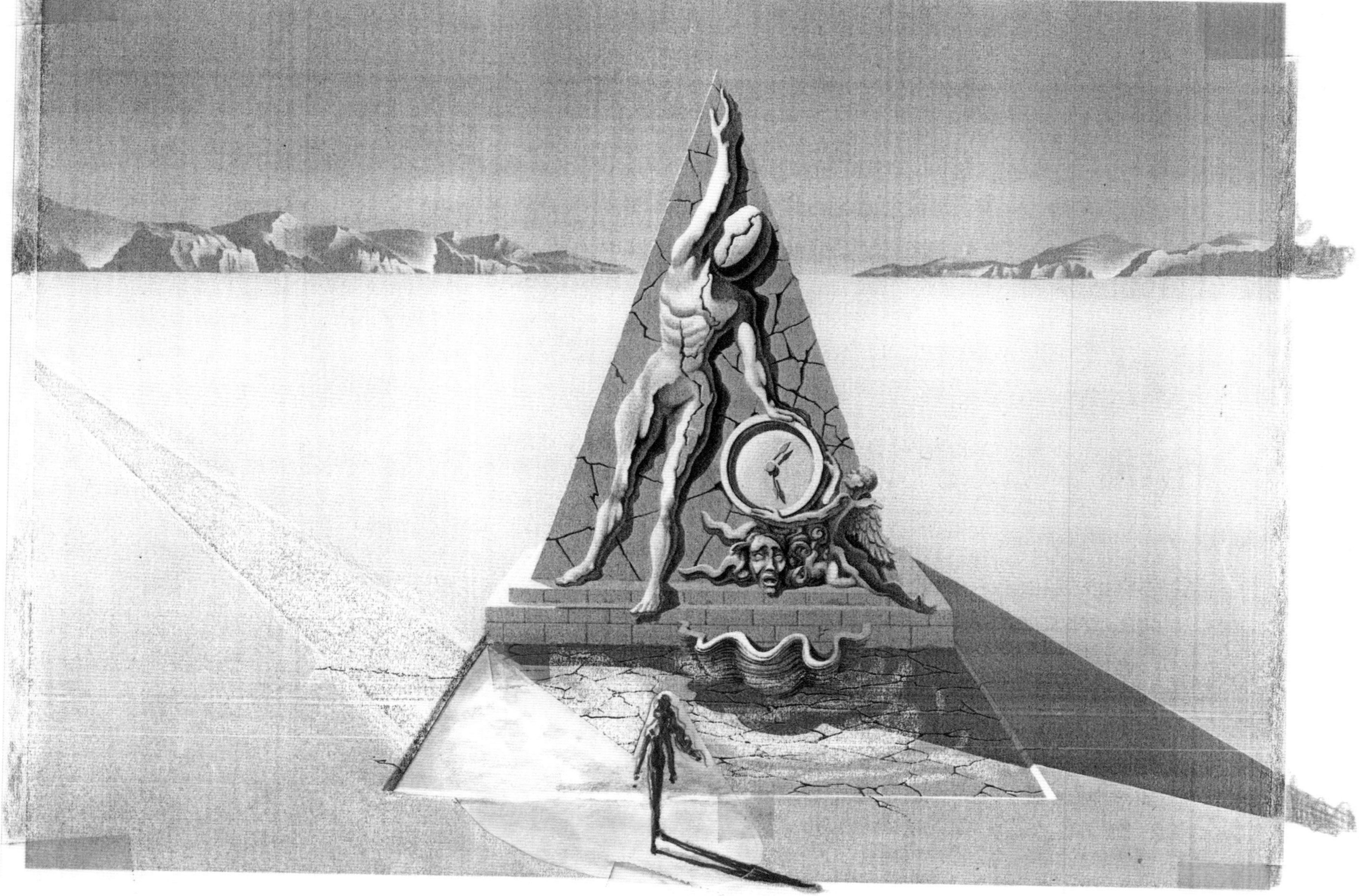

23 NEW.

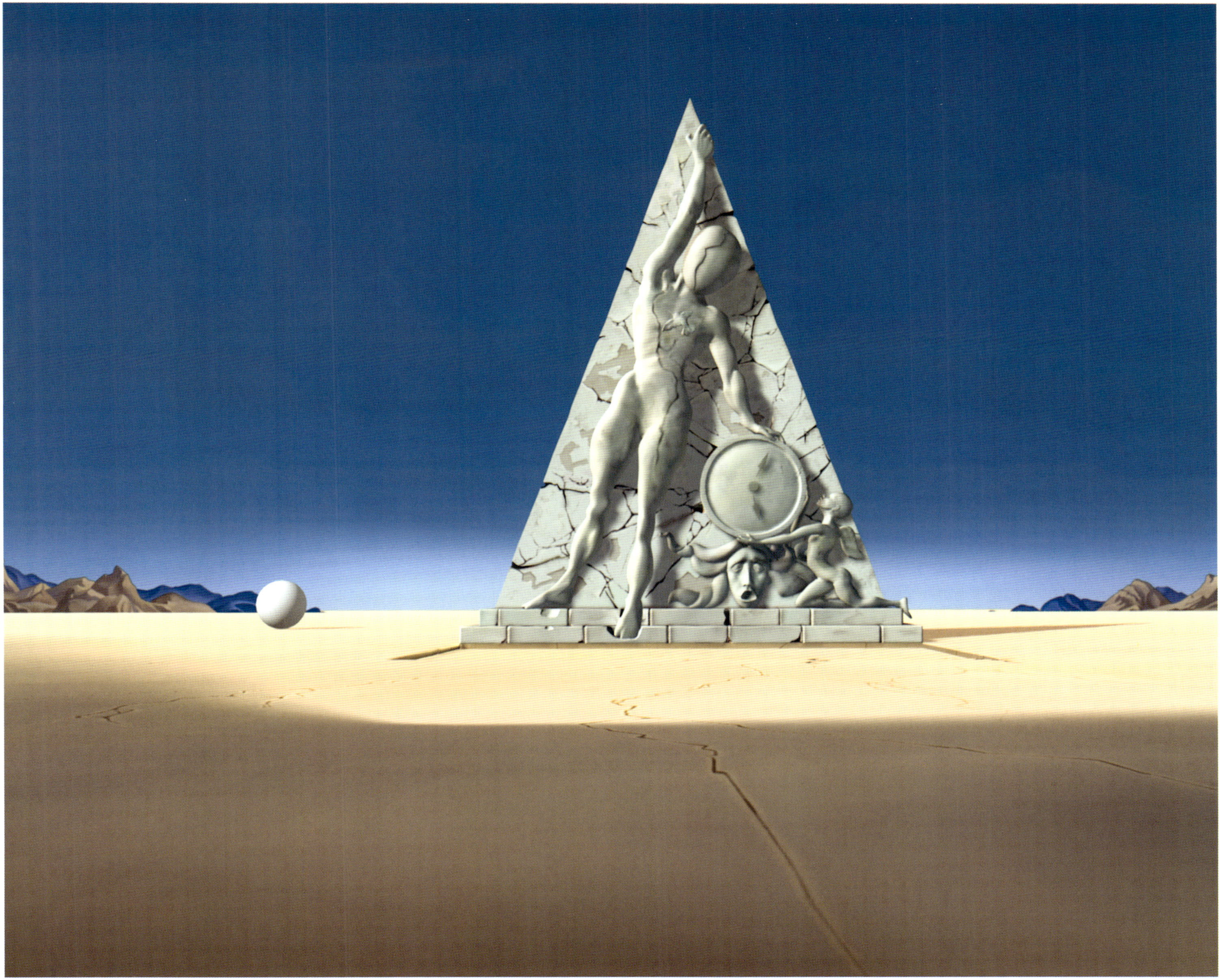

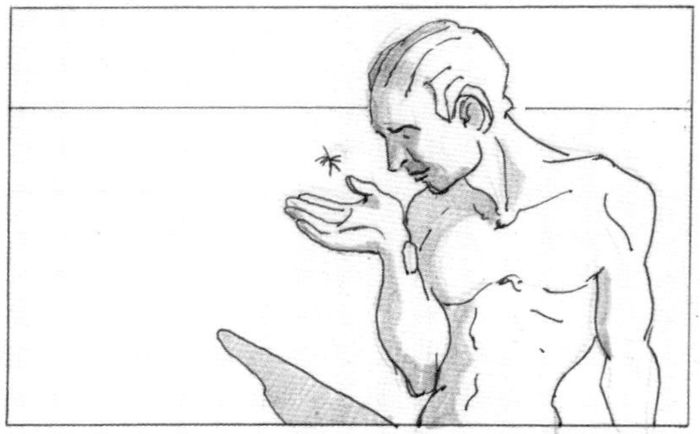

300

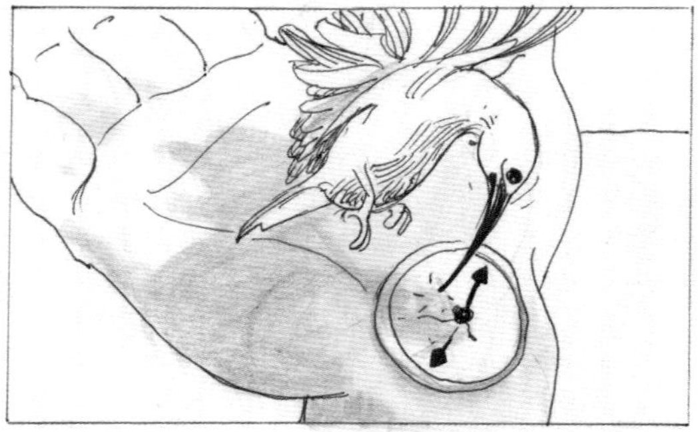

303

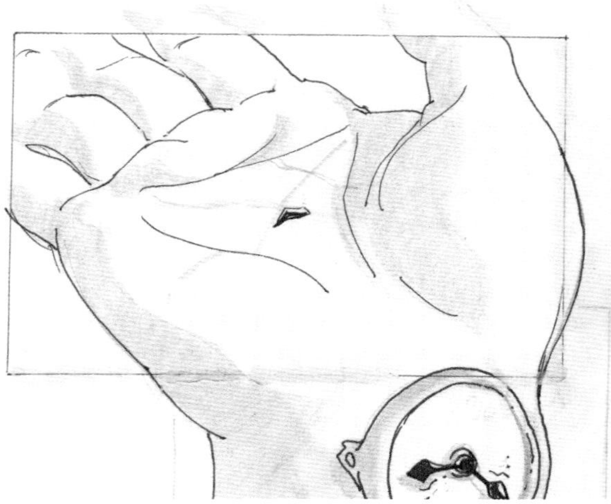

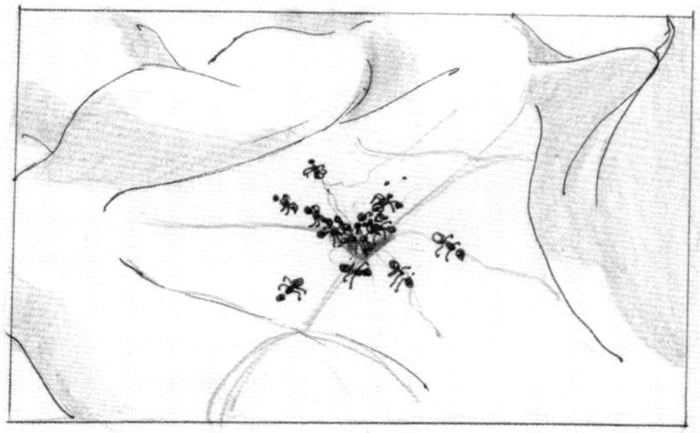

306

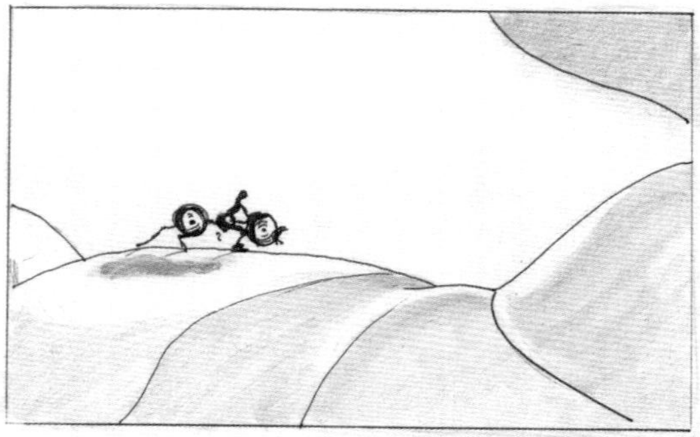

309

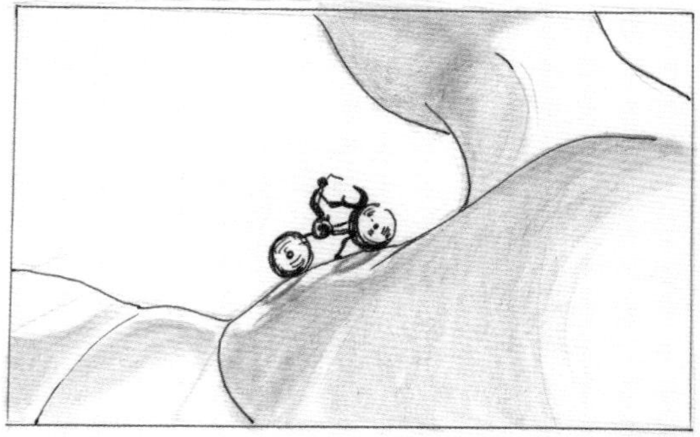

310

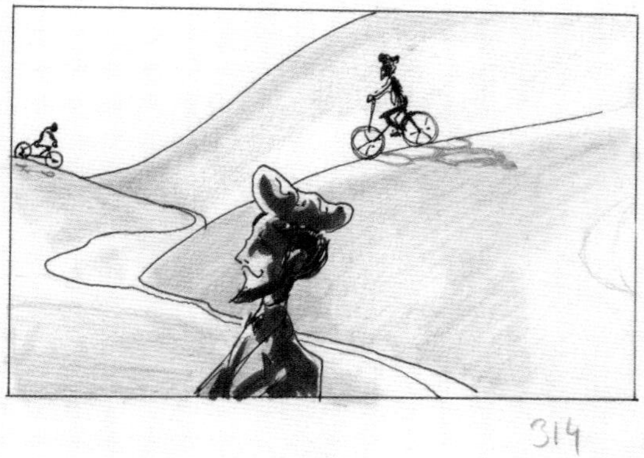

314

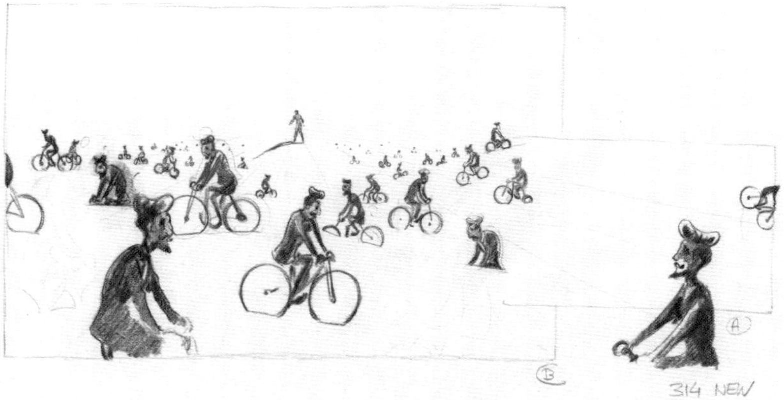

314 NEW
+
315
+
316

Page 180: Story sketches by Dominique Monfery from the 2003 production of *Destino* showing the arts-turned cyclists.

Top: Rough Animation drawing of cyclist from the 2003 production of *Destino*.

Bottom: Image from the final film, *Destino*. Only one cyclist was animated and repositioned to give the illusion of many cyclists in the shot.

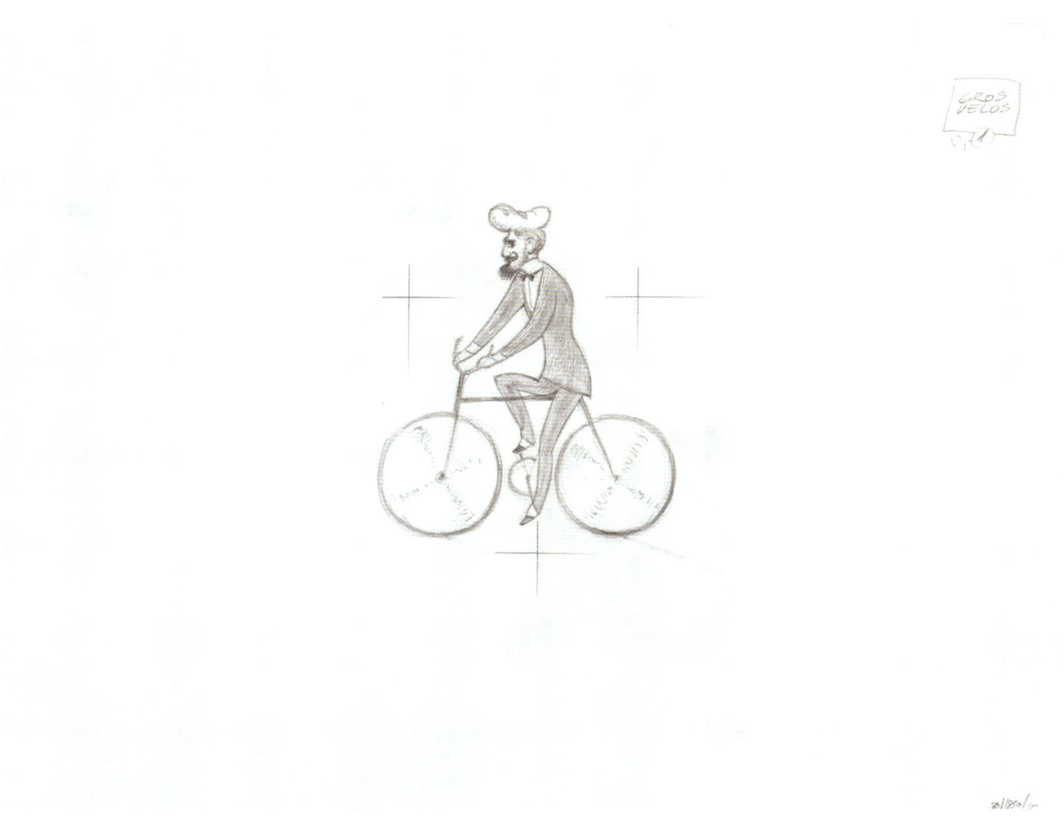

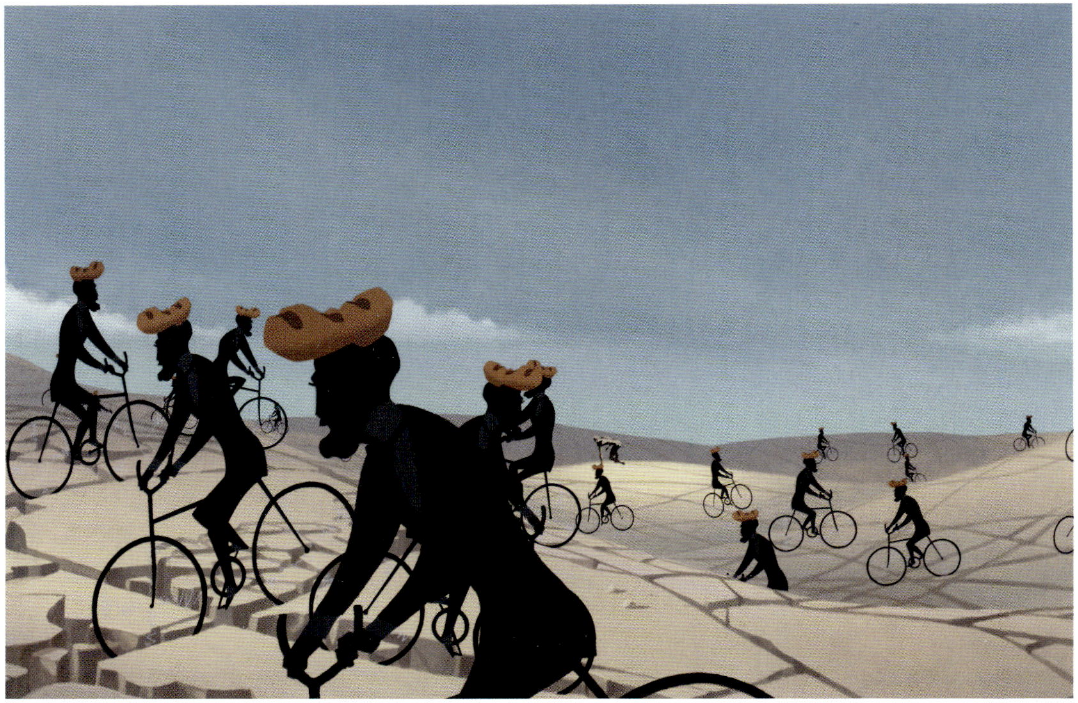

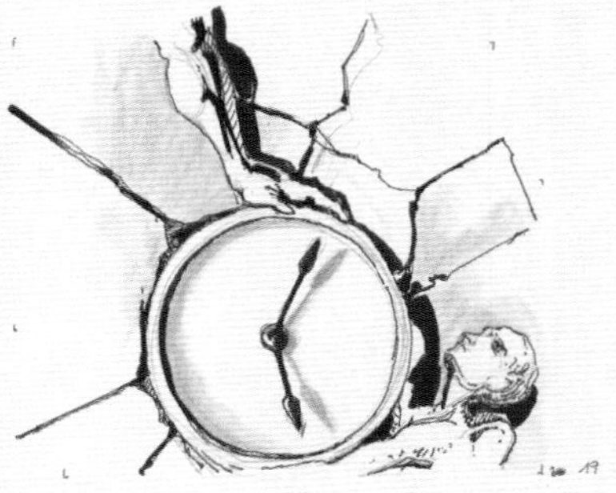

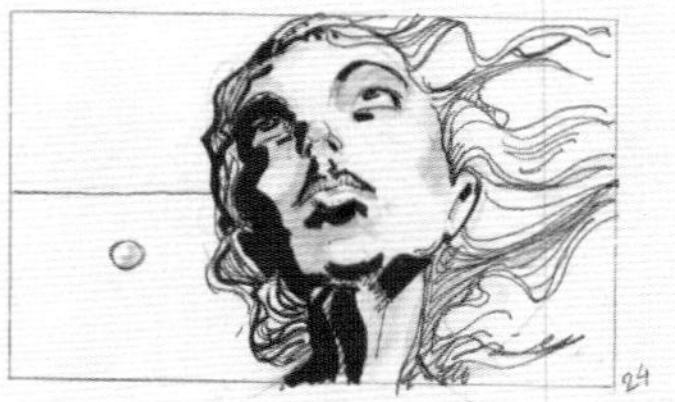

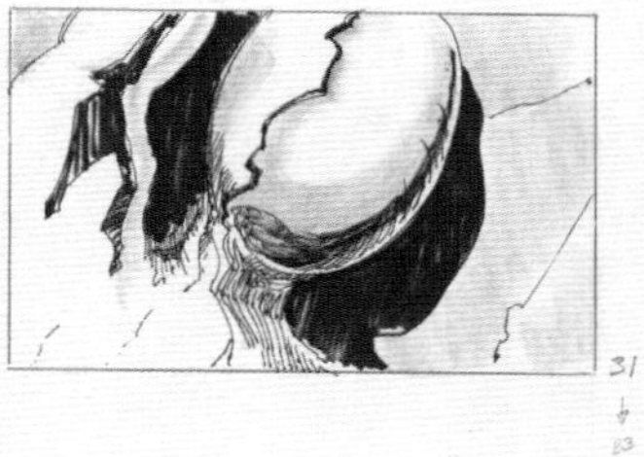

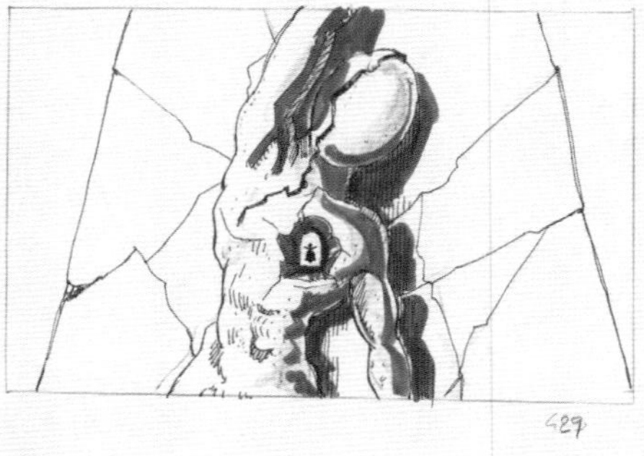

Page 182: Story sketches by Dominique Monfery from the 2003 production of *Destino*.

Story sketch by Dominique Monfery from the 2003 production of *Destino*.

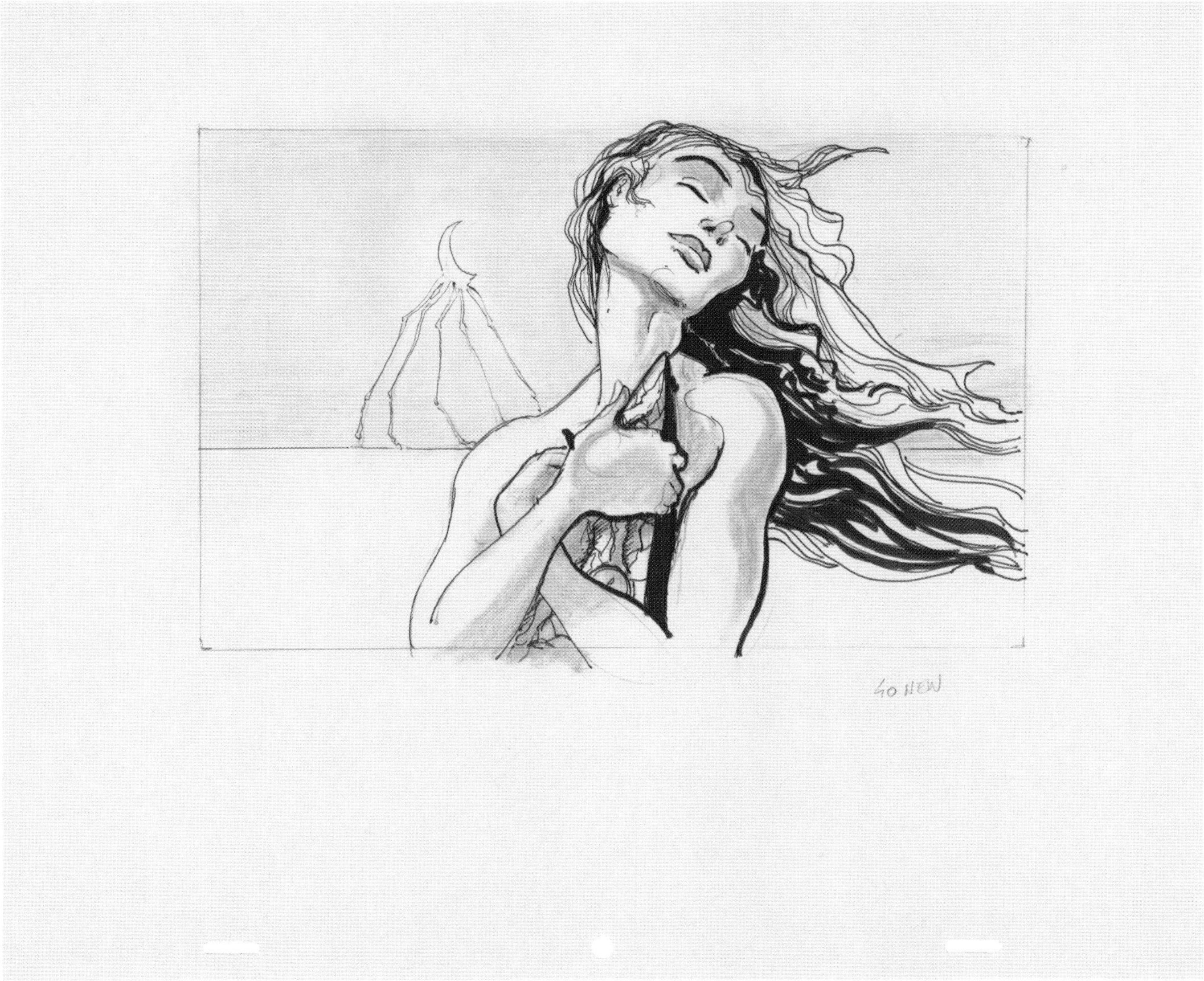

Rough animation drawing by Dominique Monfery of the "Temple of Love" sequence from *Destino* (2003).

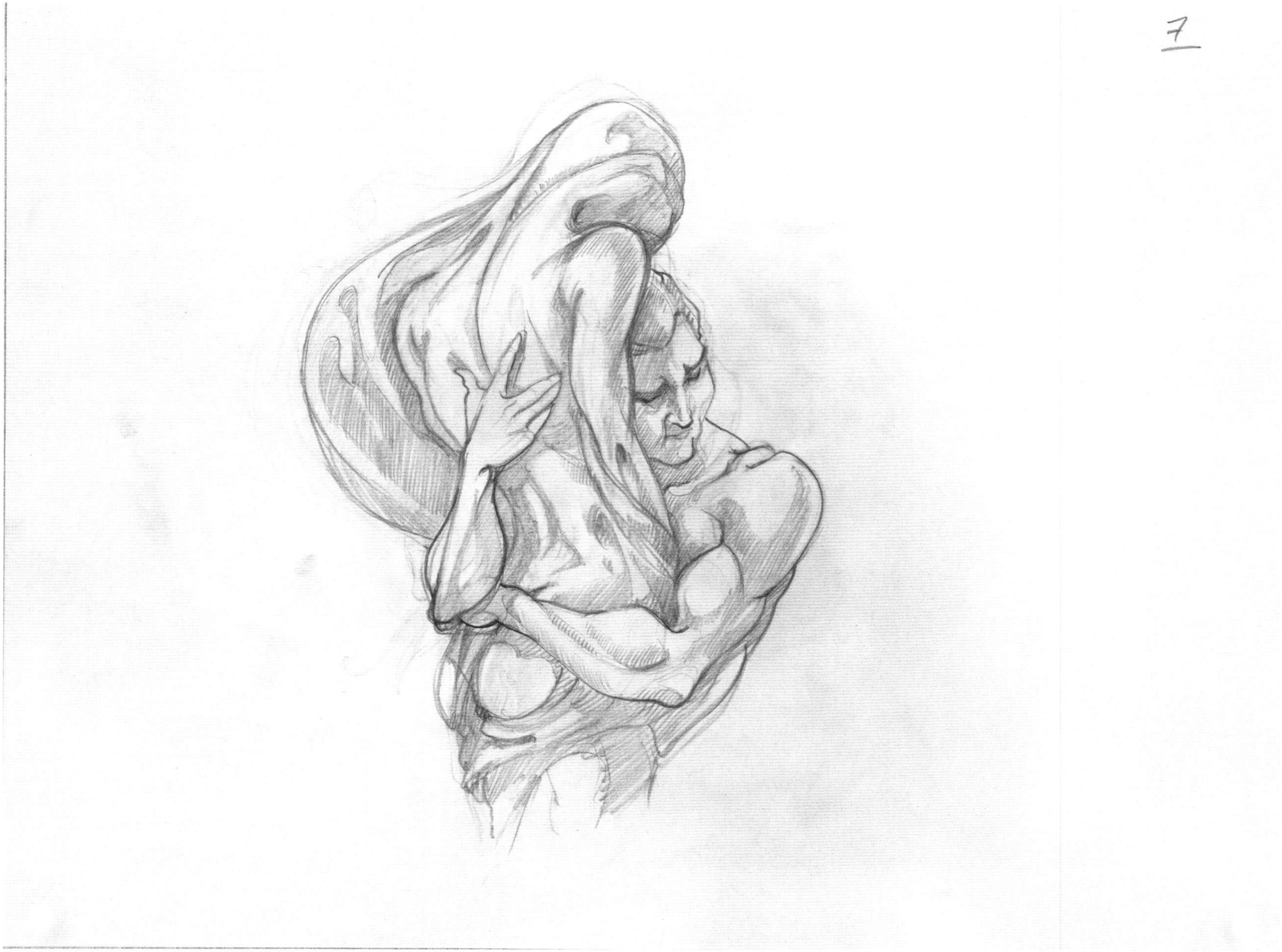

Image from the "Temple of Love" sequence from *Destino*.

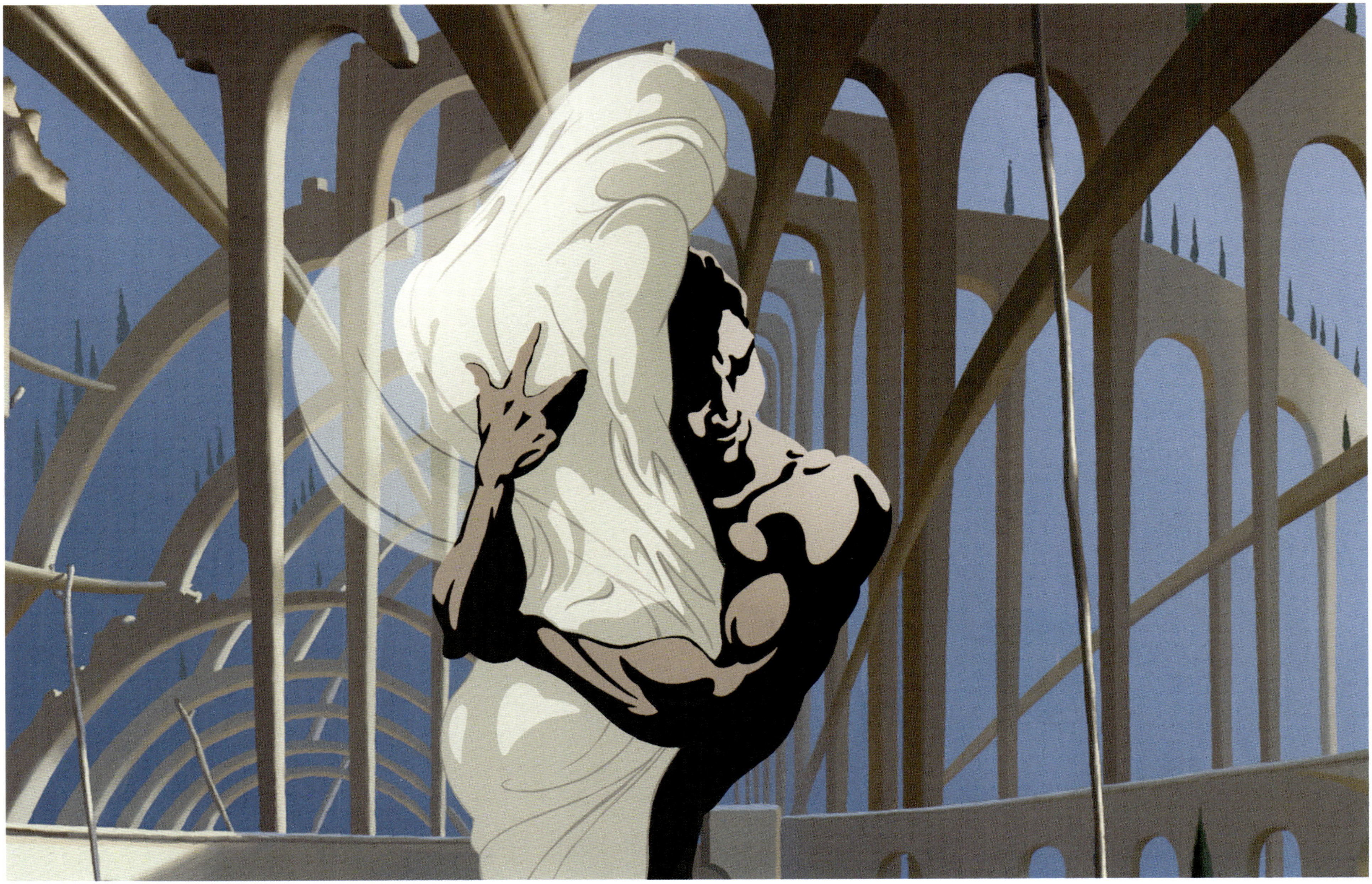

Pages 186–191: Visual development artwork for *Destino*. Courtesy of the Fundació Gala-Salvador Dalí.

The Fundació Gala-Salvador Dalí has several sketches and outlines for images in Destino. These are mainly little-known preparatory studies made in pencil and ink on oven paper (parchment or vellum) from notebooks in which Dalí would draw and redraw the images he had in his head, in a concentrated and exciting creative process that reflects the enthusiasm he felt for the project.

— Montse Aguer, Director of the Centre for Dalinian Studies, Fundació Gala-Salvador Dalí

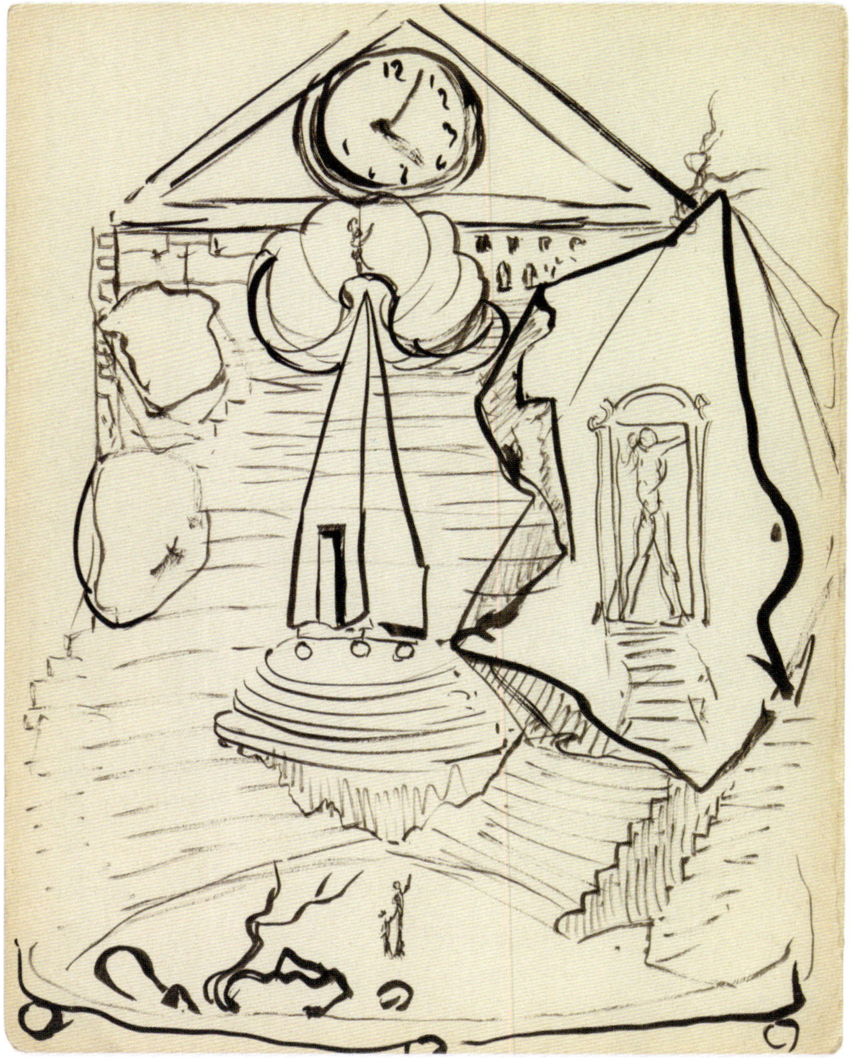

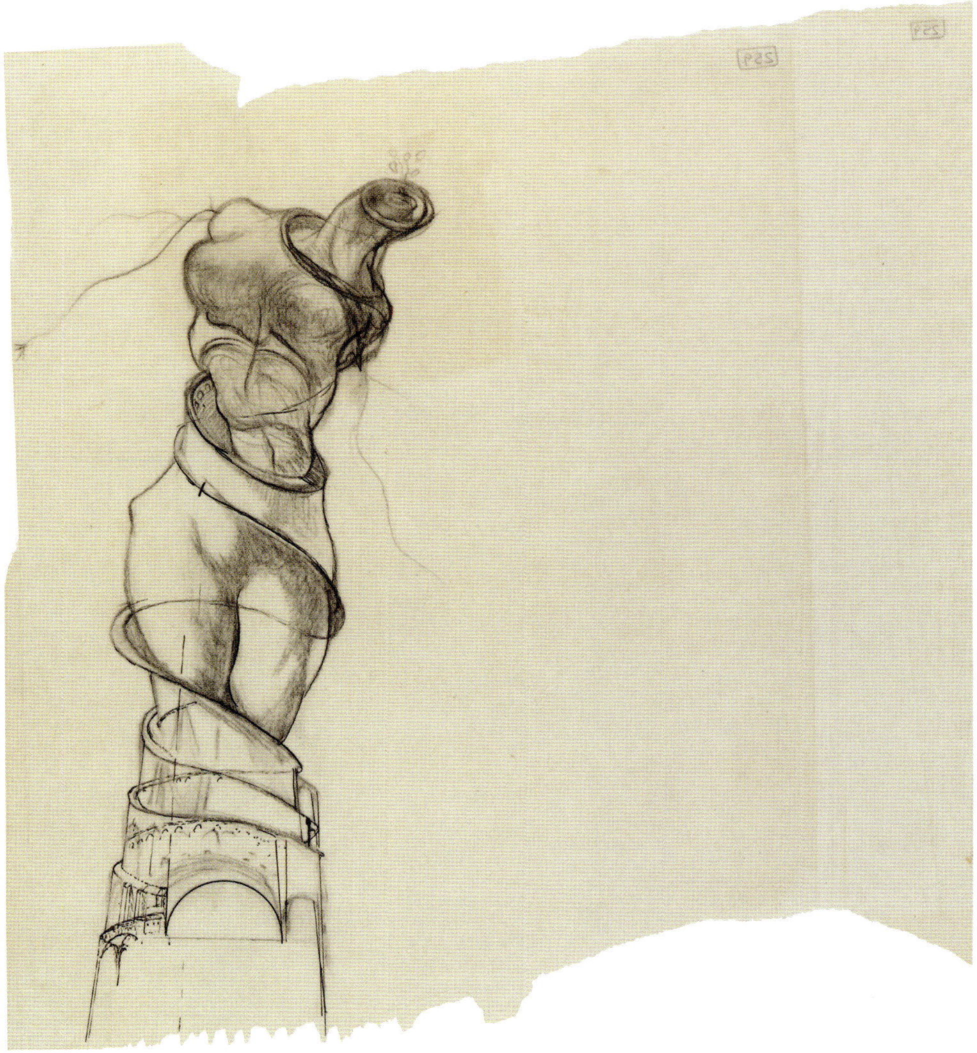

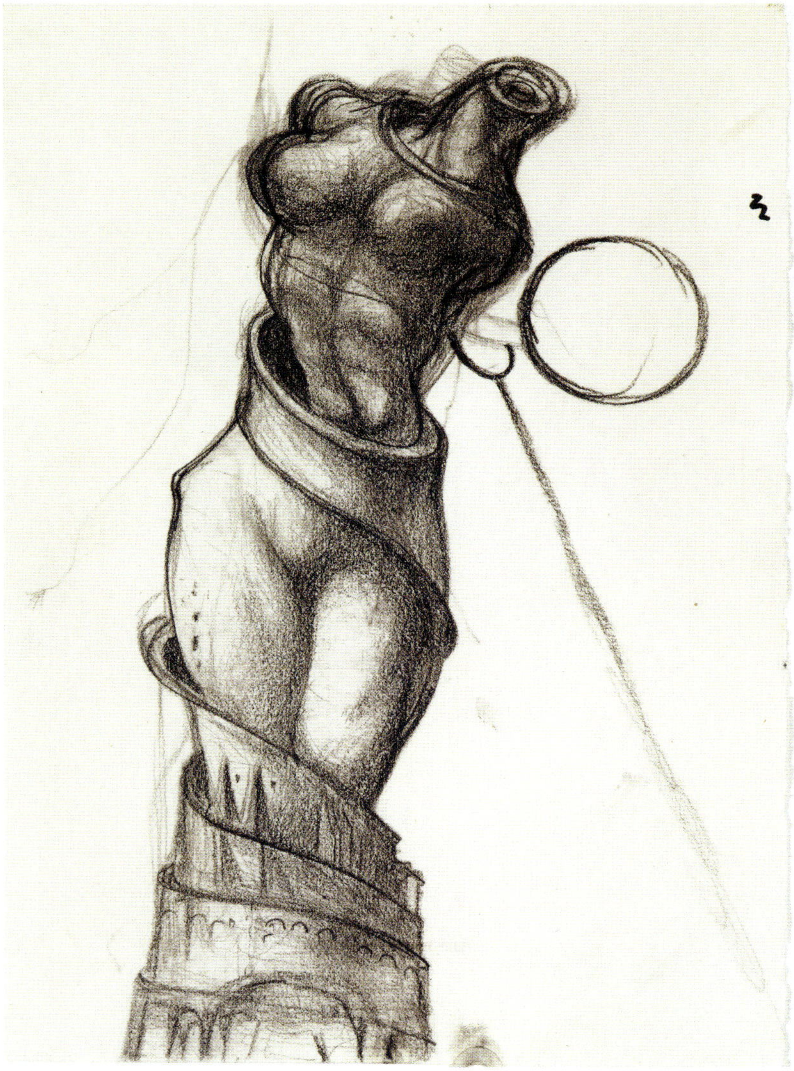

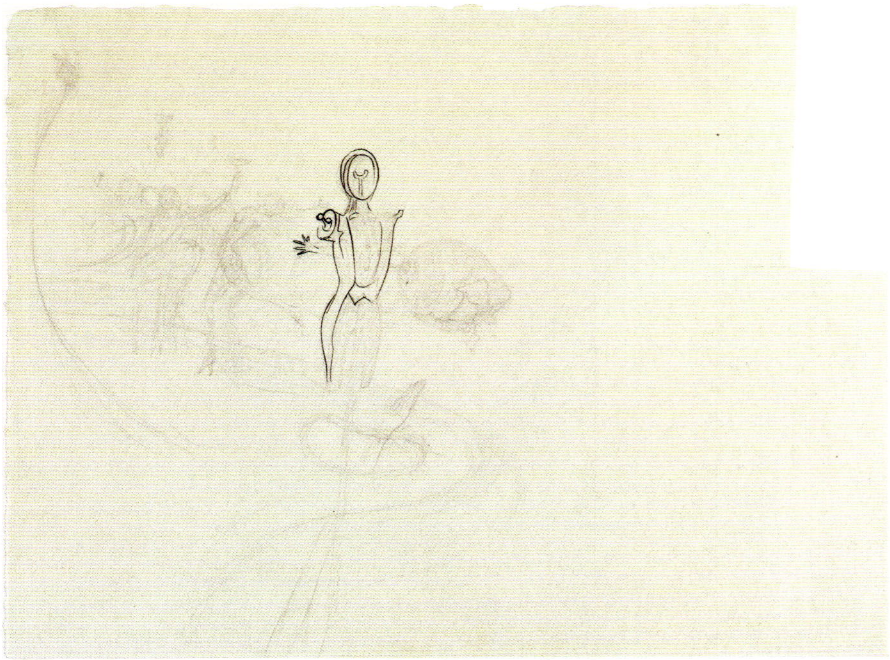

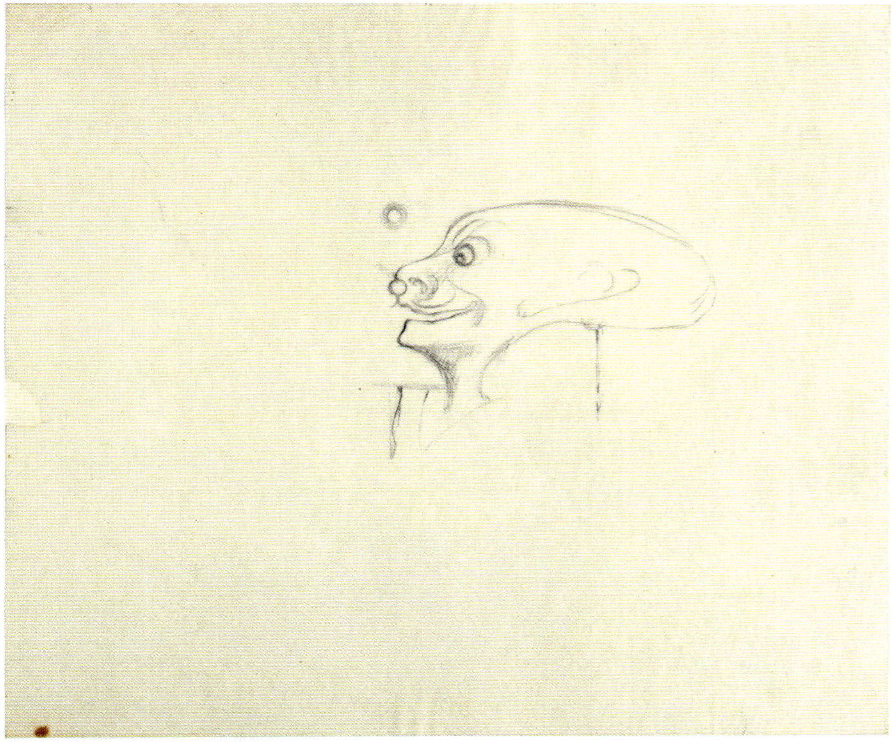

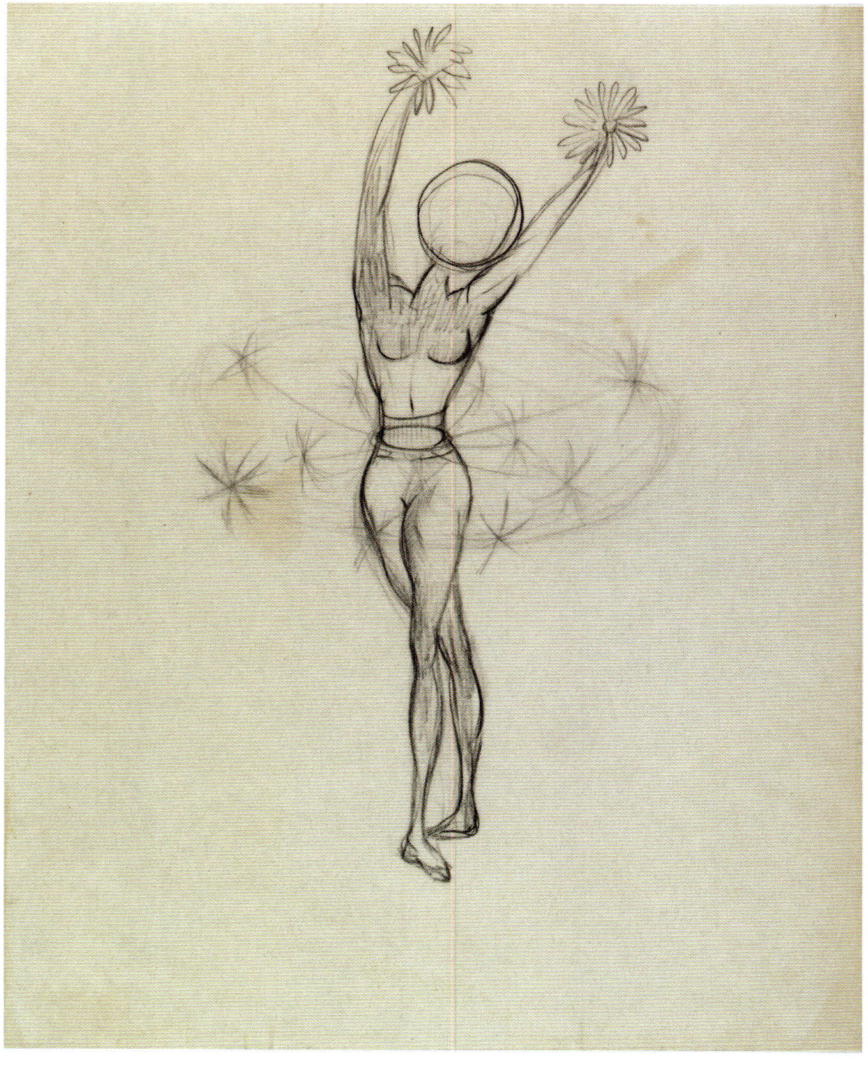

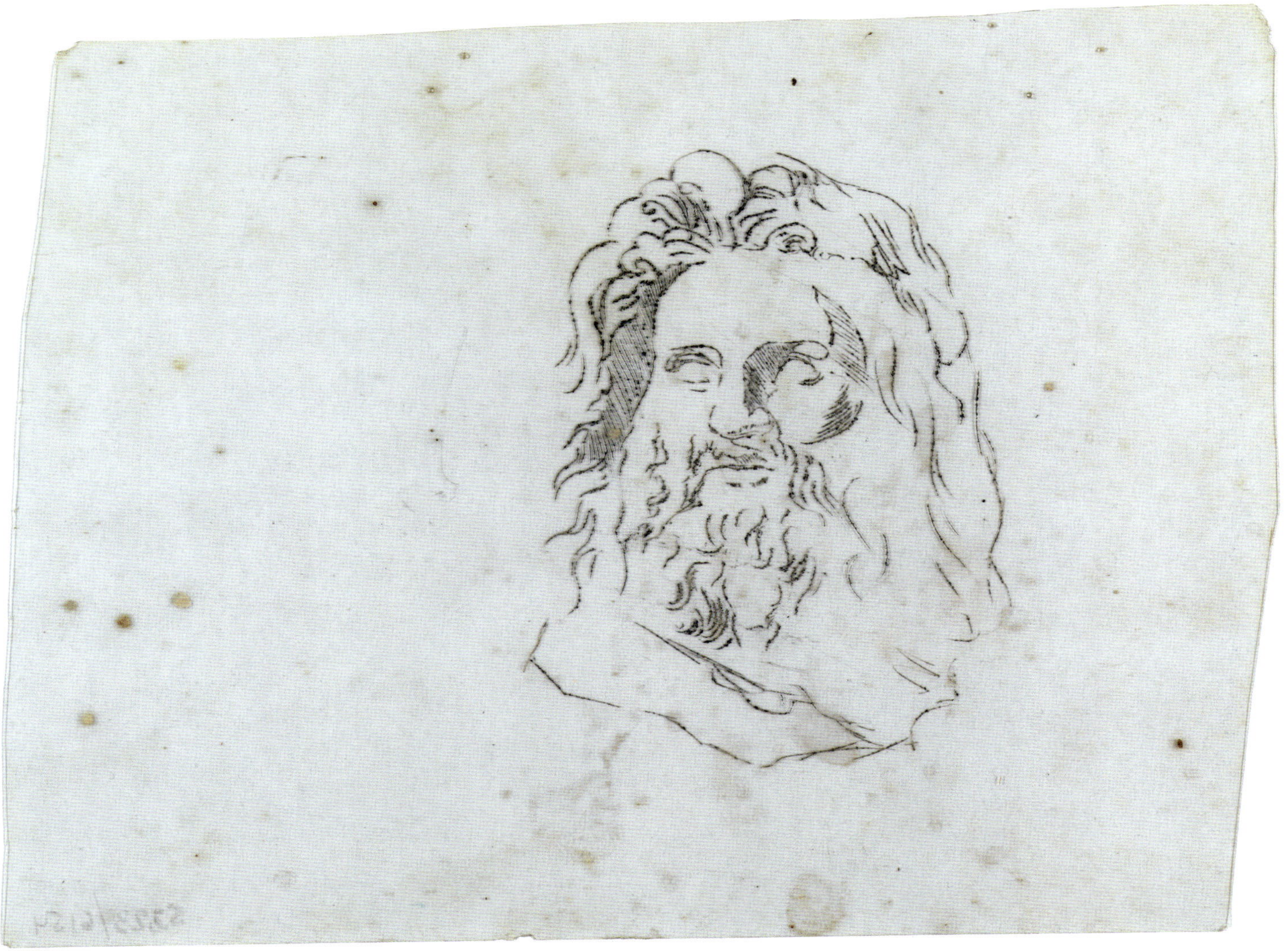

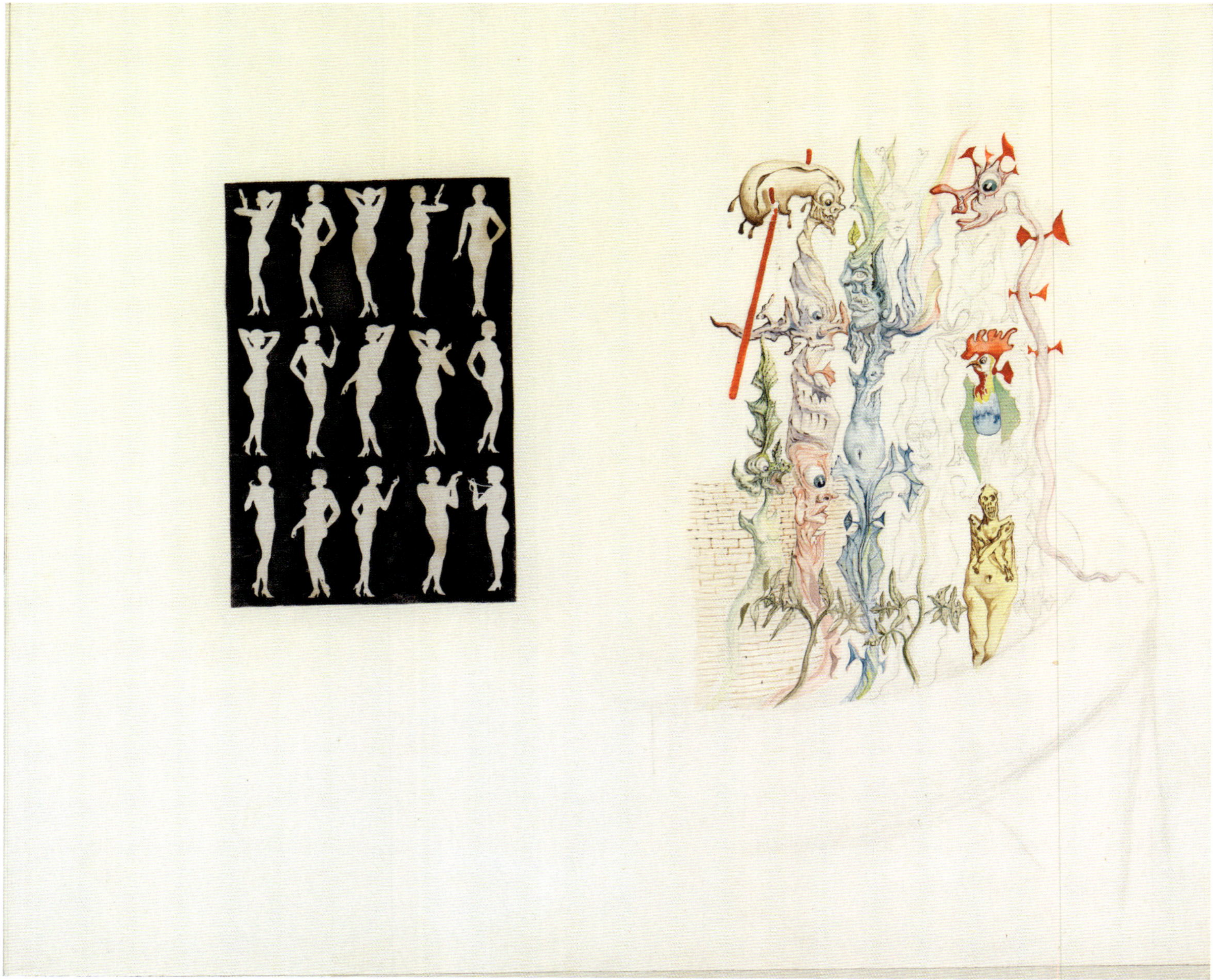

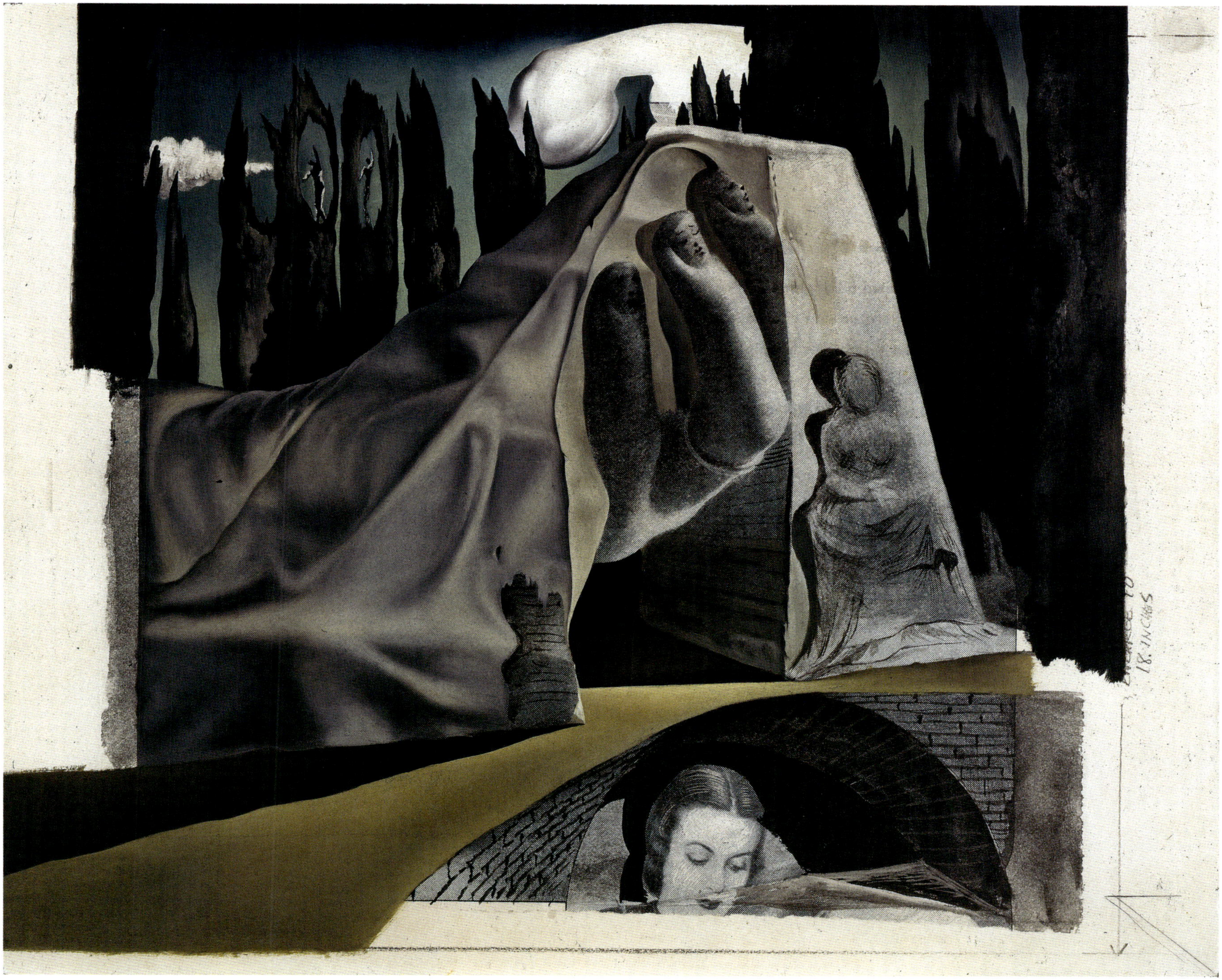
ENLARGE TO
18. INCHES

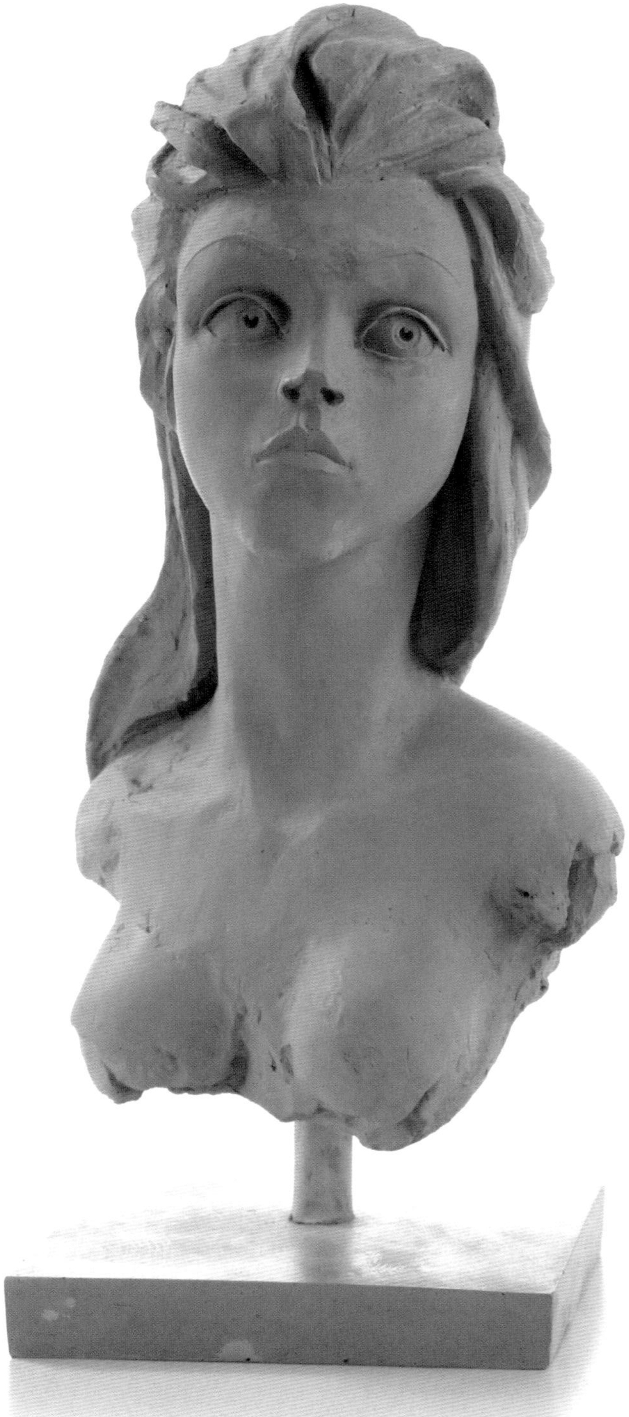
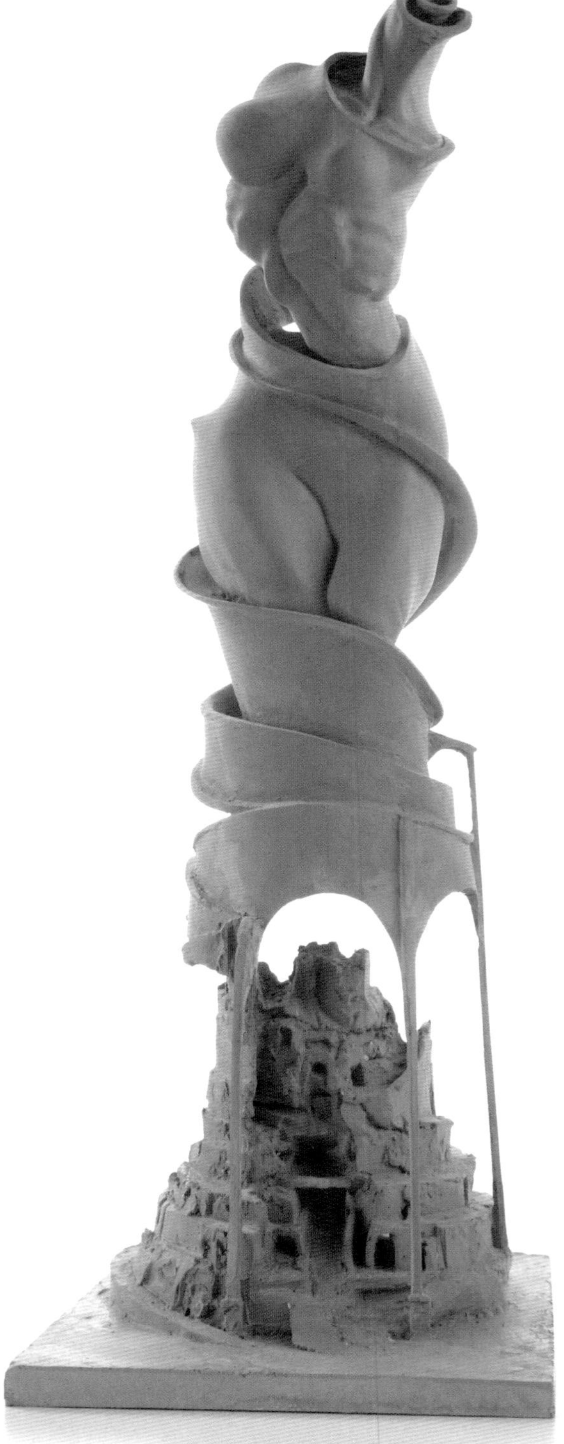

Page 192 (left): Dahlia maquette.

Page 192 (right): Torso maquette created for the 2003 production of *Destino.*

The partygoer maquettes from the original production of *Destino* (1946).

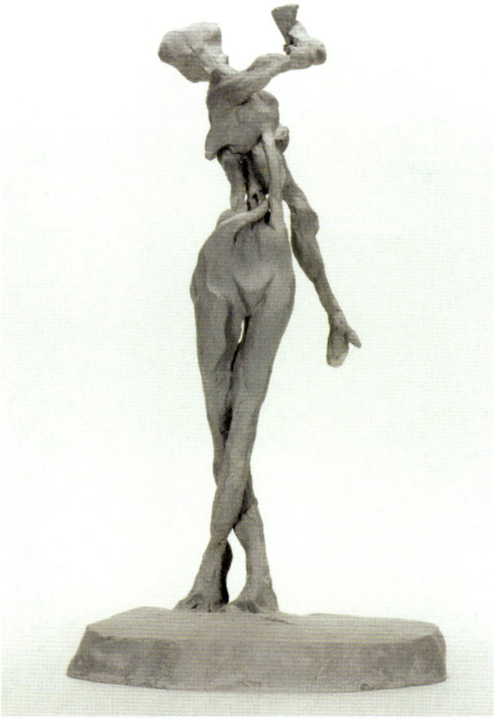

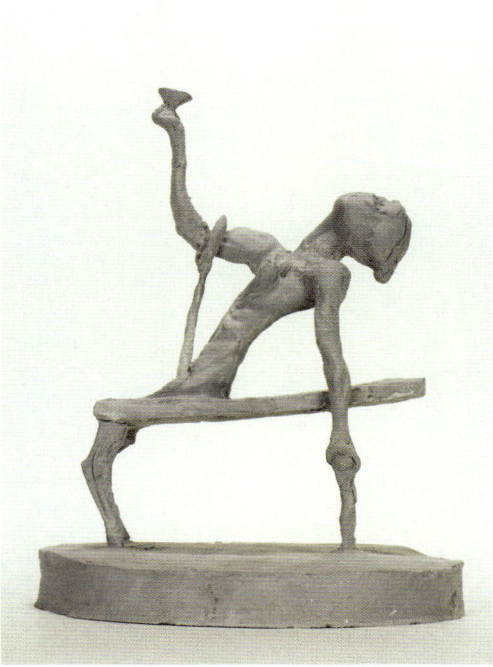

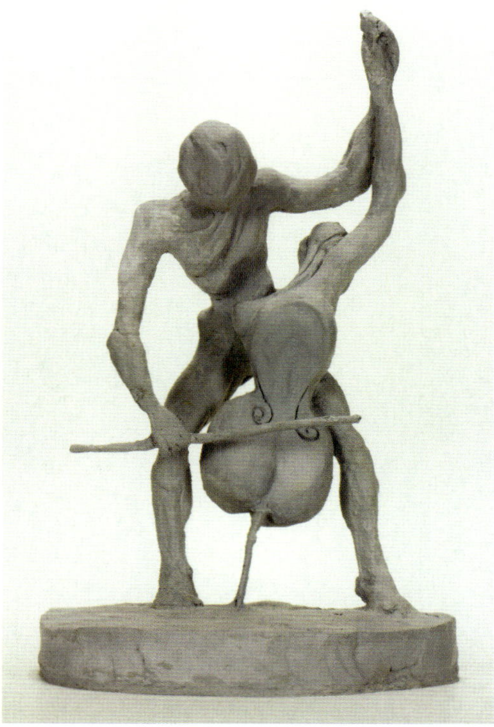

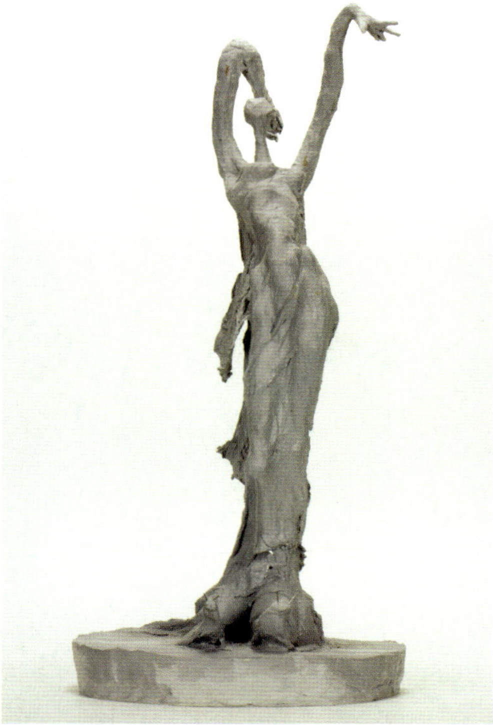

Pages 194–201: Title cards from *Destino*.

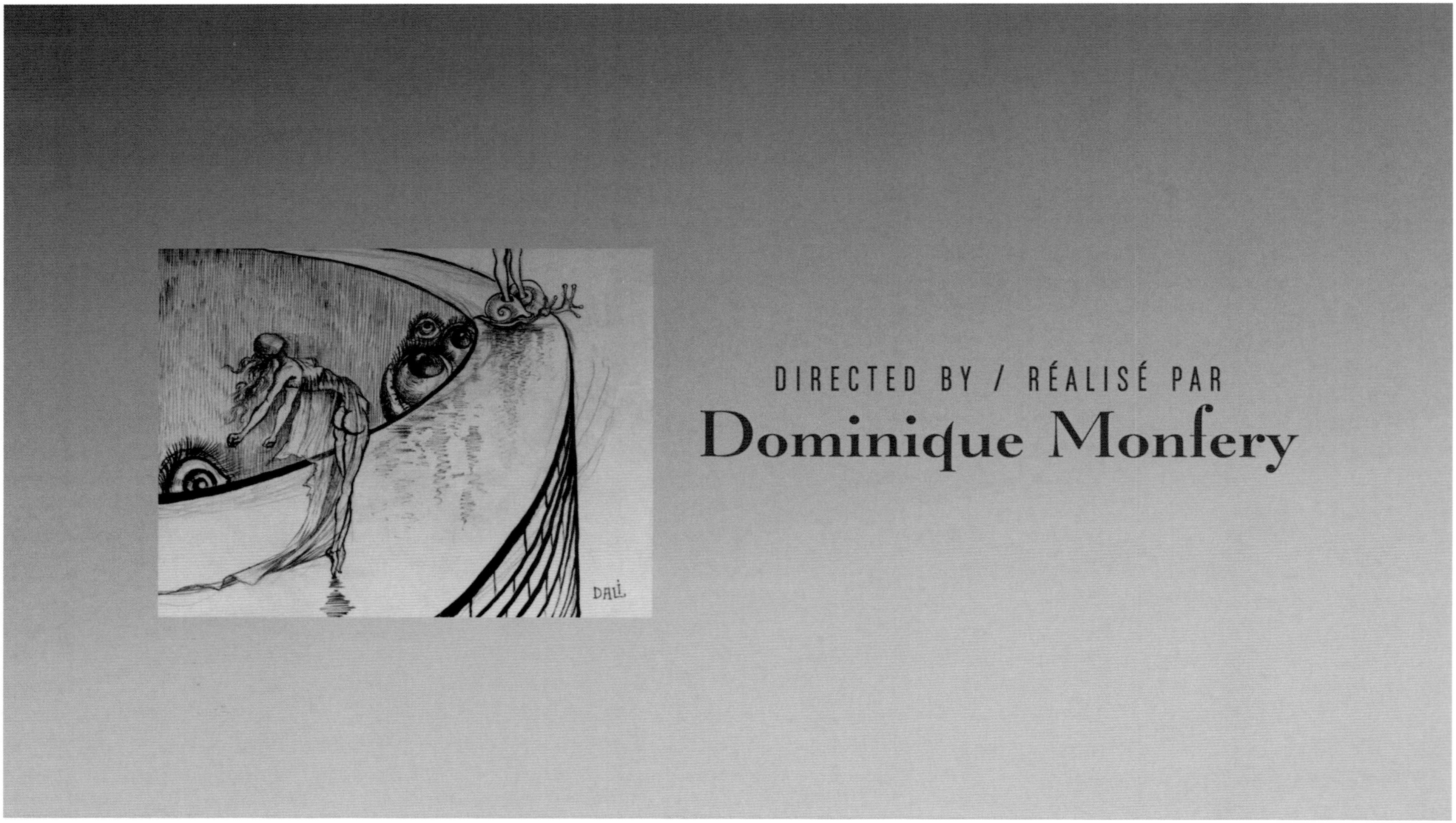

EXECUTIVE PRODUCER / PRODUCTEUR EXÉCUTIF

Roy Edward Disney

PRODUCER / PRODUCTEUR

Baker Bloodworth

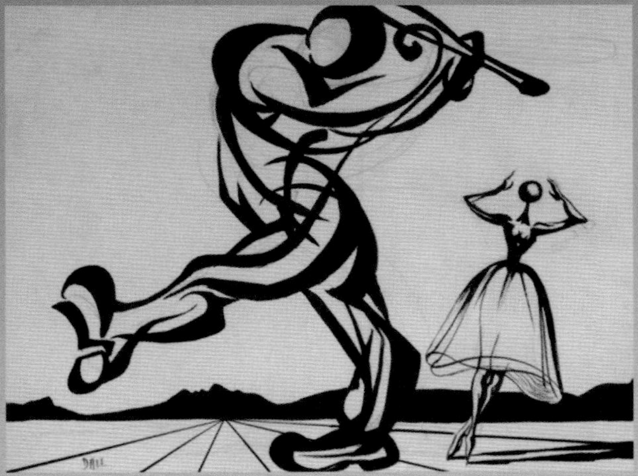

STORY BY / HISTOIRE

Salvador Dalí & John Hench

PRODUCTION DESIGNER / CONCEPTION VISUELLE

Thierry Fournier

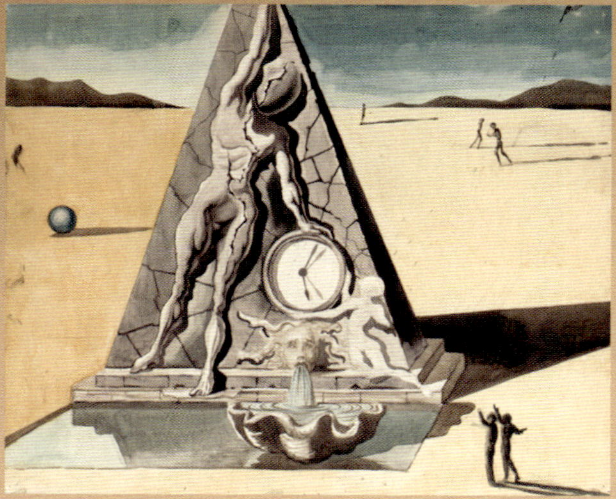

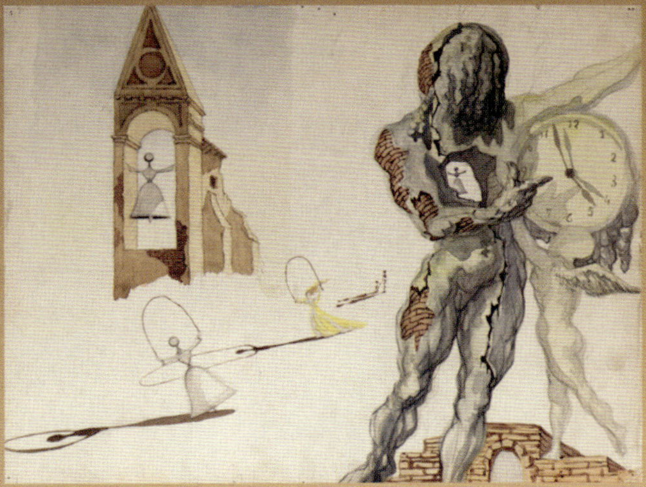

"Destino"

MUSIC BY / MUSIQUE DE

Armando Dominguez

ENGLISH LYRICS BY / PAROLES ORIGINALES DE

Ray Gilbert

PERFORMED BY / INTERPRÉTÉE PAR

Dora Luz

ADDITIONAL MUSIC BY / MUSIQUE ADDITIONNELLE

Michael Starobin

ASSOCIATE PRODUCER / PRODUCTEUR ASSOCIÉ

David A. Bossert

PRODUCTION MANAGERS / DIRECTEURS DE PRODUCTION

Coralie Cudot-Lissillour

Timothy Jason Smith

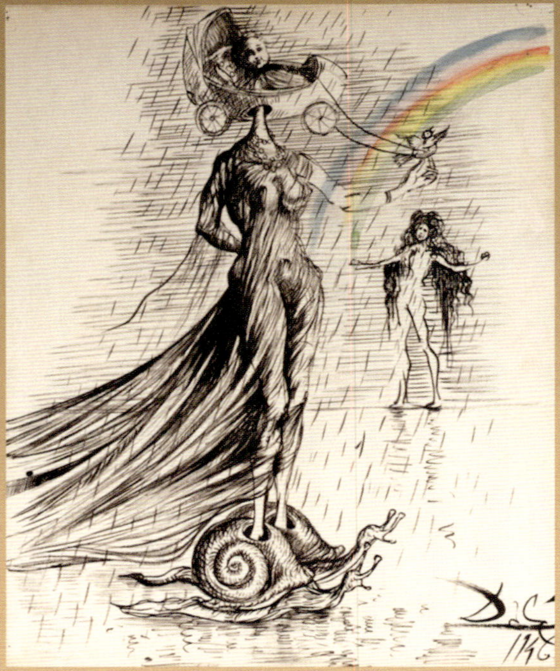

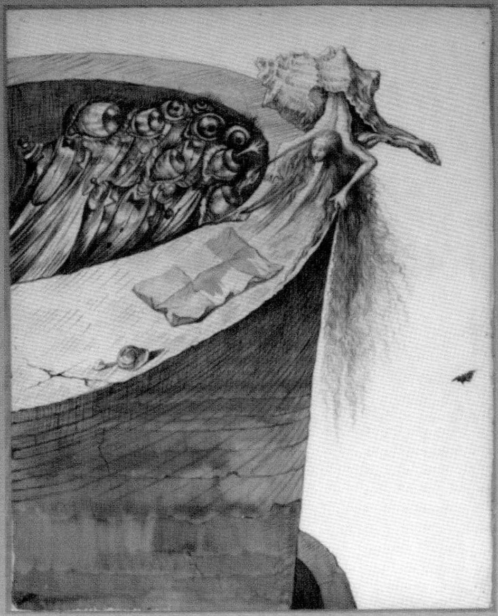

ARTISTIC SUPERVISERS / SUPERVISEURS ARTISTIQUES

STORY	Donald W. Ernst
EDITOR	Jessica Ambinder-Rojas
ASSISTANT EDITOR	Gregory F. Plotts
PARIS EDITORIAL	François Desnus
BACKGROUND	Olivier Besson
CLEAN-UP	Jeroen Dejonckheere
EFFECTS	Thierry Chaffoin
SCENE PLANNING	Raphaël Vicente
COLOR MODELS	Sylvie Bennett-Fauqué

ANIMATION

David Berthier

Dominique Monfery   Yoshimichi Tamura

VISUAL DEVELOPMENT / DÉVELOPPEMENT VISUEL

Cent Alantar   Zoltàn Maros

DIGITAL PRODUCTION /
PRODUCTION 3D

Ivan Kassabov   Nicoletta Marcialis

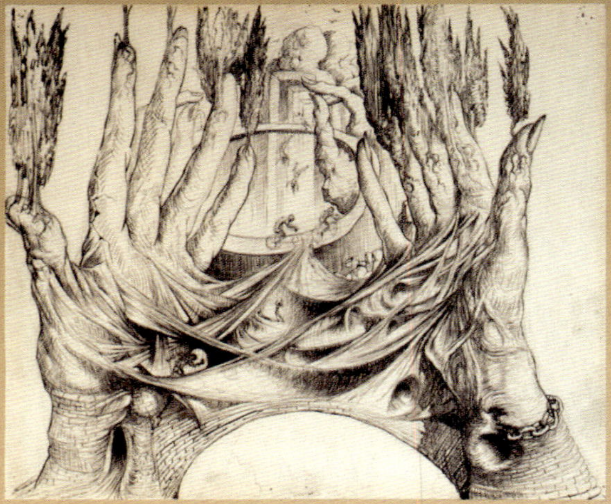

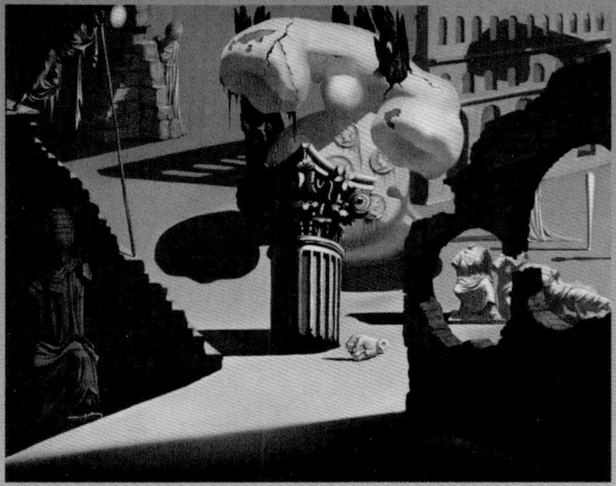

COLOR MODELS / MODÈLES COULEUR

Karen Comella
Bérangère Frésard
Ann Sorensen

CAPS SUPERVISORS / SUPERVISEURS CAPS

Mark A. Henley
Hortensia Casagran
Barbara Wiles
James Russell
Robyn L. Roberts
Timothy Gales
Holly E. Bratton
Brenda McGirl
William Fadness

END NOTES

ACT I

[1] Times Staff Writer, "Salvador Dalí Dies; Surrealist Painter was 84," *Los Angeles Times*, January 24, 1989.

[2] Montse Aguer, *The Persistence of Memory Educational Booklet* (Figueres, Spain: Fundació Gala-Salvador Dalí: D.A.S. Edicions, 2009).

[3] Salvador Dalí and Haakon Chevalier, *50 Secrets of Magic Craftsmanship* (New York: Dover, 1948) 79.

[4] Harriet S. Bee and Cassandra Heliczer, *MoMA Highlights: 350 Works from the Museum of Modern Art, New York* (New York: Museum of Modern Art, 1999) 130.

[5] Bee, *MoMA Highlights,* 130.

[6] John Hench interview, 1968.

[7] Dawn Ades, "Why Film?," *Dalí & Film* ed. by Matthew Gale (New York: Museum of Modern Art, 2007) 15.

ACT II

[1] Sara Cochran, "Spellbound," *Dalí & Film* ed. by Matthew Gale (New York: Museum of Modern Art, 2007) 174, 178.

[2] Salvador Dalí, letter to Walt Disney, 1943. St. Regis Hotel, New York, NY.

[3] Salvador and Gala Dalí, letter to Walt Disney, 18 Feb. 1945. Del Monte Lodge, Pebble Beach, CA.

[4] John Hench interview by John Canemaker, January 6, 1994, Walt Disney Imagineering, Glendale, CA.

[5] Walt Disney, letter to Salvador Dalí, 24 Dec. 1945. Burbank, CA.

[6] Jordan R. Young, "The Dali-Disney Duo: An Animated Uncompleted Collaboration," *Washington Post,* January 28, 1989.

[7] "Dalí Works at Disney," *Hollywood Daily Reporter*, August 02, 1946, Hollywood, CA.

[8] John Hench interview, 1968.

[9] John Hench interview by John Canemaker, January 6, 1994, Walt Disney Imagineering, Glendale, CA.

[10] John Hench interview, 1968.

[11] Walt Disney Studio Archives documents.

[12] Walt Disney Studio Archives documents.

[13] Jordan R. Young, "The Dali-Disney Duo: An Animated Uncompleted Collaboration," *Washington Post,* January 28, 1989.

[14] Internal Consumer Products Division memo to Frank G. Wells dated February 15, 1985.

[15] Salvador Dalí, *Salvador Dalí: The Secret Life Drawings*, (St. Petersburg, FL: Salvador Dali Museum, 1982) 260-261.

[16] John Hench interview by John Canemaker, January 6, 1994, Walt Disney Imagineering, Glendale, CA.

[17] John Canemaker, "THE NEW SEASON/FILM; The Lost Cartoon By Disney and Dalí, Fellow Surrealists," *The New York Times*, September 7, 2003.

[18] Jordan R. Young, "The Dali-Disney Duo: An Animated Uncompleted Collaboration," *Washington Post,* January 28, 1989.

[19] John Canemaker, "THE NEW SEASON/FILM; The Lost Cartoon By Disney and Dalí, Fellow Surrealists," *The New York Times*, September 7, 2003.

ACT III

[1] Walt Disney Studio Archives documents.

[2] Walter Robinson and Cathy Lebowitz, "Artworld," *Art in America*, April 1989, 288.

[3] David Bossert, *Remembering Roy E. Disney: Memories and Photos of a Storied Life* (New York: Disney Editions, 2013) chapter 10.

[4] Bossert, *Remembering Roy E. Disney,* chapter 10.

[5] "Definition of surrealism in English," Oxford Dictionaries. Oxford University Press, n.d. Web. October 13, 2014.

[6] Bossert, *Remembering Roy E. Disney,* 157.

[7] Ibid., 157.

IMAGE CREDITS

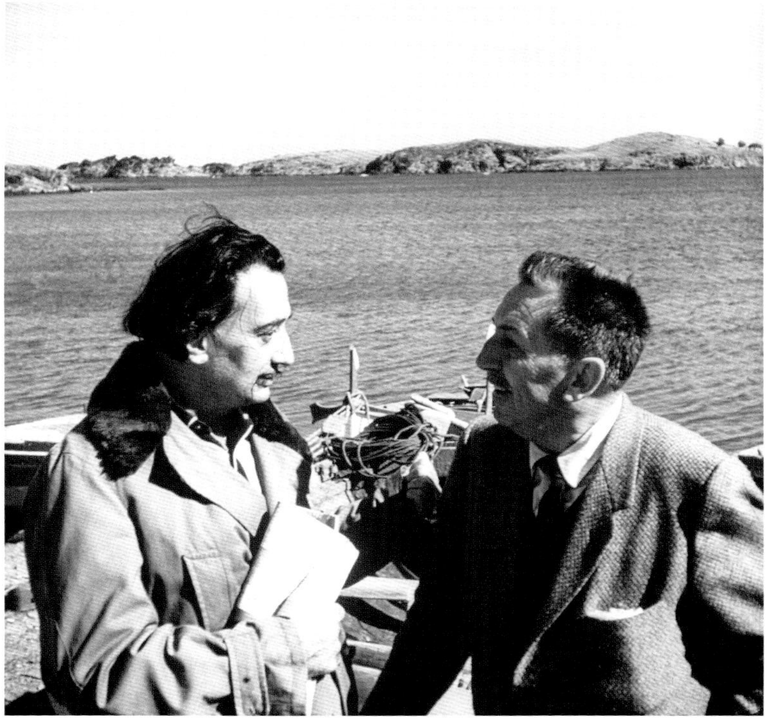

Salvador Dalí and Walt Disney in
Portlligat, Spain, circa 1957.

Final Film Images courtesy of Walt Disney Animation Studios Classic Projects:

3, 7, 10, 22, 38-39, 46, 75 (top), 76 (bottom), 77 (bottom), 99, 101 (bottom), 128-129, 133 (bottom), 151, 153, 157, 160 (bottom), 162, 175, 177 (bottom), 179, 181 (bottom), 185, 194-201, 208

Artwork courtesy of the Walt Disney Animation Studios Animation Research Library:

9, 28, 43, 45, 57, 58, 60, 63-69, 71, 73, 74, 76 (top), 77 (top, left), 90-91, 93, 96-98, 100, 103-105, 107, 109-116, 118-127, 130-132, 140, 148-150, 160 (top), 161, 171-174, 176, 177 (top), 178, 180, 181 (top), 182-184, 192-193

Photographs and Artwork courtesy of the Walt Disney Archives:

16, 18 (left), 21, 23, 32, 34-37, 40-41, 47, 50, 52, 83, 92, 94-95, 101 (top), 102, 106, 108, 133 (top), 134, 136, 138-139, 143, 145, 155, 203

Image courtesy of the Walt Disney Studios Music Library:

146

INDEX

Image from the final film, *Destino*.

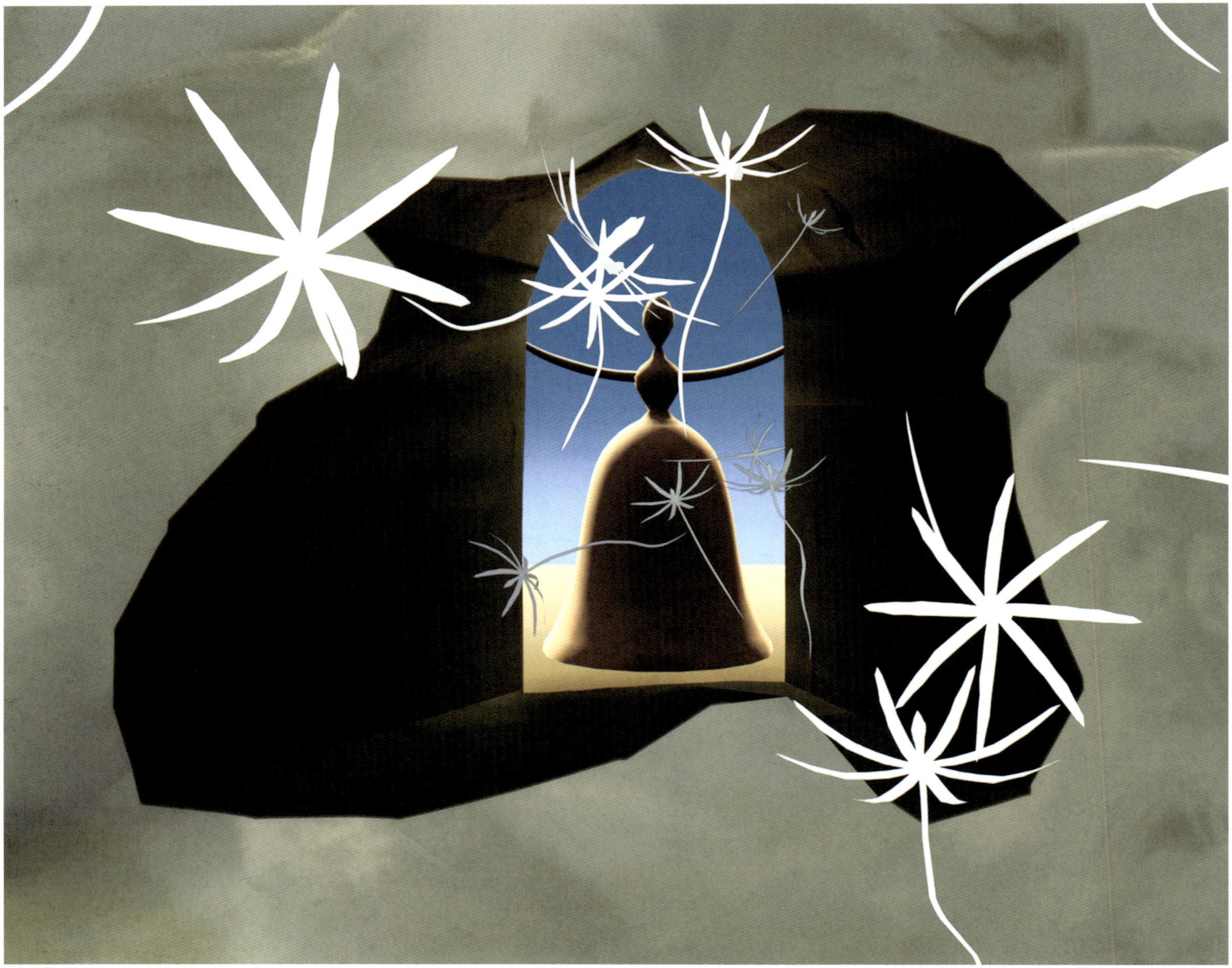